WILD THEATER

WILD THEATER

*Staging the Margins of
Baroque Ideology in
the Spanish Comedia*

Harrison Meadows

VANDERBILT UNIVERSITY PRESS
Nashville, Tennessee

Copyright 2025 by Vanderbilt University Press
All rights reserved
First printing 2025

Library of Congress Cataloging-in-Publication Data

Names: Meadows, Harrison, 1986- author.
Title: Wild theater : staging the margins of Baroque ideology in the Spanish comedia / Harrison Meadows.
Description: Nashville : Vanderbilt University Press, 2025. | Includes bibliographical references and index.
Identifiers: LCCN 2024038407 (print) | LCCN 2024038408 (ebook) | ISBN 9780826507532 (paperback) | ISBN 9780826507549 (hardcover) | ISBN 9780826507556 (epub) | ISBN 9780826507563 (pdf)
Subjects: LCSH: Spanish drama--Classical period, 1500-1700--History and criticism. | Wild men in literature.
Classification: LCC PQ6221 .M43 2025 (print) | LCC PQ6221 (ebook) | DDC 862/.308--dc23/eng/20241022
LC record available at https://lccn.loc.gov/2024038407
LC ebook record available at https://lccn.loc.gov/2024038408

Front cover image: Asher Brown Durand, *Forest in the Morning Light*, c. 1855, accession #1978.6.2. Courtesy National Gallery of Art, Washington.

*To my wild things, Fitz and Griffin.
Stay wild.*

CONTENTS

Acknowledgments ix

INTRODUCTION. Situating the Baroque Wild Figure
in Western Genealogies of Wildness 1

CHAPTER 1. The Battle of Carnival and Lent:
Premodern Antecedents of the Baroque Wild Figure 35

CHAPTER 2. Wildness as Monstrosity in the *Comedias*
of Lope de Vega 58

CHAPTER 3. Wild History: Fashioning National Identity
in the Mythological Past 89

CHAPTER 4. Of Text and Textile: Gendering Wildness
in the Spanish *Comedia* 127

CHAPTER 5. Exceptional Wildness in the Skeptical Theater
of Calderón de la Barca 165

CONCLUSION 195

EPILOGUE. Framing Bigfoot: A Genealogy of Savage
Misdirection from Segismundo to Sasquatch 201

Notes 209
Bibliography 275
Index 293

ACKNOWLEDGMENTS

WILD THEATER HAS COME to fruition through the generosity of many individuals and an abundance of institutional support. The Denbo Center for the Humanities and Arts provided crucial backing through a yearlong in-residency fellowship that allowed me dedicated time for writing in just my second year at the University of Tennessee, as well as funding for a transformative manuscript workshop. I am deeply thankful to the colleagues who participated in that workshop, including Dian Fox, Heather Hirschfeld, Bradley Nelson, and Anthony Welch, whose meticulous feedback marked a pivotal moment in refining the project's argumentation. The University of Tennessee, Knoxville College of Arts & Sciences also offered valuable subvention funding that assisted in sponsoring the publication of this work.

I owe an immense intellectual debt to my mentors. John Slater's feedback on the project along the way has been indispensable. Concisely, he is the best reader I know. Moreover, he stuck with me, and his steadfast support and commitment to professional mentorship are qualities for which I am ever grateful and will always strive to emulate. Julio Baena, my graduate director, shaped my critical approach to cultural production (i.e., everything)—an influence evident throughout these pages. His insights continue to calibrate my theoretical compass, having impressed upon me early on the wisdom of orienting due north on Cervantes (*stella cervantis*, if you will). Heather Hirschfeld, my faculty mentor, has been a steadying influence since I arrived at the University of Tennessee. She provided unwavering encouragement over the years in my progress on the project, even when I failed to heed her sage advice to insulate myself from the forces that pull on the time and energy of a junior faculty member.

I am perpetually grateful to the Association for Hispanic Classical Theater, an intellectual community whose members have contributed insights to much of the material that found its way into this book, thanks to our discussions at annual conferences and professional collaborations. I am also grateful to the external reviewers solicited by Vanderbilt University Press to evaluate the manuscript. Their thoughtful feedback helped strengthen the manuscript considerably, and I hope they find that I addressed their comments with care equal to that in which they provided them.

I would be remiss not to acknowledge my high school English teachers, Andrea Shupert and Kendra Morris, who started me down this path, long before I knew it. Kendra deserves special mention—in many ways, this book feels like the decades-delayed essay on *Sir Gawain and the Green Knight* that I never turned in during my junior year. Whether or not the final product was worth the wait, I have at least paid on interest in word count.

Personal bonds have sustained this project throughout. I am extraordinarily grateful to my parents, especially my mother, whose positive energy and unwavering support are without equal, and persist even in the face of my most cantankerous moments. To my chosen brothers, Chip, Garrett, and Drew: I cannot express how grateful I am to have old friends who I know will stick with me (even after reading this book! Buckle in.). My Knoxville family has been there for me most during the final stages of the project, especially Bernie Issa and Phillip Stokes. I would also like to recognize the special people in my graduate cohort at the University of Colorado—particularly Mark Pleiss, Taiko Haessler, Caitlin Brady Carter, and Laura Cesarco Eglin. In the early going when the ideas for this book were taking shape, I could always count on you to be a sounding board to work through an idea, to hold me accountable, and to be my most reliable co-conspirators in escaping the *sótano* for furloughs into the Boulder wild. To Mike Sullivan, thank you for offering perspective and sound counsel when it was sorely needed. Finally, there are times in life when you need a good therapist to figure it all out, but not all therapists are good ones. Eric, you are a very good therapist.

Above all, this book would not exist without my wife, Rachel. She has patiently weathered every peak and valley of this journey, celebrating the milestones and shouldering extra burdens during intense periods of writing. She makes life one worth writing books about.

Introduction
Situating the Baroque Wild Figure in Western Genealogies of Wildness

IN HIS 1588 COMEDIA *El nacimiento de Ursón y Valentín* (The Birth of Orson and Valentine), Lope de Vega introduced a character that would appear and reappear over the next century in the playwriting of the Spanish Baroque. The protagonist Ursón, after being separated at birth from his mother and brother in act 1, appears as a young adult alone in the forest at the beginning of the following act. He dons animal pelts, a costume that would become the visual marker conventional to the character type established by his example. But what exactly is Ursón? He is a Wildman, and specifically a baroque one. What makes a wild thing baroque? The answer to that question lies at the heart of the present study: to situate the baroque wild figure of the Spanish *comedia* in the genealogy of western notions of wildness. As a transhistorical figure, the Wildman (a.k.a. *Wilder Mann, wodewose, Trapajones,* Sasquatch, among many other names) has retained its cultural purchase from the earliest examples of literature such as Enkidu in *The Epic of Gilgamesh* (see Figure 0.1) to contemporary cinema and television including the 2021 adaptation of the Arthurian legend in the feature film *The Green Knight* (see Figure 0.2). Moreover, the wild figure's longevity is matched by its variability, having taken on a host of different forms across global

[2] WILD THEATER

FIGURE 0.1. The Wildman Enkidu and Gilgamesh slay Humbaba in the Cedar Forest. Enkidu is depicted covered in hair and wielding a club. Staatliche Museen zu Berlin, Vorderasiatisches Museum. Photograph by Olaf M. Teßmer, licensed under CC BY-SA 4.0.

and historical contexts.[1] Unsurprisingly, this persistence in the human imagination is reflected in the significant scholarly attention its many iterations have received. The body of scholarship is especially robust on representations of wild folk in medieval and Renaissance iconography and literature (e.g., chivalric and sentimental romance traditions), and then in Enlightenment instances that reflect early trends in scientific discourse such as, for example, ethnography (out of which the concept of the "noble savage" emerges) and psychology (when we see an uptick in recorded cases and studies carried out on feral children). However, insufficient attention has been dedicated to understanding the baroque gap that remains in the cultural history of wildness between those periods. Scholars have found medieval, Renaissance, and Enlightenment representations immensely generative objects of study as reflections of the worldview that produced them. The undertheorized baroque wild figure presents the same utility as a reflection of the large-scale epochal transitions taking place during early modernity, but has yet to be incorporated into the cultural history of the West to the same extent as in the periods that precede and follow it.

This figure—typically presented as a solitary, hirsute, club-wielding inhabitant of the marginal wilderness—became an obsession in the

FIGURE 0.2. The Green Knight as depicted in A24's *The Green Knight*, a 2021 adaptation of the fourteenth-century Arthurian poem *Sir Gawain and the Green Knight*. The hirsute Wildman finds his counterpart in the Green Man, who is usually depicted covered in leaves instead of fur. In the case of the Arthurian legend, he has green skin. In the 2021 film adaptation, his physical appearance blends tree-like characteristics with anthropomorphic traits. Screenshot, *The Green Knight*, directed by David Lowery, © A24 Films LLC, 2021.

cultural production of the Iberian Baroque, especially theater. Its direct influences in the European cultural imagination can be traced to pre-modern Carnival traditions in which costumed wild men featured prominently. Wild folk took on a variety of forms as diverse as the festive traditions and practices to which they pertained, but it was common for the wild man to play a role toward the end of festivities when he would be presented publicly and then beaten with sticks or chased out of town. Representations of this ritualistic folk spectacle can be found on display throughout the cultural production of the period, including notable examples in Boccaccio's *Decameron* (1353) and Peter Brueghel's painting *The Battle Between Carnival and Lent* (1559; see Figures 0.3 and 0.4).[2] Essential to this pre-modern concept of wildness is its allegorical nature (a nature the figure retains in regional folk festivals to the present day), for which the wild figure serves as a vehicle for some type of permissible excess or social upheaval, such as carnival revelry, the passions of youth, or a period of feasting to mark the changing of the seasons. Festivals

FIGURE 0.3. *The Battle Between Carnival and Lent*, Peter Brueghel (1559). Toward the back left, the painting depicts a Wildman (an actor wearing a costume made of leaves) carrying a club and being guided by a small procession of participants ahead and behind him. The person in front of him appears to be reading him his last rites, as was a customary element of the ritual to end Carnival festivities, portrayed in this painting as an allegorical battle against the impending Lenten season. Kunst Historisches Museum, Vienna, © KHM-Museumsverband.

of this sort do not disappear in the early modern period, neither from the court nor folk traditions (again, these traditions remain active today, see Figures 0.5–7); however, a major shift occurs during the Baroque when they come to be portrayed as dramatic characters on the emergent commercial stage in the dominant dramatic genre of the *comedia*. The folk, who are *participants* in the embodied performance of wildness in carnival traditions are shifted to the role of *spectator*, and the fullness and participatory vigor of social upheaval that permeates paratheatrical folk revelry during the premodern period is displaced by a theatricalized image of those practices in the emergence of the modern theater. Medieval folk revelry and court pageantry are harnessed for the commercial stage, where the topsy-turvy world of the carnivalesque is contained by the sobriety and imposed order of the Lenten Baroque. The carryovers, transformations, and negations of the carnivalesque into early modern

FIGURE 0.4. *The Wild Man* or *The Masquerade of Orson and Valentine* (1566). Woodcut, after Brueghel, that replicates the Wildman procession in greater detail. Courtesy of the Metropolitan Museum of Art, New York.

dramaturgy, specifically the Spanish *comedia*, are emblematic of these emerging poetic and ideological features of the incipient commercial theater in Iberia, as part of a repression of the spirit of carnival steeped into the baroque ethos. The current study presents this early modern Iberian wild figure as it develops out of medieval and Renaissance representations to then outline the contours and features that characterize its uniquely baroque form.

The conventions of wild representation on the early modern stage convey meaning differently than in medieval and Renaissance performance traditions, defined by the following fundamental shift: when the wild figure is inscribed within the bounds of baroque theatricality it simultaneously becomes modern, serving the purposes of popular entertainment that establish and reproduce the ideological commitments of a hegemonic social order. In the space of the theater, "the temporary suspension of normal social life" María Luisa Lobato describes as the spirit of medieval carnival becomes less participatory and more virtual, whereby that "temporary suspension" manifests itself only in the alienated representation of social upheaval packaged and staged to be observed at a distance by a paying audience (not participated in).

Representations of wildness were molded for the stage to embody the antitheses of dominant social values (i.e., the ideologies underpinning contemporary models of civilized order). Wildness was a thing to be domesticated, transformed, or eliminated in the unfolding of the conventional trajectory of dramatic action in the *comedia* from "order disturbed to order restored."[3] This became the theatrical and ideological utility of the wild character so often deployed by playwrights in the wake of Lope de Vega and throughout the remainder of the seventeenth century; the introduction and subsequent domestication of wildness serves as an organizing premise well-suited for the conventions of *comedia*'s fundamental structure that hinges on the disturbance and restoration of order. Importantly, as a consequence of the virtualization (or theatricalization) of the carnivalesque world-upside-down on the commercial stage, the folk become spectators rather than participants, and the regenerative, cyclical social impact of carnival revelry is diminished during the Baroque. At its expense, the spirit of Lent rises in prominence as the celebrated posture of baroque sensibilities. Rather than a period of regenerative, permissible transgression and social upheaval participated in by the folk (e.g., the quasi-theatrical allegorical ritual of reading the Wildman the terms of his death sentence in the public square to end carnival celebrations), the wild figure becomes a cautionary spectacle in the *comedia*—its domestication a thing to be watched—and whose existence has no space within the civilized order.

Following this pattern, the baroque transformation of the theatrical Wildman is defined by three interwoven characteristics: (1) its virtualization in theatrical space, (2) the poetics of *desengaño* (disillusionment) as a function of the discovery of the wild figure's "true" identity hidden behind their wild appearance, and (3) the ideological message bound up in that revelation contextualized within the play and articulated in the cultural field. Although the influence of the carnivalesque remains along with its cast of characters, wildness takes on entirely new meanings as a result of its virtualization. Following Egginton's contention that theatricality distinguishes the modern experience of space from a premodern one, the wild figure becomes modern precisely when it becomes theatrical. The "full" space of folk carnival ritual and court pageantry maintained a "hyperbolic solidity" that blurred "the distinction between the reality being represented and the reality of the representation."[4] Pre-modern spectacle, and the experience of space more broadly, is defined by presence; the wild figure drama of carnival took

FIGURE 0.5.

FIGURE 0.6.

Photos from Charles Fréger's *Wilder Mann* series, including figures of (from left to right) a Wilder Mann (Figure 0.5, Austria), Krampus (Figure 0.6, Germany, back image), and Trapajones (Figure 0.7, Cantabria, Spain). See Figure 2.1 for sixteenth-century manuscript depiction of this type of Wildman festival costume. Photos: © Charles Fréger

FIGURE 0.7.

place in the streets in and among the people, while court entertainment occurred in banquet halls where little separated the performance space from its noble audience. Modern theater is a manifestation of that presence giving way to a different organization of space where reality is cut off from its representation, as reflected in the emptying out of dramatic space onto the other side of the fourth wall.

Lope de Vega can be attributed with transforming the wild figure to maximize the ideological, economic, and theatrical possibilities of that virtualized space. The features and plot devices that characterize his wild characters become the conventions of the genre later copied or reworked by playwrights throughout the seventeenth century. Before long, the entrance of a character onto the stage wearing animal pelts would be immediately recognizable to audiences as a wild figure along with all of their corresponding traits. Lope's reconfiguration of the wild figure for the *comedia* stage draws from examples found in court masques when the young prince would participate in the performance wearing a wild mask, only to remove it at the conclusion of the choreographed spectacle to symbolize a rejection of the passions of youth and assumption of the virtues befitting his revealed royal identity. Resonating with this motif, the animal skins worn by Lope's wild figures occlude and contradict their nature rather than faithfully portraying it. In fact, the wild princes in his plays are not wild at all, and only find themselves inhabiting that state as a result of someone else's wrongdoing. Lope's plays therefore depict a displaced wildness, and the problem of wildness (which is constitutive of the dramatic conflict) can only be resolved by removing this tension between the "real" wildness of the culpable transgressor and the *appearance* of wildness projected falsely upon the wild figure as a result of the transgression. These wild figures, that is, the characters portrayed wearing animal skins, display few signs of monstrosity in their actions, which proves that what is at stake in Lope's wild figure plays is the erasure of the space between appearance and reality. This revelation of the reality (the prince's "true" identity) behind the veil of appearances (the wild mask) exemplifies the characteristically baroque poetics of *desengaño* (literally, "un-deception"), and is a distinguishing feature of the wild figures of the Spanish *comedia*. Rubio Moraga further explains how the mask takes on this function in baroque dramatic representation: *desengaño* "forms part of a social fallacy, an apparent game of tensions, in which the denouement supposes the return to the original reality, in this way negating the 'dissent' that would have been produced by the discrepancy between appearances and reality."[5] The values upheld by punishing the transgression against order that generates that discrepancy follows the logic of what Egginton calls the "major strategy of the Baroque" (a vocabulary I will rely on throughout the present study): the problem of false appearances is ultimately to be solved by revealing the reality they occlude, the resolution of which serves to affirm and uphold the values and interests of the established order (usually related to monarchical authority, national identity, ethno-religious purity, or traditional gender roles).[6] According to Oleza, these poetics of revelation essential to *desengaño* are motivated by a faith that "the discovery of true origins will return things to their rightful place."[7]

These are the ideological parameters of wild signification as developed, later to be emulated, by Lope de Vega when he transfigures the wild character into a virtualized avatar of its medieval carnivalesque predecessors. Not dissimilar from blockbuster action movies and horror films today, the Spanish *comedia* was a factory of meaning making that provided a space to alleviate cultural anxieties by portraying the satisfactory demise of believable monsters and villains. As such, they "reenact redemptive rituals of sin and punishment, wish fulfillment, and repression."[8] In noting this link between the monsters of the Baroque and modern horror cinema, Castillo identifies another feature shared by the monsters of these historically disparate entertainment genres: their capacity to resist erasure, domestication, or reincorporation into the order of things. This is also the monstrous quality of the baroque wild figure; its very presence speaks a taboo into being, its representation a threat to the order that created it for the sole purpose of subsequently disavowing its existence. In Castillo's view, this feature of the ideological monsters found in popular cultural production also can have consequences (intended or not): "Undoubtedly, some strands of horror fiction show glimpses of 'the other side' only to reaffirm the barriers that protect our rational world, but the monstrous introduces a disturbance into the cultural and moral horizon that may be difficult to contain."[9] Up for debate is the extent to which their new baroque form sought to prohibit social disruption and reinscribe or domesticate the wild figure back into a dominant cultural apparatus, but what is clear is the frequency they appeared and reappeared in *comedias* throughout the Baroque. And in so doing, each replication creates the possibility of leaving imprints on the palimpsest of baroque hegemony, traces of wildness that render dominant culture vulnerable to the "unbound forces of unreason."[10]

Evidence of wildness escaping containment can be observed even within the corpus of plays by Lope de Vega that feature a wild figure. As I will show in Lope's later wild figure plays in Chapter 2, the moment of *desengaño* is incomplete insofar as it fails to resolve identifiable aspects of the conflict set up in the action. Wildness then, understood metonymically for the order-disturbing conflict to be resolved, poses a threat to hegemony that the *comedia*'s conventions cannot always fully defend against. As Lope de Vega's own wild figure plays demonstrate, just as the *comedia* "arises as a gesture of symbolic power," it always already "harbors an unconscious symptom of its constitutive limitations."[11] In this regard, the wild figures of the Iberian stage further evince Castillo's contention that "one of the most important lessons we can learn from facing our baroque horrors . . . is that the monsters come with the house."[12]

The constitutive limitations of the *comedia* as an ideological apparatus detected in Lope's corpus can be observed to an even greater extent when tracing dramatic production over the course of the seventeenth century. The present study therefore plots a trajectory of social destabilization generated as a function of the overextension of dramatic conventions beyond their capacity to convey meaning. In some cases, the play can have a conventional ending that ostensibly restores the status quo, except the destabilizing effect introduced by the protagonist's wildness fails to be resolved in the final scene. Andrés de Claramonte's *La lindona de Galicia* (The Belle of Galicia; 1642), for instance, appears to uphold prevailing values through the domestication of the female protagonist's wildness, but the conventional marriage contract is deployed as a powerless device against her unwavering refusal to follow social norms, even in the final scene when she denies the king's marriage proposal in favor of another suitor of her choosing.[13] In other cases, the message produced by a play seems to deal in oppositional discourse more openly. For example, in Bances Candamo's *La piedra filosofal* (The Philosopher's Stone; 1693), the playwright demonstrates a knowledge of the history of literary and dramatic wild figure typologies by masterfully weaving them together in his complex and ambiguous depiction of his protagonist's wildness. Concretely, Bances leverages the conventions of these traditions to launch a subversive critique of the Habsburg monarchy at the end of the seventeenth century. Taking place in the mythological past, the protagonist opens the play by physically subduing a lion to defend the royal party on the road to Cádiz, where they are traveling to worship at the temple of Hercules. Set in this mythological and geographic context, the main character's hyperbolic display of fitness establishes the character's symbolic kinship to Hercules, a figure indelibly connected to the Iberian Peninsula and the mythological origins of Spanish identity. (Rendering the play's allusion even more transparent, Hercules is portrayed in iconography as a wild man wielding a club and wearing the pelts of the Nemean lion he famously slayed; see Figure 0.8.) These elements set in motion Bances's mythological allegory, which goes on to traverse the

FIGURE 0.8. Francisco de Zurburán, *Hércules lucha con la hidra de Lerna*, 1634, oil on canvas, 133 × 167 cm (inventory no. P001249). Madrid, Museo Nacional del Prado. © Photographic Archive Museo Nacional del Prado.

rise and fall of Spanish imperial hegemony in three acts. By the end of the play, the protagonist, who previously evoked Hercules as a beacon of competence and ability, has lost his grip on reality and suffers what would now be called a mental-health crisis. Nevertheless, he ascends the throne despite having transformed into a different type of wild man. Depicted through his descent into madness, he now echoes the lovesick wild man of the sentimental romance tradition.[14] This crisis of political authority in *La piedra filosofal* reflects the state of Spanish political affairs in the final decade of the seventeenth century.

These initial examples provided here illustrate both the symbolic flexibility of the wild figure, and also the ideological trajectory of its representation over the course of the seventeenth century. Moreover, these instances are representative of the types of oppositional values for which the wild figure stands in as a symbolic theatrical vessel, and its capacity as either a transgressive or subversive force. Wildness transgresses ideologies that would seek to contain and reincorporate it back into the hegemonic body in domesticated form, but it is also inherently subversive, containing within it the seeds of opposition, which (whether consciously or not on the part of playwrights) is always up for grabs in the *comedia* as a contested site for the reproduction or transformation of dominant cultural values. In this action-packed drama that spans the length of the Spanish Baroque, wild figures are cast in a leading role. This book shines a spotlight downstage for their monologue.

THE BAROQUE, COLONIALITY, AND MODERNITY

I have already begun to rely heavily on certain critical terminology that will continue to feature throughout the study, specifically related to concepts including the Baroque, modernity, and ideology. Because it is one of the objectives of *Wild Theater* to develop more nuanced conceptualizations of this terminology as illuminated by the baroque wild man, it is important to rehearse a history of the usage of this critically essential vocabulary. For Hispanists, an inflection point in that history can be found in the influential (even if controversial) work of José Antonio Maravall. In his foundational studies on ideology and culture in sixteenth- and seventeenth-century Spain, Maravall resisted a common understanding of the Baroque as primarily an aesthetic movement, traditionally presented as "a complex of literary or pseudo-artistic aberrations saturated with bad taste that Counter-Reformation Catholicism had cultivated in the countries subject to Rome."[15] Rather, he argued for a broader scope of the term that encompassed the entire period "in its constituent characteristics articulated within a political, economic, and social context."[16] Concisely, Maravall considered the Baroque a "historical structure." In so doing, he builds off Wölfflin's study in *Renaissance and Baroque*, which established the view of the Baroque as a modern break from the classicism of Renaissance style; nevertheless, however accurately Wölfflin identified the major features of baroque aesthetics, Maravall's approach "opens up new analytical dimensions" by putting "baroque style into a broader socio-cultural framework."[17] Baroque aesthetics cannot be decoupled from their socio-historical context, and as a consequence, the Baroque, as defined by Maravall, "was accompanied by a complexity of resources and results that made it one of those most in need of study in order to understand the history of modern Europe."[18] This contention, that the Baroque should be considered "both as aesthetic category and as historical/cultural problem" has garnered wide acceptance, and found purchase among scholars as a useful point of access for understanding the period.[19] Egginton notes that the utility of considering the Baroque in these terms lies in its explanatory power "as the aesthetic counterpart to a problem of thought that is coterminous with that time in the West we have learned to call modernity, stretching from the sixteenth century to the present."[20]

Essential for Egginton is the notion that articulations of baroque aesthetics therefore must be understood in relation to that "problem of thought" fundamental to modernity, which

> is that the subject of knowledge can only approach the world through a veil of appearances; truth is defined as the adequation of our knowledge to the world thus veiled; hence, inquiry of any kind must be guided by the reduction of whatever difference exists between the appearances and the world as it is. The problem, or why the problem remains a problem, is that the subject of knowledge only ever obtains knowledge via his or her senses, via how things appear, and hence the truth thus sought will itself always be corrupted by appearances.[21]

Thus, even in the strictest of definitions that presents the Baroque as a set of aesthetic features, it is more than merely a "style"; it constitutes a "perspective, a way of thinking which first flourished during a specific period and which now functions as a meeting point whose traffic lights make us halt and stop to think about (the culture of) the present and (some elements of) the past."[22] If the Baroque signifies a formative stage in the emergence of modernity (or what is most often referred to as early modernity), we overlook its critical role in understanding modernity as it developed, and the vestiges of those influences that remain into the present. This is not a novel idea; in fact, a robust body of scholarship has found meaningful parallels between the seventeenth century and the late-twentieth century for which the critical vocabulary offered by the Baroque has become useful as a tool that helps us comprehend aspects of a modern worldview when it was still "early," and again at the time of its possible exhaustion: postmodernity. As such, the term "baroque" has come to be understood "not only as a phenomenon of the seventeenth century (an era traditionally associated with the Baroque), but also, more broadly, as a transhistorical state that has wider historical repercussions."[23] In this vein, studies more focused on the aesthetic, ideological, technological, and economic features of twentieth- and twenty-first-century media and entertainment have found purchase in the epochal nomenclature of the neo- and ultrabaroque.[24]

But the major contribution of Maravall's work, at the most elemental level, is his recognition of the resonances between the salient features of the Baroque and the developments that were definitory for incipient modernity, even if his work soon divided Hispanist scholarship over the accuracy of some of his major conclusions about the Baroque as a "conservative," "guided," "urban," and "mass-oriented" culture. Some of his strongest critics have largely moved on from his approach due to what they see as an over-emphasis on the deliberate nature of institutional power in baroque Spain, exercised successfully to bend the collective will of the passive masses to acquiesce to their own domination. Others look to Maravall as a point of departure, developing his approach with greater nuance with the tools offered by materialist and historicist approaches to cultural production. His contention that the dominant class deployed cultural production (theater in particular) as a tool to exert ideological control over a homogenous body of willing subjects leads Weiss to recognize the justifiable "credibility problem" of this approach that stems from its reductivism. For instance, J.H. Elliot found that Maravall's conceptualization of the Baroque as a *cultura dirigida* ("guided culture") fails to account for subject formation.[25] Ruth Mackay makes that argument more forcefully, finding "fault with Maravall for focusing on grand, epochal structures that elide the tensions and contradictions of lived history and overlook individual agency."[26] As a result, Pérez-Magallón concludes that the "fundamental shortcoming of Maravall's proposal rests in the fact that presenting baroque cultural formation as a perfectly planned unitary whole defending monarchical-aristocratic interests leaves no room for the potential interstices through which alternative cultural possibilities, however subaltern, may emerge."[27]

Scholars like Castillo and Nelson contend that claims about Maravall's rejection of the possibility of reciprocal and dynamic relations of power are overblown.[28] Nevertheless, let us presuppose for a moment that (1) Maravall's central claims place "too great an emphasis on the mechanism of deliberate control exercised over a largely passive mass of people by willing and knowing adherents to the dominant regime" and (2) as a consequence, "it is all too easy to slide towards narrowly deterministic views of art as propaganda, and ideology as a rigid set of beliefs justifying the domination of one group over others."[29] Even if those critiques are merited, they can be addressed without discarding the fundamental aims of the methodology that "the task of the historian is to reconstruct and to depict the comprehensive epochal design in which every single human fact fits and can be explained in relation to the others."[30] In lieu of picking a side—pro- or anti-Maravall—Nelson succinctly identifies how the two camps prioritize different aspects of the social context of the period, and are complimentary rather than contradictory. Citing Martín-Estudillo and Spadaccini, he notes that "there are those who were interested in historically oriented interpretations focusing on the Baroque's containment side (Maravall) while others highlight its transgressive or liberating aspects."[31]

Although certain approaches to cultural production focus on the "containment side" of cultural control and hegemony, they still can (and should) account for the dynamic and contested forces at play in historical structures, only *observed from the vantage of containment*. For instance, contributions by Raymond Williams (building on the legacy of Antonio Gramsci) in his work on cultural hegemony acknowledge the "way cultural authority is both centralized and put under pressure from the margins, illustrating the dynamic relationship between social agency and structure."[32] Importantly, careful approaches to hegemonic power "open up the possibility of recollecting what hegemony represses and, for that very reason, what is resistant to the strategies of domination."[33] Dominant culture, indeed, dominates, but what is more, it is also subject to change, which of course happens over time. Epochal structures form, transform, and ultimately give way to new epochs. By recognizing in the historical data the reality of social agency and "emergent oppositional values," it opens up the additional possibility for scholarly approaches not only to investigate the energies motivating instances of social resistance in early modern Spain, but also, from the containment side, to observe the interplay between social agency and structure as contested sites where resistance is met with "hegemonic attempts to control, transform, or incorporate" those forces.[34] We are engaging here in what Stuart Hall aptly considers "the dangerous enterprise of thinking at or beyond the limit," but these are the questions at stake in a serious consideration of representations of wild figures in a culture seemingly committed to disavowing their existence, yet in which we find them everywhere.[35] Keeping a careful reading of these critical voices in mind, my approach will seek to explain the ideology of the Baroque from its margins, where the wild figures of the Spanish *comedia* inhabit the borderlands of containment and embody cultural forces at these sites where dominant and resistant ideological discourses are contested.

Renderings of history as a process that is constantly in flux also have implications on our conceptualizations of epochal terminology like "baroque" and "modernity." Traditionally, both of the terms suggest a fundamental break from a period that came before, in this case, the "Renaissance" and "medieval," respectively. As mentioned earlier, it is Heinrich Wölfflin who can be credited for the legacy of thinking about the Baroque as a break from the Renaissance. Replacing this language of rupture, Ndalianis reframes the solidification of an identifiable Baroque rather as an "intensification" of earlier modes of thinking that underwent transformations, eventually to such an extent that they become something new. For instance, one of the major distinctions between Renaissance and baroque aesthetics in art is the apparent rejection of Renaissance classicism in the Baroque; however, Ndalianis argues that the persistence of the classical is actually essential to understanding the Baroque in the ways it "embraces the classical, integrating its features into its own complex system."[36] For example, the representation of the classical is unmistakable in the poetry of Luis de Góngora, including his integration of mythological imagery, Renaissance *topoi*, and the marked influence of Latin in his poetic lexicon (usually in the form of neologisms). And yet, Góngora becomes a quintessential example of the baroque virtuoso, not by rejecting classical elements, but as a consequence of intensifying their use, ultimately to transform his poetry into something new. The quantity and obscurity of mythological imagery, along with his penchant for syntactical complexity and the lexical and rhetorical excess of his verse, are the archetypically baroque hallmarks of his poetic aesthetic. And ultimately, the Cordovan poet exemplifies Ndalianis's definition of the baroque virtuoso. When Góngora "multiplies, complicates, and plays with classical form, manipulating it with virtuoso flair," I submit that he establishes "a dialectic that embraces the classical in its system, [and] finally subjects it to a baroque logic."[37]

But again, these aesthetic qualities are more than a question of poetic style. Poetic form is no longer an instrument that works in harmony with content to produce meaning, as was the neo-platonic ideal that motivated Renaissance verse; rather, baroque form exceeds content to become meaning itself. And importantly, the baroque aesthetics of excess exemplified in Góngora's verse evince an unmistakable shift in the semantic field that exudes "instability, polidimensionality, mutability, and fragmentarity which [Walter] Benjamin" associated with modernity.[38] Along with the baroque intensification of the classical came a corresponding shift in the relationship between art and nature, specifically, the anti-naturalism attributed to the Baroque. But again, it is not so much that the natural is absent from the Baroque. Instead of emphasizing the idealized beauty and harmony of natural form (through artistic methods that sought to reproduce the natural world mimetically), the vitality of nature and its natural forces come to be associated more with a chaotic, unregulated, and dangerous energy. Succinctly, in the Baroque, nature becomes intense. Art no longer seeks correspondence in nature, but rather opposition, a force to overcome, something to "perfect," as Gracián famously quipped.[39] The relationship between art and nature has been a dynamic one over the course of history, and the two are interpenetrating concepts "always in dialectical opposition, always on the verge of synthesis."[40] But shifts in emphasis on either side of the dialectic can be fundamental. For instance, depictions of a peaceful Arcadian landscape (*locus amoenus*) in the Renaissance pastoral gives way to a more threatening natural landscape of danger and decay, and paintings like Poussin's *Et in Arcadia ego* offer a macabre reminder that death exists in Arcadia, too. (In the painting, foregrounded upon an agrestic backdrop, a group of shepherds admire a mausoleum inscribed with the Latin phrase, *Et in Arcadia ego*; see Figure 0.9.) Essential to the Edenic landscape is its hybridity, both as the locus of communion with the present God but also the site of expulsion where death and alienation come to condition human existence. This pendulum swings from the idyllic to the dangerous in the Baroque. Left unattended, nature takes over, always poised to swallow up the artifacts of human attempts to harness or organize it, which points to the prevalence of representations of ruins in the Baroque that Walter Benjamin recognized as a symbolic landscape in literary production of the period as well as a subject in the visual arts.[41] Exemplified in the works of Piranesi, nature asserts itself as a force of entropy that has reclaimed the space where civilization had once attempted to harness it. With these being the dominant representations of nature in the Baroque, it is perhaps unsurprising that in the cultural production of the period (e.g., the Spanish *comedia*) we find a pronounced fixation on wildness as an imagined threat to social destabilization, and that the wild man would gain purchase as an emblematic monster in the cultural imagination. He is both an entity that begs domestication (Christianization, civilization, etc.) and a warning against leaving the forces of nature unattended, lest the stability of civil order fall into a state of ruin and decay.

Here, the artistic treatment of classical material and the representation of nature serve as two examples toward a definition of the Baroque as not so much a break from Renaissance sensibilities but an intensification of its conventions, which is the lens through which that epochal shift is viewed in this book. These relevant examples begin to demonstrate the ways aesthetic sensibilities are inextricable from and a reflection of the broader epistemic context of the early modern period. To continue situating baroque aesthetics into that broader epistemic context requires further exposition of its organizing characteristics. Plainly, what is modernity? What fundamental shifts does this epochal term signify as distinguished from the premodern historical formations that preceded it? In the context of the sixteenth and seventeenth centuries, modernity has broad purchase as a marker that encompasses a set of trends and events considered to be worldview-shifting, including: (1) in philosophy, the emergence of Cartesian rationalism, subjective individualism, Neostoicism, and skepticism, (2) political changes marked by the rise of the nation-state, which became the crucible in which nationalism and the democratic ideal were forged, (3) new social organizations structured around capitalism and urbanization that hastened the disappearance of feudalism, (4) technological advances that fundamentally changed the way information was disseminated thanks to the printing press, (5) innovations in navigation and technologies of war which catalyzed imperial expansion and colonial domination on a global scale, and (6) major progress in the natural sciences (especially in physics and astronomy) stimulated as a function of groundbreaking inventions in instrumentation that gave early empiricists the tools to make new dimensions of the universe measurable and observable—and therefore knowable—through prosthetic amplification (e.g., the telescope and the microscope).

But there is another side to this narrative of the world becoming modern, about which postcolonial Hispanist scholarship provides insights, and will also serve as an important critical lens for understanding the wild figure. In particular, Latin American philosophers and sociologists like Enrique Dussel, Aníbal Quijano, and Walter Mignolo argue for a shift in the telling of the history of modernity to place greater emphasis on the impact of colonialism in shaping the modern worldview and world-system. As a consequence of re-reading history in this light, these scholars ultimately recalibrate the lenses through which we view the

FIGURE 0.9. *Et in Arcadia ego*, Nicholas Poussin (1628). Courtesy of the Musée du Louvre, Paris, via Wikimedia Commons.

modern turn to factor in the impact of coloniality. Traditional paradigms in the history of ideas argue for a "modernity" that begins in the wake of developments more squarely situated in the eighteenth century including Enlightenment rationalism, democracy as a political ideal exemplified in the French Revolution, and the rise of capitalism as an economic paradigm (although, as indicated in the previous paragraph, even these developments trace back to the sixteenth century).[42] However, according to Quijano, this portrayal of the history of human civilization as "a trajectory that departed from a state of nature and culminated in Europe" serves as the foundation on which the myth of modernity's Eurocentrism is built.[43] And once established, this vantage produces a view of "the differences between Europe and non-Europe as natural (racial) differences and not consequences of a history of power."[44] This second myth is the essence of what Quijano calls the "coloniality of power," which he asserts as both a cause and constituent part of modernity, not an effect (nor a vestige of a late-medieval historical formation).[45] Seen this way, a more complete narrative of incipient modernity must begin much earlier to account for the role colonialism played in producing the modern world-system and its ideological superstructure. Castro-Gómez summarizes Dussel's contribution to this paradigm-shifting alternative history: "The modern world-system begins with the simultaneous synthesis of Spain as a 'center' and Hispanic America as its 'periphery.' Modernity and colonialism are then a mutually dependent phenomenon. There is no modernity without colonialism and no colonialism without modernity. After all, Europe could only be conceived as the center of the world-system at the moment when its transatlantic colonies became the periphery."[46] By integrating coloniality into the modern ethos, it frustrates the mythology at the heart of a depiction of modernity as the inexorable march of progress (culminated in Europe), where history is "conceived as an evolutionary continuum from the primitive to the civilized, from the traditional to the modern, from the savage to the rational, from proto-capitalism to capitalism."[47] Born out of ideas of Enlightenment philosophers like Kant and Hegel, this is what Dussel calls the "fallacy of developmentalism."[48] And noting this fallacy forces us to acknowledge the other side of modernity, the one inaugurated first by the *ego conquiro* (the "conquering self," Dussel's term) that anticipated *ego cogito* by over a century, and is in fact intrinsic to the self/other dualism essential to Cartesian subjectivity. This example can be extended to identify the coloniality at the epistemic core of modern rationalism that depends on certain essential binaries—center/periphery, self/other, subject/object, and individualism/dualism. These binaries are the building blocks for the "totalization" of modernity's Eurocentrism, which "lies in the confusion between abstract universality and the concrete world hegemony derived from Europe's position as center."[49] Colonial domination, then, cannot only be seen only as an economic, political, and military phenomenon, but also one that "involves the epistemic foundations that supported the hegemony of European models of production of knowledge in modernity."[50] Building on Edward Said's framework on orientalism, Castro-Gómez labels the vantage from which those foundations are established as the "hubris of zero degrees":

> From the perspective of zero degrees, all human knowledge is arranged on an epistemological scale that goes from the traditional to the modern, from barbarism to civilization, from the community to the individual, from tyranny to democracy, from the individual to the universal, from East to West. We face an epistemic strategy of domination, which, as we well know, continues to thrive. Coloniality is not the past of modernity; it is simply its other face.[51]

Latin America becomes resituated as an early and primary frontier for Europe to deposit its universalist designs, where "barbarians, primitives, underdeveloped people, and people of color" were conceptualized as "categories that established epistemic dependencies under different global designs (Christianization, civilizing mission, modernization and development, consumerism)," states Mignolo.[52] "These epistemic dependencies," he goes on, are "the very essence of coloniality of power."[53]

While the Baroque and coloniality (as previously defined) have not traditionally featured in conceptions of modernity, I am building a case here for the explanatory power offered by these critical vocabularies toward a sophisticated apparatus to narrate the modern turn. Most important to the present study, however, are the ways that the Baroque and coloniality (both individually and in synthesis) provide a contextual framework in the service of explaining the simultaneous rise to prominence of the wild figure in Iberian theatrical production. Returning to an example I outlined, in the Baroque, natural landscapes (the wild figure's domain) are no longer imagined as a pastoral *locus amoenus*, but rather an untamed wilderness that begs to be harnessed under the technical control of the artist (*ars*). This is the purpose of the garden in the Baroque, to bring order to the wilderness, perfecting it by subjecting it to an imposed order of geometric, architectural, and technological design. Operating on both literal and figurative levels, a political metaphor that became popularized during the period lauded the figure of the prince, whose good governance brings order to the kingdom just as the gardener maintains the orderly garden through technical skill (*techne*).[54] Poets invoked this comparison for their own craft as well, fashioning their poetic or dramatic worlds on the metafictional premise of the poet-as-gardener and the text their garden.[55] What is more, the lens of coloniality brings into focus the hierarchal dualism that is embedded in a baroque aesthetics of nature. Nature, as a wilderness, comes to be defined on the basis of its deficit—uncivilized, disordered, primitive—which becomes a rationale and implied invitation for the artist (gardener, prince, *conquistador*, ethnographer, etc.) to bring their technical skill to civilize, order, and modernize the space. In so doing, modernity's Eurocentrism betrays its epistemic coloniality; for example, early modern natural philosophers, committed to the empiricist ideal of objectivity, bear witness "to a faith in the real phenomenon of truth," according to Wallerstein. But hidden by these idealized commitments is a confusion between contingent, historical, and "local truth with universal values."[56] Through this lens, these hallmarks of the modern turn can no longer solely be viewed as the result of progress, but rather an upshot of an underlying and persisting coloniality.

Whereas art was to harmonize itself to nature in the Renaissance, in the Baroque, art and nature experience an ontological separation, becoming categorical opposites, but also unequal opposites. In this hierarchical duality, art is over nature and exists to harness, improve, order, and master it (in every sense of the term). Aesthetics transform over time as artists hone the tools at their disposal to represent the world in response to the always-changing contingencies that characterize the reality around them. Baroque aesthetics are a sign and symptom of a world becoming modern, but also of one that, once it had gone colonial, would not dispense of its epistemic coloniality, only disavow it. The Spanish *comedia* "arises as a gesture of symbolic power" in this context, and in it we find the conventions of baroque aesthetics deployed to produce meaning in the world in which coloniality had taken root.[57] In its most conventional format, the constituent elements of dramatic action in the *comedia* consist of a portrayal of the world in disorder, followed by a restoration of order produced by *desengaño* (i.e., some truth revealed to the cast of characters, resulting in the resolution of the plot). Wild figures appear in the baroque theatrical imagination, taking on these aesthetics to act symbolically within these disordered dramatic worlds (dramatic wildernesses) begging for order (civilization). Discursively, the conventions of wildness and wild figures function to respond to the epistemic preoccupations of that world, as a reflection (or artistic perfection) of the historical reality in which they were dramatically imagined and staged. When the wild figure's "true" identity is revealed (through *desengaño*) to restore order at the end of these plays, they offer a fantasy of universal(izing) truth for a world increasingly aware of historical contingency. But it is important to note that the wild figure play, baroque in its obsession with false appearances, presents a world that only *appears* to be in disarray. Its conventions reflect an attempt to put back in order categories destabilized in the wake of 1492 and the New World encounters thereafter that defied established modes of classification.[58] The savage becomes an important symbolic vehicle to present the world in this type of crisis of knowledge. As stated earlier, in the *comedia*, the wild figures are almost never wild. In the end, it is "discovered" that the character everyone in the play supposes to be wild in fact turns out to be a high-born, white, European aristocrat. This configuration of the *desengaño* is the dramatic analogue of discovery, a term "derived from a late ecclesiastical Latin word, 'disco-operto' meaning 'to uncover,' 'to reveal,' 'to expose to the gaze'" (a denotation maintained in the Spanish *descubrimiento*).[59] Then, the totalizing and Eurocentrist ideals bound up in the *desengaño*/discovery that bring the fictional world back into order dramatizes the colonial reflex to assimilate the other, or as Pagden states, "transform this 'New' world, and its inhabitants, into a likeness of the Old."[60] Representations of wildness on the sixteenth- and seventeenth-century Iberian stage therefore not only exhibit their underlying coloniality in producing meaning, but also how difficult it is to extricate those characteristics from the baroque aesthetics that characterize their dramatic transmission. In these ways, the wild man of the Spanish *comedia* is baroque and he is colonial. And by that, I mean, modern.

In the field of cultural production, the interpretive lenses of the colonial and the baroque become integral in our conception of modernity because they offer new epistemic and aesthetic dimensions to our readings of cultural practices as they took shape, providing further insight into "an interpretative *habitus* in which a symbolic activity makes sense."[61] Another critical component of these lenses is the question of form. Nelson's examination of the emerging popularity of emblems during the period cuts across many of the same fields as those I cover here related to the importance of form; in the *Persistence of Presence* he describes the material production and cultural reception of emblems to illuminate the relationship between their formal composition and meaning in the cultural field. He highlights the hybridity and ambiguity at every level of their aesthetic form, material production, and cultural reception, arguing that the constituent facets of emblem culture are indicative of a fundamental departure from "medieval conceptions of the sacred meaning of words." Rather, they gesture toward "the infinite abyss that opens up between the sign and its meaning in modernity."[62] Of most importance for the present study, the aesthetics of baroque cultural production intersect with the modern in the ways they embody this "realization of the lack of epistemological and ontological certitudes characteristic of modernity."[63] The *comedia*, itself a hybrid form (tragicomic, heteroglossic, polymetric), also manifests this distinctive attribute of the modern turn in its aesthetic and thematic fixation on the portrayal of the world as full of deception. For Nelson, to understand the parameters of cultural production as a symbolic activity, analysis of the formal composition and material practices of the medium are critical. He explains:

> The emblem appears in a world that has become multiple and conflictive, and in which the traditional hierarchy between the word and the sign has become unstable. In the end, emblematics is a medium in which the desire for presence may convincingly compensate for symbolic, historical, and social instability by evoking a unified meaning from a constitutively hybrid form.... Nevertheless, if the emblem embodies a desire for presence in the face of a world of disintegrating certainties, it also embodies this same disintegration in the dispersed and confused nature of its material production.[64]

Understood along those lines, the emblem and the *comedia*, as new forms of early modern media, are two important examples of the broader "crisis of representation" in the Baroque. Castillo and Egginton consider this crisis a product of early modernity, a period they classify as the first "age of inflationary media." "Media become inflationary," they contend, "when the scope of their representation and of the world threatens the confines of their culture's prior notions of reality."[65] The emergent crisis of reality during the early modern period arose out of the proliferation of new media (again, the *comedia* and emblems being specific examples of such media), and was reflected in their aesthetics:

> the invention of movable type and the development of a vibrant print culture, the rapid spread of the use of perspective in painting and architecture, and the rise of an urban mass theater institution conspired to provoke a crisis of reality. Books changed from unique objects to copies of an ideal text; the way perspective situated viewers created the sense that one's point of view was both unique and limited; and the distinction between actors and the characters they portrayed began to be used as a model for understanding the relationship between human knowledge and reality itself.[66]

Those manifestations (i.e., print books, perspective in painting, and theater) are signs and symptoms of this evolving relationship between "human knowledge and reality itself" where reality (truth, God, presence) was imagined as existing behind the veil of appearances and therefore inaccessible to human perception. Responses to this crisis of knowledge take shape in myriad ways. Most importantly here, the baroque aesthetics of *desengaño* (again, becoming "undeceived") are one such response to this configuration of reality where metaphysical truth is understood to exist on a separate plane beyond the limits of perception. *Desengaño* offers a solution that allows the subject to transcend that boundary and see the truth behind the veil of appearances, an effective technique indeed, but also one that requires a disavowal. This is because that truth, however persuasively represented, can only be that, a representation. It can only be offered up in the mediated form of its copy—a book, a character, a painting, or a fictional world on page, canvas, stage, or (in later periods) screen.

This configuration of reality and human knowledge underpins the conventions of baroque theatricality as a representational mode, and the poetics of *desengaño* are essential as a lens through which to understand depictions of wildness on the Iberian stage. Conventional to the wild figure *comedia*, the wild character is revealed (as part of the plot-resolving *desengaño*) to be not wild at all, but rather the long-lost prince(ss) whose identification restores social order. This theatrical structuring of space, where the false appearances of the protagonist's wildness are removed to display their "true" identity underneath, relies on "the indefinitely renewed promise of presence just beyond the next veil of mediation."[67] Therefore, in revealing "truth," *desengaño* simultaneously covers up—disavows—the inescapable tension inherent to theatrical representation where the artistic medium can only offer a theatricalized image of the "reality" or "truth," conveyed, rather than the presence of that reality itself. If these parameters lie at the heart of theatrical practice as a symbolic activity, during the Baroque, also known as an "age of monsters," it is no coincidence that the wild man would figure so prominently in representations of the monstrous "at a time when the borders of our knowledge were shifting *wildly* and 'reality' itself appeared to be up for grabs."[68] Ideologically, the *comedia* was an apparatus where those "up-for-grabs" borders were negotiated, established, and reproduced for a mass audience.[69] Depictions of wildness (i.e., that which exists beyond a border, namely, beyond *civilization*) serve as an apt vehicle to demarcate a boundary, and portrayals of the domestication of wildness show what can be transformed and co-opted back within those borders and what remains excluded—the unsalvageable savages of ideological commitments in a given context.

Wild figures always embody proscription, something that exists beyond the purview of social order—that which should not exist at all. In so doing, they demarcate a firm boundary to reassert the status quo; at the same time, they simultaneously give wildness a form in the cultural imagination that, once conceived, cannot be easily forgotten. What is more, observing culture from the margins offers a vantage point of the contested and dynamic sites where hegemony and oppositional value vie for territory, and where it cannot be taken for granted that hegemonic value wins out. As we see over the course of the seventeenth century wild figures are liable to get away from their author (in some cases more than others), and the replication of the wild figure creates a surplus that cannot always be straightforwardly reconstituted back into the boundaries of baroque ideological cartography through the mechanisms of the same dramatic conventions. Every time the wild figure appears, it pits hegemony against oppositional value to perform in a dangerous "theater of truth," where the reproduction of dominant ideology may be the most likely outcome, but not the only possible one.

CHAPTERS, CORPUS, AND SCOPE

Chapter 1 presents a dramatic history of wildness that highlights the theatrical influences out of which the baroque wild figure emerges. Understanding the ways premodern paratheatrical spectacle in the courtly and public spheres mutually influenced each other is fundamental to the emergence of modern theatrical practice and the semiotics of theatricality (i.e., the ways that meaning is produced in the symbolic space we call modern theater). As the crucible in which the baroque theatrical wild figure is forged, attention to these precursors offers critical information as a historical point of departure to shed light on the representations of wildness in the *comedia* examined in *Wild Theater*. Moving into Chapter 2, I outline the features that distinguish Lope's wild characters from earlier representations. Aside from living in the woods and wearing animal skins, in these plays wildness works on a figurative level by presenting the monstrosity of the wild figure as corresponding to socially aberrant behaviors. But it is essential to their representation during the Spanish Baroque that the wild figure's assumed monstrosity is an illusion, a perception of him or her rather than a reliable marker of their identity within the poetic logic of the plays. Therefore, their marginalization at the hands of society—or monstrification—creates a quintessentially baroque dissonance between their appearance and underlying identity. This element forms the axis around which the baroque wild figure develops into the type s/he becomes in the *comedia* corpus. Wildness is not a problem innate to the nature of these theatrical characters, but rather a superficial state of being that can only be resolved through the poetics of *desengaño* by uncovering hidden truth behind the veil of appearances. The structure of this process dramatizes the modern crisis of a world in which truth and meaning have become less accessible, while also offering a dramatic fantasy that portrays those fears assuaged through the discovery of the wild figure's "true" identity. Defined by a displaced wildness—a savage misdirection—they are given the opportunity to remove the wild mask and make their humanity known. But the parameters defining their humanity are of course ideologically and dramatically constructed, as are the values projected onto their identities in these plays related to notions of monarchical authority, the honor code, femininity and masculinity, and among others, national identity.

This last theme is taken up in Chapter 3, which examines three *comedias* that employ representations of wildness to construct notions of Spanish national identity. These include Lope de Vega's *Las Batuecas del Duque de Alba* (c. 1600), Tirso de Molina's *Las Amazonas en las Indias* (Amazons in the New World; c. 1635), and Bances Candamo's *La piedra filosofal* (1693). This specific trilogy of plays forms a unity in their participation in the forming and re-forming of a nascent sense of Spanish national identity through a collective mythological past. The similarities they share provide evidence that the playwrights are drawing from a repertoire of conventions that overlap heavily, which allows for their differences (i.e., their commitments to and rejections of that repertoire) to become particularly telling. The first two plays chronologically by Lope and Tirso affirm a national mythos rooted in Spanish exceptionalism that, in the case of Lope de Vega's play is an ethno-religious apology for European and Old-Christian hegemony, and in Tirso's work depicts the rosy recasting of the infamous deeds of the conquistador Gonzalo Pizarro (and by extension the genocidal impact of the conquest of Peru). Later, Bances Candamo engages important aspects of both earlier *comedias* to deconstruct their national-mythological objectives. He inverts the emblematic discovery space of the cave, which is of critical symbolic importance in Lope's *Las Batuecas del Duque de Alba*, and in Bances's *La piedra filosofal* the cave becomes a figurative locus of the playwright's comprehensive *critique* of Spanish national mythologies glorified by his theatrical predecessors. For Bances, the theatrical device of the cave—and by extension theater itself—is exposed as a manipulative, rather than revelatory space. The playwright lays bear the semantics of this symbolic scenographic element in his meta-theatrical *comedia de magia* to present the Spanish imperial exploits of the previous century—those celebrated in Tirso de Molina's play—as a failed project of national and global proportions.

Chapter 4 then examines the embodied performance of gender through the lens of wildness. Central to this critical aim is the recognition of the complexity of the Spanish *comedia*'s wild figures as characters, and that their constitutive wildness is one aspect that cuts across other markers of their identity, gender being fundamental. In the *comedia*, consciously or not, the portrayal of gender non-conformity through the wild figure appears to always already resist social imposition, which is usually depicted through lengthy attempts to transform their appearance and behavior to conform to established gender norms. Representative of this transformation is a focus on the sartorial; the protagonists either reluctantly or are forced to leave behind their animal skins in exchange for the appropriate markers of their class and gender. This aspect is highlighted materially in the costume design of certain wild figure plays (including ones that feature masculine and feminine wild characters alike) but also as a rhetorical device fundamental to the message produced, whether successfully or in spite of the apparent ideological objectives of the play's poetic architecture. In one concise example, a female wild character is disparagingly called a "stain" (*borrón*), literally on an item of clothing, but *borrón* also suggests the figurative connotation of a blot on the page. Yet, the character overcomes their marginalization to claim a status of power in the play's conclusion. I present dramatic wildness in these plays as a problem of text and textile—an entity that figuratively tears at the social fabric of the Baroque. Like those that haunt Lady Macbeth, the stains produced through representations of wild gender in the *comedia* are difficult to disavow; however, I deploy the term in this chapter in reappropriated and empowering form, appreciating stains, rips, and tears on an elaborate baroque garment as acts of resistance against the conservative impulses of dominant cultural apparatuses. In many or all cases, that resistance may not have been actualized at the time to subvert dominant ideologies, so this approach is meant to constitute an act of recovery that conveys their resistance as such, in a new context in which it can be realized. These *comedias* are primed to be adapted and performed for the modern stage.

If Lope de Vega provides a logical point of departure for a study on the *comedia* (as so often is the case), then Chapter 5 relies on Calderón de la Barca as a bookend to the study. The final internal chapter offers a reading of the playwright's iconic wild man of *La vida es sueño* (*Life Is a*

Dream; 1635). Segismundo merits inclusion here not because he is emblematic or quintessential as one might expect as the most famous wild man of the Spanish Baroque, but rather is treated as exceptional, as an outlier to the conventions of the subgenre. I contend that Segismundo is a character who goes through a process of personal transformation (i.e., from savage to civilized), which marks him as unlike other iterations of the type. In this chapter, Segismundo is situated among Calderón's other wild men in *En la vida todo es verdad y todo mentira* (In Life, All is Truth and Falsehood; 1658), contrasted with notable influences such as Mira de Amescua's *La rueda de la fortuna* (The Wheel of Fortune; 1603). A pervasive trope utilized in the *comedia* for the purpose of the revelation of a character's identity, and not just in wild figure plays, was the ubiquitous notion that "the blood will out," (i.e., *la fuerza de la sangre*, that the nobility of a character's nature and lineage will make their identity clear). Calderón's play signifies a theatrical questioning of the utility of this ideology at a moment when the viability of Habsburg monarchical succession had become increasingly fragile. This is where I depart from criticism in the vein of Maravall that tends to see Calderón's theater as the pinnacle of the baroque *comedia* as a repressive ideological apparatus. Rather, in my view, Calderonian dramaturgy should be situated in a space between Egginton's major and minor strategies. His plays do not shy away from acknowledging their own theatricality, and in fact, their amplified metatheatricality is the mechanism by which dominant ideologies are undermined. Like in Cervantes's *El retablo de las maravillas* (*The Marvelous Puppet Show*), Calderón's self-referential theater takes its status as a copy seriously to subvert hegemonic discourse; however, the purpose of this endeavor (unlike Cervantine satire) is not to explode the power structures hegemony maintains, but to offer alternative ideologies that can better sustain that objective. In this Calderonian dramatic poetics, *desengaño* does not function to reveal reality or truth in a metaphysical sense, but rather posits a pragmatic response to a concrete problem without necessitating a commitment to traditional baroque ideologies to assert its legitimacy. This approach to Calderón helps explain some of the unresolved complexities of the skepticism found in the playwright's dramatic production, which I see as his practical response to a world in which certainty established by *organicism* is no longer a tenable program, in Juan Carlos Rodríguez's definition of the term.[70] And importantly, that pragmatic response does not align with dominant ideologies of the Spanish Baroque to the extent that it has historically been argued.

In the outline of the internal chapters of present study offered here, my corpus comes into view. I have curated a set of works meant to be representative of the trend and its conventions of the wild figure subgenre of the Spanish *comedia*, while also attending to exceptional outliers. *Wild Theater* highlights *comedias* in which a wild figure is the protagonist or wild figures play a foregrounded role. In Oleh Mazur's type index of the wild figure during the Renaissance and Baroque, the examples in my corpus are categorized generally under his designation as the "exposure type," that is, characters who become wild figures due to a period of exposure in the wilderness as infants or adults.[71] These are the ones featured in this study because they are also the predominant form on the early modern Spanish stage. In plays that do not fall under this broad categorization, wild figures almost always appear briefly as plot devices, and without speaking roles (or minimal ones, delivering only a few lines of dialogue). These are vestiges of a distinct wild folk type than the one taken up here, which again is the most conventional and pervasive form in the playwrighting from Lope de Vega to Bances Candamo. Plays that fall outside of the scope here would be *comedias* (or proto-*comedias*) that draw primarily from pastoral or folkloric/legendary (e.g., Carolingian) traditions, where wild figures either reflect conventions of wildness from those genres or as a function of reproducing specific characters that appear in the novelesque romance source material being adapted for the stage. Such plays influenced by the pastoral include Romero de Cepeda's *Comedia salvaje* (A Savage Comedy; 1582) and two by Lope: *El ganso de oro* (The Golden Goose; 1588–95) and *El premio de la hermosura* (Beauty's Prize; c. 1609–20). In each, the wild figures serve as a device to inject dramatic action by showing up to attack and/or kidnap the lovesick nobles and disturb the peace of the idyllic *locus amoenus*, as in a similar episode found in Montemayor's *La Diana*.[72] Among works influenced by the novelesque tradition that feature wild characters in a marginal or secondary capacity count three examples of plays by Calderón de la Barca: *La puente de Mantible* (The Bridge of Mantible; 1630), *El mayor encanto, amor* (Love, the Greatest Enchantment; 1635), and *Los tres mayores prodigios* (The Three Greatest Marvels; 1636). In each of those plays, the *salvaje* character is secondary and bears the traits of the giant found in chivalric romance, appearing briefly and episodically either to assist the protagonist in a task (e.g., *Los tres mayores prodigios*) or impede the hero in his journey (as in *La puente de Mantible* and *El mayor encanto, amor*).

Also, to curate a representative corpus in the space of the present study, decisions were required that necessarily excluded certain works from being highlighted. In certain cases, that meant making careful decisions to offer an in-depth analysis of one play over others that follow a similar pattern or conventions, but I acknowledge that a different set of critical lenses could justify a corpus comprised of a different subset of *comedias*. Along those lines, I offer a brief explanation of works not highlighted in the chapters that follow, but also use this space as a means to signal potential areas for further study on the performance of wildness in the dramatic production of the Spanish Baroque. For example, *El príncipe de los montes* (The Forest Prince, attributed to Juan Pérez de Montalbán) bears significant resemblances to Calderón's *La vida es sueño*. Its date of composition roughly coincides with the play renowned as Calderón's masterpiece, which suggests that further exploration could provide meaningful insights into both works. In another instance, Luis Vélez de Guevara's representation of a female wild figure in *Amor es naturaleza* (Love Is Nature) incorporates many of the conventions and devices as Lope's *El animal de Hungría* (The Animal of Hungary) and a later play by Figueroa y Córdoba, *La sirena de Tinacria* (The Siren of Sicily). *Amor es naturaleza* therefore displays potential for further study either in the form of a comparative study or in conversation with the analysis I offer on Figueroa y Córdoba's play in Chapter 4. On the question of gendered representations of wildness, another play that could extend the conclusions made in Chapter 4 is Tirso de Molina's *El Aquiles* (Achilles; c. 1611). In the *comedia*, its protagonist, the Homeric Achilles, first appears as a wild man, having been raised by Quirón at the behest of Tetis (Achilles' mother) to avoid a prophecy of his death should he participate in the Trojan War. Achilles is only presented as a wild figure in act 1, after which Tetis disguises Achilles as a noblewoman to be received at the court of Licomedes (act 2), finally to assume his destined role as a soldier counted in the ranks of the Greek forces in act 3. Importantly, this is the only instance in a wild figure *comedia* of a male character cross-dressing as a woman; however, explicitly indicated in the opening stage directions is that Achilles be played by a female actor. Since this aspect of the play has received significant scholarly attention, in lieu of Tirso's *comedia* I have elected to include works that engage the question of wildness throughout; moreover, a main obstacle to scholarship presented by Tirso's play is its unfinished status.[73] An essential element of my approach to the *comedia* is a focus on plot resolutions to interrogate the message of a play and how it is produced. *El Aquiles*, however, concludes *en medias res* as the Greek forces arrive at the gates of Troy. The subplot of Achilles's relationship with his betrothed Deidamia remains unresolved as well, and the final lines delivered by Ulysses speak on behalf of the playwright to promise a second part to the drama, but it has either been lost or was never composed.

Thematically, *Wild Theater* explores notions of monstrosity and otherness in the dominant cultural landscape of the Spanish Baroque at the intersection of political ideology, gender, class, and race. Ultimately, I depart from approaches (Oleh Mazur's index, for example) that deploy wildness as an umbrella term to encompass the Wildman (*salvaje*), the barbarian (*bárbaro*), and indigenous Americans (*indios*). While there are important intersections between these categories to be traced along the lines of race in the context of Spain's transatlantic colonial empire (ones that I examine in Chapter 3), there are fundamental distinctions between them that risk being conflated by always consolidating them into a single grouping. Nevertheless, it is not coincidental that a heightened cultural preoccupation with center and periphery manifested through representations of wildness arises at a time when the reach of Spain's geographical borders had expanded exponentially and at an unprecedented rate. Moreover, and as I unpack in Chapter 3, effacing race in representations of wildness on the Iberian stage creates a silence that speaks volumes about the ideological matrices underpinning hegemony, the examination of which is therefore essential to the present study. There are also other important avenues that can be opened up by incorporating the wild figure subgenre (*comedia de salvajes*) into a broader corpus and approaching it through the lens of race. For instance, Vélez de Guevara's *Virtudes vencen señales* (Virtue Conquers Appearances; c. 1618) draws heavily from the conventions of the wild figure *comedias*, but instead of reworking the dramatic action to distinguish the play from earlier ones like Lope's *El nacimiento de Ursón y Valentín*, the Andalusian playwright leaves his fingerprint on the work by omitting the wild protagonist and replacing him with a Black character, whose otherness is manifested not by the visual markers of the wild figure (animal pelts) but rather portrayed by his skin color.[74] My argument about the wild folk of the *comedia* can be extended to plays about Black characters such as Vélez de Guevara's *Virtudes vencen señales* because of the inherent coloniality that pervades the ideological discourses reflected in the cultural production of the period. If, as I have maintained, the Baroque reflects an early aesthetics of the world becoming modern, the other "common thread" that "links modernity in the sixteenth century with its current version is . . . the coloniality of power."[75] In establishing colonial difference as an epistemic dimension of modernity, Mignolo argues that racism develops in the sixteenth century, born out of the commitment to the purity of blood. This early expression of racism in Iberian culture that distinguished Old-Christians from people of Jewish or Moorish descent was programmed and reproduced in the execution of the colonial enterprise, incorporating Black Africans and Amerindians into a global ethno-racial hierarchical classification system.[76] It is in this context that savagery and Blackness come to be imagined as markers of Otherness (as opposed to other characteristics or figures, or as markers of something else), deployed in cultural apparatuses such as the Spanish *comedia* in the service of establishing and reproducing hegemony. Velez's play, in which wildness and race appear to be interchangeable, reinforces the argument for coloniality as an essential epistemic dimension of modernity, and points to the possible applications of this lens to a broader set of intersecting phenomena in the baroque cultural field.[77]

To conclude the study, I look beyond the seventeenth century in the Epilogue to dedicate attention to the Baroque as an early intensification of what it means to be modern. To accomplish this, I draw parallels to cultural phenomena in our media-saturated (and mediated) world today. Circling back to discussion presented in this introduction, I return to Castillo and Egginton's work in *Medialogies: Reading Reality in the Age Inflationary Media* to highlight the aspects of the world we consider modern, however fraught the term, that are foreshadowed in the production and reception of baroque Iberian theater. Inherent to modernity is the question of mediation in the increasing complexity of its ever-evolving forms. My work examines earlier iterations of cultures of mediation in that trajectory, which I argue provides a methodological (or medialogical) foundation that allows us to bring our contemporary landscape of cultural production into sharper focus. The contemporary examples I identify in the epilogue remain centered on representations of wildness, and how those representations past and present can illuminate the context in which they are produced. Presenting a genealogy of Sasquatch as a representative example, I trace the recent boom in cryptozoology documentaries back to the wild figure of the Spanish *comedia* as a means to affirm the overall project of the present study: to explain the centrality of the margin, and deterritorialize the epistemic structuring of space based on the hierarchical duality of center/periphery. Castillo and Egginton argue "reading reality" is so important today because of the massive resources invested in sustaining the globalized economic, sociological, and ecological power structures through the mechanism of an increasingly sophisticated medialogical landscape. Therefore, it is imperative we dedicate attention to identifying the ways that literal and figurative borders are constructed by and through media—be it a Hulu documentary, a targeted news headline on Twitter/X, or a Spanish *comedia*—and as a result, the less inclined we might be to lean into the subsequent cultural impulse to construct liminal wilderness borderlands and imagine their inhabitant(s) as the monstrous and abject Other.

CHAPTER 1

The Battle of Carnival and Lent

Premodern Antecedents of the Baroque Wild Figure

> Natural law is ribaldry.
> —Giordano Bruno, 1584

> There is no greater confusion than the confounding of jest and earnest.
> —Francis Bacon, 1589

OVER THE COURSE OF history, the wild man has taken many forms in the human imagination. Cultural anthropologist Roger Bartra points to the embedded presence of the wild man in the cultural production of the West, stating that they "zealously guard the secrets of Western identity," ever-present as they "watch over the frontiers of civilization."[1] As a conceptual category and in the collective imagination, wildness serves to demarcate the ideological margins of civilization as that which looms in the symbolic forest beyond the reach of civilized society. According to Hayden White, terms associated with wildness and its corresponding qualities "are not used merely to designate a specific condition or state of being but also to confirm the value of their dialectical antithesis," namely, "civilization."[2] Therefore, wildness provides a means by which to discern the "governing relationship" between dominant culture in a particular context "of the normal or familiar" and that which deviates from those values.[3] Furthermore, when observed over time, wildness demonstrates how those borders shift perpetually to form new margins at the periphery of re-centered hegemonies, thereby supplanting what came before them, articulated by Hegel as "shapes of life grown old."[4]

Although this and other scholarship has utilized the wild figure as a tool for charting those types of paradigmatic shifts in the Western worldview from antiquity to the present, studies to date have yet to situate the wild figure of the Spanish *comedia* comprehensively within that larger history of the representation of wildness.[5] Fausta Antonucci's *El salvaje en la Comedia del Siglo de Oro* on the wild man in the theater of the Spanish Baroque is substantive, but I take up the baton in the present study in response to her comment that "there is plenty left to say."[6] Due to its popularity on the early modern stage, this book centers on how the wild figure serves as a vehicle to explore the larger aesthetic and ideological matrices of the Spanish Baroque, as well as the nature of early modern theatrical representation.

As such, my approach situates the baroque wild man more directly within the history of spectacle and performance than previous work in cultural anthropology (Bartra) and literary history (Antonucci). This offers important insights into the genealogy of the type overlooked when focusing on cultural antecedents broadly or literary ones more specifically. In the pages that follow, I offer an in-depth exposition of the Spanish wild figure that emphasizes its *theatrical* lineage, which is essential to identify and understand the features that make it a uniquely theatrical phenomenon, aspects underdeveloped in scholarship to date.[7] In Bartra's typological history of wildness in European cultural production, he argues that baroque forms develop out of two medieval and Renaissance literary models, namely, those found in chivalric and sentimental romance. In chivalric cycles that glorify the exploits of knights errant, the common foes of the genre's heroic protagonists are often wild figures, who "offered society an 'abnormal' model for behavior" in contrast to the courtly model epitomized in the actions of the knight-errant.[8] The second type—the high-born protagonists of the sentimental romances—are not wild figures at the onset of the narrative, but rather fall into a state of wildness as a symptom of their lovesickness.[9] The effects of unrequited love cause these noble youths to languish, and as they unravel emotionally, they begin to take on the physical (and allegorical) attributes of the wild man as an outward manifestation of their inner passions. It is out of this tradition that characters like Cervantes's Cardenio and Ariosto's Orlando emerge, who exemplify a transitional phase in the representation of wildness toward the end of the Renaissance. Increasingly ironic and self-aware examples like those just mentioned are evidence of the decline of "the wild delirium of the lovesick courtier" as the dominant literary schematic for wildness in the cultural production of the West.[10] However, while this model accurately portrays the evolution of literary wildness, prose sources only make up one of a greater set of representational modes where wild folk appear in medieval and Renaissance Europe. Accordingly, the chivalric and sentimental predecessors outlined by Bartra emphasize prose and other non-dramatic sources that obscure traditions that more directly impacted the representations of wildness found in baroque theatrical practice. To sketch the genealogy of the wild figures that donned animal pelts on the early modern Spanish stage, we therefore must consider the equally pervasive examples of wild folk found in previous traditions of performance and spectacle, chiefly, court pageantry and folk ritual.

CARNIVAL: WILDNESS IN MEDIEVAL AND RENAISSANCE FESTIVAL CULTURE

Paratheatrical forms are crucial to this story.[11] The representation of wildness on the Spanish stage in the sixteenth and seventeenth centuries is a unique composite of those earlier paratheatrical court and folkloric traditions that ran parallel to the development of sentimental fiction and chivalric cycles, and should be emphasized for their direct influence on the wild figures that dominate the baroque stage. Tracing wildness from classical mythology to the Enlightenment's noble savage via medieval marginalia and Renaissance chivalric and sentimental fiction only tells a portion of the story; in a sense, studies have described the history of wildness as if its many threads were woven together into a single cord. While the strands they observe can be organized in this way, there are others that frustrate this complex and not entirely unilinear trajectory of a western genealogy of wildness.

Antonucci's aforementioned monograph maps another course in the cultural history of wildness; her introduction offers an in-depth account of the medieval folkloric typologies of the wild figure, which proves an immensely useful catalogue of the recurring motifs that drive the plots of many of the wild folk *comedias*. But like Bartra, she relies heavily in her study on literary rather than dramatic sources in identifying the traditions out of which the theatrical wild figures of the Spanish Baroque emerged. While her study identifies court spectacle and folk traditions as precursors, Antonucci focuses to a greater extent, and productively so, on folkloric and mythological typologies that subtend conceptualizations of wildness in the cultural imagination of the West. She then goes on to identify and interpret those types as they appear in the *comedia* corpus, isolating the "mechanisms" of representation that mutually influenced one another in the development of the wild figure in cultural production: "The formation of the literary wild figure undoubtedly is derived from characteristics of myth and folklore, as well as the figurative arts; reciprocally, literary elements can influence the representation of the wild man valued in the figurative arts."[12] Antonucci affirms that paratheatrical festivities (e.g., court masques, pageantry, festival processions, etc.), iconography, mythology and literary types mutually influenced one another in the development of the wild figure in early modern Spain, but she also implies a privileged role for literary influences in this dynamic insofar as festive paratheatrical iterations of the type (e.g., court masques and interludes) always reflected the basic narrative elements of their literary counterparts found in chivalric romances: "the core of the narrative that sustained these representations (even if it was otherwise minimal) was equal to that of the role it played in the narrative (and ideological) structure of chivalric novels."[13] Antonucci's suggestion that literary influences were primary to the development of the theatrical wild figure of the *comedia* signals the emphasis of her overall approach that situates the mythological and folkloric influences into what she describes as the "literary tradition" of the wild figure. This philological and literary focus at the center of the project, which again, is an essential study, obscures the unique elements of medieval paradramatic traditions that factor into the genealogy of the wild figures that populate the baroque Iberian stage. These traditions, as I stated earlier, belong to medieval and Renaissance court pageantry and folk ritual, two domains whose isolation from one another diminished over the medieval and Renaissance periods, greatly contributing to the emergence of modern theatrical practice.[14] The mutual influence of these two spheres of dramatic activity—the courtly and the popular—proves crucial for accessing the aspects of the wild figure's representation in the theatrical production of the Spanish Baroque that my analysis explores.

It is beyond the scope of this study to catalogue the different genres of court spectacle in detail, provided they are explained comprehensively in the many authoritative theater histories currently available.[15] But as a brief introduction to those genres en route to providing examples where the wild figure starts showing up, the forms of paratheatrical representation that were especially popular for courtly entertainment came to be classified under the blanket term *entremés*, which encompassed any type of rehearsed spectacles including dances (*bailes*), mummeries (*momos*), masques (*máscaras*), and mysteries.[16] Other paradramatic forms include more elaborate pageantry—reenacted battle scenes or tournaments generally taken from the chivalric tradition—and royal processions, both of which included a public audience beyond the court.[17] Extravagant festivities were often organized to celebrate momentous events such as royal visits to a city, royal births, birthdays, and weddings, along with festivities around religious holiday seasons such as Christmas and Shrovetide.[18] *Entremeses* would usually take place at similar points during celebrations, most often in conjunction with banquet feasts, often performed as entertainment between courses of the meal.[19] While containing some elements of plot and spoken verse, they were mainly composed of choreographed dances by masked players.[20] Between courses of the feast, a masked figure would interrupt the meal by bursting into the hall followed by other disguised players to begin the performance. At the conclusion of the piece, one or more of the characters would remove the mask to reveal their identity. A popular genre motif featured a horde of wild figures, whose costumes and dance symbolically corresponded with the time of revelry marked by the celebrations. Notably, however, members of the royal family often participated in the masques, particularly during their youth.[21] Their identity remained "hidden" behind their disguise as they weaved through the complex choreography of the dance among the other performers in the same or similar costume. In the case of the young nobility, the wild garb served as an allegory for the passions of youth, a costume they shed in the symbolic conclusion of the dance when the mask is removed, after which they assume their appointed seat at the banquet table once their true identity has been revealed.[22] In one famous example found in Gómez Manrique's *cancionero*, the young Isabel (prior to becoming queen Isabel the Catholic) performs a masque in which all of the performers are dressed in bright plumage as the eight muses, except for Isabel, who is cloaked in animal pelts.[23]

    Medieval and Renaissance entertainment at court could become much more elaborate than the masque, however. Other types of *entremeses* were performed on occasional stages or carts that were rolled into the banquet

FIGURE 1.1, FIGURE 1.2. Leone and Pompeo Leoni, *Carlos V y el Furor*, 1564, cast bronze, 251 × 143 cm, 825 kg (inventory no. E000273). Statue of Carlos V subduing Fury. The armor worn by the figure of Carlos V is removable and was crafted so that the statue could be displayed in either format. Madrid, Museo Nacional del Prado ©Photographic Archive Museo Nacional del Prado.

hall at the appointed time. A common motif of these performances drew from the chivalric imagination, usually depicting some variation of a recurring scene in which a castle is built upon a cart and inhabited by a group of young women at court, playing as maidens upon the structure's parapets. They defend the castle—an allegory for their virtue—from the bombardment of any would-be intruders depicted either as wayward knights or, "from the fourteenth century onward, . . . the wildman in certain allegorical scenes increasingly usurps roles originally held only by his human counterparts" (see Figures 1.3 and 1.4 for iconographic depictions of this scene).[24] As in the masques and mummeries however, wildness is juxtaposed meaningfully with the depiction of royalty. One example takes place in 1399 during a banquet at the court of Martí I of Aragon in which the *entremés* featured a large boulder built on a moveable cart that was brought into the hall. Upon the craggy ephemeral scenery was perched a wounded lioness (it seems to have been a sculpture rather than an actual

FIGURE 1.3. *Attack on the Castle of Love*. Ivory carving on the back of a mirror frame depicting knights sieging the Castle of Love. On the left, one knight curiously wields a club instead of a sword, possibly hearkening to the more common appearance of Wildmen in this scene. Unknown artist, circa 1330–1350 in Paris. © Victoria and Albert Museum, London.

lioness or a costumed performer). From the rock emerge birds and other game that scatter about the hall, when armed guards appear and begin to attack the lioness. Wild men enter the scene to come to her aid and defeat the men-at-arms, and the spectacle culminates as a child emerges from the lioness's wounds, cloaked in regal vestments bearing the royal coat of arms.[25] Further confirmation of the prominence of the wild figures in allegorical spectacles can be seen in the elaborate mock chivalric tournaments and naval battles put on as part of court entertainments, and royal processions, in which figures dressed as wild men would serve in the role of crowd control, walking with the parade while brandishing their clubs to keep "the crowds that followed the parade at bay."[26]

Lobato indicates these types of paradramatic entertainments remained popular at the Habsburg court in the sixteenth and seventeenth centuries,

FIGURE 1.4. *Wild Men Storming the Castle of Love.* Glass roundel with the arms of the Huppe family of Cologne. Circa 1530 in Cologne, Germany. Historisches Museum Frankfurt (inventory no. X19608, reproduced in Timothy Husband, *The Wild Man*, 75).

even if the predominance of the comedia obscures these types of paratheatrical entertainments.[27] While there were many motives for royal celebrations that included masques, dances, and interludes, there was one time of year such events could always be expected: Carnival. Lobato stresses the prevalence of paratheatrical revelry at court that occurred during this time of year: "If there was a time of year that was especially suited for this ludic mood, Carnival stands out, which did not only inspire popular celebrations but also, and especially, festivities at the Habsburg court."[28] Because Carnival and theater had long been and remained intrinsically linked, it is therefore no coincidence that the wild figure maintains such a prominent footing in the baroque theatrical imagination, specifically because of his essential role in the drama of Carnival.[29] He is the physical embodiment of the unruly spirit of Carnival—an analogue of the Lord of Misrule; as such, the fundamental role the wild figure played in the dramatic imagination at court was rivaled in the paratheatrical and semi-ritualistic practices of the folk.[30] And in order to understand the influences that shaped the wild figure in baroque theater, it is crucial to examine the evolving dynamics of representation of the wild figure(s) as they developed simultaneously in the quasi-separate courtly and popular spheres, while also exploring examples that demonstrate just how porous the boundary between the two really was. As performers and early playwrights traversed those borders by creating entertainments for both public and courtly audiences, it created the conditions for practices in each of those spaces to be mutually influential on one another.

By the medieval period, purely seasonal agrarian festivals had long been subsumed into the Catholic liturgical calendar, as winter solstice festivals were folded into Christmas celebrations, and the lean period of late winter into pre-Lenten carnival revelry. Costumed wild men feature prominently in agrarian rituals even to this day as a symbolic reflection of a time of excess and merriment.[31] Bernheimer outlines the structural elements of the carnivalesque wild figure drama shared across representations found in festivals throughout medieval Europe. An individual, or occasionally a group, would disguise themselves as wild men using materials that varied by locality including animal pelts, leaves, or straw. This costumed figure would be paraded into the center of town toward the end of the festival and then read his last rites, thereby symbolizing the waning spirit of Carnival. Once read, other participants in this spectacle would either beat him with sticks or chase him out of town in a banishment of the sinful self or indulgent spirit of revelry to usher in the sobriety of Lent (this is the scene unfolding toward the back of the town square in Brueghel's *The Battle Between Carnival and Lent*; see Figures 0.3 and 0.4). This ritualized spectacle exemplifies Bakhtin's notion of the carnivalesque spirit of the Middle Ages and Renaissance. In his framework, modern carnival celebrations break fundamentally from medieval and Renaissance expressions, which were "filled with a pathos of change and renewal, with the sense of the gay relativity of prevailing truths and authorities."[32] For Bakhtin, medieval folk ritual formed a "second life outside officialdom" during which "there is no other life outside it. During carnival time life is subject only to its laws, that is, the laws of its own freedom. It has a universal spirit; it is a special condition of the entire world, of the world's revival and renewal, in which all take part."³³ The medieval wild figure of Carnival embodies that spirit in which social pretense and hierarchical authority recede, giving way to celebratory laughter and revelry of the folk, but of course, contained within the permissible boundaries of a delineated period of time. Nevertheless, the extent of the social upheaval and renewal ingrained in the revelry diminishes, becomes less permitted, in the early modern period. And this transition coincides meaningfully with the rise of the modern commercial theater.

MODERNIZING CARNIVAL (I): JUAN DEL ENCINA'S *ECLOGUES*

Within medieval Carnival practices, the ritualistic release and sequestration of wildness is celebrated because it exemplifies "the temporary liberation from the prevailing truth and from the established order; it marked the suspension of all hierarchical rank, privileges, norms, and prohibitions.... It was hostile to all that was immortalized and completed."³⁴ In the early modern period, however, the rise of a bourgeois elite and the consolidation of political hegemony in monarchical forms of government transformed social realities. As a consequence, the ontological laughter of the carnivalesque would be silenced by "the bourgeois conception of the completed atomized being."³⁵ The power structures that underpin class society stifle the carnivalesque impulse of renewal and regeneration, and thereby inhibit practices of the social upheaval inherent to its spirit in the name of order (as defined by prevailing civic, religious, and political ideals).³⁶ The wild man of carnival drama is no longer a lighthearted ritual that celebrated the temporary leveling of social status for the purpose of restoring it in an improved state; rather, the wild figure's positive representation transforms into a negative one. It comes to represent a destabilizing force that must be nullified. According to Juan Carlos Rodríguez, for societies organized around feudalism in the medieval period (a model determined by its *organicism*), the suspension of order creates less of a risk of destabilization because the restoration of order is secure when hierarchies are conceived as the natural and immutable organization of society, world, and cosmos. However, more is at stake in suspending those hierarchies during the rise of emerging capitalist economic and social formations defined by *animism*. Capitalism, as an essential element of the underpinning ideological matrix of modernity, necessitates the "radical change" that produces the modern notion of the self, chiefly, the "given" of the free self. It requires free subjects (that is, subjects committed to the fantasy of their own freedom), unfettered from the ties to land, lord, and lineage that determined notions of the self in a society organized by feudalism.[37] The individual now has the belief in their own freedom and the potential means to change their lot in life. Carnival practices that would allow them to participate in upheaval become more dangerous when they can feel empowered to resist; as a consequence, those practices give way to modes of cultural production that control the messaging through the professionalization of cultural production, institutionalization of modes of communication, and a proliferation of non-participatory entertainments (e.g., theater) at the expense of the social upheaval of the carnivalesque.

Bakhtin's work presents Carnival as a framework for understanding the medieval worldview, and here, its counterpart, Lent, takes over as a frame within which to view early modernity. Paula Findlen persuasively makes this case when she demonstrates how the epistemological shifts from the Renaissance to the early modern period not only can be understood along these lines, but also *were* understood explicitly in this way by early modern natural philosophers. In her analysis of the emergence of a scientific worldview we have come to designate as "modern," she asserts that "many of the practices we associated with science since the seventeenth century depended on the suppression of the ludic in order to function. They belonged not to the world of Carnival but to the triumph of Lent."[38] To illustrate this transition, Findlen traces emblematic shifts in a relatively short period of time in the expressed approaches to knowledge of three key sixteenth- and seventeenth-century natural philosophers: Giordano Bruno (1548–1600), Johannes Kepler (1571–1630), and Francis Bacon (1561–1626). Whereas Bruno emphasized the ludic in the laws of nature (which played no small part in his trouble and subsequent execution at the hands of the Roman Inquisition), Kepler was a more transitional figure who maintained a seriocomic approach to knowledge: "No natural philosopher played more elegantly or more profoundly than Johannes Kepler," states Findlen, but "theology delimited a realm of absolute seriousness" for the German mathematician: "I am earnest about Faith and I do not play with it."[39] Francis Bacon, who proves to be one of the most influential predecessors of Enlightenment philosophies of knowledge, then comes to embody the impulse to purge the ludic from approaches to knowledge, and his writings would bring that approach into the mainstream for the generation that followed. In practices of seventeenth-century natural philosophy, "toppling those Carnival deities, Nature and Folly, became an important symbol of the ascendancy of new experimental and mathematical philosophies, both of which embraced theological and philosophical seriousness (combining strictures about faith with Stoic admonitions about the disciplined mind)."[40]

Since the epistemic is reflected in the aesthetic, so is true of the aesthetic developments that characterize both the Renaissance and the Baroque. One such paradigm shift manifested itself in the development of theater as a mode of cultural production. Although seasonal folk traditions and paratheatrical court entertainment never disappeared, they were supplanted by new forms of dramatic art pioneered by writers and performers that bridged the divide between the nobility and the masses, writing plays for both royal and public audiences. It is precisely within this new space where previously distinct representations of wild figures come into contact, merge, and take on the characteristics that become conventional on the *comedia* stage of the late-sixteenth and seventeenth centuries. Generally regarded as one of the most notable predecessors of modern drama in Spain, Juan del Encina is emblematic of this period of transition that saw the emergence of the professional dramatist and the conventions of modern dramatic practice take shape. The wild figure plays a central role in these developments from premodern forms of spectacle to more definitively modern ones. In her analysis of Juan del Encina's carnival eclogues, Stern identifies the prominence of the wild man carnival drama in his work. In lieu of an actual actor dressed in animal pelts or a patchwork of leaves and sticks, Stern describes another analogous carnival tradition in which

> a straw man in ragged attire . . . is drawn in a cart to the outskirts of town, where villagers rain blows upon him while a pompous judge recites in mock-heroic verse Carnival's last will and testament. Finally the straw man is burned or drowned. Thus Carnival is expelled from the village, and since he is the village scapegoat, the townsfolk believe they have expelled with him all the sins and vice committed during the year. It is obvious, then, that the Spanish ceremony described [in Encina's eclogue] belongs to the widespread European ritual of "burying the Carnival."[41]

As Stern demonstrates, this eclogue explicitly portrays the folk tradition, but has transformed the ritual into a copy of itself to be staged as theater by actors for an audience, that is, presented as an entertainment on a stage (however abstractly or concretely defined). As such, the playwright's carnival eclogues embody the intersectionality of his drama at the crossroads of medieval and modern dramatic practice. Encina and those like him signaled the rise of the professional actor and playwright, and as part of that enterprise, the dramatist drew from this ritualistic performance tradition to compose his carnival eclogues that were staged at the ducal court.[42] Encina's status as both court entertainer and popular playwright allowed him to draw from two separate wellsprings of paratheatrical tradition, thereby enmeshing those traditions in a single dramatic space in novel ways. His use of royal and popular festive traditions of Carnival exemplifies this practice. Even more specifically, two distinct manifestations of the wild man, who had featured in both folk ritual and the court masque, inhabit the same dramatic space in Encina's carnival eclogues, the significance of which I will explain further.

However, Encina's eclogues—staged as part of the carnival festivities at court—reflect a paradigmatic shift away from the ritualized practice of social upheaval and renewal that took place during the pre-modern Carnival. Wardropper highlights how it "was characteristic of the topsy-turvy Carnival season" in medieval and Renaissance Spain that "the shepherds actually held their Carnival feast *in the royal palace* and parodied the customs of the nobility."[43] Arguing against Surtz's contention that Encina's theater maintains pre-modern spatial politics that blur the lines between spectacle and spectators in which spectators do not have to consider the notion that the staged performance is taking place elsewhere, Egginton contends that "Encina and his actors are in fact forcing their noble audience to confront them on two different planes of existence, first creating distinct, theatrical realities, and then transgressing the frame in order to incorporate their audience into the new space."[44] In agreement with Egginton's view, I submit that further conclusions can be drawn from this new structuring of theatrical space evident in Encina's eclogues, a structuring which is also emblematic of the transitions away from the participatory rituals of the medieval carnivalesque to the architectonics of modern theatrical representation. When the playwright brings theater to the court, he replaces actual shepherds with actors playing them, not for their own satisfaction, but for the entertainment of the ducal court. Consequently, in the space of the court, this shift creates a space for the Bakhtinian laughter of the folk participating in the ritual to be displaced for that of the elite who now laugh at the folk from above. In stark contrast to the suspension of hierarchical stratification that defined earlier carnival observances, Stern poses a rhetorical question that gets at the heart of the fundamental change in the nature of dramatic representation signified by these developments: "Are [the members of the ducal court] witnessing shepherds parodying their lord and lady and indulging themselves in the ducal palace, or are they watching professional actors impersonate rustics at their traditional Carnival feast?"[45] Shepherds, who once feasted at the ducal table during Carnival, have been removed from the space altogether. Now, in their place, actors play the role of shepherd, and only do so for the pleasure of the aristocratic audience.[46] Exemplified by the carnivalesque spirit of the Middle Ages, the participatory "second life" of the folk to which Bakhtin refers has all but disappeared; carnival revelry only replicates the world in an upside-down state for the elite to enjoy from the safety of their position beyond the fourth wall. Meanwhile, in the emergent corral theaters of growing urban centers, the folk become spectators, alienated observers of a spectacle presented for them (rather than ritualistic practices enacted by them and for them).[47] They become distanced by the professionalization of the modern stage and the institutionalized practices (e.g., censorship) that came to condition its production. The folk lose the wild man to the ideological apparatuses that leverage this space.

This is the context in which the wild figure of the Spanish *comedia* takes shape. It is placed inside a modern packaging for the purpose of establishing and reproducing the ideological commitments of a hegemonic social order. Playwrights such as Encina pave the way for the development of professional theater in the latter half of the sixteenth century, as the wild figure of folk ritual becomes coopted into hegemonic discourse. Lope de Vega and those of his generation began to leverage the ideological potential made possible by the mutual comprehensibility of the wild figure for audiences in the court and *corral* alike. Once the *comedia* had supplanted previous forms of dramatic art, the allegorical medieval wild man who represents the indiscrete passions of youth or a time of annual revelry gives way to a more equivocal and emblematically theatrical wild figure of the Spanish *comedia*. The wholeness and presence of carnival laughter that permeates the social fabric of the medieval world is replaced by its theatricalized image, which is a reflection of the modern separation of the realm of being from that of meaning, reality from its representation.[48]

A facet of this process of theatricalization of the carnivalesque is the simultaneous ideological instrumentalization of its representation in new media such as the *comedia*, among others. For example, we encounter new definitions of the carnival repertoire codified in institutional apparatuses like Covarrubias's early modern dictionary, *Tesoro de la lengua castellana*, which then are reproduced concretely in the *comedia* in plays such as Lope's *Las ferias de Madrid*. This can be found in Covarrubias's definition of *máscara* (mask), which suggests that the mask maintained its allegorical nature during the Baroque in specific contexts, most often and most intensely in court pageantry that carried over from the medieval period, as well as public carnival processions. Nevertheless, in Covarrubias's definition of the term we also find a discursive aside about the dangers of mask-wearing, specifically as a form disguise, suggesting the mask had taken on new meaning in the cultural field. The lexicographer offers this commentary on the problem of mask-wearing: "and when they do it with bad intentions, and put it on in order to conceal their identity, their crime is worse, and for that reason it is prohibited for anyone to carry weapons at a masque without license or their identity being made known."[49] This description of the mask coincides with stricter regulations levied by authorities against mask-wearing during carnival festivities, which even came to be prohibited. We find these circumstances dramatized in Lope's *Las ferias de Madrid* when Roberto, Claudio, Adrián, and Lucrecio, all wearing masks in the streets of Madrid, encounter a sheriff who immediately arrests them: "Don't you know you can't walk around the capital / wearing masks? / Off to jail with the lot of you."[50] But in allowing the theatrical and the carnivalesque to co-exist in the same space, Teresa Ferrer argues that it compounds the possibility for the intrinsic wildness of both the carnivalesque and theatricality to break loose from their containers:

> situating the encounter within the frame of carnival celebrations, so closely linked to the playful concealing of identities and usurpation of different roles than one inhabits during daily life, underlines the connection between this aspect of carnivalesque celebrations and the *comedia*. Like in celebrations (during festive times of year), in the *comedia*, individuals' most anarchical impulses are given free rein, letting go to show the side of oneself that is most instinctive and vital, and to give in to the part of you that feels tempted by the exploration of the limits between the permitted and the socially prohibited.[51]

Vaccari agrees, understanding the *comedia* as giving these behaviors license in the space of representation, that is, the transgressions framed within the carnivalesque are permitted insofar as they do not precipitate tragic consequences, and therefore effectually condone the temporary suspension of social codes: "Wearing a mask gives the person the possibility to have an 'other' life that coincides with the world of the changed in identity and is rooted in theatrical play."[52] On the one hand, theatrical play as manifested in the *comedia* is a permissible form, or a safe enclosure for exaggerated literalizations of artifice and appearances (*apariencias*) where those deviations can be reified and blotted out. This allows theatergoers to "get it out of their system" in the same way that carnival revelry allows a type of release confined to a limited period of time. In the realm of theatrical representation, the clandestine behaviors and mistaken identities that generate the twists and turns in the *comedia* plots are far from condoned, as the quote in Vaccari's title suggests ("Máscaras fue mi locura / mis mudanzas acabé"[53]). As such, the mask in the *comedia* is emblematic of the fundamental baroque anxiety of truth hidden behind the veil of appearances, for which all the conflict that transpires must come to an end one way or another ("mis mudanzas acabé"), be it a decision on the part of the masquerader to remove the mask to return to their prescribed social role (*ser quien es*), or imposed upon them in retribution for their transgressions. Nevertheless, to eliminate the transgressive and "recuperar *la realidad de verdad*," the ideological power harnessed by the theatrical apparatus must contend with the vestiges of the carnivalesque woven into the fabric of theatrical representation that threaten to break containment.[54]

MODERNIZING CARNIVAL (II): "CORRALLING" WILDNESS FOR THE POPULAR STAGE

Prior to the birth of the professional theater in the *corrales* in the sixteenth century, early forms of spectacle have long been demarcated along the lines of who they were for, essentially treating court entertainments and folk ritual as two separate spheres of pre-modern dramatic practice. What is clear is that the barrier between the two spheres is a porous one, which ultimately transforms and congeals into a set of performance practices that have come to define what we consider modern theater. Moreover, there are elements of earlier paratheatrical practices the two spheres always shared, namely, the cultural imagination of marginal landscapes and the characters that inhabit them. Turning to the wilderness as a symbolic spatial category serves to illuminate another aspect of the transition from premodern to early modern theatrical practices introduced in the previous section.

The prevalence of forests and mountainsides in pre-modern spectacle is evident even in the relatively scant textual record of dramatic practice in the medieval period.[55] The marginal landscape of *el monte* is that Arcadian no-space which at times is the agrestic utopia of shepherds and at others the mysterious and dangerous world of devils, wild men, *serranas*, along with a host of classical gods and monsters with a penchant for violence. The construction of this imagined space becomes even more essential to the process of signification; since court entertainments contained little to no dialogue, it was significantly more reliant on robust visual apparatuses than the spoken word to convey meaning. The same is true of folk spectacle, which explains the relative lack of information in documented sources on medieval spectacle since, by definition, the medium resists preservation in the historical record. Without dialogue, there is no play text, nor had other performance documentation become conventional, so all that remains are the descriptions of the festivities recorded by chroniclers, personal letters of those in attendance, along with a number of artistic renderings of particularly notable events (see Figure 1.5). However, even within the extant record, the recurrence of certain characters and settings in both court and folk spectacle indicates that both rely on repertoire, that is, systems of signification that according to Diana Taylor depend on embodied performance over narrative and dialogue. She argues that to gain access to the production and reception of meaning in medieval dramatic practice, we cannot rely on "the epistemic systems developed in Western thought, where writing has become the guarantor of existence itself."[56] This approach shifts emphasis away from the enduring materials found in the archive to explore repertoires of embodied performance, a process Taylor succinctly describes: "Instead of focusing on patterns of cultural expression in terms of texts and narratives, we might think about them as 'scenarios' that do not reduce gestures and embodied practices to narrative description."[57] Considering paratheatrical folk processions and semi-dramatized performance spectacles during annual festival seasons as embodied performance, we have greater access to non-spoken performance practice that are not recorded in the archive. For example, Castle identifies embodied performance as the primary mode of theatrical signification in his analysis of a carnival

FIGURE 1.5. Fifteenth-century miniature of the *Bal des Ardents* (from an illuminated manuscript of Jean Froissart's *Chroniques*, ca. 1470). The scene depicts a group of court dancers, among them Charles VI of France, dressed as wild men to perform a choreographed entertainment. To make their costumes look more realistic, they were sewn onto each performer and the fabric was soaked in resin to affix a layer of flax made to look like hair. Despite being prohibited, a torch was brought into the hall, causing the costumes to catch fire, which is depicted in the miniature. Courtesy of the British Library, Harley MS 480, f. 1r., via Wikimedia Commons.

procession that took place in Toledo in 1555. Participants dressed as wild men, devils, priests, and animals; it was their "incongruous, undulating, relentlessly fantastical forms that suggested nothing less that the return to universal chaos."[58] This is only a single instance, but is representative of the way wildness and imagined wild landscapes of medieval spectacle came to produce meaning through ritualized repetition, that is, as a *repertoire* of embodied performance drawn from and repeated over time and in varied contexts.

Two such contexts, as I have indicated thus far, are the private space of the court and the public sphere of the folk. As Gurevich has shown, these spaces were traversed ubiquitously; he suggests that "court minstrels were welcomed everywhere, the palace castle, abbey, tavern, and marketplace."[59] Nevertheless, something happens in the sixteenth century that brings these two worlds together in ways that would be fundamental in the development of the professional theater, and more importantly for the present analysis, the ideological and aesthetic features that define baroque dramatic practice. The pivot toward modernity in theatrical practice takes shape as a result of key figures such as Juan del Encina and Lope de Vega traversing the boundaries between court and plebian spheres, drawing from the repertoires of each to satisfy the tastes of both. As I argued, Encina's eclogues staged in the ducal palace signify a modern turn in so far as the drama of Carnival is replicated in theatrical space rather than enacted as an integral part of carnival revelry, for and by the folk. Whereas Encina removes elements of paratheatrical folk practice from the public sphere and brings them to the privileged space of the court, Lope represents a transference of dramatic practice in the opposite direction. He draws from the repertoire of embodied performances of the court in order to fashion it for a wider public audience on the corral stage, about which Joan Oleza states: "popular theater was not the spontaneous product of a primitive phase in the evolution of theater that extends from Lope de Rueda to the second decade of the seventeenth century, but rather the opposite: a conquest. The fruit of the struggle for a theatrical model capable of reaching greater swaths of the population than those that had pertained to school, university, and court theater."[60] The merging of the repertoires of paratheatrical practice form a new dramatic art which took shape in the *corrales* and continued to develop as the court dedicated increasing resources toward spectacular entertainments near the end of Lope's career and throughout Calderón de la Barca's.

For Diana Taylor, repertoires form by the repetition of what she calls embodied practices, which are "performances [that] function as vital acts of transfer, transmitting social knowledge, memory, and a sense of identity through reiterated ... behaviors."[61] Embodied practice so defined is particularly useful toward an understanding of stage design because it does not rely solely on the written or spoken word to investigate how meaning is produced through cultural practice; rather, it seeks to access and consider any and all vectors that condition meaning in a given context. This negotiation and conditioning of meaning outside of narrative description concisely explains the silent, or at least nonlinguistic signification of scenographic practice, which also acknowledges the instability of the repertoire as a function of the replication of embodied performances. As we see the forest staged over and over, it replicates previous iterations, but no copy is perfect, and the context of each production necessarily conditions what and how these staging practices *mean*. Taylor's definition of the term accounts for this instability in a repertoire that occurs because "the production of knowledge is always a collective effort, a series of back-and-forth conversations that produce multiple results. Versions change with each transmission, and each creates slips, misses, and new interpretations that result in a somewhat new original."[62]

During the formative period for professional theatrical practice in the latter half of the sixteenth century, as I laid out previously, Lope consolidates conventions of both court and folk drama into a new repertoire designed for the popular stage. What had been a full space of allegorical vigor in both the noble palaces and streets of medieval Iberia relied almost entirely on embodied performance rather than dialogue, and then was slowly modernized over time, that is, corralled and commodified. In so doing Lope plants the seeds that would become the dominant configurations of the *comedia nueva* repertoire. In Lope's corpus it is not a coincidence that nearly all the marginal landscapes serve as the setting for plays that revolve around the mistaken identity of the protagonist. The forest as corresponding symbolic landscape where identities remain hidden becomes one element of a repertoire of devices that also includes certain plot devices and costume design. It is no surprise that this repertoire of conventions is repeatedly drawn from because each of these aspects lend themselves to an especially baroque configuration of space, symbolic and literal: the discovery space. A discovery space—a cave in the forest, for example—is the locus where artifice can be peeled back to unveil the true nature of things and produce *desengaño*.[63] The uncultivated natural landscape of the forest exemplified this conceptualized space in specific ways in the sixteenth and seventeenth centuries. In the realm of natural science, a driving metaphor for the objectives of the proto-empirical hermetic disciplines was that of "the occult secrets locked up in the bosom of nature" as a metaphor for their epistemological model.[64] This is the brand of spectacular experimentation and manipulation of natural elements we see practiced by magician characters in the *comedias de magia*. So, the scenographic repertoire of the *monte* (forest, or wilderness) serves as an embodied practice for the transmission of specific meanings, chiefly, a visual signifier for knowledge that remains hidden; the uncultured and wild marginal landscape beckons for civilizing forces to come for the secrets it conceals in its bosom.[65]

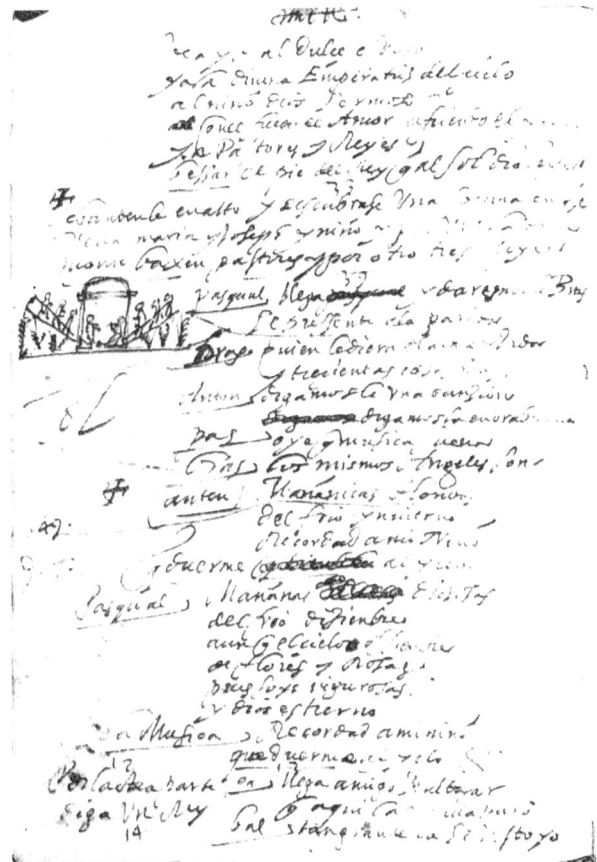

FIGURE 1.6. Autograph manuscript of Lope de Vega's *El cardenal de Belén* (Act 3, f. 10 v.), depicting marginal sketch of set design. Courtesy of comedias.org, webpage of the Association for Hispanic Classical Theater.

Lope sets a number of his earlier plays in marginal landscapes, including *El premio de la hermosura*, *El cardenal de Belén*, *El Nacimiento de Ursón y Valentín*, *El animal de Hungría*, and *El hijo de los leones* (see Figures 1.6 and 1.7).[66] The forest structure itself is an uncultured space that conceals truth, which compels the baroque impulse to bring order to that space by way of penetrating its deceitful appearances to reveal previously inaccessible truths. The forest is simultaneously a space marked by excess, supplementarity, which signifies what it lacks: order. As such, the marginal landscape lends itself to being a remarkably generative spatial

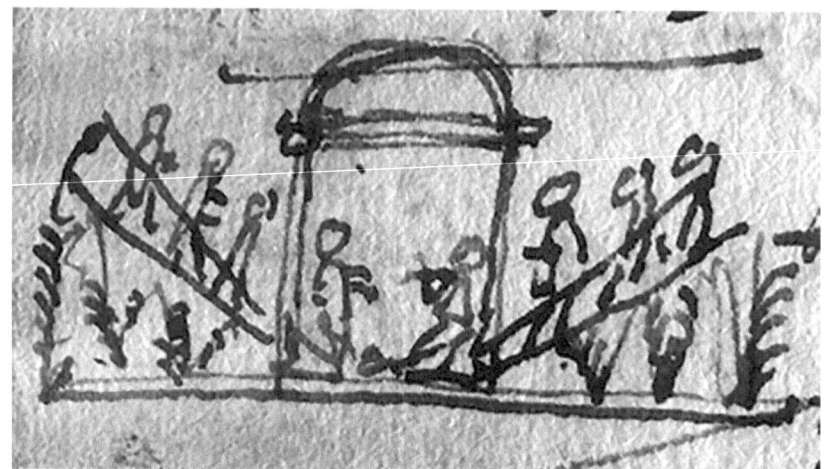

FIGURE 1.7. Detail of marginal drawing in original autograph manuscript of Lope's *El cardenal de Belén*. Biblioteca Medicea Laurenziana (Fondo Ashburnam 1898, image reproduced in Sónia Boadas, "Lope ante la puesta en escena: Las acotaciones en las comedias autógrafas," in *"Entra el editor y dice": Ecdótica y acotaciones teatrales (siglos XVI y XVII)*, 113). Licensed under CC BY 4.0 International Attribution.

metaphor as the setting for conflicts predicated on the occluded identity of its principal characters, and that are resolved by removing the veil of appearances to uncover the true nature of their identity. By producing and reproducing plays in the disordered setting of the forest, these early minimal sets on the one hand harkened back to a premodern type of negotiation on the part of the audience between the imaginative and the materially visual (or lack thereof). On the other, and more importantly, the popularity of corral theater marks a shift in the politics of power in the production and reception of dramatic practice, the nature of which marginal landscapes help us frame. Whereas the wild man is a character that appears in both premodern court and folk spectacle, the construction of *comedia* sets with a forest or craggy mountainside became an aspect of the set design within the public corrales (i.e., *el monte*), but previously had been a scenographic element more conventional to the court repertoire. Therefore, this move takes the wild man out of the space of the carnivalesque and strips him of nearly all his disruptive vitality by incorporating him into the stable and self-affirming sphere of the dramatic imagination of the court. The confined space of the corral is antithetical to the spatial politics of folk Carnival in which the spirit of misrule bleeds into the streets and flows through the city unconfined, even if to be later contained and established hierarchies restored. Lope's reconfiguration of the carnival repertoire for performances to be staged in the *corrales* therefore signifies a formal binding of the Lord of Misrule. This is the sense of "corralling" that Burningham evokes when he coins the term in *Radical Theatricality* in his discussion on "corralling the Jonglueresque." He notes the "confluence of Spanish etymologies" of the term "corral" to refer both to "a performance space fortuitously co-opted . . . from within the confines of the adjacent exterior walls of existing architectural structures" and an enclosure for herding livestock.[67] I cite his usage in the subtitle of the current section because it so concisely captures the figurative and literal confinement incurred by the wild figure in its transformation for the corral stage. Jorge Luis Castillo frames the work accomplished in the *comedia* in similar terms, stating that theatrical praxis "comes to reflect the same process of decadence that the liberating spirit of the carnivalesque suffered in being assimilated, and finally, abolished by the authoritarian world of official culture."[68] However primitively it may have been displayed in the set design of Lope's generation, the establishment of a physical "set" goes hand in hand with modern theatrical practice (absent from premodern ritualistic carnival practice). In the demarcated space of the stage (coinciding more broadly with the connotation of the *corral* as an "enclosed space"), marginal landscapes are spaces to be harnessed under the playwright's dramatic control where the wild things that lie within them are domesticated.

CHAPTER 2

Wildness as Monstrosity in the *Comedias* of Lope de Vega

> The sciences are at present masked, but if their masks were taken off, they would be revealed in all their beauty.
> —René Descartes, *Preambula* (1619)

PERHAPS IT IS MOST concise to describe the phenomenon of the theatrical wild figure of the Spanish Baroque as a revealing obsession. Its popularity and representation in the *comedia* exemplify Jeffrey Cohen's "suggestion that cultures can be read based on the monsters they create," which situates the wild figure within his definition of monster metaphors in general "as a set of symbols that are in constant flux, but whose common thread is their marginality."[1] The wild figure is a member of the repertoire of baroque monsters, and in this chapter, I will argue for its status as the Baroque's marginal monster par excellence. To draw a comparison to our current cultural context, especially in the US, Castillo and Egginton aptly identify vampires and zombies as our own examples of such monsters, each of which are revealing obsessions of the culture that produces them. In their own words, vampires serve "as an apt metaphor for the predatory practices of capital in colonial and post-colonial societies . . . [while] today's zombie hordes may best express our anxieties about capitalism's apparently inevitable byproducts: the legions of mindless, soulless consumers who sustain its endless production, and the masses of "human debris" who are left to survive the ravages of its poisoned waste."[2] The wild figure was a similarly ubiquitous monster in the theatrical production of sixteenth- and seventeenth-century Spain, and equally revealing of the cultural anxieties of the Baroque. As in the conflicts to the plots of the films, novels, and television programs in which vampires and zombies are "turned," that is, transformed from humans into monsters, the baroque wild figure stresses the correspondingly perilous and symbolic stakes within its own cultural context. Also like the zombie, the wild figure emerges as the disavowed creation of baroque society. As the personified opposite of neo-Stoic ideals of prudence, discretion, and self-control, the wild figure embodies unruly passion. And their representation—their mere existence—creates a desire to restore order through the mechanism of imposing those ideals. This distinguishes the baroque wild figure from the wild man of Carnival. The carnivalesque marks a period during which wildness is permitted, bookended by a return to order; however, in the Baroque, wildness poses a threat to civilized society that cannot exist and is the very thing that must be stamped out. Playwrights of the sixteenth- and seventeenth centuries often turned to the wild figure as a vehicle to represent the disturbance of order. Living in the forest, a deserted island, or a far-away land, they are conceived to inhabit the peripheries of the ideological map outside the bounds of prescriptive discourse. Historically understood to be the tool of a notoriously conservative culture, the *comedia*'s function in these works is to either expand the symbolic map to include the wilderness and its newly domesticated inhabitants into hegemonic social order, or to be conquered and eradicated.[3] Citing Cohen, Gordillo and Spadaccini see the baroque monster in this way as a symbolic referent, a "mode of cultural discourse" linked to epistemological turns and the construction of identity. Furthermore, the monstrous is said to spring from a "desire to name that which is difficult to apprehend and to domesticate (and therefore disempower) that which threatens."[4] However, as I will argue, their existence can only ever be disavowed, never entirely eliminated. Hayden White provides a concise description of this purpose of the wild figure: "No cultural endowment is totally adequate to the solution of all the problems with which it might be faced; yet the vitality of any culture hinges upon its power . . . to convince its least dedicated member that its fictions are truths."[5] While the reception of the plays in question often remains absent from the archive to determine exactly the responses these plays elicited, the ideological efficacy of this corpus will be evaluated based on the internal factors to which we have access. What are the symbolic or ideological features of the wild figure that pose a threat to social order? What are the mechanisms by which wildness, once unleashed, is domesticated and inscribed into re-established social order? Are there any loose ends the play fails to address? Does the resolution to the plot meet the exigencies of dramatic necessity created by the conflict? Or is there any evidence within the plays of a failure to fully resolve the disruption to order that the wild figure signifies (e.g., plot inconsistencies, how internal characters respond to the resolution, etc.)? Does wildness find ways to escape, ways that it gets away from its author's attempts to capture it?

To further explain why the wild figure emerges as a prominent form of monstrosity in the dramatic imagination of the Baroque, Elena del Río Parra's broad explanation of the cultural function of monsters during the period offers a point of departure: "The monstrous, in the end is read as a hypostatic form against the norm and in it we decipher the enigmas that disturb the always precarious balance of normality."[6] As a tool for cultural analysis, these monsters provide access into what Uebel coins as a "history of unthought": "imagining otherness necessarily involves constructing the borderlands, the boundary spaces, that contain—in the double sense, to enclose and to include—what is antithetical to the self.... Histories of unthought are thus concerned with the historical reasons for what is socially marginal or liminal becoming symbolically central."[7] As a receptacle into which those fears could be collectively deposited and cathartically disposed of (but really only stored away), the wild figure provides insight into a "history of unthought" where the borderlands of the culture of the Spanish Baroque are demarcated.

Exploring the nature of these characters' monstrosity provides critical insights into the paradoxical centrality of these marginal figures. Lope de Vega can be attributed with the theatrical innovation of the wild figure; in so doing, his *comedias* acknowledge that which exists beyond the purview of social order. On the one hand, this act demarcates a firm boundary, while on the other it simultaneously gives wildness a form in the cultural imagination—one that cannot be easily forgotten. In the plays, an important feature to note—and this is an essential quality of the wild figure of the Spanish Baroque—the wild monsters are not especially monstrous. In fact, their monstrosity is something projected onto the wild characters by external forces, in tension with their character portrayal. The wild figure's assumed monstrosity is—at least mostly—a façade, a perception of him or her based on appearances. What is more, those appearances hide crucial information about their (usually royal or aristocratic) identity and keep them from the social station originally ascribed to them. Their wildness, then, is the visual embodiment of social instability, circumstances that can only be restabilized by revealing their aristocratic identity as well as the parties responsible for their social dislocation.

Aesthetically, the dynamics of their marginalization and "monstrification" create a quintessentially baroque dissonance between their appearance and underlying identity.[8] This element forms the axis around which the baroque wild figure develops into the type s/he becomes in the *comedia* corpus. Wildness is not a problem presented as innate to these theatrical characters, but rather a superficial state of being that can only be resolved through the poetics of *desengaño*.[9] By uncovering a hidden truth behind the veil of appearances, this device "responds to and guides the visual desire to reveal that which remains concealed; it is the promise of *reality* in a world of endless illusion."[10] And that is the ideological sleight of hand in the baroque aesthetics of *desengaño*; the removal of the mask reveals the identity beneath as the "true" one, but that promised reality behind the mask is where the actual illusion takes place, where the staged version of reality is mistaken for the real one. In this scheme, wildness is purged when the wild character stops playing a role assigned to them in error to assume their place in the established order (as princess, prince, noble heir, etc.). However, even though this maneuver parades a fundamental contrast between the character's "rightful" place and their artificial role, it also imbues those categories (nobility, royal authority, honor, etc.) with universal value, when they too are contingent, local truths, hegemonically established and reproduced in the commercial theater as an ideological apparatus. This "colonization of cognitive perspectives" is accomplished thanks to a heightened sense of theatricality that opens up during the Baroque.[11] Theater is imbued with an *affective* energy that allows for the "truth" revealed behind the mask to be *effective* in moving audiences to conform to the ideological commitments avowed in the process of its revelation. But it also risks exposing its own "seams of its construction" in the process, which Egginton argues is representative of baroque aesthetics and the wide-ranging preoccupations they reflect: "Because the Baroque is theater, the theater of the Baroque offers the most vivid expression of its core; in the elements of its basic design we see the seams of its construction, and the traces of its ultimate undoing."[12] The "truths" revealed in the resolution of these plays—that version of reality presented as the way things are and ought to be—conceals the inescapability of its own artificiality, because the prince behind the wild mask is still an actor on stage playing an aristocratic character, just as ontologically theatrical as the wild man role his character was mistakenly cast to play on the world's stage within the fictional reality of the play.

Predicated on the revelation of the identity of the protagonist, restoration of order in the conclusion exemplifies the "major strategy" of baroque cultural production I referenced in the introduction. The plot device of the hidden identity revealed, which restores a character's social status and by extension social order writ large, reflects the operative mechanics of the major strategy because it "posits a separation between a representation [*the protagonist as wild man*] and the reality hidden behind it [*the protagonist's nobility or royal lineage*] in order to smuggle certain presuppositions into yet another representation that it will try to sell as reality itself."[13] In the form of commercial theater, the material production of the *comedia* takes shape in the context of new economic formations, but also responds to the social, political, and epistemological crises those formations brought about. As Nelson argues that emblem culture arises in the context of the "founding moment of modernity," so does baroque theatricality. However, this view of the symptomatic features of modernity pushes back against historical depictions that place the emergence of a modern worldview during the Enlightenment: "As historians and philosophers from José Antonio Maravall to Slavoj Žižek have argued, the founding moment of modernity is not the affirmation of transcendental certitude based on rational categories of thought by self-present Cartesian subjects, but rather the experience of the abyss out of which reason, like the emblem, dramatically arises as a gesture of symbolic power, all the while harboring an unconscious symptom of its constitutive limitations."[14] In the wild figure *comedias*, the domestication of wildness and restoration of social order assuages that longing for "transcendental certitude," but the formal limitations of theatrical representation—an ontological field necessarily closed off from presence—ensure that this closure also is prone to leave traces of its own inescapable theatricality.[15]

At the level of plot development in the dramatic works under analysis, wildness serves as a vehicle to signal persisting conflict, almost always related to a transgression against social order. So long as the wild status of the protagonist persists, the transgression that yielded those circumstances remains hidden and unpunished as well. Therefore, the resolution of the conflict occurs as a function of the revelation of the wild figure's identity, but only insofar as it also brings to light the wrongdoing of another character and the ensuing punishment thereof. Sometimes, this process is tidy in the conventional endings of the *comedias* within the vast corpus of wild figure plays. In other cases, the healing of the social wound depicted in the resolution to the conflict is more problematic. Therefore, that wound and the process by which it is treated in each of the works under scrutiny reveals the would-be existential threats to cultural hegemony and established social hierarchies, chiefly regarding ideological configurations related to political authority, gender, and nobility (as a social status and model of behavior). The introduction of wildness in these plays does not ensure its transformation, domestication, or co-optation into the bounds of dominant cultural ideologies; indeed, wildness inherently resists those processes, and the points of encounter between representations of wildness and civilization at its border become the contested sites where dominant and subversive ideologies are negotiated. This view conceives of the *comedia* as an ideological apparatus in the service of dominant culture and the reproduction of the status quo, but also that the interplay between order disturbed and order restored in each play signifies a "dialogical *encounter*" between the status quo and transgressions against it "that has the potential to reveal the lack of epistemological and ontological foundations of baroque edifices of power."[16] Wildness does not always submit willingly, and as a consequence can threaten to destabilize the ideologies motivating its dramatic domestication. With this in mind, in the pages that follow, I offer a diachronic analysis of Lope de Vega's wild figure plays: *El nacimiento de Ursón y Valentín* (c. 1588–1595), *El animal de Hungría* (c. 1608–1612), and *El hijo de los leones* (c. 1620–1622).[17]

SAVAGE MISDIRECTION IN *EL NACIMIENTO DE URSÓN Y VALENTÍN*

The earliest of the three, *El nacimiento de Ursón y Valentín*, offers a blueprint for later iterations of the baroque wild character. The story itself is well-worn, but this particular representation on the Spanish stage provides the basis for the wild characters that follow. At the opening of the play King Clodoveo is away at war, during which his advisor, Uberto, makes an advance at the queen, Margarita, who rebuffs him emphatically.

Thirsty for revenge at her scorn, Uberto accuses her of infidelity to the king upon his return. Margarita, now pregnant, is subsequently banished from court, and accompanied by the king's gardener, Luciano. On their journey, she gives birth to twins, the first of whom, Ursón, is snatched up by a she-bear and hauled into the forest, with Luciano giving chase. The other child, Valentín, grows up with his mother, without knowledge of his noble birth nor of his brother. Between the first and second acts, twenty years pass, and Valentín learns of Uberto's hand in his mother's dishonor, and vows to go to court to avenge her, although he remains unaware that his father is the king. After offering his services as a hunter to the court, Valentín is commissioned with Uberto to track down and kill a wild man—who of course happens to be Ursón—that has been terrorizing the villagers in the forest just outside Valentín's village. They come across a sleeping Ursón, when Valentín takes the opportunity to avenge his mother's honor by slaying Uberto, who subsequently confesses his crime against the queen to both Valentín and to the king before his onstage death. This leads to the anagnorisis of Margarita's identity to the king, along with Valentín as his son. Assuming all has been resolved with Ursón in Valentín's custody, Luciano appears and reveals Ursón's identity as the eldest son and heir to the throne. The play ends with the marriages of both brothers into noble families and Ursón acknowledged as heir.

Little scholarship has been dedicated to this work, although studies by José Madrigal, Oleh Mazur and most recently Fausta Antonucci and Roger Bartra provide indispensable insights into the work. While they each treat different aspects of the play, criticism generally agrees on one point. Regarding Ursón, they contend that he realizes "the outward trajectory of his state from Wildman to prince, and also, his internal trajectory from animal to human."[18] In order to align with this assertion, one has to interpret particular passages that point to Ursón's wildness at the beginning of the play, both interior and exterior. But I will argue for an alternate reading that highlights Ursón's innate regality as the lens set up by the play for audiences to interpret his behavior. The play's resolution revolves around the notion that "the truth will out" to reinforce genetic ideologies of blood-based lineage, foreshadowed in numerous instances of *la fuerza de la sangre* ("the power of the blood," or figuratively, "the blood will out") culminating in the ultimate and inevitable revelation of Ursón's identity in the final scene. I therefore find this reading more consistent with the play's ideological message and aesthetic devices. In the following scene, for example, Antonucci sees Ursón as displaying aggression and giving into his base instincts when he happens across a female villager in the forest:

> I'm accustomed to seeing the lion
> in union with the lioness,
> and therefore they are meant to be joined,
> man and woman.
> What am I waiting for? I'm off to find her.[19]

On one level, it is easy to compare his impulses to those that he observes in the animals around him in his habitat in the forest, which Mazur considers *amor ferina* (feral love).[20] In another sense, however, Ursón affirms his humanity more than he displays base emotions. He has never seen a woman before, so he must extrapolate from his experience living among the animals and observing their behavior. Through this reasoning, he arrives at the conclusion of his compatibility with the woman. Read this way, his monologue becomes a self-reflective affirmation of his own humanity that he shares with the villager. If we are to read an aggressive or savage Ursón in this passage, he has made little progress in his personal transformation arriving at the mid-point of the *comedia* when this scene takes place. And Ursón never articulates a cognizance of external or internal transformation; rather, here he is portrayed as trying to make sense of a social world that has cast him out, but also with which he senses an ineffable correspondence. Moreover, it is the fact that his innate humanity is never up for grabs that bolsters the tension of the dramatic irony waiting to be resolved in the ultimate revelation of his identity that coincides with (what is presented as) his essential regality. Internal to the world of the play, we have an example of the intended reception of this revelation when king Clodoveo comes to draw this conclusion about Ursón, that "there is nothing wild about him."[21]

Like so many *comedias*, this tension between representation and reality is the fundamental motor of the conflict. Examples abound that guide spectators to the play's emphasis on the deceptive nature of modes of representation in fulfilling their purpose as stand-ins for a supposed real object. One scene in particular draws attention to this incongruence between representation and referent, and exemplifies the extent to which the play relies on this guiding dichotomy. In a scene from act 2, two local officials (*alcaldes*) have received a communiqué from the crown requesting help in apprehending "el monstruo del monte" (the monster in the woods) that includes a drawn likeness (i.e., something akin to an early modern wanted poster or police sketch).[22] They are on patrol in the woods when one of the men unfurls the portrait as they share stories about Ursón's supposed crimes. They marvel at the features of their monster-of-interest depicted in the printed image:

> MAYOR 1: That traitor! What a face he has!
> My goodness! And here he comes,
> club and all!
> MAYOR 2: Does this animal have a tail?
> MAYOR 1: It's neither man nor meat hook.[23]

Of course, none of these characteristics accurately describe Ursón, of whose presence onstage they are unaware of until he interrupts their dialogue: "Why look at the copy / when the original is right here?"[24] When faced with the discrepancy between reality before their eyes and its representation they carry in their hands, the officials are forced to recognize the fundamental error in the prevailing assumptions about Ursón. As the two men conjecture about whether the monster has a tail (an animal feature that serves to dehumanize him), they quickly come to realize he is indeed the opposite—a human—which one of the men acknowledges explicitly when Ursón permits them to flee unharmed: "In truth he is an honorable man."[25]

What is dangerous about the representation seen here are its effects. The drawn image is disseminated as if it were accurate, and it has the power to perpetuate myths so firmly believed that those committed to them are willing to and feel justified in carrying out violence based on their premises. Meanwhile, so long as that lie continues to be believed, those who created the circumstances of this status quo (i.e., mass fear directed at a scapegoat rather than the elite perpetrators of violence) maintain their power, like Uberto here. But as this scene demonstrates, the accuracy of the representation is less stable than the two officials presume, much like in the assumptions made by the rest of the characters we see. The process of translation from reality to its representation is a "sketchy" one in which the further away from the source a representation becomes, the more disparate, deformed, and reformed it is from its referent. The same is true of Ursón. It is more precise to describe Lope's presentation of Ursón's wildness as a tension between truth and appearances than a transformation from animality to humanity, as has been contended. Antonucci hedges along these lines in stating that "what we see in of Orson's behavior, doesn't correspond at all with the stories told by the villagers."[26] Meanwhile, Mazur asserts the possibility that Ursón "is given [monstrous characteristics] as a result of superstition or fright."[27] My approach to this play takes what is presented in these remarks as minor and shifts it to a more central role in the nature of Ursón's wildness and the cultural implications of its representation. This shift in emphasis from the transformation of the wild figure to an interpretive model that hinges on the preoccupation with appearances and reality will be applicable to the wider corpus of plays as well.

When the villagers request the aid of the king to apprehend the monster of the forest that they believe Ursón to be, they provide the aforementioned bulletin that included a portrait of the supposed monster, as well as a list of his crimes. These include murder, killing of livestock, kidnapping, and rape. It is essentially a list of all the behaviors accredited to the wild man of folklore, rather than any actual behavior observed in Ursón, which leaves the audience with a decision to either believe the public outcry, or rely on the observed behaviors of Ursón in the play. In another scene, he encounters a young woman from the nearby village, to whom he speaks in a courteous manner. She is reasonably afraid of him based on the image of the wild figure perpetuated in public discourse, which again, is largely manufactured from the folkloric imagination. He treats her kindly, but she leaves him fearing for her life. Still, he permits her to leave, not entirely understanding her behavior when he says, "Your beauty is heavenly / while your fear is of this world," which not only suggests that she has misunderstood him, but also recognizes that he is aware of the monstrous image of him that has been built up in the minds of the villagers.[28] However clumsy his attempts at conversation may be, his words display honorable intentions:

> FEMALE VILLAGER: If you confess that's the case
> as you see it here before you in your power,
> then I am yours and I am a woman.
> Tell me, why would you do me harm?
> URSÓN: Me? Do harm? May heaven deny me
> the sustenance it has afforded me
> if I even thought about doing you harm,
> nor would I have the willpower to even dare it.
> Do not treat me with contempt,

>   for it is goodness you compel of me,
>   and I only would imagine taking
>   what you would give me out of the same inclination.[29]

Again, given the context, the villager understandably flees fearing for her life, but that fear derives more from the allegations made against him, which are in contrast to the words he speaks and his portrayal in the play up to this point overall. This discrepancy suggests they are exaggerated if not entirely false.

Another facet of the work further proves this to be true, when the play's emphasis on the concept of monstrosity is turned on its head. In fact, pinning monstrosity on Ursón proves to be a misdirection all along, which is made explicit upon the death of Uberto. As has been indicated by Antonucci, when Valentín kills Uberto, he is identified as having been the true baroque monster all along, not Ursón. His treason initiates the conflict to be resolved in the play, because it is his false claim about the queen's infidelity that precipitates Margarita's exile. During the hunt for Ursón, Valentín takes advantage of the moment to assassinate Uberto, affirming his monstrosity in the act: "I have come for the monster, / but he is Uberto; / die, traitor."[30] From the beginning of the play, the characters have an essential quality. Margarita is virtuous, her sons are heirs to the French throne and Uberto is a traitor. Throughout the play, Ursón displays few signs of monstrosity, other than his outward appearance, which further proves that what is at stake in the play is the opening up of a space beyond the illusions of sensory perception where reality can be put on display. This conclusion is the "major strategy" of the Baroque at play. The restoration of order affirms a set of ideological falsehoods upon which monarchical legitimacy rests, chiefly, genealogical purity, honor, and the innate superiority of the noble class. In *El nacimiento de Ursón y Valentín*, that order is put in question by the false accusations against Margarita and her subsequent exile; however, the conflict, this false appearance of her lost virtue, is resolved beyond a shadow of a doubt precisely at the moment she reveals herself to the king once he uncovers her defamation to be entirely fabricated by a resentful Uberto. The same is true of Ursón, whose monstrosity ends up being presented as merely a false projection that is put in dramatic tension with his observed behavior (and underlying virtue). The revelation of this symbolic discovery space behind the wild mask defines the play's plot trajectory, and follows a pattern indicated by Richard Glenn of Lope's early dramatic works in which "entire plays are devoted to the interplay of truth and illusion [through] a multitude of disguised characters, each having lost their real identity for one reason or another."[31]

THE WILD SUPPLEMENT: ROSAURA IN *EL ANIMAL DE HUNGRÍA*

Lope draws from *El nacimiento de Ursón y Valentín* to compose a later play featuring a wild figure, *El animal de Hungría*. While the influence of the one on the other is indisputable, the variations between them produce significant transformations in the overall meaning of the later work.[32] The plot sets up nearly identically to *El nacimiento de Ursón y Valentín*, but whereas queen Margarita takes a back seat to Ursón and Valentín in the earlier *comedia*, the conflict of *El animal de Hungría* unravels to emphasize the restoration of the defamed queen character as much as the royal offspring. In this story, queen Teodosia is the one banished from court after being accused of infidelity, in this case by her own sister, Faustina. Upon escaping her execution (she is thrown into a lion's enclosure), an extended period of time passes between scenes, and we find Faustina now wedded to the king and pregnant with the royal heir. Then one day, while joining the court entourage for a hunting retreat in the forest, she gets separated from the group. There, alone in the forest, she goes into labor and gives birth to a daughter, only for it to be immediately abducted by a wild man who appears out of nowhere. However, this supposed wild man is in fact Teodosia, who has fashioned herself as a convincing wild figure, a reputation she maintains while she goes on to raise the child—whom she names Rosaura—in the isolation of the forest.[33] In depicting the act of kidnapping by a wild figure, Lope draws from the conventional repertoire of traits that define folkloric, festival, and iconographic representations of wild folk long established in the European cultural imagination (see Figures 2.1 and 2.2).

In fact, the playwright draws from two images at once, drawing attention to one, only to replace it with another. Seen in Figure 2.1 is the depiction of the dangerous wild man who kidnaps children, which is the type that shapes the villagers' expectations of Teodosia, and later Rosaura. But they have mistaken her as the wrong type of wild figure; she is meant to be the mythical defender of children seen in Figure 2.2, in the same vein as the she-bear that abducts Ursón in *El nacimiento de Ursón y Valentín*,

FIGURE 2.1. Depiction of Wildman costume worn during 1539 Carnival in Nuremburg, Germany (*Schembartlauf*). Oxford, Bodleian Library MS. Douce 346, f. 262r. Image: © Bodleian Libraries, University of Oxford, licensed under CC BY-SA 4.0.

FIGURE 2.2. Miniature of female wild figure saving child from a dragon (in Jacob Elsner's *Gradual*, also known as the *Geese Book*, Nuremburg, 1507). New York, Morgan Library, MS M.905, vol. 2, f.122r. Image courtesy of the Opening the Geese Book website, http://geesebook.asu.edu. © 2012 Volker Schier and Corine Schleif.

not with the intention to kill, but rather to nurture and protect. One of the challenges in offering a sweeping transhistorical description of the wild figure that fully encapsulates its nature and traits are these multiple, even incompatible types that appear throughout the tradition. Lope, however, harnesses the equivocal and plural nature of the wild figure tradition as a malleable device to be molded into the baroque dramatic shape it takes on in *El animal de Hungría*.[34] By taking two competing images in the wild folk tradition, the play presents one—harmful, violent, masculine—on the level of false appearances that conceals the second—protective, maternal, feminine—until the appointed time for the first to be removed to reveal the underlying nature of this wild figure.[35] This is an especially baroque dramatic maneuver in so far as it superimposes the two wild figure types onto the dichotomy of *ser/parecer* (to be / to seem, i.e., reality/appearances); what is more, the two types produce meaning in a system of baroque theatrical signification whereby truth is veiled within a discovery space to be revealed in the play's conclusion.

Toward the end of act 1, a parallel plot is introduced, as three Spanish sailors maroon a young child named Felipe on a mountainside in Hungary, the same area inhabited by Teodosia, and also in the proximity of the village where most of the action takes place. Lauro, a villager, rescues him and when act 2 begins, enough time has elapsed for Rosaura and Felipe now to appear as young adults. They meet one day in the woods, and in the typical hastened pace common in Lope's *comedias*, they quickly fall in love and express their intent to marry. Their happiness is unfortunately short-lived, interrupted by a group of villagers who happen across them in search of the titular "animal of Hungary." Incorrectly believing they have apprehended Teodosia, the villagers threaten to incarcerate Rosaura, but Felipe swoops in to defend his recently betrothed, and ends up killing one of the villagers. After being detained, Felipe awaits his execution in punishment for this crime, when an ambassador fortuitously arrives at court on behalf of the Count of Barcelona, searching for the count's long-lost nephew, left to die as a child by the count's predecessor to protect his claim to power. This child is ultimately identified as Felipe, thereby resolving one of the two primary conflicts of the work. The false accusation against Teodosia, and the true identity of Rosaura, however, remain unknown until the king of England subsequently arrives to restore the vilified Teodosia's name, who we learn is his daughter. At precisely this moment, Teodosia appears dressed as a villager to reveal herself as the banished queen and uncovers Faustina's plot to poison the king to keep her secret hidden. Once the food is confirmed to be poisoned, Teodosia finds herself vindicated, and the work concludes as Faustina accepts her punishment to join a convent, while all parties agree on what has now become Rosaura and Felipe's *royal* engagement (linking the royal families of Hungary, England, and Aragon).

As in *El nacimiento de Ursón y Valentín*, there are scenes in *El animal de Hungría* that display its fundamental concern for the reliability of representation. When the king first arrives to the outskirts of the village with his hunting party, members of the town council approach him with a petition to rid them of the "animal" that terrorizes their village. Bartolo, one of the villagers, provides the following information about the beast, or *fiera*, as he calls it: "Their portrait has been circulated / and verses are sung everyday / of their misdeeds."[36] Here we have two methods by which to identify the wild man (again, actually a woman, in this case, presumed to be male up until the end of the play); however, much as in *El nacimiento de Ursón y Valentín*, both of these methods prove fundamentally unreliable. If her disseminated "retrato impreso" (a copy/portrait of her likeness) had been accurate as Bartolo's assertion implies, in a scene when Lauro crosses paths with Teodosia, he would not find himself so surprised by her beauty ("upon seeing your rare beauty"), nor disabused of his expectation of the male figure in the portrait.[37] Furthermore, the *romances* (ballads) written and sung about the terror of the forest increase a sense that the story had become that of legend, rather than any sort of objective reporting.[38] Again, the ultimate proof of this is the villagers' prevailing assumption that the monster is male. Their misperceptions about Teodosia illuminate important aspects of her function in the work and in the wider corpus of wild figure plays. As the king questions the town council about why they have not been able to hunt down this animal themselves, Bartolo gives the excuse that they do not have many weapons and that the animal is very intelligent, also alleging that, like Ursón, "he enjoys forcing himself on young women."[39] Nevertheless, this accusation has less to do with determining its credibility and more with the dramatic irony it creates; because the audience knows what the villagers do not, chiefly, that the wild figure is in fact a woman, the accusation itself emphasizes the extent to which the villagers' suppositions are categorically false. Bartolo continues in his erroneous description to further highlight this point: "*he* is basically a person, more or less, . . . but as big as a giant."[40] These last two citations suggest that not only are they objectively mistaken regarding her gender, they draw from folkloric descriptions of the wild figure that they then superimpose on Teodosia. Echoing into the world today (and its enduring epistemic coloniality), Lope appears to be capturing an all-too-familiar social impulse to demonize the outsider by portraying them as criminal invaders posing a threat of violence against the body politic, imagined as homogenous and unified.[41]

What is more, the audience has further evidence to the contrary in Teodosia's observed behavior through her interactions with individuals who cross her path in the forest. Although Ursón does overtly attempt to frighten them without intent to cause harm, Teodosia does not even feign ferocity when she comes across villagers. Upon meeting the villager Llorente, she immediately attempts to calm his fear: "fear not, fellow, trust that I mean you no harm."[42] Llorente, like all characters in his situation, is initially incapable of believing what he hears: "Oh, sir, by God I plead that you / take pity on me! / Your eyes are like fire!"[43] Llorente is unable to see past her wild appearance and in turn projects all the folkloric characteristics he "knows" to be true about "him." However, unlike similar exchanges in *El nacimiento de Ursón y Valentín*, Teodosia is able to persuade him to realize that her appearance and identity do not correspond. In the following dialogue, Teodosia affirms her innocence of the crimes for which she is accused, and Llorente comes to realize that appearances belie reality:

> LLORENTE: there are those who have come through these hills
> and have told about
> everything you've stolen and eaten,
> and have promised to kill you.
> TEODOSIA: Try and try they may,
> it's not the first time.
> LLORENTE: It turns out you aren't as wild
> as they say in the village.[44]

Again, as this conversation shows, Lope's wild figure plays engage more with anagnorisis than transformation.[45] This brief exchange between her and Llorente is one of a number of revelations that take place over the course of the work that change the perception of Teodosia, and in other situations, Rosaura as well. Due to the fact that Teodosia did not actually grow up in the forest, she differs as a wild character from others that appear on the seventeenth-century Spanish stage, and Lope gives no evidence that she transformed into the "fiera de los montes" that the villagers describe her to be. Nevertheless, they believe her to be very much a wild thing, while the audience has every reason to be convinced that the accusations against her are false based on her observed interactions with the villagers, and should additionally lead one to ask the same questions about Ursón.

Rosaura, however, is unlike Teodosia in that she shares the experience of being raised in the forest with other iterations of the wild figure type such as Ursón. Though her character does develop in the sense that she learns from the new experiences with the villagers she encounters, she at no point is the livestock-killing, murdering creature described by them over the course of the play and alluded to in the ballads referenced by Bartolo. Teodosia offers a concise explanation of the nature of Rosaura's wildness, which informs how the audiences should interpret her character as well: "You are a wild beast because you are treated / as a beast, and hunted everywhere / by man in his cruelty."[46] The onus of culpability for their mistaken identities lies on the villagers, and according to Teodosia, who they are and how they are perceived are completely disparate. Their innate nobility is incompatible with the monstrosity ascribed to them.

Rosaura even arrives at Teodosia's conclusion on her own. When the audience meets the adolescent Rosaura at the beginning of act 2, she consciously acknowledges Teodosia's affirmation that her wildness is only an exterior imposition—one that is in contradiction to her noble identity. Using her limited social experience as a basis, in a dialogue with Teodosia she articulates a philosophy on the essential dichotomy between animal and human that resonates with contemporary theology of the period:

> If they call me an animal,
> why is it said that heaven
> is my natural home,
> and that this veil
> covers a natural soul?
> If I have a soul and was created
> for heaven, I am not a beast.
> ...
> If I am a beast, I see all other beasts
> with their partner at their side;
> the does of these banks
> have mated with the bucks,
> mother, and not by any other way.
> If it is that I am an animal,
> with what animal did *you* mate?[47]

Toward the end of this quote, we see very similar logic to the one expressed by Ursón ("and so it is that man / and woman should be together"[48]), again leading one to question any sense of "animality," provided their own rational extrapolations about their biology. But she also goes a step further to provide a theological defense of her human status. In accordance with doctrine affirmed at the Fifth Lateran Council, she acknowledges her immortal soul, which qualifies her to receive salvation and enjoy a heavenly afterlife; in depicting her natural ability to reason in concordance with official doctrine, the play urges the audience to find Rosaura's assertion of her human status persuasive, as well as provide further evidence that contradicts the dehumanized portrayals maintained by popular belief. In addition to serving this dramatic function, Rosaura's argument performs a great deal of ideological heavy lifting by reinforcing the authority of official church doctrine as natural truth, self-evident even to someone with no familiarity with the doctrine itself or even contact with civilized society outside of Teodosia.[49]

Perception once again fails to accurately comprehend reality, and when Felipe meets Rosaura, he quite literally comes face to face with such a realization:

> Brush away your hair to show your face,
> I do not mean you any harm.
> (That face will dissuade me
> of the fear that I had because of them [the hairs covering
>   her face]).[50]

His *desengaño* reveals what lies behind the veil of her unkempt appearance. Rosaura's beauty is initially shocking to Felipe, because the animal within should have been reflected by her outward appearance as well. His perplexity is captured by his initial response, articulated rhetorically in the following question: "This is what they call an animal in / Hungary?"[51] Her outward beauty and inner rational mind (demonstrated in the passage cited in the previous paragraph) are actually in harmony, only thinly veiled behind the unkempt appearance that Felipe is able to see beyond when she pulls back her hair to show her face. Her hair, then, becomes a type of baroque curtain behind which lies a discovery space where Felipe and the external audience see the truth previously concealed. At each turn, the method by which any conflict or tension is resolved occurs through similarly structured revelations throughout the work. While transformation does occur in Rosaura as she learns more and more about the society to which she will ultimately pertain, her character development is neither the mechanism by which the conflict of the play is resolved nor the determining factor that triggers her conversion from wild to civilized. She joins the ranks of civilized society not as the end result of an incremental process of education or gradual molding into a model citizen; she discards her animal pelts as the necessary consequence of the revelation of her identity as the daughter of the king, irrespective of her actions up to that point (including her involvement in the murder of one of the villagers).

The poetics of reversal seen in Felipe's expectations of what he imagines Rosaura to be and what she actually is also apply to one other critical scene in the play's dénouement. In the final scene, it is not the king's sense of justice, but rather Rosaura's that leads to the resolution of the plot. That is, the wild figure, who is supposed to stand in as a representation of everything that poses a threat to established order, becomes the catalyst for its restoration. When the king decrees the execution of Felipe for having slain Riselo, he affirms his authority by stating, "I mandate what reason *is*, and the king, in imitation (*imitatio*) of God awards favor and punishment."[52] While the play presents his authority to make such a statement as beyond question, Rosaura's response indicates that in this particular case, he may not have enough information to declare such a sentence of execution on Felipe: "I don't know about laws, but I will say this is an unjust outrage."[53] At this moment, much of the crucial information about the case before him remains unknown to the king, not least of which are his own relation to his daughter Rosaura, along with Felipe's still undiscovered nobility. What is more, the assumptions of the status quo get in the way of an accurate understanding of the events that transpired leading to the death of Riselo at the hands of Felipe. The power dynamic that presumes the guilt of the wild monster (Rosaura) and the expected innocence of the villager (Riselo) conditions the criminal interpretation of Felipe's actions. Occluded are the complexities of the event and those that lead to it. For one, Felipe was acting to defend Rosaura from Riselo, whose efforts to capture or kill Rosaura were carried out with the support of the state. They were indeed encouraged, and as in *El nacimiento de Ursón y Valentín*, when the order of the status quo comes into question, the imperative of maintaining it takes precedence while truth and justice become secondary. Subjects like Riselo are unwitting agents of the state who are compelled to act, often violently, and even at the expense of their own self-interest in service of an ideological apparatus that allows them to become collateral damage (no entity, neither individual nor institutional is held responsible for Riselo's death in the play).

In *El animal de Hungría*, the entire enterprise to maintain order that compelled Riselo's actions was unjust because, as I have argued, it occurs under the false pretense that Rosaura is a wild beast. In the administration of punishment that transpires after Riselo's death, all of these elements prevent the king from having full knowledge of the complexities of the situation. As a result, a space is created in which the play presents the uncultured Rosaura acting in a way that displays a greater sense of justice than the king, who should be its most authoritative arbiter. Arising from this dramatic irony, the play presents it as vindicated when Rosaura takes justice into her own hands, thereby constituting a role reversal with the king. This reversal is affirmed visually and symbolically when she escapes from her imprisonment offstage to reappear wielding a club (*bastón*). This visual metaphor is made even clearer in the dialogue with the explicit reference to the *bastón* that plays on its double meaning. *Bastón* can refer both to a wild figure's club, but also a *bastón de mando*, a monarch's scepter. In this scene, the figures of the king and the wild woman are juxtaposed, the significance of which is consolidated in the dual image of the *bastón*. Here, in the final scenes of the *comedia*, baroque sensibilities would consider the image of Rosaura wielding this instrument a monstrous inversion of social hierarchies (with regard to political authority and gender); in these moments of turmoil, the wild monster holding a club usurps the king in the visual field, whose scepter (i.e., the visual symbol of his authority) is also absent from the dialogue and stage directions. However, as the scene unfolds, Rosaura's agency is critical to the subsequent restoration of order, in contrast to the king's failure to discern truth from falsehood, and as a consequence, to respond prudently to the complexities of the situation at hand (one with political ramifications if he were to unwittingly execute the heir to the throne of a foreign monarchy). Rosaura succeeds in halting Felipe's execution long enough for his identity as the son of the king of Aragon to be revealed. Again, the ostensibly monstrous in these works constantly challenges the presumed reality of its own representation.

What Rosaura accomplishes in the final scene is to create circumstances in which Faustina must confess to her deception that had long condemned her sister to a life in the forest, where she became the object of many more false accusations. The perceived breach in the honor code signified by Teodosia's infidelity creates an imbalance in the social order that brings into existence two distinct monsters: one that is monstrous in appearance (Teodosia), and one whose being (*ser*) epitomizes cultural monstrosity by transgressing the bonds of family and of her word (Faustina). It is precisely this doubling of monstrosity, this savage misdirection, that must be resolved in order for honor to be restored through the symbolic elimination of wildness that takes place when characters discard their animal pelts to reveal the identity hidden beneath them. Bartra draws this conclusion in his analysis of female wild characters in Lope's corpus that the "true monster" is never the wild woman, but rather another character.[54] In this case that applies to Faustina, who is sent to a convent. The same notion applies to *El nacimiento de Ursón y Valentín* in which Uberto plays this role. In other words, in both cases monstrosity is defined symbolically by the taking on of characteristics understood as transgressive to baroque order. Textual evidence further affirms this transfer of monstrous identification from one character to another, which signals the resolution to the conflict through the mechanisms of baroque *desengaño*. In act 3, Faustina attributes her inability to produce another heir after Rosaura has been abducted to a self-proclaimed monstrosity:

> So wild and cruel I have been,
> and for that reason
> may the heavens punish me
> by withholding succession,
> because in malice and treachery
> I have been a monster on earth:
> I killed my innocent sister,
> as well as her chaste honor.[55]

Her father, the king of England, identifies her similarly in the closing of the play: "Lock this beast away."[56] Nevertheless, the anxiety assuaged by convincingly identifying the "real" monster exudes the ideological paradox of baroque aesthetics at its core. The mechanics of signification underlying the dramatic technique of anagnorisis reflect the impact of "any ideological edifice that may be manipulating the subject, as the subject can be made to desire any thing, person, or idea that plays the role of the stopgap and thereby helps to create the illusion of self-identity and completion."[57] At the macro-level of the totalitarian state, "completion" becomes a unified, homogenous society within which every constituent part plays its role effectively.[58] Anagnorisis, the dramatic technique that promises, in pulling back the deceptive veil of appearances, to allege the presentation of truth is what Žižek calls a "fantasy screen." The ideological commitments upheld in the conventional *comedia* ending advertise truths as if they were inherent, immutable, real, or as Egginton and Nelson contend, imbued with *presence*. Yet, in the representational medium of theater (as opposed to presentational), this type of "Real Presence" constitutes a "fantasy screen, ... a scenario filling out the empty space of a fundamental impossibility, a screen masking a void."[59] Inevitably, however, the totalitarian project is stymied by some "fundamental blockage" that "prevents society from achieving its full identity as a closed homogenous reality."[60] While the actual blockage to such totalitarian projects are the injustices and inhumanity at their core, cultural production like the *comedia* serves as a fantasy screen to displace and obscure those blockages, replacing them with transgressive figures (e.g., the wild figure) that can safely be perceived as "simple deviations, contingent deformations and degenerations of the 'normal' functioning of society, . . . and as such abolishable through the amelioration of the system"; however, the "true" monsters (e.g., injustice) "are necessary products of the system itself—the points at which 'truth', the immanent antagonistic character of the system, erupts."[61] As dramatic literary artifacts, Lope's wild figure plays exemplify the ideological magic trick employed in these *comedias* to draw the spectator's gaze away from the inherent antagonism of the system. Through the resolution of the plot and the anagnorisis of the identities of Teodosia, Rosaura and Felipe, these *comedias* are structured to offer up the information revealed as reality itself, along with the ideological commitments it affirms (monarchical authority, genealogical purity, superiority of the nobility, gender hierarchies). At the same time, due to the architecture of theatrical representation (the theatricality at its core being its disavowed "fundamental blockage"), as well as the mechanism of anagnorisis that inherently relies on that architecture to produce meaning, the truths offered as reality point to the fundamentally ideological nature of those assertions, behind which can only be a void, however safely disavowed it may be.

Nevertheless, in the case of *El animal de Hungría*, this domestication of wildness, that is, the erasure of monstrosity that is supposed to occur when Faustina's transgressions come to light is incomplete. In the conventional calculus of the *comedia* whereby order restored should entirely cancel out the order disturbed, this plot resolution leaves behind a wild remainder. Going unaccounted for in the conclusion is the genealogical problem of Rosaura being Faustina's biological daughter, not Teodosia's. Although Faustina is stripped of royal legitimacy, Rosaura retains her privileges as royal offspring. If her mother's claim as rightful queen is nullified, at the very least it calls into question the claim held by her offspring, if not nullifying it as well. *El nacimiento de Ursón y Valentín* clearly presents noble virtue as an outpouring of genealogically inherited nobility. Wouldn't these ideological suppositions create the expectation that Rosaura would turn out to be wicked like her mother? Is this conclusion evidence of an emerging reconfiguration of baroque ideological matrices? Is it just an oversight on the part of the playwright? In any of these cases, Rosaura's restored royal status is taken as granted in the end without qualification. Nevertheless, she embodies an excess that frustrates completion and order perfectly restored. More precisely, Rosaura exemplifies a type of imperfect replication. Teodosia's wildness is copied onto her, but this reproduction of the wild figure in this play creates a set of circumstances that precipitate a resolution that is either inherently flawed, or at least inconsistent with the ideological affirmations of other plays in Lope's corpus. As such, Rosaura serves as a synecdoche that exemplifies the imperfect replication signified by the play overall. In *El animal de Hungría*, Lope reproduces the wild figure trope he introduced in *El nacimiento de Ursón y Valentín*, but in duplicating the constituent characters and plot devices of the earlier *comedia* in a new configuration, the play itself becomes a wild thing that proves more difficult to domesticate by means of the conventional tools of the genre. However minor a detail the problem of Rosaura's lineage may be in terms of complicating the resolution to the play, the impact of any single instance of imperfect replication such as this one becomes compounded in later iterations of the wild figure play each time the conventions of the *comedia* are called upon to eliminate the problem of wildness.

THE SAVAGE NOBLE: LEONIDO IN *EL HIJO DE LOS LEONES*

El hijo de los leones—the last extant play in Lope's corpus to feature a wild figure—demonstrates how each time *el Fénix* returns to the wild figure trope, the changes he makes to write a new play unleash wildness in ways that the conventions of the *comedia* are increasingly incapable of eliminating. The assurances of Spanish exceptionalism offered through the popular medium of the *comedia de corral* continue to be a feature of the genre throughout Lope's career and indeed over the course of the seventeenth century; nevertheless, the ideological conservatism of major forms of cultural production (e.g., in today's cultural landscape these would be Hollywood blockbusters, corporate news media, etc.) like the *comedia* become particularly revelatory when an ingrained system of values strains beneath the weight of the realities of waning political and imperial might they traditionally served to validate. But instead of acknowledging the fissures in the integrity of national identity (along with the cultural values inextricably entwined therein), cultures tend to become even more entrenched in those value systems, as if clinging to them more fervently will return society to greatness, however defined or imagined. In the *comedia*, we can observe this phenomenon playing out in the representative subset of wild figure plays analyzed in this study, each of which serves as a point to plot this trajectory of cultural crisis.

As I have suggested, through a diachronic analysis of Lope's incorporation of the wild figure into his plays over time, one begins to see this trend taking shape. In this third *comedia*, *El hijo de los leones*, Lope reconfigures the royal foundling motif, this time setting up the dramatic action around a series of abandonments that take place some twenty years prior to the opening of act 1. The audience pieces together the details of the backstory as they are disclosed by different characters over the course of the first act. We first learn of an extramarital relationship that had taken place between Lisardo (the prince of Alexandria) and Fenisa (later to be revealed that Lisardo raped Fenisa). When Lisardo learns that Fenisa is pregnant, he leaves her, citing the disparity of their social classes. With little recourse in a social context that would cast her out as a pariah, Fenisa hides the pregnancy and after giving birth takes the child into the forest, leaving him at the foot of a tree. The folktale motif of dangerous animals coming to the aid of human characters in need again serves as a plot device in this play, as a family of lions nurtures the abandoned newborn. They are later joined in raising the child by the hermit Fileno, who appropriately names the child of lions (*el hijo de los leones*) Leonido. When we actually meet Leonido as a young adult, he is still living in the forest with Fileno, and carries all of the characteristics of the wild man, or at least the expectation of one, similar to his antecedents in the two *comedias* previously analyzed in this chapter. In line with their conventional portrayal, Leonido garners the fear of the townsfolk in the nearby village as a mysterious and solitary entity that terrorizes the forest, and with increased frequency, has begun destroying the villagers' crops, killing their livestock, and kidnapping their women and children. However, the Leonido presented onstage bears little resemblance to the monster of the villagers' tales. In fact, he proves to embody the ideal citizen rather than the quintessential social outcast.

Early in the play, testimonies by the locals condition the audience's initial impressions of Leonido. Any mention of an array of general epithets such as "monstruo," "fiera," and "bárbaro" (monster, wild animal, barbarian) can immediately identify him among the townsfolk, which demonstrates the widespread frenzy he has generated. This reputation incites a formal request to the king to have him hunted and killed, a task the monarch assigns to his son, prince Lisardo (the same that abandoned Leonido's mother, Fenisa). Meanwhile, Leonido's caretaker—the elderly Fileno—lies on his deathbed, and in his final moments, he recounts to Leonido the details of finding him in the forest as an infant, and produces the piece of clothing he was wearing when he found him. In giving Leonido the garments, he hopes someone will recognize them, and as a consequence, be able to affirm Leonido's royal lineage: "May one day God grant / that you learn of your true beginnings."[62] Soon after Fileno's death, members of the royal hunting party succeed in tracking the grieving Leonido, but upon engaging with him are shocked by his courteous and eloquent manner. He impresses Lisardo to such a degree that the prince decides against slaying Leonido and actually invites him to come live at court. As Antonucci has noted, this scene echoes the meeting between the brothers Valentín and Ursón in Lope's eponymous *comedia* when, compelled by *la fuerza de la sangre* (the power of blood), they decide to refrain from killing one another despite expectation or direct order.[63] While the party passes through the village on the way back to court, Lisardo and Fenisa cross paths, and she catches the philandering eye of the prince once again. Along with the passage of time, likely more instances of enacting sexual violence, and the fact that Fenisa has changed her name to Laura, Lisardo fails to recognize her (or alternatively, Lope may simply be deploying the dramatic conventions of disguise and relying on the audience's suspension of disbelief). Upon his request, she nevertheless assents to join Leonido in accompanying the royal party back to court. In the entirely unfamiliar luxury of the royal setting, Leonido, again compelled by the natural connection he has to Fenisa (his mother), mistakes *la fuerza de la sangre* for amorous attraction; meanwhile, Lisardo has fallen for Laura/Fenisa, but remains unaware of her identity. Learning of the prince's affection for Laura/Fenisa, Leonido decides to return to the woods out of a sense of deference to Lisardo's royal authority, although his feelings for her endure. However, rather than staying at court, his mother follows him, and in so doing discovers the garments she had clothed him in as an infant, realizing he is in fact her son. She finds him, but continues to withhold this crucial piece of information while disclosing a partial version of the events that transpired years prior regarding her affair with Lisardo and his subsequent abandonment. Overcome with a sense of duty to avenge Fenisa's honor that exceeds his regard for royal authority, Leonido immediately returns to court and threatens Lisardo's life, a crime for which he is briskly sentenced to death. But then, just before his execution, Fenisa reveals herself, proclaiming Leonido to be her and

Lisardo's son. This discovery precipitates the conventional happy ending of the play by compelling the marriage between Lisardo and Fenisa to restore her honor, as well as legitimize Leonido as the royal heir. The now-prince is paired off with a princess who had conveniently just arrived at court to marry the man just acknowledged to be his father.

Antonucci maintains that in *El hijo de los leones*, as in the other two Lope plays, we observe a fundamental change in Leonido over the course of the three acts: "love does a great work on him, softening and transforming him."[64] Her interpretation of Leonido, and the wild figure subgenre in general, relies heavily on the notion of this fundamental transformation of character from wild to civilized; however, in the case of Leonido, these changes are conveyed to the audience through his own words, which are wrought with uncertainty rather than trustworthy self-identification that we can rely upon. Antonucci cites his first encounter with Fenisa as a critical moment in his transformation from wild man to prince. In Leonido's own words, Fenisa's beauty tempers his "severity to tears and softness."[65] But this self-proclaimed harshness poorly describes the portrayal of his character on display since the beginning of the work. The audience witnesses his tender-heartedness as he tearfully mourns Fileno's death ("today you will see / me bathed in tender tears").[66] In this scene, his articulation of complex emotional and psychological reflections rivals Segismundo's famous monologue at the end the second act of Calderón's *La vida es sueño* (1635), as seen in Leonido's own soliloquy:

> When I consider myself
> so rustic, wild, and terrifying,
> I envy everyone I see,
> and wish to imitate them.
> Maybe the reflective waters
> show me that I am human,
> when they lay at night amid the grass
> maybe the ripples (distorting the reflection)
> deprive me of that name ("human"),
> so that I imitate [*imitatio*] the wildest beasts
> who live with me as equals,
> and I the subject of an old man,
> who teaches and corrects me,
> governs and rules over me,

and even if I resist him
I struggle in vain,
I must be a beast; I'm not (hu)man.[67]

Although he concludes that he must be a beast, and not human, his ability to express his complex existential anxieties creates a tension coined by Christian Metz as "instant self-contradiction" whereby "the circumstances of the uttering instantly refute the affirmation of the utterance."[68] In this case, the uttering, "I must be a beast; I'm not human" betrays the utterance in so far as the very act of using language precludes him from being a being a beast. It is his voicing that he is not human that is precisely what makes him human. Moreover, the contradiction is intensified by the placement of the uttering at the end of a soliloquy in which Leonido not only speaks, but eloquently articulates his emotional state of mourning and present existential crisis. Leonido's capacity for communication through spoken language in and of itself contradicts his own conclusion; he is therefore fundamentally and immediately unlike the beasts that lack that capacity.

This contradiction, along with the fact that we never see Leonido behave in the manner the townsfolk describe, suggests that the work portrays his ostensible wildness as in direct conflict with his innate nobility. As Leonido mourns the death of Fileno, he effectively scares off a group of villagers who inadvertently come near his forest dwelling: "Where are you going, knave? / Without my license you pass through this forest?"[69] Although he succeeds in terrifying them, rather than pursue them, he allows them to flee and also prevents his lions from giving chase. This scene displays his natural inclination to exercise restraint, and his behavior here, although brusque, is far from the pernicious degree of his alleged crimes. What is more, his effortless control of the lions—the kings of the animal kingdom—is an outward manifestation of his royal blood that foreshadows the moment later in the play when it is revealed. After the villagers have fled, he immediately returns to brooding over his wildness, rendering his display of ferocity an act he adeptly performed in the prudent execution of authority over his domain, which he subsequently abandons when he no longer has an audience that requires it. What he is unable to realize, but becomes clear to the audience, is that the villagers project the expectation of wildness on Leonido, and use him as a scapegoat, while he agonizes over the role he is not even conscious he is playing.

By the third of Lope's wild figure *comedias*, it has become a convention of the subgenre that for specific reasons I have argued, we are led to believe the villagers' claims about the wild figure are exaggerated or falsified, especially provided the scant evidence in the observed behavior of the "wild" protagonists to substantiate those allegations. One example in *El hijo de los leones* confirms this claim more concretely than what is a reasonable inference in the previous two. When asked to pay his share of the annual crops and livestock in rent to the landowner, Faquín, a farmer on the lands of the nobleman Perseo, conveniently uses the wild man as a scapegoat for the lack of provisions that he is able to supply. Even though he swears "that the king would have / envied his lot, / from the first goat to the last ox," his lengthy description of the destroyed crops and livestock has the air of hyperbole, which extends to his identification of the wild man: "if a devil of a savage, a monster, or I don't know what, didn't destroy the whole village."[70] Faquín deploys a variety of monikers to describe the supposed creature, which are so generalized they lead to a semantically dubious identification of the perpetrator that ultimately has no bearing on the referent described.[71]

Lope seems to be asking the medium to do more of the heavy lifting to restore order at the end of the *El hijo de los leones* than in earlier wild folk plays. The affective charge portrayed in the despair of Fenisa as she recounts the story of her rape in act 1 and her remorse upon considering the eventualities that befell her newborn in the forest ("I'm sure—oh how terrible!—the wild animals buried him").[72] The audience hears of her resolve to reject the advances of prince Lisardo, only for him to sneak into her chambers one night while her father is away to rape her in her sleep. Although this honor plot is conventional, what sets this depiction apart is the explicit detailed description of the rape. In lieu of glossing over what took place through euphemisms or readings between the lines to diminish their emotional impact, Fenisa's impassioned description of the events elicit a confrontation with her trauma. As a consequence, this creates dramatic exigencies that go beyond resolving the honor plot through recognition and marriage, but also that respond to her expressed emotional trauma. In *El hijo de los leones*, Lope must rely more heavily on the conventions of the *comedia* to provide a happy ending. The marriage between Fenisa and Lisardo conventionally resolves the honor plot, but bridging the gap between the actual and the ideal stretches "the boundaries of conventional comic reintegration."[73] Furthermore, in *El hijo de los leones*, the resolution reunites a son with a father and mother, the latter of which was so compelled by baroque notions of honor, that she leaves him at the foot of a tree as an infant, in spite of him being "so beautiful he would have been enough to console my [lost] honor."[74] In *El nacimiento de Valentín y Ursón*, Uberto dies by the hand of Valentín—who becomes a wild man as a result of Uberto's false claim against the honor of his mother—thereby eliminating the threat he posed to the integrity of social order in comprehensive fashion. Less so, Faustina, although having committed a similar crime—fabricating the story of her sister's infidelity—is forced to join a convent. In this third play, Lisardo marries the victim of his offense, only admitting to his fault when there was no denying it. Moreover, Lope never deals with the issue of Lisardo's lack of fitness to rule, highlighted throughout the work in relation to Leonido's inclination to act valiantly and win the affection of those around him. The "real" baroque monster of the play is not only permitted to live, but he is also afforded the same role in society as previous to his transgression. Increasingly, in Lope's corpus of wild figure plays, the monster lingers. His or her death becomes increasingly symbolic, or elided altogether. In *El hijo de los leones*, the display of ideological precepts conventionally upheld occurs at the expense of dramatic exigency. This is not to say that this would or would not have been perceived or led to a questioning of those precepts, but rather that a diachronic analysis of this mini-corpus of Lope de Vega's wild figure plays demonstrates an intensification of internal tensions that the playwright relies on the conventions of the *comedia* to resolve.

As a component in the system of meaning making of the *comedia* the wild figure exists thanks to the baroque aesthetic of containment driven by Counter-Reformation values, but also is the very thing that tests the integrity of the mechanisms in place to hold the center. And wildness tends to risk getting away from its author, leaving excesses and deformity in its wake—a baroque monster indeed. In this sense, the wild figure poses the threat of "spilling over into its container" and as such, creates texts that are themselves *monstrous*.[75] This baroque impulse to control and contain that motivates the conflict of these plays falls in line with Maravall's propagandistic model of cultural production, but we must nuance our readings to account for the ideological complexity found among these works, both intertextually entwined but also unique signifiers in dynamic relationship with the ideological matrices of the period. On that dynamic, "in the structural interplay between change and conservatism" Weiss notes, "the desire to control and contain (*dirigismo*) wins out."[76] That *desire* to imagine monsters simply for the purpose of cathartically containing, domesticating, or eliminating them indeed appears to be alive and well in each of Lope's plays analyzed in this chapter. Yet, we ultimately need flexible critical tools to account for the ways dramatic wildness is also always in dynamic interaction with hegemonic structures. In each of his wild figure plays, the trajectory of the dramatic action and its resolution follow a conservative logic of containment, but at the same time, it is critical that we "be equally alert to elements of oppositional discourse in his plays (whether conscious or not) whose presence is there not simply to be contained, but as the ground of future change."[77] It is not a necessary outcome that those structures fully succeed in controlling, incorporating, or transforming the defiant vigor the wild figure theatrically embodies from the margins. Furthermore, as Weiss again points out, a play will inevitably present more than one attitude in relation to the ideological matrices of hegemonic structures. On the presumption of Lope de Vega's broad conservatism, he counters, "his conservatism relative to which ideological fields?"[78] In this chapter, these methodological concerns have motivated the approach applied to explain the ideological contours of Lope de Vega's wild figure plays.

CHAPTER 3

Wild History
*Fashioning National Identity
in the Mythological Past*

THE PRESENT CHAPTER EXAMINES three *comedias* that construct notions of Spanish national identity, accomplished through the presentation of carefully arranged dramatic versions of well-known mythological and folkloric sources. Lope de Vega's *Las Batuecas del Duque de Alba* (c. 1600), Tirso de Molina's *Las Amazonas en las Indias* (1631), and Bances Candamo's *La piedra filosofal* (1693) share this semiotics, that is, they all produce meaning by relying on a system of shared conventions that I will call national mythological drama.[1] The mechanics of the system work in the following manner: the plays dramatize mythologized histories of national import to reconstruct their meaning for contemporary audiences, specifically with regard to pride of place connected to an inchoate sense of national identity. Although each of the plays share a similar methodology by fashioning national history through specific theatrical retellings of mythological, historical, and folkloric material, the earlier plays construct a starkly different image of Spain than Bances's *comedia*, staged at court in 1693. In this chapter, I argue that the time between the composition of the works—Lope and Tirso's works are first staged toward the beginning of the seventeenth century while the other near its close—suggests some shift occurred in the interim to allow for their incompatible depictions of Spanish history.

In *Las Batuecas del Duque de Alba*, Lope imbues folkloric source material with national significance, articulating the idiosyncratic elements of the plot to correspond meaningfully with the epic narrative of the final events of the Reconquista when Granada falls to the forces of the Catholic Monarchs. The play glorifies this historical moment by retelling it as an ethno-religious apology for European and Old-Christian hegemony, two facets comprising a Spanish national identity ascribed to by dominant culture during the period. Many similarities can be found between Lope's *Batuecas* play and Tirso de Molina's *Trilogía de los Pizarros*, especially the third installment in *Las Amazonas en las Indias*. Tirso's defense of Pizarro in the trilogy, like Lope in *Las Batuecas*, casts a community of wild folk—in this case a civilization of Amazons—to mythologize a national-historical drama that exalts one of the most prominent figures in the Spanish imperial project: Gonzalo Pizarro. The enigmatic closure of the play questions the success of this gesture, however, and it would seem that wild representation resists its container. Of interest here are the ways wildness is deployed to establish national identity during "the period most associated with the birth of a national literature," but also fracturing under its own weight almost from the onset.[2] In the final decade of the century, Bances Candamo's *La piedra filosofal* is a play that signifies an early emptying out of those national mythologies; rather than celebrate the collective past, Bances recasts elements of a national origin mythology as an allegory for Spanish imperial failure and decline.

In this chapter, I explore the ways the compositional elements of each play are configured to mythologize the national past. To achieve this objective, I rely on Tyrrell's explanation of the dynamics of national myth formation defined as "tales that rest on 'invented tradition,' [which] have some basis in fact, but have been embellished, or selected; they are used for various purposes of national solidarity or the advance of group and class interests."[3] In discussing the nature of national mythologies of the United States, which are applicable to the current discussion, Tyrrell adds:

> In contrast to the concept of legend or classical mythology, national myth . . . does not necessarily assume an essentially fabricated status. It can be a mixture of invention, exaggeration, de-contextualization, and erasure. Nevertheless, aspects of the national narrative that function as myths in the United States may (indeed it might be said *must*) be founded

on certain facts and ring true by expressing features considered as the essence of individual or national character.⁴

This definition reflects the mythologizing enterprise Lope and Tirso carry out in the plays analyzed in this chapter. In so doing, their plays display an entrenched patriotism at the end of the sixteenth and early seventeenth centuries—a doubling down on national identity that is a common feature of empires in decline. However, Bances Candamo's *La piedra filosofal* is less committed to this national mythos. Put on for the court of Carlos II in the final years of the infirm king's reign that would end the Spanish Habsburg monarchical line, it looks back at the failures of the imperial project with clearer vision at a moment when the woeful condition of national affairs could not be ignored.

But what does all of this have to do with the wild figure? The logic for corpus selection in the present chapter is twofold: first, and this is rather self-explanatory, all three playwrights draw from features in the repertoire of wild representation in crafting prominent character(s) in each of the plays; second, like other chapters in this monograph, the *comedias* examined here form a miniature corpus of works that are in conversation with one another. In this case their intertextuality revolves around participation in the formation, and re-formation, of national identity during the period. Their similarities are such that, at the very least, they are drawing from a repertoire of conventions that overlap heavily, and it is their commitments to and rejections of that repertoire that helps account for their differences. And the differences are what become particularly telling and hold most of the interest here. In Lope and Tirso, the common thread is the representation of the discovery of a community of wild folk, which they compose to present particular theatrical retellings of folklore and mythology, respectively. Their retellings are acts of folklore and mythology in and of themselves that reconfigure the past in ways that shape how a collective body of subjects views itself. The plays affirm and uphold the ideologies of imperialism and a homogenous body of Christian Spanish subjects. This is epitomized in Lope's use of the discovery space of the cave in *Las Batuecas del Duque de Alba* as the locus for the revelation of national identity. The cave is where they find the physical remains of Teodosio, brother of the last Visigothic king of Spain, Rodrigo. This discovery, which coincides with the military campaign and fall of Granada in 1492, articulates the Spain of the Catholic Monarchs as inheritors of the Christian kingdoms of Visigoth

Spain prior to the arrival of Muslim inhabitants of the Iberian Peninsula in 711 CE. Tirso takes up the narrative of colonial discovery to paint the encounter of Gonzalo Pizarro with indigenous people in a positive light in *Las Amazonas en las Indias*. Bances then engages important aspects of both earlier plays to deconstruct those national-mythological objectives, and launch a comprehensive critique of empire vis-à-vis the cave as a discovery space. For Bances, the theatrical device of the cave—and by extension theater itself—becomes a manipulative, rather than revelatory space where national myth can be sold as historical reality.

This approach requires some definition of terms, specifically the modifier "national" as a facet of Iberian identity during a time when the very concept of "nation" had yet to be solidified. In explicitly political contexts, Spain was described in the plural—*las Españas*—for which no equivalent translation exists in English, an etymological curiosity that obscures the complexities of pinning down an entity that can be identified discretely as Spain (in the singular) during the sixteenth and seventeenth centuries. Across Europe, regional kingdoms were being consolidated into larger political entities, the borders of which begin to coalesce into a map that would be recognizable today, and primary markers of identity became ones of proto-national affiliation (e.g., English, French, Dutch, etc.). So even if the nation-state as we presently understand it was still very much a work-in-progress, geopolitical structures (i.e., where one resided and to whom one was subjected politically) came to demarcate sets of cultural practices and values, which produced a conceptualization of identity linked to one's geopolitical subjectivity. These markers were leveraged propagandistically to unify a populace of subjects, against which an image of the other could be constructed. Barbara Fuchs explains the dynamics of the formation of a modern national consciousness through the discourses of cultural production during the period, relying on the representations of Englishness and Spanishness in each other's literature and drama as a case study. Fuchs affirms the use of this vocabulary of national identity as appropriate for early modern European cultural production. Moreover, it has long been commonplace to attribute Lope de Vega with the birth of a Spanish national theater. Describing his playwriting as "Spanish"—or as Ignacio Arellano puts it, "radically Spanish"—obscures the longstanding debate over the extent to which the portrayal of Spain in Lope's works should qualify his theater as a "propagandistic instrument of the state."[5] While there remains robust debate over when the emergence of national identity in the current sense of the term took place,

Ryjik, affirms "if we consider Golden Age theater as an important element in the process of communication of cultural content to audiences from the intellectual elite to the lowest stratums of society, that is, in the formation of a national consciousness, it is apt to analyze the type of cultural content produced by this theater, especially in what refers to an idea of nation."[6] This is precisely the type of content we find in the plays treated in this chapter, which transmit ideas related to collective pride of place and the boundaries of that collective in ways that illuminate the formation of ideas of nation solidified in the centuries that follow.

FETISHIZING RACIAL AND RELIGIOUS PURITY IN LOPE'S *LAS BATUECAS DEL DUQUE DE ALBA*

As I have outlined to this point, relying on a broad body of scholarship to do so, the antecedents to the baroque wild figure form a collage of influences as they become manifested on the sixteenth- and seventeenth-century Spanish stage, including literary, iconographic, dramatic, historical, as well as folk sources. But within each of those genre categories, influences are not homogenous. While each iteration of the baroque wild figure displays a unique configuration of features drawing from a common repertoire of conventions, we can also point to influences outside that repertoire, that is, source material that is unique to each work. This is especially evident for Lope de Vega's *Las Batuecas del Duque de Alba* (c. 1600), which dramatizes a well-known and concrete Extremaduran folktale. Previously disseminated through oral transmission, Lope's staging of the story, along with the subsequent publication of the play, created a standardized version for a wider theater-going and reading audience. *Las Batuecas* presents the fabulous tale of a community of people living in the mountainous terrain of the Sierra de Francia near the border between Spain and Portugal. As the legend goes, a group of Visigoth soldiers fled to this area to retreat from Muslim forces, where they stayed, and where their descendants then lived in complete isolation for hundreds of years.[7] In the opening scenes of Lope's *comedia*, the setting shifts between the Batuecas and the aristocratic space of the ducal court of Alba, where we meet Brianda and Juan de Arce. They have fallen in love, but are keeping it secret because they are of different social classes (Brianda is a noblewoman and Juan de Arce a high-ranking servant of the duke). They decide to abscond together into the mountainous woods of the Batuecas, which is where they encounter the community of wild folk living there. As the play follows their stay there with the *batuecos* and the duke's ultimately successful search to find them, the action culminates in the Duke of Alba blessing Juan de Arce's betrothal to Brianda. But more importantly for the analysis here, in the conclusion, he also acknowledges the wild folk as his political subjects (the Batuecas valley is located within the territory of his ducal lands) and baptizes them as Christians.

In relying on the details of this particular tale, the play signifies something of an outlier in terms of the conventions that generally characterize the wild figure *comedias* of the Spanish Baroque. Chiefly, in Lope's *Batuecas* we encounter a community of wild folk rather than more solitary figures. As such, the elements and devices that tend to make up the plot arc of wild figure plays are also mostly absent from those considered in this chapter, although some of the tropes are reproduced (and will be identified in the analysis that follows). No interpersonal affront at court serves to catalyze the principal action, nor are there any royal foundlings whose reappearance resolves the degeneration of monarchical authority that such an affront produces. The wild figure in those plays is exemplary in its capacity to prescriptively legitimize political authority by modeling it through theatrical representation. They portray the parameters by which an individual obtains and administers legitimate political authority. In that framework, the recovery of the lost identity of the wild figure as prince necessarily and believably ensures the political stability of the kingdom. Within this popular medium, the manner in which the wild figure's identity legitimizes their authority and establishes order gives shape to the intense commitments to political ideologies on monarchical legitimacy that were fundamental in early modern Spanish political thought. In *Las Batuecas*, the question of political authority is not absent—the play's finale maintains traditional political hierarchies by establishing the Duke of Alba as the rightful regional authority over the *batuecos*—while the most prominent message of the play relates more directly to the construction of Spanish national identity through the consolidation of a collective mythology.[8]

The folkloric source material for *Las Batuecas* proves appropriate for highlighting the collective by relating a story about a group of wild folk rather than an individual. As in other wild figure *comedias*, the plot hinges on the recuperation of lost identity, just on a larger scale. Concisely, the play presents the discovery of a community residing in the Extremaduran wilderness who have lived in seclusion since the eighth-century defeat of the Visigoths by the Muslim forces. It is their identity the audience is set up to be most concerned with, and upon its discovery, they recover their Spanish identity, then are legally recognized as citizens therein under the authority of the Duke of Alba. Therefore, the message is not solely concerned with the nature of an individual—namely the king—for whom the wild figure is a theatrical vehicle. Rather than a projection of the idea of the monarch *to* the masses, the representation of a community of wild folk in *Las Batuecas* presents a compelling image of collective affiliation for members of an imagined Iberian public. The community of wild folk in *Las Batuecas* signifies what Stuart Hall calls an "articulation," defined as a "non-necessary link, between a social force which is making itself, and the ideology or conceptions of the world which makes intelligible the process they are going through, which begins to bring onto the historical stage a new social position and political position, a new set of social and political subjects."[9] David Castillo offers insights into the context that brought sets of discourses to be articulated in the formation of national subjectivity, citing the "revisionist zeal of the 'organic' historians of the late 1400s and the 1500s resulted in a systematic rewriting of the past of the Iberian Peninsula and the consolidation of a national mythology of ancient origins and historical destiny of which Spaniards, especially Castilians, could be proud."[10] In Lope's play the wild folk become literalized proof of *pureza de sangre* (blood purity), for which the dramatic mode serves as a vehicle for embodied performance to present an ideological link as if it were a natural or "real" one.[11] The linkage depicts a critical aspect of *españolidad* (i.e., notions of inclusion and exclusion of those who possess it and those who do not) as corresponding to an aspect of the identity of the eighth-century Germanic Visigoths (i.e., Christianity). In so doing, the dramatic adaptation of the folktale efficiently consolidated a mythology by which ethnically European Christians claimed Spanish identity at the expense of the Muslim inhabitants of the peninsula from their arrival in 711 CE to the expulsion of even the *morisco* converts over the period of 1609 to 1614. This articulation of *españolidad* viewed the inhabitants of North African descent as foreign invaders, even though they had resided on the peninsula for more than 700 years.[12]

Much of the scholarship on *Las Batuecas* obscures this feature of the play, however. Rather than a play that draws from a European repertoire of images and source material, scholars see *Las Batuecas del Duque de Alba* as an allegorical representation of the evangelization of the Americas, and by extension a theatrical justification for the Spanish imperial project that, according to its logic, brought civilization and salvation to the inhabitants of the Americas. Rodríguez de la Flor summarizes this view: "that the conquest of America offers the historical model, on which the fictive structure of *Las Batuecas* unfolds, evinced by the synchronicity of the two phenomena, linked more than you could imagine."[13] This emphasis on the conquest of the Americas is critical to note as the prevailing historical context in which the play was written. It serves as a lens to make sense of the ideological potential that rendered these particular influences of European literary, oral, and dramatic traditions ready to be excavated and mined for their content. The mythological and folkloric material works in tandem with the representation of contact and evangelization in the service of the play's multivalent ideological project. In fact, this approach reveals that both influences—those of *conquista* and *Reconquista*—are components of a more complex dramatic apparatus designed to consolidate national identity.[14] Rodríguez de la Flor's language of "historical model" proves useful to describe the plurality of sources relied upon to compose *Las Batuecas del Duque de Alba*. Each of the historical models of the Conquest and *la Reconquista* are deployed along with the folkloric model of the discovery of the uncontacted *batuecos*, as well as the dramatic model of the wild figure, already developed by Lope in previous works. All of these "models" form part of the play's system of signification that entails (1) a portrayal of peaceful encounter, evangelization, and legal incorporation of uncontacted peoples that could be easily transferred as a template onto the narrative of the Spanish imperial project in the Americas, and (2) to affirm an Iberian history of uninterrupted ethno-European inhabitance of the peninsula upon which the exclusion of Iberians of north African descent from ethnic Spanish identity could be sustained.[15] Both of these messages, produced by the interweaving of those "models," serve the larger project to impose an ethnically European imperial ideological framework onto historical narratives, namely of *Conquista* and *Reconquista*, thereby offering a frame for the construction and consolidation of Spanish identity within the collective imagination.

Scholarship that primarily focuses on the influence of the New World narrative on Lope's play aptly highlights the following aspects of the work: (1) the representation of civilization versus barbarity in the play draws parallels to the encounter, conquest and evangelization of the Americas; (2) the notion that *Las Batuecas* forms part of a trilogy in Lope's corpus, which includes *Los guanches de Tenerife* (The Guanches of Tenerife) and *El Nuevo Mundo descubierto por Cristóbal Colón* (The New World Discovered by Christopher Columbus)—one of his few plays to explicitly present American content that also employs some of the same plot devices as *Batuecas*; and (3) two adaptations/rewritings of the play by later playwrights read the play in light of the conquest and explicitly orient the audience to see the connection to the New World in their titles. These adaptations include *El nuevo mundo en España* (The New World in Spain; 1671) by Matos Fragoso and Hoz y Mota's *El descubrimiento de las Batuecas del Duque de Alba, o, El nuevo Mundo en España* (The Discovery of the Duke of Alba's Batuecas, or, The New World in Spain; 1710).

Due to the monumental significance of the contact between the indigenous Americans and the Europeans as a result of Columbus's first voyage and the age of exploration and conquest that followed, Hispanists frame Spain as an early modern political entity in the context of empire. As outlined in the introduction, the corpus of wild figure *comedias* evinces contentions made by Latin American postcolonialist theory that there is no modernity without coloniality, and *Las Batuecas* is a play for which coloniality serves as a particularly useful lens. So without downplaying the colonial to contextualize the work nor the epistemic coloniality underpinning its salient message, the present analysis focuses on the impact of European folkloric narratives reproduced in Lope's play, specifically, the dramatic history of the wild figure. As has been established, Lope's use of this character draws heavily from the European imaginary. In this case, the wild figure indeed superimposes the known onto the unknown in order to paint the conquest narrative in a certain light (i.e., imagine the indigenous inhabitants of the Americas within the framework of wild folk), but wildness is also deployed to reconstruct a European, and in this case Iberian, historical narrative. In depicting a story about the Other, the wild figure also tells us one about the inhabitants of the center (i.e., seventeenth-century Spain). The wild *batuecos* are presented as Spanish, and produce a message about *la españolidad*, and the representation of their wildness in the play creates meaning in ways akin to other wild folk plays.

As I have indicated, the connection between Lope's work and the discovery of the New World is made evident in the two rewritings of his original. The first is Matos Fragoso's *El nuevo mundo en Castilla* (1671) and the other Hoz y Mota's *El descubrimiento de las Batuecas del Duque de Alba* (1710). The title Matos Fragoso gives his version—*El nuevo mundo en Castilla*—suggests that the author read Lope's version as placing the template of the New World discovery onto an Iberian geography. The next version of the play, another "reboot" of sorts, is by Hoz y Mota, for which there are two extant copies from the eighteenth century. While the original manuscript from 1710 is titled *Las Batuecas del Duque de Alba*, a 1766 copy bears the title(s) *El Sol en el Nuevo Mundo, o, Nuevo Mundo en Castilla* (The Sun in the New World, or, New World in Castile).[16] If these titles are any indication, the reception of the play as an allegory for the discovery of the New World is clear. The title *El Sol en el Nuevo Mundo* is especially ideologically embedded since the play takes place entirely on the Iberian Peninsula. Hall's theoretical language of articulation again serves to explain this phenomenon. Articulation provides this vocabulary thanks to its multiple connotations both as the spoken expression of an idea but also the type of link created by a trailer connection (e.g., an articulated transit bus). As a tool for cultural studies, an articulation then describes the expression of a set of ideas that are linked together, but that linkage

> is not necessary, determined, absolute and essential for all time. You have to ask under what circumstances can a connection be forged or made? The so-called "unity" of a discourse is really the articulation of different, distinct elements which can be rearticulated in different ways because they have no necessary "belongingness." The "unity" which matters is a linkage between the articulated discourse and the social forces with which it can, under certain historical conditions, but need not necessarily, be connected.[17]

Linked in these subsequent rewritings of Lope's Batuecas play are the connection between contact, evangelization, and political subjugation of Iberian wild folk with the same processes of New World indigenous peoples. And this connection is inherently "forged" in context, patent beyond the sole reference to the New World in the play, which occurs when Brianda predicts the discovery of the Americas in a moment of almost extradiegetic prophecy: "And another, second world / remains to be discovered by Columbus."[18]

Rozas identifies Brianda's reference to Columbus, which he notes is "still in prophetic form, it is intrinsically coherent with this catechism by the logical path the work follows, and also because it maintains the programed sense that the discovery of the Batuecas is similar—materially and even spiritually—to the discovery of America."[19] Brianda's mention of Columbus also forms part of what Rozas concisely summarizes as the "New World framework" for understanding the play: "*Los guanches de Tenerife* and *El Nuevo Mundo descubierto por Cristóbal Colón* are works which, without forcing it too much, we could consider a trilogy along with the *comedia*."[20] However, the play is not only an apology for the colonization and evangelization of the Americas; these allusions, while present, function differently than the ones I will highlight here (even if they betray an inescapable coloniality). They serve to affirm Spanish identity, of which the *batuecos* are always already a part as stakeholders in the mythical history of Spanish national identity. This is a mythical history also in play in the *comedia de indios* that validates Spanish destiny in evangelizing the indigenous people of the Americas by situating them as actors in a narrative the extends back to the biblical Israelites. However, apart from the other two installments in the trilogy, in the specific case of *Las Batuecas*, this ideological gesture also reproduces a leitmotif in the poetics of baroque theatrical wildness: the appearance of the other(s) who is/are actually not other at all, but rather an integral part at the heart of Spanish ideological landscape tied to its Iberian geographical center. The wild figure—the false other—provides an initial misdirection that ultimately shines a brighter light on the intended target of the theatrical process of othering, in this case Iberians of North African descent, who are erased by means of their absence, albeit a conspicuous one.[21] Lope fashions *hispanidad* through the articulation of contemporary white Christians under the Spanish crown and the Visigoths who inhabited the peninsula eight centuries prior. Presenting this link as unbroken, the play simultaneously dramatizes a national history that omits the Iberian Moors and their descendants, excluding them from sharing in that collective identity. Rodríguez de la Flor concisely summarizes this aspect of the play: "traditional legendary aspects are superimposed to create, in a mythologized variant of the story, that which resides in the collective unconscious and lacks, in a proper sense, history. The age-old national ghost of the 'loss of Spain' is given here, as in other sites of national geography, as a type of origin of the entire fable."[22]

Lope relies on the "New World framework" to superimpose the New World onto the Old, but the end goal is not the evangelization and civilizing of the wild folk inhabiting the Batuecas; rather, it is to resolve that mythologized sense of loss and affirm the link between ethno-European Christian goths and the Old Christian Spaniards of the seventeenth century. The play ultimately uses the representation of the assumed other (the wild folk) to prime the audience to be thinking along the lines of who is other, only to emphasize the identity of the true Other (as positioned ideologically by the play), in this case the Muslim civilizations that inhabited the Iberian Peninsula from 711 to 1492. Again, the *comedia* betrays its commitment to New World evangelization and colonial domination, but its explicit concern is with guiding the audience toward a reception of the play that internalizes mythologies about national identity. The following verses spoken by the Duke of Alba mark the resolution of the conflict, and follow the "New World framework" that Rozas suggests drives the plot:

> Friends, my name is exalted
> greatly in being your Lord
> of the abundant land inherited
> from the illustrious ancestors
> that are the first of my line.
> I baptize you all.[23]

This speech act accomplishes two specific goals: first, it validates the incorporation of the *batuecos* under the Duke's political authority and second, it baptizes them as Christians. It must not be overlooked that this proclamation reproduces the events and top-down political organization of empire that characterized contact with the indigenous peoples of the Americas, as well as their ensuing political incorporation under the Spanish monarchy and evangelization. At the same time, to emphasize these similarities is to obscure the parameters that condition the peaceful subjugation (there is no need for pacification) of the *batuecos*, who willingly acknowledge the duke's authority, even before his cited proclamation. When the duke and the wild folk first come into contact, Triso is the first to speak to Alba, offering a sentiment that is then echoed by Giroto:

> TRISO: Everyone embraces you, great Duke;
>   according to what you have told us,
>   it is a true and clear obligation,
>   because you are our lord,
>   this being your mountain.
> GIROTO: We are all fortunate
>   that from such high lineage [blood]
>   we would come to have such a master.[24]

On the one hand, this is a fantasy of the Conquest, presented to an audience willing to accept such a rosy portrayal of contact, conquest, and evangelization with all of the ideological values and none of the violence.[25] On the other, the events leading up to their encounter with the Duke set up the audience to identify meaningful bonds of affiliation between the *batuecos* and the "civilized" members of the Duke's entourage (a synecdoche of the Spanish populace writ large). This fundamentally affects the audience's perception and reception of their identity. Chiefly, their classification as other is false, and whereas indigenous people remain "other" in representations of evangelization, the point here, as in the wild figure subgenre in general, is that the wild folk always already form part of the collective political body as defined within the ideological parameters perpetuated by dramatic art of the period. In this case, the highlighted aspect of their shared identity—Visigothic ancestry—is proof of an essential facet of the identity constructed by the representation (Old Christian, European).

Scholars such as Rozas have noted that the primitive community represented is by no means a utopia, nor an affirmation of the pre-civilized Golden age inhabited by the noble savage: "but soon we realize that is not quite the Arcadia, nor a golden age, themes to which Lope was so partial."[26] From the vantage of coloniality, it is expected to find the "fallacy of developmentalism" embedded in the discourse of the play whereby *batuecos* beckon to emerge from their primitive political organization by submitting to the established political paradigms championed in the play.[27] Like the Amerindians their representation evokes, they are "conceptualized as the tabula rasa" upon which those paradigms "could and should be inscribed."[28] In this case, their infighting at the beginning of the play is evidence of their need for properly administered political order under the Duke of Alba's political authority. (This is another resonance shared with the *comedia de indios*.) All that is required for this to transpire is the Duke's proclamation, rather than any process of civilizing transformation. This is because the play constructs Spanish identity through the affirmation of their a priori affiliation. Brianda provides the first inkling of this ultimate realization of sameness when she notes, "even though you look wild, your intentions are pious."[29] Moreover, that they speak Spanish is more than the result of theatrical necessity for the sake of audience intelligibility, but rather another means by which the play continues to point to these bonds of affiliation tied to their common Visigoth ancestry. Again it is Brianda who notices that the *batuecos* speak Spanish, whose surprise the audience should share. Rhetorically, she asks, "How is that you've lived here, / without God, and without order [literally: the Law], / and you speak Castilian like this?"[30] Darinto's response alludes to the king Rodrigo without explicitly stating his name, the first in a series of references that point to the *batuecos'* link to the last Visigoth king:

> It is said, a fleeing king
> came to live in this area,
> and some shepherds
> or soldiers from a war
> holed up in this sierra
> that you see.[31]

When Don Juan de Arce learns who they are, he even takes for granted an aspect of their identity that later is essential for their own realization of Spanish identity: "heaven / would have it that these *Castilians* / since that time are / without knowledge that they are *Christians*" (emphasis my own).[32] Again, the *batuecos* are Spanish Christians all along, which makes the play about the process of all involved parties coming to realize that this is the case. This unfolding understanding of the bond that links them vis-à-vis Rodrigo culminates in the revelation of the meaning of the letters inscribed on the shield found in a cave in the Batuecas valley by the duke's party as they search for Brianda and Juan de Arce. The letters on the shield, "T.D.S.R.," identify the human remains also found in the cave, which are those of its owner: *Teodosilo sobrino de Rodrigo* (Teodosilo, nephew of Rodrigo).[33]

The recovered remains of Teodosilo leads to the recognition of the *batuecos* as "descendants of the Gothic kings," which the Duke and Ramiro de Lara explicitly understand through the lens of the *Reconquista*: "The cadaver that was in that cave, / they say was King Rodrigo's nephew; / that fleeing from the African Moors / he died in those hills."[34] Lara also makes reference to the period of time elapsed since Teodosilo's death: "it has been six hundred years since [that shield] was painted."[35] As is true in Lope's other wild folk plays, the *batuecos* are not wild at all—that is, they are not marginal or other, but rather central and integral to the facet of Spanish identity being constructed in a given dramatic iteration of the wild figure. In this case, the aspect (re)presented in the play not only suggests that Spanish national identity can be traced to before the arrival of North Africans to the peninsula in 711 CE, but also that the thread was never broken, that the Old Christian lineage remained pure and intact, only tucked away and waiting to be found.[36]

The recovery of Teodosilo's remains and their importance to the Reconquista also ties into the secondary plot of *Las Batuecas del Duque de Alba*. Updates on the developments of Ferdinand and Isabella's campaign to take Granada dominate conversations among the members of the duke's household over the course of the play. When Ramiro de Lara arrives from the royal court in act 2, news from the battle front proves most pressing before they can move on to discuss matters related to the primary plot (Lara's request to marry Brianda). When asked by the duke how the king and queen are faring, Lara communicates that they are well, and are en route to Granada. He makes particular mention that Isabel has accompanied Fernando: "The bellicose catholic queen / accompanies her Fernando to war, / which enlivens so many."[37] He also brings word to the duke that the king wishes for him to assume the title of viceroy of Castilla while the crown is in Granada, rather than join the war effort himself. Outside of the interpersonal conflicts that drive the plot, the issue of the war in Granada is of greatest importance. The conquest is subtext (which is not to say less important); the Reconquista is text, both figuratively but also quite literally. The letters on Teodosilo's shield—the shield as text—signify the explicit message to be conveyed by the play. The writing on the shield conveys the identity and affiliation of the *batuecos*, articulated to produce meaning in the contemporary context of 1492.[38] The Duke then has the shield sent to Fernando on the battlefront, a gesture for which the intended message is made clear.[39] The shield symbolizes the loss of the peninsula to Muslim occupation, or more precisely related to the figurative imagery of the shield, the inability to defend the Iberian Peninsula from Muslim takeover. With the shield in tow, the Catholic kings are to reclaim victory by participating in the final push to retake the peninsula for God and country. To my knowledge, the sending of the shield is an invention by Lope, but not a casual one. The physical presence of the shield with Fernando and Isabella in Granada articulates a linkage between Rodrigo's forces from 711 CE and the Catholic troops in 1492 through their shared purpose in defending the peninsula of Muslim occupation, which the play presents as natural and necessary to Spanish national identity. Returning to Stuart Hall's notion of articulation, the density of the visual metaphor of the shield creates linkages between the two periods with remarkable complexity, and the intensity with which they render the connections comprehensible requires the ideological commitments of the specific context in which Lope pens the work.

A NEW WORLD FOR OLD WORLD MYTHOLOGY IN TIRSO DE MOLINA'S *AMAZONAS EN LAS INDIAS*

Even if at first glance Tirso foregrounds New World settings in a number of his plays, especially the Pizarro trilogy, the representations of wild folk, namely the mythological race of the Amazons, are steeped in European ethno-mythologies.[40] Readers might be inclined to privilege the Mercedarian's view of the New World as unique because he spent time as a monk in Santo Domingo, it should be noted that his travels never took him to South America where *Las Amazonas en las Indias* (1631) takes place, even if his approach to conquest shares in the Eurocentric colonial worldview steeped in the *ego conquiro*. Moreover, like Lope's *Batuecas*, Tirso's impetus for writing the Pizarro trilogy seems to have had more to do with personal connections between playwright and the descendants of notable historical figures that appear in the plays. Written between eight and twelve years after his return from the New World, "the actual circumstances that motivated the writing of the trilogy were the years he lived in Trujillo [Cáceres] and his direct contact with the descendants of the Pizarro conquistadors."[41] Zugasti offers a careful analysis of the importance of historical veracity in the play, situating Tirso in a larger conversation during the period among critics and practitioners on the classical debate on the distinct nature and objectives of the two types of literature: history and poetry. Zugasti considers passages from Aristotle to Lopez-Pinciano to Bances Candamo, as well as excerpts from Golden Age plays in which characters weigh in on the matter, including Tirso.[42] In *Los cigarrales de Toledo* (The Country Estates of Toledo), for example, a group of playgoers discuss the historicity of a staging of the playwright's own *El vergonzoso en palacio* (Bashful at Court), in which the prevailing opinion expressed by internal characters suggests that playwriting provides ample room for poetic license and less concern for objective history: "As if Apollo's license reached into historical memory and couldn't build, atop the foundation of actual people, imaginary buildings of clever invention!"[43] Mayberry traces this dramatic convention of allowing a certain amount of poetic license at the expense of historical flexibility back to Antiquity: "even Aeschylus, the inventor of the

Greek trilogy, was willing to manipulate and modify the actual events of a legend in order to conform with the religious idea which motivated the drama."[44] While these prescriptive poetics and artistic precedents help to gauge the possibilities one might find with regard to the importance of historical accuracy versus poetic license, I will turn to *Amazonas en las Indias* to let practice determine theory rather than the other way around. More specifically, I will examine the dramatic function of the two wild folk characters, Menalipe and Martesia, as mythological, rather than historical, figures that shed light on the *comedia*'s overall ideological project.

It is of course possible that Tirso believed in the existence of the Amazons, as it was a topic debated in contemporary chronicles, with some writers of the conquest affirming their existence and others rejecting it.[45] In either case, his credulity or incredulity on this topic is tangential to their fictional portrayal in his play, which, like all representations of the Amazons in the period, constitutes a fabulous projection of the European imagination onto the American landscape. Moreover, in a play that otherwise dramatizes events that can be found in contemporary chronicles, the Amazons Menalipe and Martesia appear to be the only purely fabricated characters on the part of the playwright.[46] While previous scholarship has carried out careful studies to identify the sources Tirso draws from for the historical events dramatized in the play, I will turn my focus to the Amazons as outliers beyond the scope of this type of historical-biographical approach, an approach that has produced a consensus on the play that in *Amazonas en las Indias*, Tirso attempts to restore the image of Gonzalo Pizarro, as he does with the Pizarro family name in general in the trilogy as a whole.[47] Zugasti states it concisely in his edition of the trilogy: "Tirso's objective is the political reaffirmation of Gonzalo Pizarro, and for that it was necessary to combat his reputation as a dissident with the opposite image: he remained loyal to the crown, but his friends betrayed him and he ended up the scapegoat of a movement that never gained support."[48] As clear as this message may be, in trying to rewrite the official history, it becomes impossible for Tirso to revive the image of Gonzalo *and* celebrate the conquest; in fact, the extent to which the play is critical of Gonzalo's contemporaries in Perú that fought or were deployed against him, creates ambiguity about whether the play is meant to paint the conquest of Perú—or at least the fallout of the civil war initiated by the death of Almagro—in a positive light at all. Whether this was done consciously or not, the message produced cannot be ignored, and leaves us with a limited number of possibilities related to authorial intention which we can articulate. Two options emerge; either the play "got away from the author" or by the time of the play's composition, rosy depictions of the conquest were no longer tenable. In either case, a natural dramatic consequence of exalting Gonzalo Pizarro is a critique of empire, suggesting the notion that, had things turned out differently and Gonzalo had become governor of Lima, the turmoil of the ensuing period would have been avoided. Deploying the conventions of tragic drama, the mystic Amazon characters become mouthpieces of the cosmic determinacy made manifest as tragic destiny; it is the predetermined fate of the tragic hero, written immutably in the stars.

The critical tools offered by theater and performance studies shed light on two elements of the play that are essential to the mechanics of the message it conveys: the theatrical wild figure and the poetics of tragedy. These features of *Amazonas en las Indias* are also the conventions of the work unique to its status as a work of theater, with their own developments in the history of spectacle. Moreover, the two elements—wildness and tragedy—are inextricably entwined, as I will argue in the present analysis. Mayberry identifies this connection as well, concisely articulating the importance of the relationship between the Amazons (i.e., wild figures) and tragic drama: "[the Amazons] deserve the title role because of their vital function in the dramatic structure of the tragedy."[49] Scholars from McKendrick and Valentín de Pedro to Miró Quesada Sosa downplayed the importance of the Amazon characters in the play, while Green argued to restore their importance by noting they "provide [Tirso] with a means for telling the future" and act "as a counterpart of the chorus in Greek tragedy in this play."[50] These comments paved the way for Mayberry's in-depth study explaining their essential role in the tragedy in greater detail. As the tragic chorus, the warrior queen and sorceress "appear anywhere and at any moment . . . as prophetic commentators on the action."[51] Specifically, they appear when Gonzalo Pizarro—the tragic hero—commits an error related to his tragic flaw, to comment on its consequences. Mayberry identifies his flaw and Martesia and Menalipe's function in making it known to the audience:

> It was a stroke of genius on Tirso's part that the Amazons should be the instrument by which is revealed the tragic error or *hamartia* which Aristotle defined as essential to a tragic hero. Being a great nobleman and solider, Gonzalo fulfills Aristotle's further definition of the tragic hero. As in the

ancient concept of tragic irony, the hero's flaw has noble aspects. Gonzalo fails to restore utopia in the New World because of his tragic inclination to compromise. Gonzalo is always motivated by high ideals, but step-by-step his compromises lead to treason.[52]

Mayberry's analysis of the Amazons' impact on the development of tragedy is impressive, but the article (along with other scholarship on the play) looks at Menalipe and Martesia as characters only within the frame of other historical and contemporary examples of Amazons, without contextualizing their representation as iterations in a broader set of representations of wild figures. The conventions of their portrayal reflect those of the wild figure subgenre, the consideration of which informs a deeper understanding of the Amazons' critical function to the play's meaning. First, I will further outline their constitutive role in the play's tragic makeup, to then identify the features of their theatrical wildness, which are essential to the dramatic mechanics of the play's message.

The poetics of tragic action give greater weight to the events that transpire to precipitate Gonzalo Pizarro's downfall. Tragedy imbues the play with the gravitas of history—immutable, but not necessarily just. This fits Bushnell's encompassing definition of "tragedy's subject," which "is the relationship between the individual and the community in the face of a necessity that we may call the gods or history, and tragedy is performed to transform those who experience it."[53] That last clause, "to transform those who experience it," describes Tirso's play maybe more narrowly than the quote suggests. The work relies on tragic irony—Gonzalo's justifiable actions in "the face of a necessity" that give cause to his treasonous downfall—in order to "transform," or more plainly, *change* public opinion (at least among the Spanish noble and royal elite at the time of the play's composition). This objective pertained to a larger project of the Pizarro descendants when Tirso penned the trilogy in support of reclamation case for the title of *marqués*, which had been granted to Francisco in 1537 but not passed on after his death.[54] Green convincingly argues the three *comedias* are "occasional plays, a pageant in three parts prepared by Tirso to commemorate the creation, in 1631, ... [and] revival of the title of *Marqués de Indias*" which granted the title and lands in Spain to Juan Hernando Pizarro, the great grandson of Francisco.[55] 1631 falls toward the end of the period Tirso is composing the trilogy in the city of Trujillo, which is adjacent to La Zarza and within the lands included Pizarro's newly reinstated marquisate.

Grady's materialist approach to tragedy is critical of how "traditional theories of tragedy have understood that tragedy continually disrupts order and calls it in doubt, but they assume that at the end of the play, traditional order is reestablished and the good prevails."[56] Rather, Grady contends, historical contexts like early modern Europe and fifth-century BCE Greece, when established notions of the ordering of the world (social, epistemological, cosmological, etc.) are cast in doubt, are "precisely the points of the most creative upsurge in the writing of tragedy."[57] In Tirso's play, the representation of Gonzalo's death reflects this poetics of tragic necessity because it suggests that justice does not always prevail, and the tragic mode is deployed to protest against the depiction of the tragic hero found in the official history. The Amazons Menalipe and Martesia are the axis upon which this resistance turns. Gonzalo's predetermined fate is again emblematic of Grady's materialist theorization of early modern tragedy that is concerned with order, but presents a universe "that appears indifferent to moral orders, and what order is reestablished—or fails to be reestablished—is a (merely) human and historical matter which perhaps helps chart for us, provisionally, the limits of the human under great duress."[58] Martesia predicts the future about Gonzalo's fate and the way he will be remembered while Menalipe offers the protagonist an alternative path that would result in a utopian American fantasy. At stake in *Amazonas en las Indias* is a change in the course of history, the offer of an imagined history in which Gonzalo is deserving of a nontragic end. But the whims of history do not afford him this end, and he is ultimately painted as a villain in the official narrative. But the play itself, then, becomes a resistance to established order as manifested in that official history. Because the play presents him as our hero and recasts those that went against him—the "winners" of history—as villains, it is not without implicit and explicit critique of the imperial project, or at least its administration, as well as the leaders at the helm (including Carlos V and Philip II) who fail to manage it prudently and justly.

It is therefore significant for my purposes here that wild folk, as the only nonhistorical characters who appear in the play, serve as the mouthpieces who voice this alternative vision of Pizarro, and in so doing, whether purposely or inadvertently, become the vehicles responsible for the act of frustrating a celebration of conquest. This serves another example through which the wild figure becomes the locus of ideological negotiation, and in this case the coherence of the play's salient message to redeem Gonzalo Pizarro's image runs the risk of being in tension with a larger set of ideological commitments related to the conquest. The positionality of the Amazon characters frustrates a positive narrative of the imperial project, and these wild figures inhabit the site at which the play's ideological commitments are assembled to be made coherent, but that coherence is not guaranteed. By means of constructing an "other" who speaks truth (which is a convention of the *comedia de indios*), the play seeks to incorporate Gonzalo Pizarro into the dominant conquest narrative, but it also invests the other with agency within the dynamics of the dramatic action. As a consequence of the positive representation of the Amazons in the play (especially the legitimacy of their political authority), it complicates the range of possible responses when Martesia promises to defend their land against the Spanish: "prevent revenge / against all who, / from their ruthless nation, / intend to conquer our land, / tyrannize our home."[59] Therefore, dramatic exigency makes potential responses at odds with traditional ideological commitments to the conquest. At the very least, identifying the "good guys" becomes conflicted as a result of Tirso's portrayal of the Amazons as prudent and dignified rulers and the Spanish as poor administrators of empire. The wild figures here seem to resist domestication by diffusing the centripetal impulse of a unified ideology when, as in the earlier example, they say the quiet parts out loud.[60]

In identifying Tirso's influences for the Amazons in the play, scholarship has offered a number of possibilities for the dramatist's inspiration for Menalipe and Martesia, but they have primarily focused on previous examples of Amazons specifically with which the playwright would have been familiar. Zugasti summarizes those sources:

> This abundance of sources indicates that for many people in the sixteenth and seventeenth centuries, they considered reality what today we would call a fable. There were differing opinions about the existence of the Amazons: las Casas, López de Gómara, or Fernández de Oviedo refuted the veracity of the myth, but we have seen that Colón, Cortés, and Orellana among many others were believers. As late as 1641, Cristóbal de Acuña (author of *Nuevo descubrimiento del gran río de las Amazonas*) believed firmly in their existence. Tirso doesn't enter into this dialectic, but it seems evident that for him everything was myth: he treats it in jest, the magical quality attributed to them points to a literary vision, never a realist one.[61]

The careful philological studies carried out by investigating references to the Amazons in both contemporary and classical sources miss the more immediate dramatic influences on the work, chiefly, the representations of wildness so popular in Iberian dramatic practice during the period. More concretely, the play displays a number of conventions of staging wildness that point to its participation in this developing repertoire of wild representation.[62] The image of the Amazons in popular culture, along with other classical mythological "monsters," became more of a fascination as a result of the exploration of the unknown after 1492, but the representation of the mythological and monstrous is not unique to Tirso's Spain, neither geographically nor chronologically. The idea of a community of cannibal women living in isolation deep in the forest has certainly held a prominent space in the cultural imagination of the West both before Tirso's play and since; however, what should be of most interest to historicist cultural scholarship is what makes a specific depiction of the Amazons in one context stand apart from others. In the case of *Amazonas en las Indias* the influences that best help explain their character traits and how they produce meaning within the *comedia* are the conventions of the wild figure subgenre that it draws from and of which it is a unique configuration of that subgenre's constituent features, rather than the transhistorical characteristics that make characters like Martesia and Menalipe identifiable as Amazons.

Those conventions in the theatrical wild figure repertoire materialize in *Amazonas en las Indias* at their first appearance on the stage. As I indicated in each of the plays in Lope's wild figure corpus, Tirso's play incorporates a scene in which the audience first sees the wild figure encounter a "civilized" character. Usually it is a villager character who is initially terrified to have happened across the infamous wild monster well known to terrorize the locality. What happens next often depends on the gender of the wild figure, but common to all of the scenes is that they hinge in some way on the motif of misrecognition. For wild men, they may make peaceable but unsuccessful attempts to engage the villager, but the villager cannot overcome their fear and flees as mortified as when they arrived. For wild women, the villager character, usually male, is surprised to find out that the wild figure is female, and also beautiful. This is the case when Caravajal first encounters Martesia in Tirso's *Amazonas*. After she identifies herself as an oracle, he responds, "How is it that you're a witch but you're not old?"[63] This comment is telling; we are made aware of the specific parameters of Caravajal's misrecognition, unable to categorize the figure in front of him, beautiful but dangerous, young but capable of inexplicable magic, and speaking in his native tongue. This last item is the other critical aspect that shows up more in these first encounter scenes: the surprise at the eloquence of the wild figure in speaking perfect Castilian, or speaking it comprehensibly at all. Like Lope in *Las Batuecas del Duque de Alba,* Tirso contends with competing forces in writing a play in which distinct communities (linguistic, geographical, etc.) come into contact. First, playwrights like Tirso and Lope must navigate the pragmatic realities of dramaturgy in the time. For example, at the most basic level, the characters, especially the principal ones, have to speak. But this creates a plot hole that is intensified in plays like *Las Batuecas del Duque de Alba* and *Amazonas en las Indias.* It lacks verisimilitude that the *batuecos* would speak Castilian, and even more so the Amazons, who have never been in contact with speakers of Spanish across the Atlantic Ocean. To resolve this implausibility, characters like Ramiro in *Las Batuecas* and Caravajal in *Amazonas* mirror the audience's incredulity by openly asking how it is that the wild folk before them speak Spanish, thereby giving their wild interlocutors the opportunity to resolve the problem of mutual comprehensibility.[64] Caravajal asks the question to Martesia outright:

> How is it that you speak the language
> that Spain extracted from the mines of Rome?
> Who taught you the style
> of the eloquent Castilian tongue?[65]

In other instances, the eloquence of the wild figure is noteworthy and antithetical to their monstrosity, but this is a unique instance in which other characters acknowledge this as uncanny. The wild figure—here the Amazon—is not supposed to be able to speak, but they are doing so adeptly, and in this case the unexpected speech of the wild figure is reproduced as a convention of the subgenre while also being reconfigured into a unique new form. In other instances, this surprise is produced by the expectation that the wild figure is something-other-than-human who resides in the allegorical periphery of the forest—outside the civilized center, but only just. In *Amazonas en las Indias,* the spatial metaphor prevails, but is exploded on a global scale, situated not in the margins of the local, but rather an imperial periphery. But in creating a scenario in which Martesia's ability to speak Spanish is uncanny, Tirso resolves this with an equally uncanny solution that prefigures the *comedias de magia* that would become increasingly popular toward the end of the seventeenth century and into the eighteenth. Martesia responds to Caravajal's dismay with a lengthy discourse on her abilities as a powerful magician, of which I will cite representative excerpts:

> You doubt, my discrete fellow, but don't be frightened
> that from the divinity in my chest
> I am an oracle, marvel of this land.
> Men and animals alike
> venerate my absolute precepts;
> tigers, lions
> serpents, basilisks,
> inhabitants of this craggy terrain,
> they will come if I called them, in droves;
>
> ...
>
> Stairways to heaven,
> I ride on the winds
> and imitating the sun (admired by the *indio*)
> my acumen, like his [i.e., the sun's], the planets orbit.
> Are you frightened now
> (if that verifies your experience)
> that she who shines, shines so brightly
> might be aware of any skill
> and speak all the words your language
> could imagine uttering?[66]

An aspect of Martesia's response is worth contextualizing because it has led to incomplete or imprecise readings of the character. The device Tirso relies on here to sidestep the problem of mutual comprehensibility is by no means the most sophisticated in so far as it smacks of inserting a deus ex machina to resolve a seemingly irresolvable problem. However, Martesia's powers serve multiple roles in the drama, and therefore do a lot of work for Tirso, which I will outline further; moreover, the nature of these powers and their implications suggest something more complicated is going on than "providing [Tirso] with a means for telling the future" and beyond their role "as a counterpart of the chorus in Greek tragedy in this play,"[67] however important those two factors are.

While it may seem like an easy way out for Tirso to make Martesia a sorceress and therefore able to communicate with Caravajal, this representation signifies a new configuration of one theatrical repertoire—the wild figure—and an early iteration of another, the mage figure in the *comedia de magia*. This blending of features contextualizes Martesia as a rather more complex character than first meets the eye as a unique blend of wild figure, mythological race, and natural magician.[68] In fact, the aspects pulled from the repertoire of wildness serve as a bridge to reveal the links between all three character types, and make sense of them. Put differently, Tirso's decision to make Martesia a sorceress does not take place in a vacuum, even though the wielding of natural magic is not a conventional trait attributed to historical and contemporary representations of the Amazons. On the one hand, certain powers Martesia exercises over the natural world ("tigers, lions, serpents, basilisks, inhabitants of this craggy terrain, they will come if I called them, and in droves") reflect those often connected to the wild figure.[69] In this case, that refers to communion with the beasts of the animal kingdom and amicable dominion over them, like Leonido in *Hijo de los leones*, who can command the lions to do his bidding (or in the play, call them off from attacking a villager). On the other hand, Martesia's abilities are more akin to those of someone proficient in the hermetic disciplines (e.g., alchemy, metallurgy, distillation, etc.), like those displayed by court magicians in the *comedia de magia*. The natural world is essential to these characters as well, but rather than communion with nature, they have a technical expertise in the manipulation of the natural world. The objective of their magical enterprise is often articulated as that of seeking to discover a secret hidden in the bosom of nature (hence, "hermetic," i.e., that which is enclosed or sealed off). What is of note here is that there is no literary precedent for the Amazons practicing natural magic. This appears to be Tirso's invention, but it still represents a borrowing and a reconfiguring of conventions to produce the innovation of the Amazon sorceress character. We can identify those borrowings, and make better sense of how they work to produce meaning in his text based on the playwright's commitment to the conventions he's borrowing from (wild folk, practitioners of natural magic), and the *swerving* he does to produce something new (Amazon characters with traits from those other two repertoires). By recognizing the Amazons' characteristics conventional to theatrical wild figures, it takes us the step needed to bridge the gap between Martesia and the representative set of court magicians—both historical and literary—who practice a similar brand of natural magic to that of Martesia.

It becomes clear that Tirso is drawing from the repertoire of representations of hermeticism not only in Martesia's ability to manipulate natural elements, but also in the way she articulates the source that produces her magical powers. Science historian William Eamon explains the role of practitioners of natural magic in the fifteenth and sixteenth centuries—known as professors of secrets—as predecessors to the well-known empiricists of the seventeenth century like Robert Boyle and Christian Huygens. Professors of secrets were often figures that gained notoriety in the upper echelons of society and courts across Europe. As interest in the practice of hermetic magic grew, especially among the nobility, societies (often secret ones) dedicated to the practice of natural magic were formed. Emblematic of the conceptualization of knowledge as a secret to be uncovered, one such secret society formed in Rome was the Accademia dei Lincei (the Lincean Academy, or literally, Academy of the Linx), counting among its members not only Galileo, but also one of the most renowned practitioners of the hermetic disciplines, Giambattista Della Porta. They chose the lynx as their namesake and emblem because of their objective "to penetrate into the inside of things in order to know their causes and the operations of nature that work internally, just as it is said of the lynx that it sees not just what is in front of it, but what is hidden inside."[70] Eamon shows that the metaphor of the hunt to uncover the secrets hidden in nature was *the* metaphor par excellence used by practitioners of proto-empirical hermetic science, which gained purchase more broadly in representations of natural magic during the period. Martesia conceptualizes her power by relying on this metaphor: "Don't be frightened; / that by the divinity enclosed in my bosom / I am an oracle."[71] Here, Martesia describes herself as that very secret, her supernatural powers ("divinity") are enclosed within her nature. This line prefigures the play's final stage directions that constitute an analogous visual metaphor as Martesia and Menalipe are literally enclosed by nature: "The forest opens and encloses the two women."[72]

Although Martesia synecdochally represents the power of nature (i.e., she is the secret of nature itself), she also wields her power in ways that allude to representations of court magicians in the *comedia de magia*. This manifests itself in two ways. First is Martesia's expertise. Her ability to wield natural magic makes suprarational knowledge accessible, which leads to the second trait she shares with theatrical representations of court magicians on the baroque Iberian stage: her role as advisor to the crown. Conventionally, like Martesia, these characters are enlisted by the sovereign to use their powers to provide information that is critically important to the political situation at hand.[73] In this case, she is advisor to her sister Menalipe, for whom she conjures natural elements to report events taking place near and far and she can also tap into them to predict the future. Reading the Amazon characters metonymically as stand-ins for the natural American landscape (as literalized secrets of nature) makes the play's closure all the more powerful. That utopia, that secret enclosed in the bosom of nature, buries itself farther into the natural world, withdrawing deeper into the literal and metaphorical forest to abscond from the destructive and hierarchical Europeans that "attempt from their cruel nation to conquer our provinces, tyrannize our homeland."[74]

When we meet the Amazons in act 1 and learn the mythological weight of their genealogy, it is clear that the Spanish vis-à-vis Gonzalo Pizarro and Caravajal have every reason to fear the cannibalistic man-eating warrior women they encounter during their cinnamon expedition. And it is on the Amazons' terms that the physical combat between them comes to a halt. They pacify their Spanish opponents and choose peace instead of imposing their will to vanquish their foe. This prudent self-discipline samples from the increasingly conventional wild figure motif—the wild figure that is just as dangerous as expected, but chooses to wield that power with restraint. They are the wild things that do not turn out to be all that wild after all. Moreover, they exude authority by physically and mentally overpowering the play's heroes while accurately telling the future, and it is that authority that underpins the tragic logic of Gonzalo Pizarro's inevitable death as a consequence of failing to heed their prophetic warning.

Akin to the indigenous characters in the *comedia de indios*, the Amazons play the role of the other, constructed to be the unexpected messengers of the ideological truth(s) for which the play is a vehicle.[75] But unlike the *comedia de indios*, their message is disregarded, triggering the events to unfold toward a tragic and violent end in lieu of comedic closure and order restored. In this sense, the Amazons' dramatic function aligns closely with that of the *gracioso* in the *comedia*, who unexpectedly offer perceptive observations on the action (sometimes unwittingly) obscured by their unrefined delivery and given little credence by the noble protagonists because of their subordinate social station. The Amazons in Tirso's play and *gracioso* of the *comedia* both function as mouthpieces for disregarded oppositional wisdom, even if aesthetically the dignified, austere regality of the Amazons is in stark contrast to the plebeian image of the *gracioso*. They are two such types of a recurring phenomenon in the cultural imagination of the West that can take a variety of forms.

Foucault explains the role played by this figure through the representative figure of the madman:

> From the depths of the Middle Ages, a man was mad if his speech could not be said to form part of the common discourse of men. His words were considered nul [sic] and void, without truth or significance, worthless as evidence, inadmissible in the authentication of acts or contracts. . . . And yet, in contrast to all others, his words were credited with strange powers, *of revealing some hidden truth*, of *predicting the future*, of revealing, in all their naivete, *what the wise were unable to perceive*. . . . For centuries the words of the mad man either fell into a void—rejected the moment they were proffered—or else men deciphered in them a naïve or cunning reason, *rationality more rational than that of a rational man*. At all events, whether excluded or secretly invested with reason, the *madman's speech did not strictly exist*. . . . Whatever the madman said, it was taken for mere noise; he was credited with words in a symbolic sense, in the theatre, in which he stepped forward, unarmed and reconciled, playing his role: that of masked truth.[76]

Even if it is the most explicit message, the play's truth conveyed about Gonzalo Pizarro is hardly the most impactful message conveyed by Menalipe and Martesia. The authority of the wild women's discourse that seeks to redeem Gonzalo's image in the official historical narrative bleeds over into their discourse overall. Martesia's affirmation of the ruthless conquest is prophetic in its utterance (the temporal reality within the play), but then evaluative in the uttered (the message it conveys presented in the context of the play's staging in the 1630s). Any access to the bountiful American utopia "enclosed in their bosom" remains closed off, forced deeper and deeper into the wilderness in the period of colonial violence that ensued in the period from the historical moment portrayed and the composition of the work in 1631. For readers today in the pre-apocalyptic times on the cusp of climate unviability, the symbolism of Martesia and Menalipe disappearing as the forest encloses around them in the final moments of the play rings with a greater finality augmented by the culminating weight of history since the play was written. In a sense, this moment channels some of Martesia's prophetic power, pointing to a world that would become increasingly violent toward nature to the point that there are increasingly fewer spaces for "la divinidad que encierra mi pecho" (the divinity held within my bosom) to escape the destructive impulses of civilization.

SAILING BEYOND THE PILLARS: EMPIRICISM AND EMPIRE IN BANCES CANDAMO'S *LA PIEDRA FILOSOFAL*

Written by Bances Candamo and staged for a royal audience in 1693, *La piedra filosofal* is set in the mythological past on the edge of the then-known world, near the pillars of Hercules in Cádiz. Bances's work presents a dramatic allegory of Spanish identity, adapting the version of the fabled naming of the Iberian Peninsula found in Alfonso X's *Estoria de España* (History of Spain).[77] The play diverges in significant ways from the *Estoria*, but the salient elements are reproduced. Following Alfonso's version, the play opens as king Hispán and his daughter Iberia are joined by their royal entourage en route to visit the temple of Hercules, where we find them discussing preparations to receive three suitors from distant kingdoms who will compete for Iberia's hand. Finding a viable suitor for Iberia serves as the basis for a plot that foregrounds Hispán's motivation to secure succession. However, the play hardly veils a critical perspective of Hispán's approach, and by extension a critique on the question of succession and empire acutely applicable to the Habsburg monarchy toward the end of the seventeenth century. In that context, this poses a major problem provided these political themes were explicitly prohibited by Queen Regent Mariana de Austria at the time of its staging at court, which may provide a clue for Bances's abrupt departure from his role as official court playwright shortly after putting on *La piedra filosofal*. The work also displays a keen awareness of contemporary scientific discourse, deploying the imagery and language of early modern empiricism to reframe origin mythologies of the nascent Spanish state.[78] More concretely, the play presents its audience with an experiment gone wrong, and this empirical failure dramatizes the imperial ones that had come to define Habsburg rule under Felipe IV and Carlos II. Setting the play in Cádiz, *La piedra filosofal* evokes the imagery of the pillars of Hercules, which were an emblematic motif for the Habsburg monarchy and imperial project going back to Carlos I, who incorporated the pillars into the royal coat of arms. The pillars also came to represent the imperial ethos that motivated sailing beyond them. We also see a concomitant

FIGURE 3.1. Frontispiece of Andrés García de Céspedes's *Regimiento de navegación* (1606). Courtesy of Yale University Beinecke Rare Book and Manuscript Library, MS Taylor 237.

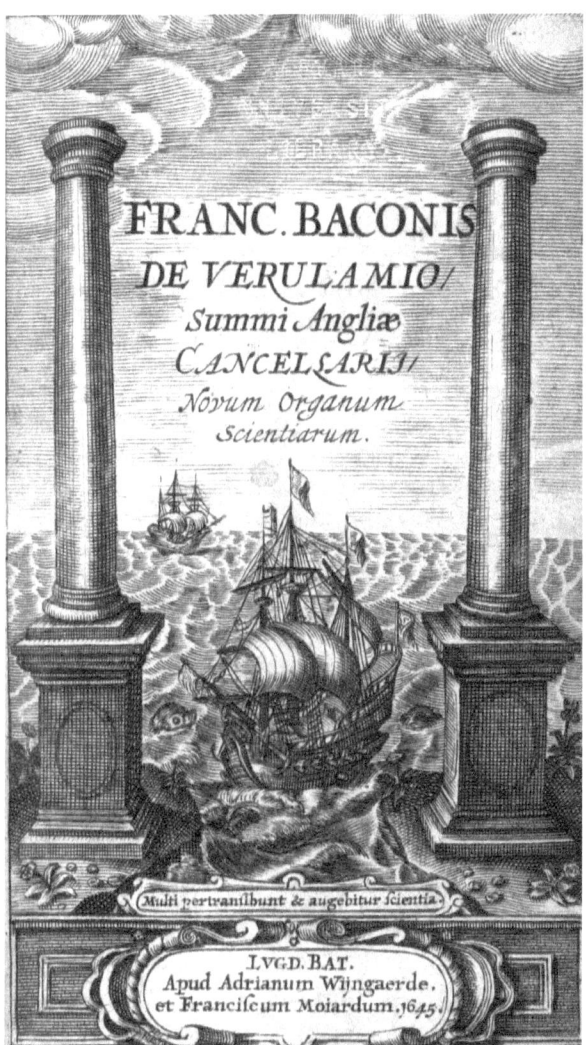

FIGURE 3.2. Frontispiece of Francis Bacon's *Novum Organum* (1645 edition). Courtesy of Houghton Library, Harvard University, EC.B1328.620ib.

emblematic use of the pillars by early modern empiricists (they appear on the frontispiece of Francis Bacon's *Novum Organum*, for example; see Figure 3.2). Bances's *comedia* combines these emblem traditions into a dense theatrical metaphor to look back at *plus ultra* (i.e., sailing through pillars, literally and figuratively) as a failed project, and the promise of the unexplored as a compelling illusion.

The invocation of alchemy made by the play goes beyond the reference to the philosopher's stone in the title; in fact, Bances's most noticeable departure from the version of the story found in Alfonso X's *Estoria* is the incorporation of natural magic and hermetic science practiced by the character Rocas. Hispán calls on the magus Rocas at the beginning of the play to set up a magical experiment (*experiencia*) to assist him in determining whom he should pick to wed Iberia (in early modern Spanish, the term *experiencia* is used to describe what would be called an experiment in the vernacular today). From the opening stage directions, we can identify Rocas as a practitioner of natural magic: "To one side [of the stage] music can be heard off in the distance, and from the other side voices, martial drums and trumpets, and in the center a discovery space within a grotto appears Rocas, an old philosopher, in rustic attire, among books, globes, quadrants, and other mathematical instruments."[79] These opening stage directions echo those found in an earlier wild figure play by Calderón, *En la vida todo es verdad y todo mentira*, which I highlight in Chapter 5.[80] Here, Bances departs from the Calderonian model by placing the natural magician in the discovery space of the cave, where in *En la vida* the cave is where the royal hunting party finds the two Wildman protagonists. Although the constituent elements are configured differently, both works explore political authority and epistemology (i.e., in a given context, prevailing notions on the nature of truth and how we establish matters of fact) through depictions of proto-empirical experimentation and natural magic. As will become clear, the explicit intertextuality between *La piedra filosofal* and Calderón's *En la vida todo es verdad y todo mentira* evinces the ways Bances draws from the repertoire of theatrical wildness to compose his play, while also addressing themes that correspond to those conventional to the corpus of wild figure *comedias* that precede it. The other major element of relevance that merits the inclusion of Bances's play in a study on theatrical wildness on the early modern Iberian stage is the characterization of the protagonist, Hispalo. He enters the fold by dramatic happenstance, but his introduction is not without careful attention to creating figurative meaning in ways that intersect with a baroque repertoire of theatrical wildness. When the royal hunting party finds themselves in mortal danger upon encountering a lion in the initial scenes of the play, Hispalo—who just happens to be passing through the same area—subdues the alpha predator. Perhaps the most famous scene evoked here is the famous episode in *Cantar de mío Cid* when Ruy Díaz pacifies the lion and humiliates the *infantes de*

Carrión. But it also parallels (and even more closely) the analogous scene as Leonido first appears in Lope's *El hijo de los leones*, when the lions are obedient to his commands, which serves as a metaphor to point to his royal identity and fitness to wield political authority at the end of the work. In *La piedra filosofal*, Bances inverts the lion/king imagery of this visual metaphor, depicting Hispalo as larger-than-life and heroic as an initial point of reference for the subsequent portrayal of his psychological deterioration that ultimately becomes incapacitating with respect to his suitability as Iberia's suitor and fitness to succeed Hispán as monarch.

Returning to the figure of Rocas, in the history of ideas, the approach to knowledge of the natural world applied by figures like him—known as professors of secrets—marks an initial epistemological shift away from scholasticism and toward proto-empirical methodologies for establishing a matter of fact. As Teofilo Ruiz describes it, "the Hermetic magus has been seen as a bridge between the ethereal world of magic and the hard-nosed world of scientific fact."[81] As I introduced earlier, their practice of natural magic like alchemy demonstrates a value in experimentation and observation over theory, a process often framed as an attempt to reveal the secrets of nature through the manipulation of natural materials—hence, professor of secrets. Although the observational methodology practiced by the professors of secrets was greatly influential on the development of early modern empiricism, they tend to be remembered more for their status as magicians than precursors to the scientific method; nevertheless, the figure of the court magician was a particularly popular character in *comedias* during the latter part of the seventeenth century and into the eighteenth.[82]

La piedra filosofal opens with the image of the professor of secrets, as well as the search for secrets metaphorically bound up in the figure of Rocas, whose knowledge and expertise Hispán and Iberia wish to employ. Figuratively, the secrets for which they search exist in the magus's hidden grotto—and more precisely through the knowledge contained within Rocas himself. Identified by his books, beakers and mathematical instruments that surround him, Rocas, the natural magician is literally hidden in the natural world. This imagery assembled within the tableau of the grotto represents hermetic science, and it is the alterations to the narrative produced by the introduction of Rocas, a novel character not found in the *Estoria* that refashion the national origin myth conveyed in *La piedra filosofal*. Hispán commissions Rocas to gather information on Iberia's suitors so that he can make an informed decision about whom he selects for her to wed. Like Basilio in *La vida es sueño*, as the basis for making a decision with massive political ramifications, Hispán turns to hermetic science in lieu of his own prudence, the baroque virtue par excellence in the art of governing. The candidates include Hispalo, Tersandro and Numidio, each hailing from different parts of the known world. He sets out to accomplish this task by creating a magical space within which he can observe Hispalo's behavior in certain situations, particularly to see how he would react in a courtly setting.[83] Hispán clearly instructs Rocas regarding his ultimate purpose in selecting a suitor for his daughter:

> With foreign princes
> I want to avoid alliances
> that extend the limits
> of my empire's borders;
> when monarchies have
> lands and reputation,
> all a king needs to maintain them
> is prudence, with authority
> over his dominion;
> but if a certain line is crossed,
> so begins the decline.[84]

In this quote, Hispán provides the parameters for the outcome he desires, and the consequences of choosing poorly. By selecting a foreign prince, he realizes the dangers of exceeding the kingdom's reach beyond its administrative capacity. From these instructions, we have a framework by which to judge the outcome of this enterprise.

With that in mind, in the space of the magical sequence created by Rocas, ostensibly to test Hispán's political fitness, the three suitors are required to resolve one of the great problems that hinder the island's prosperity. Hispalo is to build a bridge from the island to the mainland, Tersandro must concoct a way to filter salt water to make it potable, and Numidio is to fortify Cádiz by constructing a wall that encircles the (then) island.[85] The first to finish their prescribed task wins the hand of Iberia. With the help of Rocas, Hispalo succeeds in building the bridge. Rocas, and again, still within the illusory space of the magical experiment, commits an act of treason when he colludes with the second suitor Tersandro so that he can abscond with Iberia. Hispalo justly punishes Rocas in his first act of governance. Indignant that Hispalo would turn against him after he had been such a decisive influence in his success in the competition to win Iberia's hand, Rocas abruptly concludes the magical sequence and condemns Hispalo to the king as being unfit to rule the kingdom (this time in the plane of "reality" within the work). We thus learn of Rocas's ulterior motives from the beginning; he leverages his involvement to ensure first and foremost that he benefits from the outcome. Surreptitiously, Rocas reports to Hispán that his subject failed the test, even though he acted justly by the dominant political ideologies of the day.

Unaware that Rocas's experiment is an illusion, Hispalo loses grip on reality as a result of the magician's ruse, which precipitates the perceptual crisis that is the basis of the mental instability he displays for the rest of the work. This scene inverts the episode in *El conde Lucanor* between the dean of Santiago and the necromancer don Illán, in which Illán creates a magical space in order to observe how the dean will respond to his rising star, and if he will be true to his word in offering recompense to don Illán for assisting him in his quest for ecclesiastical supremacy. When the dean never makes good on his promise, and even if one considers the pragmatism of don Illán harsh, the dean's ingratitude is the cause for his just deserts. This scene in *La piedra filosofal* plays out differently in nuanced, but significant ways. Primarily, the roles of the magician and his subject are reversed. In *La piedra filosofal*, the magician Rocas desires his own personal gain, and leverages his magical experiment to ensure it. He solicits Hispalo (not the other way around), and does so to potentially bolster his case as the match, for which Hispalo shows gratitude. Furthermore, Hispalo proves to be a capable ruler within the illusory sequence of events when he justly punishes Rocas for committing treason, rather than allowing himself to be beholden to an advisor in exchange for political favors. Therefore, Rocas's deception within the magical enchantment becomes an act of treason in reality (that is, the reality of the dramatic action). It constitutes a betrayal of his responsibility to the king by putting his own personal gain over his loyalty to the king, which also jeopardizes the governance of the kingdom. Moreover, the king's prudence is called into question due to his inability to select trustworthy advisors nor perceive their corruption.

Within Rocas's illusion, Hispalo's task in the competition against the other suitors is to construct a bridge from Cádiz to the mainland, while the other suitors must respectively create a sea-water filtration system and build a wall to fortify the island. Each of these grand-scale engineering projects stand to strengthen Hispán's kingdom, providing military, economic and public health infrastructure. All of these endeavors are of national importance (centralized metonymically on the Mediterranean island), as is the result of Hispán and Iberia's search for her husband and future king of Spain, the premise of the play's action. The opening setting of the play in Rocas's peripheral habitat and then subsequently near the pillars of Hercules at the edge of the known world exemplify a prevailing interest in exploring limits and liminality found in the *comedia* (e.g., the limits of knowledge and the knowable, borders, boundaries, physical versus magical space, reality versus theatricality, sanity and insanity).[86] As I mentioned, in the context of the late seventeenth century the image of sailing through the pillars of Hercules becomes emblematic for practitioners of empiricism. This image, which appeared on the frontispiece of notable works such as García de Céspedes's *Regimiento de navegación* (1606) and Bacon's *Novum Organum* (1620), carried immense symbolic weight during the early modern period as a representation of transcending "the traditional limits of knowledge" (see frontispiece images in Figures 3.1 and 3.2).[87] Hispán's national project is to grow his kingdom through the correct choice of marriage for his daughter, for which he relies on Rocas's pseudo-scientific expertise. In other words, Hispán's aims are both imperial and empirical; however, the vehicle for his enterprise of *plus ultra*—the illusory space of Rocas's magical experiment—ends in failure. Sailing through the pillars is a failed exercise, and the promise offered by the illusion is a compelling one, so much so that it precipitates madness. Unable to discern between illusion and reality after Rocas's experiment, Hispalo comes unhinged. Rocas is an unreliable empiricist who manipulates the variables of his experiment to achieve particular results. And the consequences of his self-interest are national in scope; Hispalo never recovers from his psychological episode, even once he has discovered Rocas's deception and after being restored as heir to the throne and his engagement to Iberia is back on. So, the play ends with a mentally incapacitated heir and Hispán's imperial project in a precarious position.

Hispalo is like Segismundo from *La vida es sueño* and Eraclio from *En la vida todo es verdad y todo mentira* insofar as he continues to distrust the reality around him at the end of *La piedra filosofal*; however, there is no determinable *desengaño* in the play's final scenes. His profound uncertainty about reality results in a psychological break rather than a healthy skeptical or Neostoic worldview, such as those displayed by his

Calderonian dramatic predecessors. He never regains his wits, and again unlike Segismundo and Eraclio, he does not arrive at a satisfactory moral philosophy to supersede the anxiety of doubt. At one moment toward the end of the work, though, he seems to have recuperated some sense of stability:

> so I hold within me
> the philosopher's stone;
> I shall be content with myself
> given that the perception
> of the well-instructed man
> turns the bad into good
> and the tragic into the festive.[88]

Segismundo's response to a similar situation encourages prudence in the face of perceptual doubt, to *obrar bien*, whereas Hispalo resolves to perceive good as bad, or, in theatrical terms, transpose tragedy for comedy. For Hispalo, the world is upside-down. His solution is to actively change his perception and misunderstand (*convierte*) the reality around him, even as the walls are crumbling around him. Moreover, we can interpret Hispalo through the lens of the other characters. For instance, Iberia's concerns for his mental state remain resolute, and her final verdict on the topic is clear in the final lines of dialogue to close the play:

> So it was
> Rocas's illusion, conjuring
> black shadows from the abyss,
> that to Hispalo (what punishment!)
> I showed affection (what agony!)
> and favor; which caused
> his confused judgment
> between truth and deception
> to appear to everyone he'd gone mad.[89]

Thus, the play ends with the future of the monarchy in the hands of a mad king whose betrothed suggests she wishes him dead ("may you kill Hispalo, / lest he be the one chosen as your successor").[90] In one sense, the appearance of a conventional *comedia* ending appears intact through the union of Hispalo and Iberia overseen by the king, along with the discovery of the misdeeds of the deceitful Rocas. Nevertheless, it is a tragic farce of the conventional comedic marriage ritual. Echoing the grotto of Rocas's habitat, the presentation of this particular conclusion takes on qualities that can only be understood as grotesque.[91] The constituent parts of the conventional ending are all there, but each is deformed or in the wrong place. The resolution seems unsatisfactory precisely because it presents recognizable conventions but inverts them. An example of this can be seen in the ways the conventions of wildness are turned upside down in the play; Hispalo, who evokes the image of Hercules—strong, capable, and fit—at the beginning of the play, has become the wild man of sentimental romance in the final scene, entirely out of touch with reality. Hispalo's discourse on the philosopher's stone as a metaphor for a healthy approach in the face of doubt rings hollow as a functional response the existential crisis he has suffered. Just as transforming ore into gold was a fantasy of transubstantiation that remained elusive for alchemists, so too is it here for Hispalo. The philosopher's stone is for Hispalo what Laureola's letters are for Leriano at the end of Diego de San Pedro's *Cárcel de amor* (Prison of Love) when he responds to her rejection by eating her letters as a type of epistolary communion, as if each torn piece of paper were a eucharist wafer. Both the philosopher's stone and Leriano's attempt to ingest words made flesh are spectacular displays of the desire for unattainable presence in the despair of absence.

In Bances's play, the philosopher's stone becomes an organizing metaphor for how to respond to an irresolvable problem. But the cure-all of the philosopher's stone is put on display as a totalizing fantasy, and exposes the colonial epistemic frameworks that underpin that fantasy, rather than justifying a contingent ideological framework as inalienable, universal truth. *La piedra filosofal* is a play in which representations of conventions are so distorted that a space is opened up for ideological critique as a possible *habitus* in cultural discourse (critique of empire, Salic law, monarchical authority, and the white and Iberian origins of Spanish national identity). We are left with a mad king treating a funeral (tragedy) as if it were a wedding (comedy) ("turns the bad into good / and the tragic into the festive").[92] This is the world upside down, without any of the festive revelry of actual carnival celebration. The parallels to the infirm Carlos II are patent, the problem of succession openly displayed, and finally, the play presents a critique of the Spanish colonial enterprise through the complex recasting of the mythological and empirical significance of the metaphor of sailing through the pillars of Hercules.

CHAPTER 4

Of Text and Textile
Gendering Wildness in the Spanish Comedia

FOLDS IN THE FABRIC OF THE BAROQUE

ONE RECURRING THEME IN this analysis of wildness on the baroque stage is how it serves as an adaptable vehicle for playwrights to dramatize transgressions against prescribed rules for social normativity. In the previous chapter the dramatic introduction and assimilation of the wild Other was presented as "arising out of the necessity to reconstruct" Spanish national identity in response to the perceived threats presented by non-white, non-Christian *indios* and Muslims to a common national historical narrative.[1] Theater, especially the playwriting of Lope and Tirso, was a means to "rethink the idea of Spain and make it comprehensible as singular and homogenous," an ideological project that "demanded the symbolic integration of any excluded group."[2] But far from the spirit of democratic *inclusion*, as Moisés Castillo notes, the theater was a place to watch the *assimilation* of the Other unfold, be it manifested in representations of indigenous Americans or Muslims, rural farmers, or women.[3] It is this last entry in Castillo's list that I will take up in the present chapter, but I will broaden his terminology to encompass gender more generally, because the hegemonic impulses that motivate the construction of the ideal woman as a normative gender category also motivate the social pre- and proscriptions that constitute notions of idealized masculinity. In the dramatic works treated in this chapter, transgressions against gender norms in the context of baroque Spain are what constitute the wildness of the theatrical wild folk, which sets into conventional motion a conflict and its resolution that revolves around their domestication and reintegration into the hegemonic fold. As I have argued throughout this study, theater offers a symbolic contact zone between civilization and wildness, and in each of the plays analyzed in this chapter, early modern notions of gender as a natural category (i.e., civilization) face evidence that threatens the integrity of the system posed by the existence of femininities and masculinities that diverge from established norms (i.e., wildness). These are the "victims of modernity" according to Dussel, "victims of an irrational act that contradicts modernity's ideal of rationality."[4] And this contradiction would threaten the disintegration of that system if it were not for "the civilizing and exculpating myths" at the core of every totalitarian project that justifies violence as a means to ameliorate the Other to the system and maintain itself as a homogenous, unified whole.[5]

However, that is not to say they pose no threat. Even in plays that most clearly rely on wildness as the dramatic vessel for the Other simply for the sake of domesticating them and upholding the status quo, their representation in the public sphere creates a dialectic between margin and center where oppositional and dominant ideologies are negotiated. In his approach to representations of *habla de negros* on the early modern Spanish stage, Nicholas R. Jones argues that the "control and gaze of white poetic and dramatic practitioners cannot sustain a seamless denigration of Blackness."[6] In his chapter on portrayals of black women on the Iberian stage, Jones evinces what he calls "radical performances": "in many of those moments when antiblack racism and misogyny appear to (re)produce their most aberrant and abject representations of the black women characters, these ... figures inhabit the limits of habla de negros language and aesthetic form, performing moments of spectacular visibility, at times despite and beyond [the author's] intentions."[7] I by no means wish to suggest that Jones's approach can be unproblematically extended to representations of wild women—characters who in the end usually turn out to be white aristocrats. They do not constitute the same phenomena as the "radical performances" of Blackness, nor representations of Black women more specifically (although the hegemonic discourses that motivate hierarchical oppression on the basis of both race and gender share a coloniality at their core). And acknowledging the importance of these distinctions, I posit that the broad application of Jones's framework lies in its assertion that the echoes of the lived experience of the marginalized can be "rendered legible" in the space of representation "regardless of the ideologies espoused by the authors."[8] Even if misogyny or traditional ideologies of masculinity drive the domestication of the wild women and men characters in the plays analyzed in this chapter, my aim is to demonstrate that the theatrical staging of that process amplifies its performativity immediately in contradiction with the ideological commitment to biological determinism that the play ostensibly reproduces. Therefore, in spite of the apparent objective of the *comedia* as a normative apparatus of control over women's bodies and behaviors, the theatrical representation of gendered wildness and the performative nature of its domestication staged in the *comedia* lay bare the ideological scaffolding at the center of such an enterprise.[9] By dint of their very existence, wild women in the *comedia* embody a tearing at the seams of ideology by performing gender that compromises the "truth" that necessitates the domesticated and docile woman, in spite of this being the expressed "reality" the plays seek to affirm.

Before proceeding, these comments require an important point of clarification. As will be clear in my analysis, my critical perspective is that the plays I have included participate in the "major strategy" of the Baroque in the service of reproducing dominant ideologies and to suppress dissention. And my contention is not that the *comedias* presented in this chapter necessarily subvert the status quo or can be shown to have demonstrably resulted in audiences questioning dominant ideologies of gender. Then, as now, for ideology to be sustained and reproduced, it requires the cognitive dissonance of a body of adherents to mistake the performative for the innate, natural and, inalienable. That is precisely what is at stake in the gendered performance of wildness in these plays, and I do not seek to make direct claims about the likelihood of original audiences' perception of the contradictions underpinning their theatrically performed content. The objective of my examination of these works, rather, is to reverse engineer the ideological blueprint of this dramatic enterprise and the theatrical mechanisms that make it function. In so doing, I offer these examples to recover the agency of a set of characters resisting wildly, even as the dominant structures of power in place sought to neutralize the force of their opposition.

As a tool for a historicist analysis of the *comedia*, the wild woman character effectively pinpoints the critical defense points posted along in the ideological ramparts of the Baroque, where weak spots in its perimeter can be identified by the places guarded most aggressively. In the *comedias* discussed here, the transformations the wild characters undergo—usually depicted through lengthy attempts to change their appearance and behavior to conform to established gender norms—displays a marked emphasis on the sartorial; metonymic of their domestication, the wild women reluctantly leave behind their animal skins in exchange for the elaborate dress of the noble elite and wild men replace their club for a sword and military uniform. This aspect is highlighted materially in the costume design of the wild figure plays, but also as a rhetorical device fundamental to the message produced, whether successfully or in spite of the apparent ideological objectives of the play's poetic architecture. Here I will rely on the figurative illustration of the Baroque as a woven fabric, which I develop into an organizing metaphor for the analysis in this chapter that is useful in succinctly capturing the relationship between wild figures, ideology, and gender performance in early modern Iberian dramaturgy. Specifically, this chapter presents dramatic wildness in the *comedia* as a problem of text and textile—an entity that figuratively tears at the social fabric of the Baroque. By transgressing gender norms, the embodied performance of female wildness produces the salient problem of the text (i.e., its conflict), and that problem is manifested materially through the conventional visual marker of wildness in period costume design: animal pelts. In lieu of the ornate extravagance characteristic of baroque fashion, their appearance is emblematically *lacking* in textile, just as their existence on the baroque stage exemplifies the locus of the "lack," the point where the presence of truth (in this case, gendered behavior determined through biological necessity) is incompatible with the medium conveying the message: theater. Again, wild figures, as I will show, resist the complex "architectonics" of theatrical representation that permit—encourage even—the disavowal required to sustain a commitment to "the indefinitely renewed promise of presence just beyond the next veil of mediation."[10]

The staging of that truth occurs in the conventional resolutions to *comedia* plots defined by the poetics of *desengaño* ("becoming undeceived") in which the character(s) come to see the world of veiled appearances for what they are and recognize the truth they occlude. The truths revealed by restoring the order disturbed in the conflict of the play offer an example of the world the way it is supposed to be, and the values—presented as inalienable truths—that underpin the reality thus displayed. Yet, for a genre seemingly obsessed with affirming normativity in the conventional *comedia* resolutions, of the approximately 3,000 verses of any given *comedia*, 2,700 of them or more consist of order disturbed, in Reichenberger's framework, while just a few hundred at the end of the play depict that order restored.[11] But imagining conflict—that is, the world the way is *not* supposed to be—is as much an ideological imperative as it is a necessity of dramatic action. This conventional structure of the *comedia* arises out of this ritualistic necessity; presenting transgressions that demand the Law to redeem or neutralize the threat it poses to the system proves an expedient mechanism for legitimizing the Law and consolidating subjective obedience. However, as a result of the normative and transgressive inhabiting the same space, sites of representation are sites of negotiation, and whether intentionally or not, are liable to become sites of contestation. In the *comedia*, the normative and the transgressive often become intertwined to complicate their disambiguation in conventional endings. Dale Pratt views an equally precarious tendency as inherent to the production of meaning in the *autos sacramentales* (a genre of one-act eucharist plays put on for Corpus Christi that were especially popular in Spain). He conceptualizes the nature of allegory in Calderón's *autos* in the following way:

> *Culpa* (the allegorical character Guilt) seems very enchanting onstage, and the wages of sin seem to be theatrical life (at least for the duration of the *auto*) rather than oblivion. . . . These doctrinally suspect images threaten the cohesion and message of the allegorical victory at the end of each *auto*, yet paradoxically sustain the action which makes possible said victory.[12]

Likewise, the duration of the wild figures' portrayal as wild inhabits significantly more space than the ultimately domesticated version of themselves in the resolution of the play, and playwrights display varying degrees of success in combatting the formidable resistance posed by the dramatic exigencies create as a result of the introduction of wildness into the play.

As I have begun to outline, the ways that text and textile are linked to one another in the wild figure plays offer a useful conceptual framework for understanding their ideological architecture. I will establish the coherence and utility of their connection by offering a particularly illustrative example that occurs at a critical moment in the action of Andrés de Claramonte's *La lindona de Galicia*. The play opens with García, the protagonist and newly crowned king of Galicia deliberating over his marriage prospects. His moralist advisers steer him toward the match that is most politically expedient, and away from marrying his mistress and the mother of his child—the eponymous Lindona. In a description that epitomizes the ideological problem of the wild figure, one of the advisors states, "Lindona is a stain."[13] As García's pregnant paramour, Lindona embodies transgression in the context of the prescriptive norms of baroque sexuality, and for that reason, she is a stain, which could also be translated as a blot on the page. This disparaging remark consolidates the merging elements of text, textile, and ideology concisely in one word. The consequence of her transgression is that she be erased, which in this case means consigning her to oblivion through García's marriage to another woman. Her and García's affair represents a blot that mars the fabric of the Baroque, but also one that resists erasure. The transgressive presence that Lindona represents is disavowed through his marriage to the queen of Portugal, but the erasure her banishment from court signifies is only a partial one. Moreover, we also learn that their daughter, who has been presumed dead, has survived. She is the embodiment of an excess—the excess that spills over onto a garment that García's marriage to the queen of Portugal cannot wash clean. Notably, Lindona and her daughter (named Linda) both become wild women, and as such the transgression that precipitates the conflict becomes embodied symbolically as wildness. The only way to resolve this problem of wildness that looms as a specter over the legitimacy of García's reign and ultimately leads to his (temporary) downfall is by reversing the initial wrong by means of the prescriptive logic of baroque ideological commitments. In this case, the problem relates to the stain on Lindona's honor created by conceiving a child out of wedlock, which also renders that child illegitimate. The play tidily resolves these issues by creating a scenario for a conventional wedding between Lindona and García to conclude the play. Lindona, whose spatial movement is organized both literally and figuratively, returns from the marginal wilderness to the center of centers of civilization, the royal court. Her daughter endures a process of domestication; she is taught to speak Spanish and proper court etiquette (including how to dress, walk in high heels, etc.). On the surface, the blot on Lindona's honor and on the fabric of the Baroque that had produced wild figures has been washed clean. But as I will show through extended analysis, a closer look at the play's resolution suggests that remnants of the stain remain embedded in the fabric, and traces of wildness can still be perceived despite the superficial domestication presented to resolve the play. In a reversal of García's advisor's appellation of Lindona as a stain, she embodies Hélène Cixious's charge to "take a look around, and cut through!"[14] It is only when she decides, and on her own terms, that she accepts the marriage contract with García to repair the ideological fabric of the Baroque in the conclusion of the play.[15] Of course, any garment that undergoes mending or is darned is added to, or conversely when cleaned it wears away at the fibers, the signs of which become more visible over time the more it is repaired and washed. Maybe not initially perceptible, however, the integrity of the garment has been compromised. Any inevitable assertion to the contrary is a disavowal. The wild woman, whose garments are defined by their lack, embodies this disavowal. Like Lindona who is the odd (wo)man out in every sense of the term, the wild woman's existence is supplementary, and must be concealed within one of Delueze's baroque folds.[16]

Deleuze's conceptual geography of the Baroque assists here in the inherent supplementary nature of a fold; it implies what is more than necessary to create a surface. What appears to be a gap in the fabric is in fact one surface. The wild figure emerges from one of those folds, and is swallowed up by them, disavowed only inasmuch as they are occluded from view. But they do not fall into a limitless abyss, rather they return to the fold; they "slink away in defeat, only to be resurrected" in a later *comedia*.[17] Moreover, Deleuze's baroque cartography imagines the texture of the fold as an important characteristic to understand the distinctions between western and eastern philosophy. The fold "which seems to predominate in the Occident" is made of cloth.[18] This metaphorical baroque cloth is intrinsic to the ideological function of the wild character in the Spanish *comedia*, the explanation of which will be a common thread weaved throughout my analysis in this chapter.

STAINS AS SIGN AND SYMPTOM IN CLARAMONTE'S *LA LINDONA DE GALICIA*

The well-worn historical narrative of the chaotic succession of Sancho III (1000–1035 CE) serves as the backdrop to Claramonte's *La lindona de Galicia* (1642).[19] Upon the death of his father, Sancho declares himself king of Galicia, León, and Castilla. His younger brother, García, wants Galicia for himself, and a heated argument ensues between the two that ends in García heading back to Galicia to reign, and Sancho readying his troops to take it by force. Before the first appearance of a wild character, the theme of wildness is introduced during this discussion when Sancho calls his brother a wild beast (*fiero*) for his open and unbridled ambition. Therefore, wildness is the conceptual framework for proscribed behavior unbefitting a prince, who should act with prudence, "the political virtue par excellence."[20] It is precisely García's inability to display prudence in handling the contingencies of a complex situation with significant political consequences that becomes both catalyst and motor for the dramatic action.

After the exchange in the opening scene between García and his brother over their claim to the throne of Galicia, the setting transitions to Galicia, where most of the action takes place for the rest of the play. Upon his arrival to A Coruña, the audience learns that García is betrothed to Lindona, a local woman with whom he already has a young child. It is not unusual for wild folk *comedias* to depict regions like Galicia as peripheral wildscapes in relation to an imagined geographical and symbolic center of Madrid (even if that sense is displaced when these plays were performed outside of the capital across the Iberian Peninsula, as the ones in this book most certainly were). That geographic marginality is embodied linguistically in gallego-portugués spoken by Lindona that contrasts with the Castilian spoken by the rest of the characters in the king's court. While she is not, at least not initially, a wild woman, marking Lindona's speech as different thus draws explicit attention to her marginality from the start; moreover, it will become clear that Claramonte's attention to the linguistic is a feature emphasized by design in his representation of wildness when, later on, Lindona's daughter never learns to speak as a child because she is raised in isolation by a she-bear.[21] Even though the play has not received much critical attention, this aspect gives it a unique quality—one that affects the reception of the female protagonist Lindona.[22] From her first utterance, she is identified as a marginalized figure due to her linguistic difference from each of the other characters in the play. Furthermore, her status as an unmarried mother, followed by García's abandonment, amplifies her marginalization as a woman when she becomes powerless to restore her lost honor (at least at first). Her and García's cultural transgression is sexual in nature, but could be repaired through their proposed marriage, but this course of action is interrupted in the scene following García's return to Galicia, when two royal ambassadors arrive from the south to contract his marriage to the Portuguese princess, Leonor—a union that would bring together the two regions under one crown. García's dilemma requires that he scorn the woman he loves for the politically expedient match. Aside from the emotional distress García endures, the social consequences (which have real effects) of this decision are disproportionately skewed against Lindona, who as a result loses her honor, while he remains unblemished within the cultural order, even maintaining his place in its highest seat of authority as reigning monarch, even if only briefly. Scenarios in which infidelity precipitates cultural exile for the woman while the man remains essentially unscathed are common generators of plot conflict in the *comedia*.[23] That which makes *La lindona de Galicia* stand out are the ways the conflict is imagined literally and figuratively as producing wildness, and what is more, wildness that reproduces itself and resists containment. While the values of good governance are reaffirmed convincingly in the resolution of *La lindona de Galicia* through generic conventions that restore social order after a period of upheaval, the simultaneous domestication of the wild women remains incomplete. The present analysis examines the implications of this partial domestication, and how gender and wildness uniquely intersect to illuminate the limits baked into the nature of ideological apparatuses like the *comedia*.

Just before learning of the Portuguese ambassadors' arrival, Basco and Mendo (two of García's advisors) enter to discuss García's marriage prospects without him present. Mendo takes the position that García's commitments to Lindona take precedent, while Basco argues for the political expediency of the match with the Portuguese princess. The conversation portrays two sides of an important political debate taking shape during the early modern period related to the nature of prudence as the most important political virtue of a prince in the execution of their office. Prudence in this context is imbued with specific connotations that require some contextualization, especially its relation to the concept of reason of state, another important term in political philosophy during the period. Reason of state broadly defined is "the application of reason to the problems of government, the criterion whereby the means to certain political ends deemed advisable for the preservation of the commonwealth is to be judged."[24] Machiavelli's view of reason of state in *The Prince* (1532) is the point of departure in the debate. As can be seen from this definition, prudence, that is, the prince's capacity to discern the best course of action in complex circumstances, is essential. With some exceptions, Spanish political thinkers found that Machiavelli's definition of prudence went too far in moving "the term toward a more secular meaning, often akin to 'political dexterity.'"[25] In Spain, "reason of state" became an expression that could be deployed as a metonym for Machiavelli's political pragmatism, and for his critics, the term was often deployed as a strawman to describe Machiavellian statecraft as the political philosophy of the self-interested tyrant; however, in contemporary political treatises published in Spain, one finds more nuance on the question of reason of state that political philosophers and theologians such as Diego de Saavedra Fajardo, Juan de Mariana, and Pedro de Ribadeneira—to name but a few—dedicate significant attention. In response to Machiavelli, they tend to restore a greater emphasis on prudence as a moral virtue as well as a political one, about which they argue "for some sort of accommodation between the ethical demands of Catholicism and the pragmatic necessity for a certain, limited kind of political deceit."[26]

In the conversation between Basco and Mendo about García's decision to marry either Lindona or Leonor, underlying their debate is an ideological disagreement on reason of state, which motivates their divergent views on the most prudent course of action in the present circumstances. More specifically they clash on the question of political prudence that determines the ethical limits of deception for a prince in the execution of statecraft. One aspect on which the two advisors can agree are the stakes, chiefly, that handling the situation imprudently jeopardizes the legitimacy of García's right to rule. Basco contends that it would not be prudent for the king to marry his lover: "She cannot be queen who was first the king's mistress."[27] The underlying logic is driven by the notion that political decisions, especially ones as important as marriage, should be leveraged to maximize political benefit, in this case expanding the prince's claim to power. For Basco, the imprudence of García marrying Lindona is less related to a moral code or social conservatism, and more pragmatically concerned with García squandering the opportunity to consolidate and expand his geopolitical influence. His counsel encourages García to follow the path of political expediency that aligns with a definition of reason of state that encourages deception if it is of benefit to the state. In a figurative symmetry that dramatizes this contemporary political debate, Mendo embodies a position more aligned with the ethicist side of the ideological aisle, and is slow to agree with Basco's reason of state logic. He cites the ulterior and selfish motives of Basco's guidance: "What wild envy! What a deceitful mask!"[28] Juxtaposed with Basco's position, these verses stake a claim in the debate over the appropriate course of action for García, suggesting that the deception required to abandon Lindona and their child goes beyond the limits of what the ethicist political philosophers would define as the prudence of a Christian prince. Moreover, García fails to see the deception noted in Mendo's words, which is a critical factor in his inability to make a disinterested decision unaffected by circumstances. For Saavedra Fajardo, navigating the contingencies of a situation is essential to his definition of prudence and the appropriate limits of deception; in a list of specific factors a prince must successfully navigate, he argues that to govern effectively the prince should beware of opinions, his own passion, and the sinister intentions of advisors, "provided that reason of State is the art of deceiving without being deceived."[29] In *La lindona de Galicia*, love, contrasting advice, and the duplicitous motives of the advisor Basco are precisely the obstacles García faces in the decision between his commitment to Lindona and the expediency of the Portuguese match. His inability to act with the calculated restraint required of a leader to deceive (within ethical bounds) without being deceived precipitates the political and interpersonal turmoil that erupts at the end of act 1.

Therefore, the plot conflict itself dramatizes this contemporary debate in political ideologies (in which the political advisors are metonymic of their respective sides of the debate for which they serve as mouthpieces) for audiences to observe the merits of ethicist political philosophy of reason of state pitted against its more strictly Machiavellian counterpart that values political expediency over all else. If by following Basco's position and marrying Leonor, García precipitates the conflict, it therefore sheds light on the way we are to interpret the values that underpin its logic, observe their consequences as imagined for us over the course of the play, as well as the values that underscore the alternative position (in this case, Mendo's ethicist approach, which will later provide the mechanisms to resolve that conflict). But it will become clear that Basco's attempt to erase the *borrón* (stain) that Lindona signifies cannot be carried out so easily, which exemplifies the function of the wild woman in the *comedia*. In this play, Lindona, as the wild woman, is a problem in the text that needs to be erased, but she resists erasure. She has already been added in; she is woven into the fabric of the play—and more broadly, into ideology itself—in ways that prevent her disappearance. Ideology, like theater, is always liable to show the "seams of its construction" because it is ideological to its core, just as theater can only be theatrical, in spite of the expressed aim of both in asserting the presence of what they claim to be Truth, which necessarily is of a different order and always resides somewhere else.[30]

García initially and vehemently resists the match by launching an extended plea against Basco's reason of state logic. The king's discourse lands as compelling, at least emotionally, as he asserts that he neither desires to abandon Lindona, nor would it be right to commit such an act that nullifies everything he holds dear. It is revealing that he articulates what scorning Lindona means in explicitly political terms: "that isn't being a king, that's being a tyrant."[31] Importantly, according to the ethicist reason of state values ultimately affirmed by the play, the interpersonal tyranny that figuratively characterizes his decision to abandon Lindona is just as applicable on a political level as well. Moralist political philosophers like Pedro de Ribadeneira sought to put "Christian ethical principles back into . . . statecraft, and a major part of this enterprise was to recuperate the notion of virtue" absent in Machiavelli's work.[32] From this perspective on reason of state, García's decision to abandon Lindona at the expense of her honor and the legitimacy of the child lacks prudence as a moral virtue, which cannot be extricated from its political implications for a Christian prince. By falling prey to Basco's deception and subsequently acting out of self-interest to consolidate power at any cost, García undermines the legitimacy of his political authority—the definition of tyrannical rule—by failing to display the requisite prudence required of the prince according to Saavedra Fajardo's definition of the term as a political virtue.[33] As a consequence of his tyranny, García acknowledges the gravity of what is at stake for Lindona if he marries the Portuguese Leonor, describing it as murder (*homicida*), depicting her loss of honor as a type of social death often described as such during the period. During García's passionate speech against the plan to marry the Portuguese queen, Basco responds with empty, although convincing cliches such as "Listen, sir, for your passion blinds you," which ultimately lead to García's concession.[34] Here is another example pointing to García's inability to dispassionately approach the situation, an essential skill in the prudent execution of governance in contemporary Spanish political thought.[35] The king goes on to question Basco's reason of state logic by relying on vocabulary explicitly informed by contemporary political discourse:

> Reason of state is
> the peace of the kingdom,
> we must tell lies that are unfaithful
> with reason of state,

and the seat is occupied by the copy
at the expense of the original.
Leonor, along with the kingdom, have been able
to abandon you, Linda, deceived.[36]

The "copy" here (*el traslado*) refers to the portrait of Leonor, whom he must choose in lieu of the original, Lindona. The juxtaposition of Lindona and the portrait of Leonor sets up ironic tension at play in García's capitulation that derives from the common baroque conceit of presence and absence—specifically depicted here as copy versus original. Here García is presented as being appropriately skeptical of appearances over reality, which, in the context of baroque aesthetic conventions and ideological commitments inclined to be distrustful of appearances, makes a convincing argument that further questions the validity of the reason of state argument thus far offered as self-evident by Basco.

Basco's definition of reason of state that privileges the political benefits of consolidating alliances and political power through arranged royal marriages also comes into conflict with one final point of emphasis offered by Diego de Saavedra Fajardo; in *Empresa 60*, the political philosopher offers a warning to those heads of state who would show preference to their own affairs over matters of state:

> Also put in danger are those hereditary monarchies when the successor, forgetting the most principal of his duties, views the servitude of his subjects as their natural condition; and not recognizing their greatness, rejects them and governs them like slaves, tending more to his own objectives and satiating his appetites than to the public good, converts domination into tyranny; it is where the prince holds the people in such low regard and in return they hate and abhor his person and his actions, that the reciprocal union dissolves between king and kingdom, when it should be that the king obeys and the people are in charge, for the benefit of everyone: the former enjoys the splendor and authority of governing, and the latter the happiness of being well-governed.[37]

Revising Machiavelli, Saavedra Fajardo contends that the prince should primarily serve his subjects and the public good, over doing whatever is expedient to maintain his power. This is not a rejection of reason of state, but rather Saavedra Fajardo's definition of it. In this case, an appropriate application of reason of state suggests that García should avoid basing his decision on personal desire, but a closer look at the excerpt from Saavedra Fajardo makes its application more complicated. Even though García's primary motivation is personally driven, its moral precepts are in line with the ideological commitments to the honor code, and from Mendo's ethicist position, García dishonors his subjects by lacking the virtue to keep to his word and marry Lindona. Meanwhile Basco's pragmatism insists that marrying Leonor would consolidate the power of the two kingdoms, thereby rendering the deception required to remove Lindona from the picture as both a necessary and permissible means to a politically expedient end. In this play, the virtue of the prince is inherently entwined to reason of state, defined here as Saavedra Fajardo defines it as the greatest public good, rather than the consolidation and maintenance of monarchical power. This latter definition presented through its theatrical mouthpiece Basco initially wins out, but does so at the expense of peace in the kingdom ("paces del Reyno tal").[38] Despite its purpose to maintain the stability of the monarchy, Basco's guidance relies too greatly on the maintenance of power and turns out to be self-interested, while also lacking virtue, based on the illusory promise of a truth located elsewhere (literally Portugal, but of most importance is that the locus of peace and stability that has been promised from afar is unreliable).

When Lindona first enters and learns of her fate, her affectively evocative reaction to the news of García's proposed marriage to the Portuguese princess helps us better understand what the play is saying about this debate, and continues to diminish the force of Basco's argument as she heaps grievances on her previously betrothed. The emotionally stirring nature of her diatribe against García and his royal court strengthens the force of her argument.[39] Lindona shares in Antigone's plight in her unsuccessful and tragic attempt, however emotionally compelling, to persuade a king who has gone back on his word. It is also suggestive that by Lindona's side stands her and García's daughter, still unnamed at this point in the play. Provided the relative scarcity of children on the early modern Spanish stage, this presence would have been conspicuous, maximizing the impact of the verbal blows meted out by Lindona as the legitimacy of the child at stake is made tangible. After Basco insensitively informs her, "your seat is occupied" as she enters the throne room for what she believes to be her coronation, her initial incredulity also reinforces the extent to which García's affront against her should strike as nearly inconceivable.[40] She replies, "I am your wife, / quit this nonsense."[41] Once the reality of the situation sets in, her discourse shifts as she issues a litany of pointed reminders of García's commitments and the significance of going back on his word. When he asserts that he must marry Leonor for reason of state, Lindona posits that such a rationale does not nullify all other obligations:

> What about your word, and your hand?
> . . .
> And my honor, and of this child's?
> . . .
> women, let my example be a warning;
> behold who men are:
> was it for this that you've come
> to A Coruña?[42]

From her perspective, above and beyond their mutual love, García's word, their betrothal, her honor, and their offspring win out over Basco's definition reason of state, which the play (following popular reception of Machiavellian political philosophy in Spain) comes across as overly shrewd and self-interested, that is, lacking virtue and therefore prudence also. The careful use of physical space in the scene mirrors the poetic conceit developed through juxtaposition of presence and absence in the verse, which visually reinforces the impact of García's abandonment. Learning of her abrupt dismissal, Lindona is physically and emotionally present in stark contrast to Leonor's representation by proxy both in her portrait and two ambassadors. When she articulates her response as her daughter stands physically by her side on the stage, the visual signification of their presence is striking, intensified precisely by the absence of Leonor, who only exists in representative form through her ambassadors who have arrived as her proxy for the ceremony; moreover, the only visual evidence of her existence is equally representative: the portrait of her brought by the Portuguese ambassadors. In the physical staging of this scene, it becomes clear that García has chosen what he earlier described as a "sombra" (shadow)—the portrait of Leonor—over emotions he has felt, pledges he has made, and a child he has fathered. This scene depicts the baroque preoccupation with relying too heavily on appearances and representation as Basco persuades García to make a choice based on not one but two representations of Leonor (her portrait and the ambassadors serving as her representatives), while also being persuaded by a misguided confidence in the reliability of representational signification (i.e., the portrait):

> A blur [borrón], all of which is life,
> and a self, all of which is feeling;
> a wonder reduced
> to the rarest beauty,
> which is sovereign, jealous,
> incredible [peregrina], and singular,
> speaks without speaking,
> with greater force than if it actually spoke.[43]

Note that Basco uses the same term here to describe Leonor's portrait that he had previously applied to Lindona: "borrón." When describing Lindona the term was employed in the sense that she was a stain that required removal, while here he uses the term to emphasize the portrait as mimetic of life; it is true to life in so far as the truth can be blurred and difficult to discern, but its strange beauty speaks for itself. But his repetition of *borrón* when describing Leonor suggests more than a coincidence, and one that betrays a meaningful dramatic irony. His portrayal of the Portuguese princess in these verses unwittingly evokes his previous comment identifying Lindona as the "borrón," which the text suggests is actually the person (or one of the people) described in this passage also. As he goes about describing the qualities of the portrayed image as indicative of the match García should choose, it is clear he refers to Leonor but importantly, what Basco offers here is an inadvertent description of someone else, really two people (with the same name): Lindona and her daughter Linda. In so doing, he unintentionally acknowledges the decision García *should* have chosen both for himself and for reason of state defined as the option in the best interests of "peace in the kingdom" over an expansionist political mentality.[44] So it turns out Basco is correct that the beauty García should choose is the *borrón*, but the problem becomes that he urges the king to select someone else. Moreover, the verses in question foreshadow an unmistakable description of his and Lindona's daughter later in the play. First, by connecting *borrón* to beauty ("la belleza más rara"), these verses on beauty rather explicitly signal a connection to the names of mother and daughter, Lindona and Linda, that also denote beauty. And even more notably, Linda is a beauty that "speaks" ("está hablando," i.e., her existence determines much of what happens in the play) without speaking (when she next appears as an adolescent, she cannot communicate through verbal communication as a result of language deprivation from living alone in the forest from birth). Therefore, Basco gets at the truth of the matter (according to the poetic logic of the play), but misidentifies the object(s) to which he is referring: Lindona y Linda. The surreptitious advisor guides García to misinterpret this description of who to choose, an error that stems from Basco's definition of reason of state. García's inability to discern the appropriate course of action, compounded by his subsequent reliance on the poor counsel, are the errors that catalyze García's demise. The greatest good for the kingdom derives from virtuous actions of the king, which can only be achieved when the signified (Lindona/Linda) is properly aligned by its signifier (Basco's offered description) as the king's choice for a match. Conversely, when reason of state (the signifier) is aligned with incorrect signifieds (e.g., self-preservation and consolidation of power), its application leads to conflict in the kingdom. However, when defined correctly (at least as presented by the play) as Saavedra Fajardo defines it (the prince as administrator of the public good in the service of the people), it results in peace in the kingdom ("paces en Reyna tal"). Claramonte sets up a complex symmetry here between political philosophy and interpersonal conflict that together serve as motors for the plot when their misinterpretation leads to conflict. They later condition the parameters for its resolution when García comes to identify correctly the "borrón" he was to have chosen all along—Lindona, the stain that was actually the truth, in all its difficult splendor.

But when García selects Leonor, it signifies catastrophe for Lindona, which she expresses in ways that expose the ideological scaffolding that motivates García's decision-making apparatus. One rhetorical strategy she deploys is an attack on his national identity, stating, "Castilian, which is worse than being Galician,"[45] which suggests that the behavior "reasonable" (i.e., reason of state, *razón de estado*) in Castile is reprehensible in Galicia. Difference, in this case the cultural differences that subtend values and condition decisions, deconstructs the essential qualities that García's ideological commitments presuppose. This portion of her speech creates a pause that questions the self-evident nature of García's decision. She also pinpoints a cultural anxiety within the patriarchal, male-dominated power structure of baroque Spain when she calls into question García's masculinity. In a scene that highlights her vulnerability to that order as a scorned and abandoned mother, she appears strong and, at moments, perhaps even subversive. Her entreaty ("women, beware") to the women that accompany her in the scene (who would have been her ladies-in-waiting) goes beyond the fourth wall as she continues to condemn García, calling him a "false gentleman" (*falso cavaleyro*) who

> deceives,
> two-faced;
> if he makes a promise to God,
> he will just as soon break his word.[46]

There can be no objection to the veracity of her commentary. García did, indeed, fail to fulfill his promises, and Lindona's reproach at no point seems unfounded. As a result, she pinpoints a serious conflict within the political realm of ideology: is prudence defined by pragmatism even if it requires deception, or is it defined by uncompromising virtue through keeping one's word? Repeatedly, the play provides more compelling evidence of the latter. Announcing her double vulnerability to the dominant culture as Galician—highlighted by her speaking gallego-portugués—and as a woman, audiences are presented with the affective quandary of feeling compassion for the emotionally and ideologically compelling grievances of the forsaken protagonist or the primacy of a value system that renders her powerless to the whims of the ineffective and inconstant García.

This final scene of act 1 then ends chaotically, which is a fact that has been downplayed in criticism. Antonucci states that the scene ends with the arrival of Sancho to overthrow García, and "the affronted Lindona abandoning her young child."[47] The stage directions are clear, however, that what happens next is rather more sudden and jarring. In the culmination of emotions running increasingly high, Lindona takes her daughter in her clutches and heaves her through a castle window that overlooks the craggy bay of A Coruña. A clear allusion to *La vida es sueño*, this moment is even more intense than its parallel in Calderón's play, due to the fact that it is her own child. This results in an equally more difficult interpretation of the plot development. Whereas in Calderón's play Segismundo heaves the servant from the window as evidence of the protagonist's monstrous characteristics that he has yet to overcome, in *La lindona de Galicia*, the consequences of her violent act continue to condition the events as they unfold for the remainder of the work (unlike the Polish soldier largely forgotten in *La vida es sueño*). However, like Segismundo, Lindona's character development is incomplete when this takes place during the abrupt closing of act 1. At this moment, the audience is left bewildered when the act ends to consider this startling shift in her character that, from a modern perspective, could be described as something akin to a psychotic break. Her warm relationship both with García and to her child previous to this moment enhance the shock of the incident, and clearly display that something has changed abruptly in Lindona, particularly after she delivers nearly one-hundred lines of well-reasoned arguments for why García should not renege on his word. As the act comes to a close, Lindona does not have to wait long to exact revenge on the unfaithful García as his brother Sancho arrives to successfully overthrow him. García is subsequently left with Lindona for her to dispense justice as she pleases. Given this charge, she imprisons him.

At the beginning of the act 2, years have passed. Sancho has died, and his brother Fernando reigns over the kingdoms of Castile, León, and Galicia. García remains in Lindona's custody, and we also meet Sancho's son Ramiro, who, having grown tired of life at his uncle's court, sets off to the forests of Galicia with his hunting party. They happen across a young woman, dressed in animal pelts, who appears to delight in their presence, although the only words she speaks are to repeat the final word of everything Ramiro and his lackey say. She then flees into the woods, but her beauty and the enigma of her echo fascinates them, so they decide to give chase. The erotic trope of the men as hunters and the woman as prey is made explicit in this scene. But their hunt is interrupted, when the young men stumble upon Lindona's castle, where García remains imprisoned. Lindona is away when they arrive, so they speak with the prisoner. In hearing of his plight, they pledge to return to save him. Eventually, Ramiro's hunting party finds the young woman they were previously following, and they take her back to Fernando's court, where she receives a tutor. They come to learn that she mimicked their speech because she had never had any contact with humans, and therefore never learned language. It has yet to be directly revealed in the dialogue, but it is clear that the young woman is Linda, who we later learn had been rescued by a she-bear after miraculously surviving defenestration. Antonucci notes that Linda—not to be confused with her mother Lindona—is the only wild character to appear on the baroque stage not being able to produce spoken language and is therefore "a very lifelike wild woman."[48] Upon receiving the report from Ramiro about the imprisoned García in a remote Galician castle, king Fernando decides to travel northwest to liberate his brother as the second act concludes.

The elements of the plot replicate some of those seen previously in the wild figure corpus such as the she-bear that snatches away Ursón in *El nacimiento de Ursón y Valentín* along with the agrestic and wooded Arcadian landscape where nearly all of the wild character plays take place, at least in part. By also bringing classical myth to the fore in the direct allusions to the tragic narratives of Echo and Callisto in Ovid's *Metamorphoses*, Claramonte "swerves" from both Lope and also classical mythology by interweaving these literary and dramatic antecedents together into his *comedia* in order to improve upon their premises.[49] With wildness as his vehicle, he deploys the conventions of the genre to bring happy endings where they had previously been absent. Figurative of the state of disarray brought on by García's poor governance, then, is the emergence of two wild characters—Lindona and Linda—whose domestication becomes the mechanism by which the plot is resolved. As such, wildness becomes an apt metaphor for dramatic conflict as it stands in as the antithesis to both the ordered state *and* the domesticated *ángel de la casa* (angel of the house), about which a broader claim can be made: wildness is the very thing at stake in the fixations on both ideological affirmations—social order and domestic order—that dominate the *comedia* overall. It is no wonder that sixteenth- and seventeenth-century playwrights turn to the explicit representation of wildness so frequently to dramatize the trajectory of conflict and resolution to the action. And identifying the obsession with wildness in the *comedia* renders even more emblematic the traditional conceptualization of the *comedia* plot as order disturbed (i.e., wildness) to order restored. However, in Claramonte's attempt to blot out the *borrón* of wildness created in the wake of the conflict and invert tragedy through the conventions of the *comedia*, the tenuous nature of this process becomes palpable through the depiction of how contrived it appears in his play. The playwright's resurrection of Echo and Calisto as part of the endeavor to inscribe gender normativity upon his wild characters resists his effort at every turn; as playwrights continued to return to the well to draw on the wildness motif, when the wild woman cuts through the fabric of the Baroque like in this play, we see playwrights relying more heavily on the conventions of the *comedia* to sew it back together before she emerges to take a look around.

Again, the resonance with Echo's narrative from Ovid becomes clear when Linda appears in the forest and is only capable of mimicking the noises uttered by Ramiro and his servant Mormojón. She spies the two hunters just as Echo does when she observes Narcissus in the Ovidian myth, but is unable to communicate with them. According to the Ovidian narrative, Echo's voice has been taken away by Juno, while in the play, she never learns language due to her childhood in the forest, completely secluded from other humans. While the cause of their inability to use language may be distinct, there are notable comparisons to be made between the two characters from this point in the plot forward. Unable to communicate with Narcissus, Echo resorts to showing her affection by any means necessary. She throws her arms around him, and he immediately flees in response. Adding insult to injury, he exclaims, "I would die before I give you a chance at me."[50] Scorned, she retreats to the woods, wasting away until nothing is left but her voice. Linda inverts Echo's narrative. Under the tutelage of Doña Elvira at Fernando's court, Linda begins to produce language, and makes some developments in her manners, but never completely transforms into a cultured elite. Unlike in later works such as *La sirena de Tinacria*, very few lines portray Elvira's lessons, except one important moment that parallels Narcissus's rejection of Echo in Ovid's *Metamorphoses*. In one scene, Ramiro enters and the stage directions indicate that Linda quickly goes to Ramiro and hugs him. There are of course exceptions, but dramatists generally do not add copious stage directions, and they tend to be related to scenography and music. That makes it more noticeable when they diverge from the conventional practice to include stage directions related to the acting of a scene, especially ones as specific as those here. This would suggest that Linda's enthusiastic embrace is essential in some way, which is confirmed in Elvira's response. Like in the Echo narrative, her behavior is rebuked for breaking from decorum. Elvira reproaches her for this behavior, imploring, "Never go to hug a man; / it isn't an appropriate way to show love."[51] Unfazed by her advance, Ramiro, aside from being attracted to her physically, finds her uncultured behavior and lack of language endearing, if not enthralling. Even though Elvira tells her that it is indecent to offer an embrace in such a manner, the object of her desire never rejects her—in fact, rather the opposite. Unlike Narcissus, Ramiro responds to her love in kind. Unrequited love kills Echo, tragically reducing her to the paradox of the present absence that constitutes an echo, whose existence manifests the impossibility of completion idealized in shared love. *La lindona de Galicia* attempts to give Echo a happy ending in which she recuperates her voice by means of acquiring the culture of her "rescuers" (i.e., colonizers). Ironically, Claramonte's swerve from the myth tale fails to achieve this purpose without forfeiting ideological ground elsewhere. By providing this comedic closure to the action, Linda's behavior is dismissive of the behaviors proscribed by decorum. Her embrace is permitted, even if to Elvira's displeasure. As a result of the wild pupil's resistance to domestication, the premise of Elvira's instruction seems hollow. Claramonte replicates literary antecedents to improve upon them, or at least transform them for his dramatic ends to produce a new result; however, the reconfiguration of those elements resists such an endeavor as they are negotiated in the play, creating dramatic exigencies that compromise the playwright's ability to accomplish one objective without ceding ideological territory.

The other mythological allusion made prominent in *La lindona de Galicia* is the story of Callisto, who belonged to Diana's band of nymphs. In one form or another, Callisto is frequently present in the wild figure *comedias* as I mentioned in my analysis of Lope's *El nacimiento de Ursón y Valentín* and *El animal de Hungría* in Chapter 2 of this study. Represented as a she-bear, she appears in this work to rescue Linda from the crags beneath the castle after having been thrown from the window. The she-bear in folkloric literature is ubiquitously depicted as a maternal protector, even (and most often) of human children who find themselves abandoned. These elements come together in Callisto's myth tale in Ovid, which begins one day in the forest when Jupiter catches a glimpse of Callisto reposing in the Arcadian landscape. Aware of the strict vow of chastity adhered to by Diana's nymphs, Zeus disguises himself as Diana, and he uses this deception to rape her. Her ensuing pregnancy is soon discovered by Diana, who responds swiftly and unequivocally by casting her out. Then Juno, to punish Callisto for her husband's infidelity, transforms her into a she-bear. Like Echo, as a bear she loses her voice and ability to communicate with the human world, and most importantly with Arcas, her son who will never recognize her. The longing that she expresses to know her child is clear in Ovid's telling of the story, and her human drive to connect with her child supersedes otherwise aggressive instincts assumed upon becoming a bear. A truly tragic figure, Callisto is the victim of both sides of patriarchal violence, first represented by Jupiter's sexual assault, followed by being demonized and expelled from the micro-society of Diana's nymphs for failing to comply with a strict social code even when the circumstances were entirely beyond her control. The she-bears of the wild woman *comedias*, channeling Callisto, nurture those whom cultural order has unjustly expelled. García's rejection of Lindona, like Jupiter's of Callisto, is portrayed as unjust, and as a result initiates the major conflict of the work. The she-bear appears to fulfill her crucial role in this play in order to facilitate the cultural recuperation of those whom society has punished for others' transgressions. Callisto mothers these wild characters in a way that empowers them to be the agents of their own restoration. Due to her upbringing in the ursine care of her surrogate mother, Linda lacks the trappings of culture, which leads her to call for pause at every culturally charged moment of the play. Despite Claramonte's attempt to domesticate Linda through the royal maidservant's instruction, as a daughter of Callisto, she pushes back at the boundaries that define cultural norms, and calls into question their essential nature. Surprisingly, she is not punished; rather, she transforms those boundaries to achieve her own desires, resolve the conflict between her parents, and win a small victory for all those who identify with Callisto's plight. Callisto is the wild woman play's ghost of Tom Joad; she makes many an appearance just when she is needed, only to fade into the background, almost unnoticed.

The resolution to the play still dramatizes an obsession with completion, the healing of all social ills and righting of all wrongs represented by hasty marriages, but it does not entirely reflect the prescriptive boundaries expected from the ideological framework of the Baroque. As the complete cast of characters arrives at Lindona's castle to rescue the imprisoned García, the aged prisoner identifies Linda as his daughter from her pendant she was also wearing when Lindona flung her from the window.[52] Although her survival is initially difficult to believe for those present in this scene, Ordoñez—one of Sancho's advisors—appears and recounts the tale of her survival. On the day he arrived with Sancho to overthrow García, Ordoñez witnesses the child's fall, and attempts to save her, but cannot reach her before a she-bear snatches her up and carries her off into the forest, where she grows up to become the young woman currently in their presence. With Fernando pleased to see his long-lost brother again and Lindona acquitted of wrongdoing at the revelation that her daughter is still alive, the king proposes marriage to Linda. Her response and their ensuing exchange is unexpected:

> FERNANDO: You, Linda, give me your hand.
> LINDA: What for?
> FERNANDO: To be the owner of my soul.
> LINDA: That's love?
> FERNANDO: Love in an eternal bond,
>   with you as my wife.

LINDA: But I,
> by jealousy, am in love
> with the Prince; and I wish for my love
> to shine upon him;
> for him I'm no longer wild,
> for him I'm no longer a monster,
> to him I owe this reason
> and to his love my understanding.[53]

Thus, Linda rejects the king's proposal. He accepts her decision and blesses the marriage between her and Ramiro. As soon as they join hands, Lindona looks to García, and says, "Give me that hand of yours."[54] Her daughter paves the way for her to speak, recuperating an ability dearly lost by Echo, but regained in *La lindona de Galicia* by the two female protagonists. Their voice breaks the rules of traditional gender performance usually expected from the Spanish *comedia*. Of course, they do not completely break free from the cultural milieu to which they pertain, but Linda obtains a literal and figurative voice to exert agency within that system. The raw materials Claramonte put into play seem to have gotten away from him as his wild woman Linda maintains elements of her wildness even in the conclusion. As a darned spot, she refuses to get "out"; rather, she is weaved into the fabric of the Baroque.

Fernando's response to Linda's rejection is initially perplexing. One might expect that he, the king, take offense at the affront. This moment of closure contrasts with García's decision that had precipitated the conflict of the work. Unlike García in act 1, he chooses not to resist what clearly is presented to be the right course of action at the conclusion of *La lindona de Galicia*. García's abandonment of Lindona due to faulty ideological imperatives in act 1 precipitates his downfall, while Fernando permits love for its own sake as a virtue, and considers all the contingencies of the circumstances to show prudence by choosing to ignore any affront to his honor caused by Linda's rejection. And his honor does not seem to be at stake when he chooses not to obsess over it. This situation is not a perfect parallel to García's reason of state dilemma; however, García suffers for his inability to discern the right course amid the conflicting complexities of a situation, fails to hide his emotion, ultimately displaying a lack of prudence as result. Conversely, in response to the rejection, Fernando never betrays his emotions, and permits Ramiro and Linda to marry. Poetically, contrasting the violence of Zeus and the anger of

Diana toward Callisto, Fernando accepts the rejection of Linda and her betrothal, which produces a final applause that commends his gracious and liberal spirit, the preferred representation of the exercise of monarchical authority in the *comedia*.

BAROQUE UPCYCLED COUTURE: REFASHIONING WILDNESS IN FIGUEROA Y CÓRDOBA'S *LA SIRENA DE TINACRIA*

A common feature of the literature and playwriting of the Spanish Baroque is the prevalence of content drawn from classical mythology. Claramonte and Figueroa y Córdoba are no exceptions, with the latter making explicit reference to the Odyssean repertoire of monsters in the title of his wild figure play, *La sirena de Tinacria* (1678). Like in *La lindona de Galicia*, the overall prevalence of Arcadian mythology informs the interpretations of the wild woman *comedias*. Figueroa y Córdoba's work draws from the same plot conventions of the royal foundling motif found throughout this corpus. The wild woman of this *comedia*, Ismenia, is also the titular protagonist, which becomes clear from the opening lines of the play. Like the sirens of classical mythology, she lives in the forest on an island and possesses an enchanting singing voice (a behavior she will be reprimanded for during her transition to aristocratic society). When Federico arrives shipwrecked on her island, he is enchanted by her physical beauty and euphonic singing, about which he confesses to be "blind and bewildered."[55] However, as Linda inverts the tragic sequences of the Eco and Callisto myths in *La lindona de Galicia*, so too does Ismenia with regard to the sirens. Rather than destroying all men that have the misfortune of sailing near her island (Diana or Medusa are two other defenders of their feminine domains), she is the agent that initiates the resolution to the conflict of the plot. Moreover, the characterization of Ismenia as a siren is a purely figurative one, a linguistic marker attributed to her outward appearance (*parecer*) in the play rather than a description of an intrinsic or immutable trait that constitutes her being (*ser*). "Siren" is a garment she wears, or rather an external signifier; *La sirena de Tinacria* is a play that explores the relationship of fashion—the clothes we wear as outward signifiers—to the self, specifically whether a change of clothes can change the person underneath. Figueroa y Córdoba's *comedia* would suggest that question (and therefore the answer) is rather more complicated in ways that evince a meaningful shift from Renaissance to baroque conceptualizations of the link between outward appearances and interior being.

The play foregrounds Ismenia's clothes as meaningful to her state of being. At the beginning of the play, she dons the conventional animal pelts as markers of her wildness, and later dresses for court in a show of her new status as a member of the social elite. As such, the play emphasizes Ismenia's clothes as a visual metaphor for social inscription. Important to note here is that fashion and clothing were conceived of differently during the Renaissance than they are today, which conditions their representation in cultural production. Fashion, in the modern sense, as the ever-changing cultural appeal for certain styles of clothing, took shape during the Renaissance, with references of the term appearing in the sixteenth century.[56] Rosalind Jones and Peter Stallybrass's foundational study *Renaissance Clothing and the Materials of Memory* explains that fashion also had another meaning related to the relationship of clothing to the wearer that is more closely associated with the modern use of the verb form "to fashion," that is, a process by which something is molded or shaped. These two meanings, which have since disassociated in the etymology of the term, affect the way we read clothes and their relationship to the individual during early modernity. Jones argues for a notion of "deep wearing" during the Renaissance, whereby clothing was not just an exterior marker of an interior reality (e.g., mourning, social status, etc.), but rather imagined a more intrinsic relationship by which clothing inscribed meaning onto the wearer. Clothing was not ornamental, but constitutive: "For it was investiture, the putting on of clothes, that quite literally constituted a person as a monarch or a freeman of a guild or a household servant. Investiture was, in other words, the means by which a person was given a form, a shape, a depth."[57] It is this power of clothes that can fashion (i.e., mold) a person and inscribe meaning onto the wearer so that their nature is transformed. Jones cites an early modern English text that employs the term "transnaturing" as a concise critical vocabulary for this semiotics of clothes wearing.[58] The sartorial domestication of Ismenia in *La sirena de Tinacria* is motivated by confidence in the power of wardrobe to "transnature" her from wild to civilized, that is, "mold and shape [her] both physically and socially, to constitute a subject."[59] But these ideologies of clothing breakdown in the play by means of the heightened sense of separation between exterior and interior that is tantamount to a meaningful shift in worldview from the

Renaissance to the Baroque. The intensified presentation of separation between appearances and reality that is essential to a baroque aesthetics of artifice reflects this transition, and is leveraged to its maximum potential in the theater. But unlike the penniless squire in *Lazarillo de Tormes* whose representation lays bare this ontological separation of one's worth and identity from the clothes they wear, the ideological posture of *La sirena de Tinacria* is less clear.[60] What *is* evident in the *comedia*, however, is that Ismenia finds herself subjected to a literal reshaping of her body when she puts on the elaborate trappings of baroque dress. And success in inscribing Ismenia within the bounds of accepted female subjectivity must contend with the possibility of the breakdown of that process. Her domestication is the site where her gender is fashioned, and where the mode of theatrical representation must pull off a compelling trick to obscure its own theatricality for this transformation to be successful. This creates a site of contention where the social necessity of her transformation and its breakdown vie for space, where this transformation to attest gender norms is only as compelling as it can be made to appear natural, lest the seams of gender's performative core be exposed. But this is precisely the trick theater is best at pulling off, in the service of the modern impulse to disavow the emptiness at the center of totalizing ideologies and enforce them as if they were true, natural, and necessary. In the following analysis of *La sirena de Tinacria*, I will outline what is at stake in the possible readings regarding Ismenia's theatrical domestication as it relates to dominant gender ideologies of the period.

At the beginning of the play, Ismenia articulates having always desired to be liberated from the seclusion of her island, but when her wish comes true, finds that not all of the customs of civilization are to her liking. Almost simultaneous to Federico's shipwreck on Ismenia's Island, members of the Duchess of Tinacria's entourage arrive. They snatch her up and bring her to the court of the duchess, Matilde. Like Linda, Ismenia is assigned a tutor—Flora—to teach her "palace etiquette," and she thus trades her animal pelts, bow, and arrows for a farthingale and chopines (platform shoes lampooned with some frequency in the *comedia* by making them exaggeratedly tall and difficult to walk in).[61] The audience learns that the process is not going particularly smoothly when Federico's conversation with the gracioso Talego is interrupted by her animated indignance heard from offstage: "Go ahead and make fun of me you peasants / and take off these clothes."[62] Ismenia then enters the stage with Flora as Talego and Federico hide in the wings to watch the episode unfold. Intended to provoke laughter, underneath the surface of the scene exists a tacit—unintended even—criticism of the social norms in play, as is so often true with humor.[63] The chopines cause her particular strife, about which she chides Flora's nonchalance about the ease in which "all of them are able to walk around in the palace in such a way."[64] When Flora elaborates regarding why women wear them, she remarks that they make them taller, to which Ismenia aptly quips:

> That's not true
>
> ...
>
> because if a woman
> falls from her place
> wearing those, when they're on the ground
> they can't get any shorter.[65]

Her reasoning here exemplifies how the wild women of the Spanish *comedia*, due to their lack of exposure to the norms that condition social behavior, are able to innocently expose their artificiality through lighthearted criticism. But the levity of the physical comedy should not obscure the ideological commitments deconstructed by Ismenia's failed attempts to adequately perform the gendered fashion that should come naturally to her. Cirnigliaro's work on early modern fashion identifies the significance of this failure when she posits that "sartorial practices impacted and ultimately molded constructions of female subjectivities," and that chopines in particular "reveal societal negotiations with elevation, transgression and movement."[66] This is evident in Ismenia's cited commentary. Even though it is meant to be comic, her immediate response to Flora's rationale behind wearing chopines still "reveals societal negotiations" when she succinctly states, "That's not true." This utterance concisely places ideology (i.e., notions of socially constructed truth) up for grabs. This scene demonstrates how society is imposed onto the subject, molding and re-shaping Ismenia's body through shoes that make her taller, along with bodices and farthingales that both constrict and expand her body, literally pulling and compressing her in every direction—a feeling she befittingly describes as "the strangest torment."[67] The attire highlighted in this scene thus dramatizes the fashioning of Ismenia. On the one hand the narrow set of social prescriptions one must perform to adhere to normative subjectivity entails a tightening or constricting, exemplified by the tightening of the bodice. On the other hand, there is the farthingale that structures and enlarges the lower half of the dress. Any characteristic, desire, or behavior to which anyone is inclined but transgresses cultural norms—i.e., does not fit within the constraints of the bodice—must be occluded, space for which the farthingale provides.[68] For Ismenia, the prescriptions of courtly culture are initially oppressive, as much as her corset is constricting. She refuses to conceal any facet of her nature, outwardly represented by her frequent petition to have her animal pelts and bow returned to her. In response, Matilde (the duchess hosting Ismenia at her court) reflects the performative nature of culture, in this instance so closely tied to gender performance: "with time and experience / you will get the hang of it."[69] Matilde echoes Judith Butler's contention regarding the legitimation of gender ideology through repetition: "As in other ritual social dramas, the action of gender requires a performance that is *repeated*. This repetition is at once a reenactment and reexperiencing of a set of meanings already socially established; and it is the mundane and ritualized form of their legitimation."[70] Ismenia compellingly questions these behaviors at every chance she gets, which challenges the essentiality of gender norms, even if her transgressive tendencies are ultimately suppressed.

Thanks to Flora's instruction, Matilde's prediction comes to pass, about which Flora boasts to Talego:

> Ismenia, once haughty and vain,
> has become a courtier,
> and forgetting rustic
> extremes, lives subject
> to reason.[71]

Clearly meant as a compliment, Flora's words escape their intended meaning. To arrive at her definition of "reason," we have observed the process of inscription on Ismenia's body required to internalize its precepts as coherent and stable. From this point forward, the outward signs of Ismenia's wild upbringing disappear; nevertheless, the interpretation of her behavior as a reflection of her past is less clear. She may gracefully don the clothes that Flora has instructed her to wear, but Ismenia remains openly incredulous at the culturally constructed performance of her gender that is expected of her over the course of the play.

One such instance where this becomes clear occurs when Enrique's ambassador arrives to Matilde's court to propose her marriage to Enrique, the Duke of Calabria. Enrique has felt an affront to his honor due to Matilde's refusal to give audience to his ambassador, who indicates the duke's response to such a slight: "your opinion has been slighted, / you being a man who doesn't suffer insults to your reputation."[72] The ambassador goes on to disclose that if she doesn't contract a marriage with Enrique, they will go to war. Ismenia interrupts the ambassador and rebukes him for speaking to a duchess in such a disrespectful manner:

> That's enough!
> My patience has worn thin!
> Insolent ambassador,
> with haughty arrogance
> you cunningly reduce
> deeds to mere words!
> ...
> Show appropriate appreciation to find yourself
> in the presence of her Highness.[73]

Matilde apologizes for Ismenia's outburst, which the ambassador shrugs off because, in his words, "she's a woman"—a slight as much a trivialization of Ismenia as it is an insult to the duchess as well. Matilde displays prudence in diplomatic restraint—much to Ismenia's chagrin—and even Federico, disguised under the name of Lisardo, is moved to action as he draws his sword and admonishes Enrique's representative. Sufficiently exasperated by the reception he has received at the Tinacrian court, the ambassador requests Matilde's final decision, to which she, equally ready to end the audience, firmly replies, "Ismenia has already sufficiently responded."[74] A subtle foreshadowing to when Ismenia will have this authority once she has assumed her still hidden role as the legitimate duchess, she is celebrated for this significant breach of social decorum along the lines of gender and political order.

Ismenia's behavior continues to follow this tack, and is quick to challenge cultural norms that she fails to understand. Ismenia tires of Federico's transparent inability to see past her presumed lowly birth, for which she admonishes him to embrace their shared love for one another rather than worry about concerns she considers insubstantial. She insightfully remarks:

> I've seen it on your lips
> so many times, that not

being your equal, it would be unworthy
of your high birth
and a personal affront
to deceive a woman.[75]

Even after joining the ranks of aristocratic society, Ismenia remains incapable of understanding the importance of caste, which is another instance in which the play is incapable of completely erasing such a doubt. This is palatable, however, because beneath all of her layers, she is indeed of noble birth, the "true" Duchess of Tinacria. At this point in the development in the plot, the audience is aware that she is the duchess, and this dramatic irony therefore makes it so their love is not taboo, but the dramatic irony is significant, as Ismenia and Federico are yet to be aware of this. There have been moments when various characters seem to note that there is something about Ismenia they cannot quite put their finger on that belies her wild upbringing (it is *la fuerza de la sangre*, "the blood will out"), but as far as they both know, her humble beginnings reflect her social station. That her plea rings emotionally compelling, along with Federico's constant inner turmoil at the situation, implies that the strictures of cultural prescription weigh heavily on them both. Just before she admonishes him as quoted, Federico bemoans his unquenchable attraction for Ismenia:

By my faith I cannot
go after her, nor does she deserve it,
that I would deceive the one I love.
May she leave my heart so that my
love can find its equal in Matilde.[76]

Deep down, Federico knows that he loves Ismenia, but that he must spurn her for Matilde because he cannot marry a woman beneath his class. If their situation were as they believe it to be at this moment, the impossibility of their relationship would still incite grief and pity for their plight, even though in this case the point is rendered moot at the revelation of her identity as rightful heir to the dukedom of Tinacria. In *La sirena de Tinacria*, the dramatic irony of their true identities makes this impossibility easily overlooked up until the very last moment of the work. While they are unaware of Ismenia's hidden aristocratic identity, their despair and honest questioning of the rules that prohibit their match creates a space for an affective response in the audience to prioritize true love over social proscription; however, the audience always knows they actually *can* fall in love, which diminishes the impact of their emotional struggle and ultimately undermines the subversive vigor of their would-be forbidden love.

So just how conservative is the conventional ending to *La sirena de Tinacria*? Alberto, a count who had been loyal to Ismenia's father (the Duke of Tinacria who was usurped by his brother, Matilde's father), realizes Ismenia's identity at the end of act 2 upon seeing the ruby given to her by Arnesto. At this moment, he vows to help reveal her true identity (about which she remains unaware). Simultaneously, he is the only character aside from Talego with knowledge of Federico's identity as the Duke of Barcelona. He has thus far been hiding under the alias of Lisardo, guised as an ambassador from his own court. Federico divulges to Arnesto his love for Ismenia, but ultimate obligation to marry the Duchess of Tinacria. In another stroke of dramatic irony, Arnesto promises to help him contract the marriage with the Duchess of Tinacria, but of course the audience knows he is actually referring to Ismenia, the rightful heiress to the dukedom. With these pieces in place, Enrique's army arrives to invade Tinacria as recompense for Matilde's affront in rejecting his proposal.[77] In response, Matilde leads her own forces into battle from the front line. One of Enrique's soldiers apprises him of this situation that the Duchess of Tinacria has prepared her troops and is leading them into battle. Dramatic exigency has us pulling for her victory over Enrique, and her active role leading her army in the battle occupies a decidedly masculine space, which pushes against straightforward prescriptions for the performance of gender.

Once the battle ends, the conflict is resolved hastily. Enrique yields to Federico on the battlefield, followed by Arnesto fulfilling his promise to reveal Ismenia as the rightful heir to the dukedom of Tinacria. Now that Ismenia's noble status has been made known, Federico can marry the duchess of Tinacria, except now, that person is Ismenia, his true love. Matilde, who would have been an infant when her father usurped the ducal seat, peacefully concedes to her cousin:

> And I, Ismenia,
> did not have any part in your disgrace
> whatsoever, with these arms
> I return to you the scepter.[78]

The vanquished Enrique offers his hand to Matilde, who dutifully accepts it. The play then ends as Ismenia conventionally requests that the audience "pardon its many faults."[79]

The abrupt nature of this ending, which is not at all uncommon to the *comedia*, reduces its overall effect to celebrate dominant cultural ideologies. This required convention contrasts with the events that lead up to the denouement, driven by two female characters whose behavior pushes against the boundaries of prescribed gender performance. Ismenia and Matilde speak up and out as champions of their own desires and in their own best interest, while Federico is the inconstant lover who is incapable of making up his mind. They are not punished for their actions, but neither do they resolve the conflict in the way that one should expect given their character development over the course of the narrative. I have demonstrated those developments throughout my analysis of this work, and the conclusion prescriptively undermines the subversive force embodied by Ismenia and Matilde up to this point. Matilde gives her hand to Enrique in the final lines of the play, but it is important to note that she does so after rejecting the premise under which it was initially contracted—her father's will.[80] This constitutes a symbolic, yet subtle, rejection of the divine Logos when she rejects the proposal via the ambassador earlier in the play, reversed in the final scene. The compulsory ending of Matilde's contracted marriage to Enrique therefore is in tension with the development of her character throughout the play. In this sense, Figueroa y Córdoba's work seems to renege on the system of values that it sets up in the first three thousand verses of the play. This resolution comes across as more of a coda to the events that transpire, and the types of reactions the two female protagonists exhibit throughout. The tears in the fabric of the Baroque caused by the conflict are not darned particularly well, about which Connor elaborates in regard to the conventional *comedia* ending in general:

> To say that such conflicts are merely structures of the comic genre is to deny comedy's essential ambiguity, its paradoxical ability to explore the most intense subversions of the very society that constructs it and to then undo, in an order-restoring conclusion its own deconstruction of the dominant system, as if to say, 'just kidding.'[81]

In the end however, it is difficult to make a claim about the extent to which the "just kidding" in *La sirena de Tinacria* compromised or destabilized the integrity of ideology's artifice, or if contradictions in the play's finale really proves hegemony's dominance, misdirecting the gaze to obscure those contradictions. Another Arcadian myth from Ovid's *Metamorphoses* sheds light on this ambiguity so inherent in the *comedia*, and observed in *La sirena de Tinacria*. After Diana transforms Actaeon into a deer to be ripped apart by his own hounds, the narrative concludes with the following closure (or lack thereof):

> And gossip argued
> All up and down the land, and every which way;
> Some thought the goddess was too merciless
> And others praised her; maidenhood, they claimed,
> Deserved just such stern acts of reckoning,
> And both sides found good reasoning for their judgment.[82]

Comedia scholars are going to find good reasoning for the judgment of *La sirena de Tinacria* on either side of the critical interpretation of the play's finale. Is the conventional closure sufficient to maintain the ideologies it ostensibly celebrates? Probably so. But the play offers a striking display of female agency within the ideological matrices of the period; moreover, it is a play begging to be adapted and performed for audiences today. Both Matilde and Ismenia are decisive and influential, essentially two sides of the same coin, one the noble duchess and the other the Amazon. Raised in diametrically disparate locations—the court and the forest—both procure agency in the male-dominated society they inhabit. Through their performance of gender, the wild woman and the duchess of *La sirena de Tinacria* pull at the seams of the fabric of the cultural order to which they pertain. And even if their agency was only introduced into the space of representation to avow traditional gender norms in the end, by the 1670's, the dramatic conventions of the *comedia* start to give way to the competing demands of artistic innovation, a familiar repertoire of theatrical wildness, and ideological orthodoxy.

Cross-dressing as a form or misrecognition and disguise pervades theatrical production as an integral facet of the baroque dramatic aesthetic. In the plays analyzed above, it is not cross-dressing per se, but rather a form of animal drag that the wild protagonist put on in their roles as wild women. Still, the conservative closure of the plays treated in this chapter, which is true of most *comedias*, appears to remain as they remove their animal-skin cloaks and replace them with aristocratic dress corresponding to their social station. To decide what to make of the subversive or repressive energy of this transformation, Boyle's *Unruly Women* offers a balanced perspective to calibrate approaches to the wild women of the seventeenth-century theater. Boyle contends: "women stood at a complex intersection of pressing social preoccupations: the moral and pragmatic debates concerning the proper place and exemplary status of women; the regulation and staging of women's speech and bodies; and lastly, the economic and social interdependence between custodial institutions and public theatre as dramatic sites of rehabilitation."[83] By making sense of the wild women in the plays that I have analyzed in this chapter, I make no intention of binding them or diminishing their "unruly" status. I offer to illuminate their complexity, and allow them to exist in their particularity, while at the same time suggesting that there are common threads that run throughout the corpus here discussed. No longer subsumed under the blanket masculine term wild *man*, the wild women of the *comedia* gain a unique voice of their own, one that illuminates the study of gender performance in the *comedia*, and offers a more precise understanding of the ideological function of the genre, both as a containment apparatus of cultural control, and one where the oppositional ideologies it guards against threaten "to spill over into its container."[84]

Gender trouble manifests itself in numerous and complex ways in the Spanish *comedia*. One of the most common, as is true of disguise in the *comedia* in general, is cross-dressing, which includes the performance of characteristics that go beyond a simple change in wardrobe. The *comedia* dictates that the character's true and right nature lies at an essential level that is depicted in the resolution of each work; however, theater is a medium that also must contend with its own limits, lest it betray the theatricality at its core. At risk is revealing the notion that one's identity is merely another role being played by an actor or actress, and defined by "what he or she does, says, or wears" and not by who they "are."[85] Therefore, theater exemplifies Butler's assertion that at the fundamental level,

> gender is an identity tenuously constituted in time, instituted in an exterior space through a stylized repetition of acts.... These acts, gestures, enactments, generally construed, are performative in the sense that the essence or identity that they otherwise purport to express are fabrications manufactured and sustained through corporeal signs and other discursive means ... acts and gestures articulated and enacted desires create the

illusion of an interior and organizing gender core, an illusion discursively maintained.[86]

During the Baroque, theater becomes a site where this illusion is discursively maintained, where the interplay of appearance and reality sustains the organicism of a predetermined set of characteristics that define gender or social class. In spite of the heightened sense of performativity exalted in baroque cultural production, the poetics of *desengaño* reveal a truth that stabilizes performativity. However, because the reality revealed behind the veil of performance is itself another performance, the *comedia* must always contend with its own theatricality, and over the course of the Baroque, its conventions appear to be giving way under the weight of that purpose. As proof, those conventions would indeed ultimately give way in the following century to new aesthetics of cultural production in the service of hegemonic reproduction: Neoclassicism (followed by Romanticism, etc.).

A play that embodies this volatile essence at the heart of theater is the last *comedia* penned by Calderón de la Barca, *Hado y divisa de Leonido y Marfisa* (The Tokens of Fate of Leonido and Marfisa; 1680). The analysis that follows on the gender-bending female protagonist of the play also serves also as a transition to the chapter that follows, dedicated to representations of wildness in Calderón. The *comedia*'s obsession with appearance and reality promises to expose the artificial for what truly lies beneath, but in Calderón's works we see an acceptance of the contradiction that lies at the core of theatricality. In Calderón, that underlying layer of essential qualities beneath the deceptive world of appearances is acknowledged as yet another theatrical plane. However, where Cervantes responds with the minor strategy to reveal the empty space behind the curtain and subvert hegemony, Calderón's philosophical dramaturgy constitutes a middle strategy that accepts the theatrical limitations of *desengaño* and by extension the *comedia* as an ideological apparatus.[87] Moreover, his theater is critical of dominant ideologies, but only in as much as they were no longer tenable nor able to be reproduced through the same conventions of the *comedia*. Instead of disavowing the theatricality at the core of baroque *desengaño*, Calderón takes it as a given, and in so doing retools the *comedia* as a medium to bolster a weakened hegemony with more sustainable alternative ideologies in the political and social context of Habsburg Spain under Felipe IV and Carlos II. As an example, *Hado y divisa de Leonido y Marfisa* is an elaborate court play staged in March of 1680 that has clear political undertones that address the young Carlos II, and also features the wild woman Marfisa.[88] In many ways this play replicates the plot of *En la vida todo es verdad y todo mentira* (see analysis in Chapter 5), but the playwright replaces one of the male children with a female character, both the progeny of the king Casimiro. Casimiro leaves them in the forest to protect them from harm during a violent uprising, where the son, Leonido, is nursed by a lion until being found fortuitously by the Duke of Cantabria who takes him into his care. His twin sister, Marfisa, however is found by the wild man Argante to grow up living in a cave on the island of Sicily (Trinacria in the play).

Unlike Teodosia and Rosaura in Lope's *El animal de Hungría*, whose animal pelts become accidental drag when she is mistaken for a man, Marfisa's feminine identity is never misinterpreted as a result of her conventional wild woman appearance. She also never becomes the feared monster of the forest either, a convention of the character that diminishes over the course of seventeenth-century representation. In this play, the goal is not to reveal the humanity beneath the wild mask, but rather depict a character putting on a mask, and wearing it to successfully restore order, even if that requires dissimulation and transgressive gender performance. Gender hybridity is the marker of Rosaura's monstrous representation in *La vida es sueño*, but in *Hado y divisa de Leonido y Marfisa*, Marfisa's cross-dressing provides her access to power, which is required to resolve the play. Marfisa's success in passing as a man occurs because her behavior before donning Leonido's armor is more congruent with gender performance typically ascribed to traditional masculinity. Due to the fact that this cross-dressing episode takes place in the final scene of the play, the audience never sees any other behavior from Marfisa than those typical of the wild character at the beginning of other plays within this corpus. She goes through no process of acculturation, and the only clothes we see her wear are androgynous animal pelts and the masculine armor belonging to her brother. At no point is she chastised for behaving in a way that is dissonant to her gender, nor provided a cultural education like Linda of *La lindona de Galicia* or Ismenia of *La sirena de Tinacria*. Rather, it is her decision to fight for the honor of her brother by pretending to be him, through which she restores both herself and Leonido to their royal lineage. At different moments being either timid or brash, Leonido fails to accomplish his two main goals: to restore his name and to win the hand of Arminda. First, he overcompensates for being called a coward by hatching a plan that fails so badly it leads to the death of his servant. Incapable of achieving his own desires, Marfisa stands in as his substitute, ready to duel for her brother's honor, and as a result liberates herself as well. From her first appearance in act 1 of the play, she expresses her desire to escape the cave (labeled by Quintero as a feminine space) where her surrogate father has kept her sequestered her entire life.[89] *Hado y divisa de Leonido y Marfisa* leaves little to no space for prescribed gender norms, and an abundance of liberty for Marfisa to perform gender traits traditionally ascribed to men, and what is more, performs the role not only without correction, but in order to restore her brother's honor and her own, which includes the resolution to the conflict of the plot. In this particular play, it is not that her wildness requires erasure, but rather the wildness—her wildness and the play's—that resists its container (or cave) to be the agent of restoring a cultural order in disarray.

CHAPTER 5

Exceptional Wildness in the Skeptical Theater of Calderón de la Barca

> The prison doesn't fail to produce delinquents.
> —Michel Foucault

> Dreams of reason create monsters.
> —Francisco de Goya

ALONE AND LOCKED AWAY in his tower, Segismundo weeps the tears of an abandoned son. This is our first glimpse of one of the most iconic characters in all of the *comedia*, the protagonist of Pedro Calderón de la Barca's masterpiece, *La vida es sueño*. Well-known to Spanish theater enthusiasts and extensively studied in scholarship, Segismundo has attained a certain singularity, immediately identifiable by a now irreducible set of visual markers: he first appears alone, chained inside a solitary tower, and wearing animal pelts (the ubiquitous *vestido de pieles* of the wild figure). In fact, the tower and the animal-skinned cloak are aspects of this depiction that are essential to making Segismundo both unique and recognizable. The poetic logic of the character's animal pelts is patent; plenty of ink has been spent analyzing the symmetry between this exterior appearance and his inner psychological state: he is half man, half beast, prone to violent fits of passion, yet also capable of delivering monologues with the finesse of a master poet and the depth of an existential philosopher. Nevertheless, Segismundo's representation as the hirsute prince in the tower has become so iconic, we have come to overlook that these visual elements make little sense in the otherwise realistic depiction of character and wardrobe in *La vida es sueño*.

Typically, wild men reside in the forest, which is a stable convention in the poetic, folkloric, literary, dramatic, and more recently, cryptozoological history of the type. Whereas Segismundo's tower is secluded and away from court, it is markedly distinct from the natural landscape that surrounds it. Moreover, we have little reason to accept on its face that the protagonist would be supplied with animal pelts, over more normal clothes. Presumably all of his provisions are supplied by Clotaldo, the courtier who has been assigned as Segismundo's caretaker by his father Basilio, king of Poland. Returning to this basic point that the juxtaposition of the tower and the animal skins creates a visual dissonance, it stands to further the complexities of the poetic logic of this opening depiction of the protagonist. Chiefly, this scene makes more sense poetically by situating Segismundo within the repertoire of wild figures of the *comedia*, which, as I have outlined, was well established by the composition of *La vida es sueño* in the late 1620s.[1] In fact, the popularity of the theatrical wild figure by this point requires further attention to consider how Segismundo fits into this tradition, which is a question of repertoire, but also of reception. Although Golden Age scholars have effectively parsed out the symbolic complexities of the animal pelts worn by Segismundo as an outward reflection of his inner psychological state, the extent to which those complexities are conveyed to a live audience (then or now) bears asking. To that end, it also changes the way we imagine theatergoers' response to Calderón's character when he first appears onstage during the original staging in 1635. Segismundo does draw ample attention to his own hybridity in the spoken verse (i.e., he articulates himself as part man, part beast, which is reflected in the costume design), but the audience, playwright (*poeta*), and director (*autor de comedias*) start from a different point of departure in the production and reception of meaning when it can be expected that the animal skins will make Segismundo immediately recognizable as a wild man derived from the ones they had seen portrayed previously on the *comedia* stage.

This last point is fundamental to the aspects of the work that are opened up by contextualizing Segismundo within the baroque repertoire of theatrical wildness more explicitly. Calderón's wild man is in direct conversation with pre-existing repertoires, knowledge of which provides access to consider how his wild man replicates those conventions, as well as the ways the playwright molds Segismundo to make him his own. As a result, new insights into the hybridity signified by the tower/animal pelts dichotomy come into focus, which also contextualize Segismundo's exceptional wildness with relation to the *comedia*'s wild figure subgenre. The character merits inclusion in the corpus examined in this book not because he is emblematic or quintessential, but rather exceptional, an outlier to the conventions of the subgenre. It may be unsurprising to those familiar with Calderón that *his* wild man would stand out, but this approach sheds light on some of the meaningful ways the playwright swerves from conventions with ingenious effect. My main contention is that Segismundo is a character who goes through a process of transformation (i.e., from savage to civilized), which constitutes both a process of learning restraint (or more precisely, self regulation) and coping with existential doubt. I will then situate Segismundo among Calderón's other wild figures in *En la vida todo es verdad y todo mentira* (1659), contrasting them with notable influences such as Mira de Amescua's *La rueda de la fortuna* (1603). As can be seen in the dates of those plays (and along with his final *comedia*, *Hado y divisa de Leonido y Marfisa* in 1680), the playwright returns to the concept of wildness for inspiration at moments near the beginning, middle, and then again at the end of his career, which offers a symmetry to the plays examined here.

Scholarship has traced the marked evidence of the influence of the wild man tradition on Calderón de la Barca's drama, especially as it relates to Segismundo in *La vida es sueño*.[2] Deyermond primarily considers folkloric sources as influences, describing Segismundo as a "standard wild man of the medieval tradition" in his "setting, dwelling, and clothes," but distinguishes Calderón's protagonist in one significant way.[3] Segismundo does not choose to deny society for a life in the forest, but rather this life is forced upon him, and he is even worse than the wild characters raised by wild animals because he still receives a courtly education that makes him conscious of "the restraint on his liberty."[4] According to Deyermond, this ultimately makes him a more dangerous wild man because he develops animosity against those who have kept him chained. Whereas Deyermond compares Segismundo to the iconographic and literary wild figures of the medieval period, Antonucci notes the importance of situating Calderón's Segismundo in a theatrical genealogy of the type "in the sense that his character and its trajectory in *Life Is a Dream* is constructed through staging that derives from the theatrical tradition of the wild man."[5] Antonucci enumerates the characteristics that Segismundo shares with the wild figure of the baroque Spanish stage, which include his wearing of animal pelts, instinctual aggression, the instigation of new feelings that arise from encountering someone of the opposite sex for the first time, the tutor character, and a rebellion against a father figure that ends in victory for the wild character and her/his ultimate recuperation of their rightful role as successor to a seat of power.[6] This list also serves as a useful tool to consolidate the constituent elements of the repertoire of wildness overall, from which dramatists are drawing from in the composition of their wild figure *comedias*. Rather than provide an exhaustive treatment of the wild man in Calderón, Antonucci articulates the explicit objective of her treatment of wildness in the playwright's drama to demonstrate that the wild figure continued to be influential for playwrights after Lope de Vega.[7] In what follows, I also cannot claim to explore the theme exhaustively, but I do offer an analysis of examples of the character in Calderón's corpus that further situates the wild figure within that theatrical lineage, and how it develops within the corpus of the dramatist over the course of his career.[8]

The locus of my deviation from Antonucci's assessment of the wild figure in earlier playwrights is precisely where our perspectives coincide regarding the aspect of Segismundo's character that renders him exceptional in a theatrical history of wildness on the stage of the Spanish Baroque. Chiefly, we *do* observe a transformation in Segismundo that I argued was secondary or non-existent in Lope de Vega's wild figures. Whereas Lope's plays are more concerned with the eventual revelation of the identity of the wild figure rather than their development from a state of wildness to civilized, Calderón emphasizes character development, which constitutes a significant shift. The poetics of revelation that resolve his wild figure plays depict a metaphorical space just behind the animal skins (i.e., the wild mask) that can be accessed and then relied upon to establish order and constitute the subjects within that order. This organization of space in Lope's theatrical poetics suggests a greater ability to disavow epistemological instability inherent to the constitutive limitations of the theatrical mode. Even if, as I argue in Chapter 2 of this study, that revelation opens up just another theatrical space to present the ideological as if it were real, it reflects a belief in the ability to access the truth within the baroque politics of space that emphasize artifice and reality, surface and depth. Calderón, on the other hand, shifts focus to the character as a result of an exacerbated consciousness of that organization of space whereby the world of appearances has been further cut off from the reality that is supposed to be behind it. It is a world that not only permits the evolution of the wild protagonist but in fact requires it in order to overcome the trauma of being cut off from the divine Logos.[9] This trauma is presented as twofold in the case of Segismundo. First, he must learn to cope with the Father's rejection, and second, the existential crisis represented in the unresolved question of whether he is dreaming or awake.[10] Unmoored by these traumas through the end of the second act, he ultimately achieves a functional skepticism that grounds the stability of his sense of self and ethical commitments, even though Truth remains inaccessible behind a curtain (now full of Deleuzian folds) that theatrical representation (and by extension representation itself, i.e., the Symbolic) can no longer provide access. According to Vitse, Calderón's heroes are "all children and all confronted with the silence, the abdication, or the aggression of their parents; these heroes at the twilight of Divinity formulate for us the first response to our modern tragedy as humans cut off from God."[11] In the analysis that follows I will demonstrate this preoccupation with theatrical space as a salient feature of Calderón's wild figure plays, and the significance of this swerve by the playwright from earlier iterations of the type. As a result of the ambiguity at the end of these plays, I will propose we reconsider the "aristocratic heroism" depicted in the protagonists' character development to observe individuals learning to cope (with various degrees of success) in a world where modes of representation (and therefore modes of being) no longer provide reliable access to metaphysical truths.[12]

OF TOWERS AND BEASTS: HYBRID CONTRADICTIONS IN *LA VIDA ES SUEÑO*

I will further examine Rosaura in this section, but her lines that open *La vida es sueño* convey a sense of contradictory hybridity that parallels the poetic dimensions of Segismundo depicted in animal skins imprisoned in the tower I began to introduce earlier. Like Rosaura's description of her horse as a "violent hippogryph" (*violento hipogrifo*), the two iconic elements of Segismundo's first appearance onstage—the tower and fur pelts—are out of place together; more precisely, they form a hybrid contradiction. Moreover, they add another layer to the hybrid contradiction signified by Segismundo as man/beast, crafted along the lines of interior/ exterior. His wild outward appearance reflects his inner psychological state, but also represents a hybrid contradiction of a wild exterior appearance that betrays the human beneath the animal pelts. Segismundo indeed exemplifies the inherent contradiction in the term *Wildman* itself. The tower, then, forms yet another of these hybrid contradictions both within it and outside it. Materially and figuratively embedded in the prison built by Basilio are the contrivances of modern civilization. It is a manmade edifice, constructed to imprison Segismundo for the purposes of reason of state (however misguided) to avoid his suspected tyrannical rule that would endanger social order. Within the tower, he is constantly surveilled by Clotaldo, who also is charged with his intellectual and social formation (i.e., civilizing him). The tower becomes the site and symbol of the control imposed on the subject, and the power that enforces it. This visual and spatial organization bears the hallmarks of the modern sequestration of social delinquents through penal justice, in this case despotically applied, for Segismundo's only crime was "being born."[13] The civilized and civilizing tower that contains the wild man (or as I will argue, may well produce him) is a hybrid contradiction, a beacon of civilization that requires violence to maintain itself, and that it disavows by placing that violence out of sight and locking it shut.[14] Within the hybrid contradiction of the tower (i.e., civilized/violent) resides another; it is a type of Russian doll with Segismundo the wild man at the center. And there is also one further exterior layer, the tower situated in the natural landscape described by Rosaura in the opening scene in terms that reflect the tension I have thus described, as a rustic palace amongst the craggy topography: "Amongst the bald crags lies (*yacer*) a rustic palace."[15]

The tower is conceptualized in the play-text as this hybrid contradiction on other occasions too, most notably in its depiction by Segismundo as a cradle and a grave, "cradle and tomb," which parallels the way his father Basilio describes the womb of his mother Clorilene, who died giving birth to Segismundo: "she would give him that living tomb that was her womb."[16] This verse appears in a more extended conceit that juxtaposes life and death paradoxically to portray Segismundo's birth and Clorilene's death as simultaneous events that produced the "monster in the form of man."[17] Bárbara Mujica notes this connection, describing "the womb-coffin that the tower signifies."[18] With these explicit parallels in poetic language that situate Segismundo in the space of a living coffin, Calderón gestures toward the idea of the tower as womb, but once again turns away from it to create yet another aspect of its increasingly complex and multi-faceted portrayal as a hybrid contradiction. Whereas his mother's womb was a type of coffin, the tower is a different type. The feminine space of the womb is replaced with the masculine space of the phallic tower, which links it more closely to the patriarchal violence of Basilio, whose agency is behind the psychological suffering experienced by Segismundo in the phallus-coffin of the father's design. Turning again to the repertoire of wild representation on the baroque stage, it is also important to note that Segismundo is the first and only wild figure to appear in a tower. In *comedias* both before and after *La vida es sueño*, if a space is referenced as the forest abode of the pelt-wearing wild figure, it is invariably described as a grotto or a cave. Again Calderón draws our attention to this convention when Rosaura nearly cites Góngora's *Polifemo* to describe the entrance to the tower: "The door /—more like a horrible mouth, actually— / is open."[19] Góngora, who draws from the repertoire of the wild figure in his portrayal of Polyphemus, also paints the imagery of "horrible mouth" as the opening to the giant cyclops's home, but it is a cavernous and grotesque grotto. So Rosaura's allusion in *La vida es sueño* gives us a point of reference to a space where we would normally find a cave or a grotto, but in this case it is replaced with the tower, thereby making the meaning produced by the tower a site of contention rather than convention. In the traditional depiction of nature as feminine, the cavern as womb more directly reflects the symbolic spatiality of the feminine maternal, but Calderón diverges from the repertoire when he places his wild man in the tower—a prison where there was once a home and a phallus where there once was a womb. Considering Segismundo in the context of the wild figure repertoire therefore illuminates our interpretation of the overtly masculine and paternal violence conveyed by the tower as an existential and literal prison, a coffin of despair in the face of the absent Father/Logos. Itself a hybrid contradiction, the tower begets hybrid contradictions; as the device that defines the embodiment of conflict (i.e., Segismundo and Rosaura) and the one that generates it, the ending of the play refers back to the tower in such a way that allows us to evaluate the mechanisms that transform Segismundo and Rosaura from hybrid contradictions into the aristocratic roles they play in the end, but also the vestiges of violence required to "harmonize" those contradictions and allow them to assume their "rightful" role. In the analysis that follows, I will offer examples of this conflict, but also posit a new methodology for reading Calderonian *comedias*. Rather than assume that the plot will be fully resolved, from which we can derive conclusions about the ideological commitments that underpin such a resolution and make it satisfactory, I posit a more ambiguous Calderón that never entirely points to an inalienable truth behind the veil. Instead, his plays rely on *desengaño* to guide the audience to a satisfaction in partial closure produced because of (and not in spite of) an acknowledgment of the limits of the conventions of theatrical representation, and by extension the limitations of human perception itself. Calderón's characters that learn to cope in a world defined by irresolvable contingencies and existential doubt are the ones that manage a fortunate conclusion, while those who demand certainty but inevitably find it beyond their grasp tend to either meet tragic ends themselves or cause them for others.

In order to arrive at this conclusion, it first requires a closer examination of the dual conflicts that make up the plot of *La vida es sueño*, starting with Rosaura, whose opening lines inaugurate the conceit developed around hybrid contradictions advanced over the course of the work. Rosaura's invective goes beyond the first verse noted earlier, which is aimed at the horse that has just thrown her:

> You headlong hippogriff
> who matches the gale in rushing to and fro,
> you lightning-bolt
> without a flash,
> you dull-plumed bird, you scaleless fish,
> you beast without natural instinct,
> tell me where
> you lead me stumbling through this labyrinth
> of naked crags![20]

De Armas notes the inability to control one's horse as a reflection of an inner nature unable to control one's passions, linking her state to that of Segismundo at the beginning of the play.[21] A number of scholars have analyzed the relation of the hippogryph imagery of the initial scene with monstrosity. González Echevarría clearly states that the mention of the hippogryph inaugurates Calderón's "monstrous art."[22] Küpper elaborates on this notion, contending that the hippogryph functions as a "projection" of Rosaura's inner self—a hybrid being who transgresses her place in "the great chain of being."[23] Importantly, Rosaura has arrived at this state of conflict-producing hybrid contradiction not as a result of her own wrongdoing, but rather of her abandonment both by her father, Clotaldo and her betrothed, Astolfo. Clotaldo's own assessment admits that the question of honor is precarious, and that Rosaura's arrival to avenge the affront against her is righteous:

> But if an affront has already
> transpired, and nobody
> divulged it—since honor
> is of such a fragile material
> that with just one action it shatters
> or is stained by a breeze—
> what more can you do, what more
> can one who is noble, for their part,
> at the cost of so many risks
> come to look for him?[24]

In Clotaldo's words, the loss of honor is a matter for which one does not maintain all of the culpability, but rather can often hang in the balance of the actions of another. If that is the case for the stranger who has just arrived from Moscovia (he has noticed that Rosaura has his sword, and therefore must be his son, as Rosaura is still disguised as a man), then the same reality extends to Rosaura's situation as well. The dramatic irony of this scene produced by Rosaura's successful male disguise begs the question about whether Clotaldo would have the same response if Rosaura were not successfully passing as a man and leveraging the social capital it affords. As a consequence, a double standard is presented in a way that may not destabilize ideologies of honor on its own, but is reinforced dramatically by invoking pity for the character standing before Clotaldo (and not scorn). The dramatic irony of the scene—the tension between him treating her as if she were a man, while the audience knows that she is not—creates a scenario where the logic of Clotaldo's remarks are rendered affectively charged to apply to Rosaura, regardless of her gender.

The poetics of baroque theatrical wildness help explain the nature of Rosaura's monstrosity as presented in *La vida es sueño*. She is of the same ilk as the other perceived monsters in Spanish drama, who are often wild men or women. *Her* transgressions do not result in her becoming a monster; rather, the transgressions of others—principally Astolfo and Clotaldo—monstrify her; they turn her into a hybrid contradiction. Abandoned by father and betrothed, Rosaura's identity fragments into competing identities. The symptoms of that fragmentation are rendered dramatically through hybrid visual and poetic metaphors that portray her as monstrous. And the resolution to the affront against her honor is matched poetically in the play by resolving the expressed hybrid contradictions that constitute her monstrosity. Foucault's definition of the monster applies:

> From the Middle Ages to the eighteenth century, . . . the monster is essentially a mixture. It is the mixture of two realms, the animal and the human. . . . It is the blending, the mixture of two species. . . . It is the mixture of two individuals. . . . It is the mixture of two sexes. . . . It is a mixture of life and death. . . . Finally, it is a mixture of forms.[25]

In baroque theater, we see these mixtures—of species, of sexes, and of forms—dramatized frequently, and dramatized with particular intensity in *La vida es sueño*, where physiological traits take on the nature of metaphor. Rosaura inaugurates this aspect of the work, as she exudes that "mixture"—and thus her monstrosity. By calling her horse a hippogryph—a creature defined by the combination of horse and gryphon (itself a mixture of lion and eagle)—Rosaura projects herself onto the beast in a way that reflects her character throughout the play.[26] Rosaura's representation oscillates between male and female, a hybrid contradiction that is not resolved until the end, and for which Rosaura verbalizes its monstrous effect: "being / a monster of two species, among these feminine fineries / masculine weapons adorn me."[27] Mixture defines her in other moments as well, the result of which renders her immobile and formless: "I am an immoveable shape (*bulto*) of fire and ice."[28] These words play on the expectation of a poetic conceit that conventionally serves to describe the inaccessibility—and sometimes cruelty—of beauty. In contrast, Rosaura is the opposite of this ideal form, an indeterminate shape, or maybe more precisely, "mass." Derrida offers a complementary definition to Foucault's hybrid as that which is formless, and therefore unrecognizable. This interplay of hybridity and amorphism define Rosaura throughout *La vida es sueño*, or rather, render her beyond definition; therefore, she remains unrecognizable both to herself and to the other characters so long as she is forced to perform hybridity contrary to her will.

When she begins to relate her story to Segismundo in act 1, Clotaldo enters the stage and interrupts her just as she is only able to speak two words: "I am . . ."[29] This ellipsis spans the entirety of the work until she has the opportunity to recount the details of her story to Segismundo in act 3, who appears to disregard everything she has said and rejects her help. He responds in this manner in order to attain the throne, which her story encourages him to accomplish more hastily with the second impetus to arrange her marriage to Astolfo and thus restore her honor. Up to this point, it is her loss of honor that keeps her from fulfilling her social role (the famous *soy quien soy* [I am who I am]), which compounds on itself as she is continually forced to play a series of transgressive roles that go against her nature and keep her from being able to finish the sentence to articulate who she *is*.[30] As a result, she becomes a fragmented, hybrid being whose very life is at stake, implied when she mistakenly places her faith in her father, Clotaldo: "and I trust Clotaldo's intentions, / for I owe him gratitude / for my honor and life."[31] This line is stated before she learns he is her father who had abandoned her mother, because he continues to withhold that information from her, about which there are two possible interpretations. In the first option, he is being prudent and discrete in handling the contingencies of the scenario and waiting for the right moment to ensure Rosaura's honor is restored. Alternatively, he is acting out of his own self-interest and preservation. I find more textual evidence for this latter option. At the end of act 1, when he still thinks Rosaura is a man, Clotaldo learns that Rosaura's affront is with Astolfo.[32] He erroneously assumes no affront has occurred because Astolfo, a duke, cannot dishonor someone below his station, like the male commoner Rosaura has disguised herself as. Relieved, Clotaldo is quick to advise her to return home, fully willing to send her away without revealing himself as her father nor her noble status.[33] So she is technically accurate that Clotaldo holds the key to her restored honor, but does not realize at this point that it is out of necessity, and at a moment when it remains suspect that her faith in Clotaldo is merited. But in this moment, we observe the precarity of her situation when her only hope lies at the whim of a self-interested and absent father rather than a sense that paternal figures will be faithful stewards of their authority and carry out their responsibility to their children's safety. With her honor at risk, and therefore her life at stake, she remains Foucault's monster as a mixture of life and death provided the potential for either constitutes her being and hangs in the balance of Clotaldo's (in)constancy.

As sixteenth- and seventeenth-century treatises explicitly note, monsters by definition were bereft of humanity. In *La vida es sueño*, it is not a physiological trait that monstrifies Rosaura, that deprives her of human life, but rather the affront to her honor. Life and honor are the axes upon which her monstrosity revolves, without which her sense of self and outward portrayal thereof remains hybrid and contrary to her aristocratic identity. In the conventional ending of *La vida es sueño*—if read as such—Rosaura's honor is restored once she is acknowledged by her father and betrothed to Astolfo. Ultimately, she fails to exercise agency over her own restoration; that task belongs to Segismundo, and her conclusion is riddled with ambiguity. On the one hand, she petitions Segismundo to "impedir y deshacer" (impede and undo) Astolfo from marrying Estrella, about which a conservative interpretation would assume that she also desires to marry him in order to recuperate her honor. On the other, the text of the play never explicitly demonstrates that Rosaura is keen to see such an outcome come to pass. In her plea to Segismundo, Rosaura is enjoined to carry out vengeance alongside him with sword drawn. Given that she only appeals for the obstruction of the marriage between Astolfo and Estrella, is it safe to assume that she yearns to marry the man who abandoned her? Is the closure at the end affirming of the ideologies that produce it, or, like Cervantes in *La fuerza de la sangre*, are those ideologies extended poetically to their untenable emotional and logical breaking point? The answer is debated in scholarship. According to Dian Fox, both Clotaldo and Astolfo only agree to honor their responsibilities once they no longer have the option to pursue their own personal gain, where Clotaldo "is so bent on preserving his reputation that, were circumstances less satisfying, he would probably continue to withhold recognition from his daughter" and Astolfo's refusal to marry someone beneath his station clearly shows that he "originally gave his word to Rosaura fully intending to break it."[34] Furthermore, the final lines of the play fail to provide convincing closure to the conflict, and their meaning can entirely depend on the manner in which they are delivered. After the enthroned Segismundo sends the soldier to the tower, his father responds, "your ingenuity astonishes everyone."[35] The baroque poetics of *admiratio* suggest a more conflicted and ambiguous reaction than mere admiration, which is obscured by a modern use or direct translation of *admirar*. This ambivalence continues in the following responses by both Astolfo and Rosaura, respectively:

> ASTOLFO: "What a change in state!"
> ROSAURA: "How discreet and prudent!"[36]

And Segismundo then offers a key to reading their responses in this way when he wonders why they appear so surprised: "What's so astonishing?

What has you so startled?"[37] It therefore remains unclear the extent to which Rosaura's monstrosity is adequately dealt with in *La vida es sueño*. According to Ruth El Saffar, Rosaura and her mother Violante remain conflictive undercurrents whose disruptive agency is never resolved in *La vida es sueño*.[38] But if understood conventionally, her betrothal to Astolfo and her father's acknowledgment of his paternity restore her honor and erase the behaviors and characteristics that monstrify her throughout the play; however, in Calderonian fashion, simply too much ambiguity remains at the end of the playwright's masterpiece to assume such a tidy and orthodox resolution to the conflict.

Segismundo's character development from monster to prince occurs similarly to that of Rosaura, which may be expected given their parallels as "victims of paternal injustice."[39] Even though the wild character helps make sense of Rosaura's character, she is not properly a wild woman. When Segismundo first appears in animal pelts, however, there is no mistaking the connection to the wild figure of the Spanish *comedia*. Like Rosaura and the wild characters before him, the monstrification of Segismundo is something enacted upon him—his imprisonment in the tower—rather than an act or behavior that would define him as such. He eventually lives up to his reputation, unlike many of the wild figures before him, but the play puts into question whether his violent behavior and sexual appetite are predetermined by fate (if we, like Basilio, believe Clorilene's prophetic dream) or conditioned by the shackles that bind Segismundo to the tower away from civilization that make his wildness a self-fulfilling prophecy. Mujica offers a compelling argument that the play depicts Segismundo's personal trajectory defined by his ability to overcome his fits of passion and rage not only to display Neostoic self-restraint but also to take personal responsibility for his actions.[40] Moreover, as Deyermond aptly notes, Segismundo does not choose a life secluded from human contact, but rather has this life violently foisted upon him.[41] As should be clear by now, this element roots him firmly in the wild figure tradition of children abandoned at birth, which precipitates a heightened sense of anxiety about the nature of his identity that he, like earlier iterations of the type, clearly articulates. Unlike previous examples however, his existential doubt grounded in the rejection of the father is critical to his character trajectory in *La vida es sueño* in ways that are less developed in previous examples. Whereas Rosaura's self-knowledge is defined by doubt and apprehension, structurally mirrored in the play by the two-act ellipses of her inability to complete the phrase,

"I am . . ."[42], Segismundo demonstrates certainty about his identity, even if it is a tragic certainty. His anxiety reaches the point of delusion—that is, circumstances lead him to distort his perception of reality—when he declares himself a monster, precisely due to his self-identification as a mixture of forms:

> Although I may be in this state,
> I am not obligated to you,
> and I can demand that you account
> for the time you've stolen from me,
> liberty, life, and honor
> . . .
> and I know what I am—
> a composite of man and beast.[43]

This is the most assured, yet laden with anxiety, statement of any character about their place in the order of things seen thus far in the wild figure *comedia* corpus. Segismundo *knows* that his nature, his very being, is bifurcated, a monstrous mixture of man and beast. The result strips him of his honor, that in this baroque context, is equivalent to his humanity, and life itself. His father, the king, and therefore arbiter of meaning, creates the monster in the tower; he too is a monster and both monsters must be eliminated or transformed for the conflictive sequence to be resolved. This inner conflict in the protagonist can also be understood as a Foucauldian mixture of life and death, which is evident from Segismundo's first lines:

> with me here,
> I know so little of the world
> that cradle and tomb
> this tower has been for me
> . . .
> I only behold
> this rustic desert
> where I, miserable, live,
> being a living skeleton,
> being an animate corpse.[44]

This mixture of animal and beast, life and death, has been interpreted in various ways. De Armas makes the comparison of Segismundo to a lion in the opening scene, whose relation to the tale of Hercules situates him within the pantheon of myth. While I do not dispute the mythological aspects of the play uncovered by de Armas, Segismundo's appearance in relation to the lion places him in the wild figure literary tradition as well. Aside from the Leonido of *El hijo de los leones*, Calderón creates two of his own wild Leonido characters, the first in *En la vida todo es verdad y todo mentira*, and later in his final comedia, *Hado y divisa de Leonido y Marfisa*. So, although the connection between Hercules and lions is a valid one, it is infused in the literary genealogy of the plays of this corpus also.

De Armas unpacks this theme even more by identifying the inherent unbalanced nature of the lion: Segismundo "he should be king, but first must repress, as a human, the excesses of the lion."[45] De Armas also gives a lengthy description of Galenic imbalance within the protagonist, noting Segismundo's speech when he describes his bondage in relation to the four elements: bird/air (1. 133), beast/land (l. 133), fish/water (l. 143) and Mt. Etna/fire (l. 164). His description of the fish and volcano demonstrates imbalance, alluding to the well-worn metaphor of the trickle that becomes an ocean, along with the explosive nature of the volcano, each indicating an excess of sadness and misfortune (water) and choler (fire).[46] This analysis sheds light on the mythological aspects of Segismundo, but also points to the representation of his character as a hybrid contradiction, that is, monster. Both Derrida's and Foucault's definitions of the concept apply here as well. The protagonist's humoral imbalance creates the image of an entity whose borders and boundaries are not where they should be, which, according to Río Parra's research cited in Chapter 2, bears repeating here. She demonstrates that early modern treatises on the topic consider the monstrous as an ideological perversion of the normal: "The monstrous, in the end is read as a hypostatic form against the norm and in it we decipher the enigmas that disturb the always precarious balance of normality."[47] Imbalance, mixture, and amorphism define Segismundo's monstrosity within the framework of the early modern conception of the term, within which Calderón's portrayal develops the character specifically through the poetic conceit of hybrid contradictions that persist until they are resolved once Segismundo's assumes his rightful place as prince of Poland after transforming into the idealized prudent figure of the monarch. Or does he?

Cultural transgression creates a breach in the Baroque, out of which the monster is born. It is then required that it be sufficiently dealt with and that breach be closed satisfactorily. Essential to the conflict in *La vida es sueño*, identities dissolve into multiple forms that are contrary to their nature. Segismundo becomes a man-beast hybrid while Rosaura's hippogryph (literally, her horse) is a hybrid projection of the inarticulable self (when she cannot finish the sentence "I am . . ." in act 1 of the play). In regard to Segismundo, the method by which his monstrous qualities are erased, however, is not through anagnorisis, as is the case in every other wild play during this period, but rather through transformation. This facet of the work is yet another indication of its exceptional nature, that is also significant to the play's complexity, if not equally problematic to its interpretation. As I mentioned, the conclusion of the work poses as many problems as it does provide a satisfactory conventional resolution to the conflict. While I previously treated the characters' responses to Segismundo's edicts to restore order, here I will examine his actions themselves. In particular, the return of the soldier to the tower has always perplexed readers of the play, and has captivated critics since Parker's comments encouraged further attention to the closing scene. It remains true that we "are impelled to ask what it means" forty years later, as critics continue to debate its interpretation.[48] In *La vida es sueño*, what do we make of the imprisoned soldier? His return to the tower is more than a scar left from the suture of baroque order; he is a new monster of culture created before the wound can be stitched, and the play ends where it began, with another prisoner in the tower.[49]

Parker notes this "circular structure" of *La vida es sueño*, contending that the scene dramatizes the breakdown of the allegory of Segismundo as a Christ figure who restores order, and acknowledges the "cosmic guilt incurred by mankind" whose "greatest crime is being born."[50] Cascardi more specifically describes the political element of this problematic ending as the "inability of absolute power to conceal its violent origins."[51] Greer develops the theses of both critics compellingly, even if, as she concedes, Parker "probably would have rejected" the conclusions she reaches in the process.[52] Greer views the parallel between Rosaura and Segismundo in their concomitant pursuits of justice (Rosaura) and power (Segismundo). Drawing comparisons from Calderón's contemporary Pascal, Greer contends that the Spanish dramatist constructs a dichotomy between earthly and divine justice, for which the former will inevitably be flawed. Unlike the ending of Calderón's *auto sacramental* with the same title in which the presentation of the eucharist "can be figured as a perfectly innocent and voluntary sacrifice in payment of an infinite guilt," the *comedia La vida es sueño* presents "the contingent and impure world of human experience."[53] As a result, the conclusion of Calderón's *comedia* "consists of a partially justified rebellion paid for [by the soldier] involuntarily, at the mandate of power. In such circumstances, the union of absolute power and perfect justice is an *hipogrifo* whom no one can master."[54] One conflict is resolved, but only for another to remain: the ultimate problem of history, conflict itself. The "resolution" presented within the play's final lines exemplifies the dividing line among scholars to interpret the *comedia* as a purely ideological genre or one capable of subversive ends. I maintain a view here of a Calderón that offers an ideological middle ground, one that acknowledges the violence and contingencies of civilized order, but rather than subvert or resist them, offer consolations for how to best navigate them. The conclusion of *La vida es sueño* signals the inability of ideology to satisfy its own promise of completion and enclosure, but then offers a model for proceeding despite existential uncertainty and political contingency, however imperfect but acceptable. To an even greater degree, a later play in Calderón's oeuvre, *En la vida todo es verdad y todo mentira* portrays dominant political ideologies on monarchical authority as a fantasy, while offering a pragmatic and available alternative that does not require exploding the status quo.

HUNTING FOR THE SECRETS OF NATURE IN *EN LA VIDA TODO ES VERDAD Y TODO MENTIRA*

Later in his career, Calderón would return to the wild figure repertoire in his *comedia*, *En la vida todo es verdad y todo mentira* (1659). As the title implies, the skeptical premise of *En la vida* echoes that of *La vida es sueño*. The link between the two works is further evinced by the wild figures featured in the later play. However, the singular wild figure in *La vida es sueño* proliferates in *En la vida todo es verdad y todo mentira*. What was one in the earlier *comedia* multiplies into three: Focas, now emperor, was raised by wolves in the forest, and the two wild man protagonists, Eraclio and Leonido, who emerge from their cave in the forest when we meet them in act 1. Conventional to the genre, they have been raised by a surrogate father, in this case the hermit Astolfo. When Calderón returns to the repertoire of wildness, innovation requires variation from previous iterations of the wild figure type, even within his own dramatic corpus (i.e., Segismundo). In reviving the wild figure in *En la vida*, repetition also constitutes a duplication—literally—a wild multiplier effect by which the transgression of Focas in the usurpation of the imperial throne of Constantinople begets even more wildness in the form of two wild figures: Eraclio and Leonido. Their wildness becomes the major problem of the play, and in this instance, Calderón relies on the convention of mistaken identity (rather than personal transformation) as the motor of conflict to be resolved through anagnorisis of the true identities of the wild protagonists. We learn in the exposition that one of them is the heir to the throne of Constantinople (we do not know which one), although it remains doubly ambiguous which of the two has legitimate claim to the throne, because the play withholds that information. First, it is only made known that one of the two is the son of the emperor Focas, while the other belongs to Mauricio, the previous emperor usurped by Focas approximately twenty years before the opening of the play. In addition to their uncertain paternity, a further question emerges regarding right to rule; Focas seeks to identify his successor, but as Focas is a usurper, Mauricio's heir maintains a claim to the imperial throne—one that Focas wishes to stamp out by also finding and killing his predecessor's son. However, when Calderón unleashes wildness again in *En la vida*, its tendency to get away from its author and resist the ideological fantasy of completeness is less evident in the ending of this play; rather, Calderón taps into the unruly force of wildness precisely to accept that certain ideological paradigms (in this case related to monarchical authority and succession) were no longer sustainable, while also offering a pragmatic response to a world where notions of truth and falsehood are no longer stable categories.

While both *La vida es sueño* and *En la vida* present a worldview defined by its pragmatic skepticism as a response to existential doubt, the later play is also heavily influenced by Mira de Amescua's *La rueda de la fortuna* (1603). In fact, it should be considered a rewriting of Amescua's earlier wild figure *comedia*. Their historical settings coincide, both loosely following the bloody transition of power of Byzantine Constantinople from the emperor Maurice (582–602 CE) to Phocas (602–610 CE), and then ultimately to the subsequent emperor, Heraclius (610–641 CE). These historical narratives inspire the plot of both *comedias*, and even though *La rueda de la fortuna* gives reference to the year 1303, it clearly alludes to the turbulent lives of the Byzantine emperors six centuries previous. Valbuena Prat and Cotarelo hold Amescua's play in low esteem due to its chaotic emplotments, and while it is indeed a whirlwind, it should be lauded for what it *does* accomplish, which is that it successfully dramatizes a complex idea—the relationship between fortune and free will—in decidedly entertaining fashion.[55] However, there is another facet that becomes apparent in the hectic development of the plot and the series of ascensions to and subsequent abdications of the imperial throne depicted in *La rueda de la fortuna*. The three emperors to succeed Mauricio—Leoncio, Focas, and Heraclio, respectively—are each installed by distinct methodologies of election, which serves to repudiate each of those models until ultimately affirming the paradigm of Salic Law in a show of dramatic exemplarity, Heraclio establishes his rightful claim to the throne as Mauricio's heir in the finale.[56] As the play draws to a close, only Heraclio's ascent to the throne is presented as legitimate in the play based on the model of primogeniture. This model is the "story" of history that the play tells, mirrored in the inherent qualities ascribed to Heraclio. In *La rueda de la fortuna*, his clear fitness to rule is evidence of his royal blood, and vice versa; his actions are inextricably linked to his identity as the son of the legitimate king, and flow forth from his royal blood as part of his nature.

Most importantly for the present analysis, Mira de Amescua's work never casts any doubt about Heraclio's identity as Mauricio's son and heir. In *La rueda de la fortuna*, like in Lope's wild figure plays that treat the topic of royal succession, the blood always outs. In Mira de Amescua's play, various scenes clearly depict *la fuerza de la sangre* and foreshadow Heraclio's ascension in the denouement of the dramatic action. This initially occurs in the first act when he falls asleep on the throne, and dreams of being emperor.[57] Although he does not know it at the time, this dream evinces an inner reality, a shadow that eventually is made external and real upon learning of his identity, and results in him becoming emperor.[58] His capacity as a soldier and natural grace in navigating court culture negates his "formative" years living in seclusion as a wild man; it is his nature, not nurture, that forms who he is and manifests itself in this manner throughout the work. Finally, even though on a mission to oust the emperor, he wells up with compassion upon encountering him, mortally wounded, in the palace. Seeing his blood spilt, Heraclio expresses his ineffable sympathy for the man who he would soon learn to be his dying father:

> Seeing your blood spilt,
> and with such pitiful agony,

>   the blood that gives me life
>   feels unsettled in my veins,
>   even though I'm not your assassin.[59]

These inner feelings result from the "true" connection that bonds the two characters: their blood. Blood legitimizes Heraclio's ascension to the imperial throne, which is confirmed by his behavior and affinity for all things related to the duties of a prince.

Mira's *La rueda de la fortuna* emphatically affirms that the blood will out in this instance of *la fuerza de la sangre* depicted through the visual metaphor of Mauricio literally bleeding out that produces Heraclio's numinous sense of the connection to his father. In contrast to the primogeniture model of legitimate political authority, Calderón subtly deconstructs it in in his portrayal of this chaotic succession of Byzantine emperors Mauricio, Phocas, and Heraclius in *En la vida todo es verdad y todo mentira*.[60] In Focas's extended monologue in the opening act of Calderón's version, he reproduces one of Focas's lines in Mira's play, nearly verbatim: "I was sustained by wolf's milk as a young child."[61] In reworking the plot, Calderón omits the most treacherous character from Mira's work, Teodosio, but transfers his villainy onto Focas in *En la vida*, who is developed into the primary antagonist in the play. We see Teodosio's reflection in Calderón's Focas made explicit from the outset when, in the opening scene, he describes his "insatiable thirst for blood," which is a near citation of Teodosio's comment in *La rueda de la fortuna*: "It's insatiable, that is, my thirst to drink human blood."[62] But there are subtle but illuminating differences between these characters' articulation of being bloodthirsty. Moreover, those nuanced differences on the nature of blood are emblematic of the ideological concerns on which Calderón's *comedia* hinges, and how they diverge from the commitments that underpin the resolution of Mira de Amescua's text. Teodosio's bloodthirst represents a straightforward portrayal of his penchant for violence and the tyrannical administration of political authority, evidence within the circular logic that he would be unfit to rule because he is not actually Mauricio's son. Mauricio rejects him outright later in the play, but the underlying reality of his common blood as an essential aspect of the nature of his character makes his desire for blood all the more meaningful; here, his comment constitutes a disavowal of the blood he lacks (i.e., noble blood), which manifests itself in a blood fetish. It is an outward and insatiable desire to drink the blood of others so as to incorporate their blood into his own to make up for his lack.⁶³ For Calderón's Focas, his hydropic thirst can also be read on (at least) two levels. Like in the case of Teodosio, Focas's comment straightforwardly alludes to his own penchant for violence, proof of which is made clear in his tyrannical abuse of power as well as the violent usurpation of Mauricio's throne.⁶⁴ On a figurative level, Focas's bloodthirst betrays a different underlying anxiety foreshadowed in his comment here, and central to the obsession with blood as presented in *En la vida*. Motivating Focas's desire for blood is an *epistemological* problem (rather than Heraclio's ontological one in *La rueda de la fortuna*). Whereas Teodosio's blood was an irresolvable problem inherent to his nature and constitutive of his being, Focas's preoccupation with blood becomes a concise organizing metaphor for his desire for knowledge, specifically knowledge about blood: the identity of his son. Questioning the intrinsic linkage between nature and appearances is inconceivable in Mira de Amescua's play (the blood, specifically Heraclio's, will *always* out). Focas on the other hand spends the entirety of *En la vida* clinging to this epistemological premise as he attempts to quench a thirst for knowledge about his blood. But it proves unreliable, which points to a recognition in Calderonian drama of the fracturing of a worldview in which the "the blood will out" remains a matter of fact. The dramatic world of *En la vida* signals a bleeding out of such ideological commitments, which are emblematic of the cultural crisis of the Spanish Baroque, especially in the realm of the political when the problem of Habsburg succession and imperial decline threatened the viability of the monarchy itself. Nevertheless, by acknowledging the pervasive philosophical and political uncertainty as a reality, Calderón's play proposes an optimistic solution to the problem of doubt that frustrates scholarly perspectives about the ideological conservatism of the playwright's drama. The vocabulary of "bleeding out" here offers a critical framework to explain the complexities of the philosophical skepticism presented in *En la vida todo es verdad y todo mentira* as that pragmatic response to a world in which certainty established by nature is no longer a tenable paradigm.

Focas begins his epistemological quest to quench his (ultimately insatiable) thirst for blood (i.e., knowledge) by returning to his birthplace in search of his lost son. He immediately encounters the first hurdle in this enterprise when he meets Eraclio and Leonido, two young wild men, either of which could be his heir. Constituting the main conflict of the play, the work is primarily concerned with the methodology by which Focas establishes this "matter of fact" about the identity of his son. Unlike the poetics of transformation that organize Segismundo's plotline in *La vida es sueño*, this play returns to the conventional structure of the wild figure subgenre that hinges on mistaken identity resolved through anagnorisis. In *En la vida*, Focas is the transgressive figure whose actions represent a savage misdirection in so far as the consequences of his coup d'état are redirected and experienced by others, which is savage in its own right, but also because the product of his transgression produces savages (in this case not one, but two wild men). *En la vida* again resembles the wild figure plays more closely because the question of succession revolves around the anagnorisis of the identity of the rightful heir to the throne.

As part of the exposition recounted in the opening scenes, we learn that both of the wild figures, now young men, were born during the wartorn chaos of Focas's insurrection approximately twenty years prior to the beginning of the play. Teodosia, the empress and Mauricio's wife, in fact gives birth to a son as Focas's troops are invading the imperial palace, whom she relinquishes to Astolfo so that they can flee to safety. As he successfully escapes with the child into the forest, they happen upon Irífile, Focas's partner, who is also now in active childbirth, which she ultimately does not survive. Astolfo finds himself with a second newborn entrusted to his care, both of whom he goes on to raise in the seclusion of the forest landscape of Trinacria (modern-day Sicily).⁶⁵ After nearly two decades with no other human contact, one day Eraclio and Leonido hear the distant sounds of martial drums from what turns out to be Focas's troops now on the island. When they ultimately reach the cave that has served as their forest abode, Focas demands that Astolfo identify the two young men. He refuses to provide any information beyond confirming that one of the young men is in fact Focas's son, and that the other is Mauricio's heir. In response, Focas pleads with himself to guide him to the right test (*experiencia*) that he can carry out to obtain the knowledge he seeks:

> Won't you tell me, reason,
> what test I might
> carry out on them that
> would be a way to reveal the truth [*desengaño*]?⁶⁶

These verses lay the foundation for the pseudo-empiricism Focas will rely upon to acquire the knowledge he desires and establish it as a matter of fact. With the preservation of his imperial bloodline at stake, he enlists Lisipo to assist him, a court magician who had been banished by Federico, the duke of Calabria, for making a prophecy against him and in favor of Focas. At the emperor's request to set up this *experiencia* (a term which, in early modern Spanish, shares the fundamental characteristics of an experiment—a set of tests that serve to discover previously unknown knowledge through first-hand experience), Lisipo conjures an illusory palace within which Focas can observe Eraclio and Leonido in a courtly setting.[67] This relies on the premise that observing their behavior in this closed environment will be a reliable indicator to determine each of his subjects' identities. Focas's confidence about accurately making this determination is based on the following criterion: "that natural passion / through experiments will tell / which is my son and which one is not."[68] Here, "natural passion" refers to *la fuerza de la sangre*; he assumes the blood will out and his heir will become self-evident. Astolfo argues against the reliability of Focas's designs, questioning the ability to draw any such conclusions provided he did not participate in their upbringing: "Don't believe in tests about a son raised by someone else."[69] It is comments like these by likeable characters that guide the audience's expectations to be dubious about the experiment's success, and they should be given appropriate weight in determining the message about the flaws and ultimate failures of Focas's experiment to which the play gestures throughout.

The first act closes the way it begins: with a hunt. Focas's epistemological thirst for blood—to track down his own and spill that of another—brings him to the Trinacrian wilderness to open the play.[70] In our first encounter with him, we find him penetrating the dense wilderness with his entourage, not on a literal hunt exactly, but it has the look of one, the only difference being the quarry they are hunting, in this case figuratively.[71] In a play that gives great care to symmetry, the figurative hunt that opens the act is replicated at its close with the pretense of a real one (one that turns out to be faked). Focas concocts the ruse of a hunt to separate Leonido and Eraclio from his entourage in order to reduce the variables that could affect his ability to observe them effectively in the isolated environment of Lisipo's conjured palace. The figurative significance of the hunt, as it relates to Focas's epistemological project dramatized in the play, illuminates an even greater degree of complexity to Calderón's philosophical theater in *En la vida*. According to science historian William Eamon, the hunt, specifically the hunt for "the occult secrets locked up in the bosom of nature," was a popular metaphor that described the objectives of the early modern natural philosopher, which became well-worn in proto-scientific treatises during the period.[72] As an example, Eamon offers the famed professor of secrets Giambattista Della Porta's *Magiae naturalis*, an emblematic work that he contends "reads like a manifesto for a new scientific methodology: that of science as a *venatio*, a hunt for 'new secrets of nature.'"[73] The complexities with which this metaphor for the hunt is dramatized to correspond with Focas's epistemological objectives is striking. First, searching for the secrets of nature aptly describes his endeavor, with multiple allusions and explicit depictions of the hunt in act 1 as further gestures toward this driving metaphor. Additionally, the question of blood, specifically that the blood will out, organizes Focas's enterprise spatially as a matter of interior (nature, blood) and exterior (appearances, behavior), which represents a further complexity that resonates with the language of peering into the inside of things that was part of the conceptualization of science as a *venatio*. As I referenced in Chapter 3, the renowned Academy of Lincei was a group in Italy founded in 1603 dedicated to the study of natural philosophy. They chose the lynx as their namesake and emblem because of the objective of the academy, according to Francesco Stelluti, "to penetrate into the inside of things in order to know their causes and the operations of nature that work internally, just as it is said of the lynx that it sees not just what is in front of it, but what is hidden inside."[74] Within the palace experiment the court magus Lisipo creates false versions of other characters whom Eraclio and Leonido would recognize, including one named Ismenia, a handmaid of Cintia, queen of Trinacria. At one moment during the magical experiment, the false Ismenia uses this language to describe the function of the illusory castle as an epistemological apparatus: "Lisipo's design is to discover the interior."[75] By describing the "experiment" (*experiencia*) as the search for the interior of the young men to learn the secrets of their nature that are hidden there, Ismenia's lines are firmly in dialogue with a specific vein of Renaissance natural philosophy.

And finally, it is Lisipo's craft as court magician that makes this *experiencia* possible. Described as a mage or magician (*mago*), he should be situated in the history of science as an example of a theatricalized professor of secrets, which is another facet of Calderón's work that corresponds to the development of empirical inquiry taking shape throughout Europe during the seventeenth century.[76] Lisipo resembles (with some embellishment) the professor of secrets, a transitional figure that stood between the practitioners of hermetic natural magic and early empiricists like Boyle, Huygens, and Bacon who, thanks to the narrative of the scientific revolution, have come to be much more renowned for their contributions to the development of early modern technical and observational experimentation than the "masters of experience" that preceded them. The hermetic disciplines of natural magic marked a shift toward experimentation over theory in order to reveal the secrets of nature by experience through the manipulation of natural materials. While these disciplines (e.g., alchemy) remained influential in Renaissance science, the shift toward experimentalism can be seen in the craft of the professor of secrets, "for whom trueness to nature was measured not by the yardstick of ancient authority but by direct experience."[77] The spectacular nature of Lisipo's craft embodies the ethos and aesthetic attributed to the professor of secrets characterized by "his passionate quest for secrets, his craving for rarities, his cultivation of wonder, and his tendency to view science as a theatrical performance designed to delight and astonish spectators."[78] Calderón taps into this method of demonstration in Lisipo's magical palace, a type of spectacular laboratory theater (within the spectacle of the play itself) with Focas as spectator, which is created to demonstrate one of nature's secrets in a theatrical display of wonderment. Focas, again imagining this process through blood-related imagery, even describes Lisipo's experiment in alchemical terms as the forge by which he will assess the quality of their hearts ("aquilatados los pechos en la forja"). The one, his son, will be the gold to whom he will show favor, and the other, Mauricio's son, will be the dross to be discarded.[79] Regalado notes the proto-scientific nature of the palace scene as well, while also suggesting, although not explicitly, the relevance of the hunt. He posits that the palace experiment, or the play within a play, begins when Focas concocts the hunt in the forest where the marvelous palace appears, and where the test subjects, Eraclio and Leonido, will soon arrive.[80] Built for the same purpose as other early modern instruments such as the telescope, microscope, or air-pump, the instrument of the palace functions in its "capacity to enhance perception, and to constitute new perceptual objects."[81] Slater elaborates on the theatricality of those instruments in operational practice, which they share with didactic theater like the Calderonian *autos sacramentales*: "Both the plays and laboratory appurtenances have a didactic utility, and both contrive to create or isolate conditions to make very particular aspects of the world available as spectacle."[82]

Lisipo's illusory palace serves as a type of laboratory theater as well, the outcome of which has eluded scholarship on the question of whether the play affirms the identification of Eraclio as Mauricio's heir as a plausibly reached matter of fact.[83] That is, Focas accurately discerns that Leonido is his son, and the mass of soldiers correctly install Eraclio as emperor at the end of the work. The dominant view posits this play is a dramatic representation of the fallibility of the senses, which one must acknowledge in order to act prudently in the face of uncertainty. Cruickshank takes Mauricio's paternity of Eraclio for granted, a perspective summarized by Mujica as the following: "the recognition for the impossibility of knowledge is not cause for despair, but a basis for the formation of a healthy moral outlook based on prudence" and that "although Calderón proceeds from skeptical premises, he is not a true skeptic in the sense that he does assume the existence of an objective reality which is revealed to his characters at the end of the play."[84] This objective reality is of course that Eraclio's virtuous behavior substantiates his royal blood and right to rule, while Leonido's impudence identifies him as the usurper Focas's son. While there is no denying that such an interpretation reflects the dominant political philosophy of the period, I find no textual evidence to indicate precisely when it becomes clear that Eraclio is Mauricio's son, and therefore heir to the imperial throne. In fact, the play seems to be simultaneously guiding its audience to want Eraclio to be victorious, while also frustrating the certainties necessary to substantiate such a conclusion. In other words, Calderón seems to be tricking us, and making us enjoy it. Astolfo, the only character with knowledge of their true identities, never reveals this information, a fact the play highlights on multiple occasions. Hildner puts forth this interpretation: "the verifiable evidence regarding the young men's identities are not as conclusive as they seem. First, the examination of their conduct carried out by Focas does not provide indisputable results. Each [character] exhibits characteristics that neither connect him exclusively to Focas nor the deceased Mauricio."[85]

My analysis here is indebted to Hildner's essay, which informs my examination of Lisipo's metatheatrical laboratory. Within the architecture of this structure is a play within a play, or more precisely here, a laboratory spectacle within a more straightforwardly theatrical one. This creates an internal audience of spectators of the palace experiment (Focas observing Eraclio and Leonido), and an external one (beyond the fourth wall), which allows that external audience to evaluate the outcome of the performance, based not only on their perception but also by observing how each of the internal spectators evaluates the same spectacle from the other side of the fourth wall. Internally, Lisipo plays the role of *virtuoso* whose skill is required in order for the dramatic experiment to be carried out, a demonstration for which the observers do not know the outcome.

This demonstration is marked by dissimulation and theatricality, with Eraclio's and Leonido's performance on display for an internal audience within an enclosed, artificial space. At one point, Lisipo even provides lines for the characters he has conjured within his internal drama, to which each responds to their director: "Yes I'll say it, I am here / to obey you."[86]

Once underway, obstacles impede Focas's certainty throughout the entirety of the experiment. In his observation of Eraclio and Leonido, he encounters "traces, signs, and clues" that are supposed to "lead to the discovery of nature's hidden causes," but the "signs" do not meet his expectations to detect a paternal affiliation successfully ("a quien con mis señas halle"). He determines the differences between Eraclio and Leonido, but they only serve to distinguish them from each other, and he appreciates different qualities in each. At every turn, Leonido acts brashly, while Eraclio displays prudence and courtesy. Focas seems to be seeing himself in Leonido, while observing what he knows to be right behavior in Eraclio, but that still does not signify certainty about their identities for him or the audience. By the end of act 2, one of Lisipo's false characters asks him about what he has learned from the experiment thus far, to which he responds, "everything and nothing," that both of their behaviors please him and therefore he still has his doubts.[87] Furthermore, Focas is a poor observer. At one point, while looking on from a hidden vantage, he actually falls asleep, which leads to one of the most important moments in the development of the plot. He is discovered sleeping, and Leonido decides to take fate into his own hands and slay the sleeping emperor. Eraclio succeeds in detaining him, but amid the skirmish Focas awakens to find the young men standing over him with swords drawn. He is mistaken in believing Leonido, who contends that he was in fact trying to stop Eraclio from committing the act. From Leonido's false account, Focas believes he has uncovered the truth. Ironically, Leonido's behavior in this particular moment reflects the villainy that the audience has come to expect from Focas, and adds to the suspicion that Leonido may in fact be Focas's progeny. Nevertheless, at the precise moment he is least capable of observing their behavior, Focas finds what he considers the decisive evidence for which he set up the experiment. Focas attempts to manufacture *la fuerza de la sangre*, expecting to feel a numinous connection with one of the young men, but never experiences the inexplicable sensation of consanguinity so clearly presented in other works. In his attempt to peer inside into the true nature of the blood that runs through the veins of his son and heir, he falls prey to the deception of appearances. But it should also be noted, even if he had observed this critical moment, *la fuerza de la sangre* never manifests itself in a play that dedicates significant attention gesturing toward it.

From this moment forward, Leonido is presumed to be Focas's heir, the palace disappears, and toward the end of act 3, Eraclio and his surrogate father Astolfo are sent off in a leaky boat to carry out Focas's initial aim to kill whichever pretender was not his son. At this moment, a fleet of ships appears on the horizon captained by Federico, the Duke of Calabria. He rescues the two marooned characters and takes them back to shore to overthrow the tyrannous Focas. Eraclio assassinates Focas, spares a contrite Leonido, and the victorious army chants Eraclio's name and installs him as emperor, to the cheers of the soldiers. Upon Focas's death and Eraclio's ascension to the imperial throne, baroque order appears to have been restored, but the space between the veil and the "reality" to which it supposedly refers is more tenuous in this work than any up to this point.

This conclusion of *En la vida* is persuasively ambiguous. Along with the soldiers, the audience sees Eraclio crowned emperor, and has been guided throughout the *comedia* to approve this outcome, even though no substantial evidence has been given to affirm his legitimacy. The reality to which the veil (the *comedia*/representation) refers is ideological to the extent that it persuasively affirms a particular version of that reality—Focas is a monster who must be blotted out, and Eraclio should be emperor. As persuasive as that "reality" may be, the problem is that this conclusion is reached by means of a methodology incapable of making such a claim. The defining characteristic put forth by the play that legitimizes Eraclio's rule is primogeniture. Calderón provides his audiences with a model for their reception by means of the mass of soldiers presented in the play celebrating the new emperor in support of the conclusion. On the surface, it would seem that justice has been served and the rightful character has assumed the throne. So, rather than a play that seeks to reassure its audience of the "necessary yet ineffable substratum of reality (the theological truth behind the worldly deceptions)," what we ultimately see in the end is a play that stages "a means by which people arrive at a politically acceptable consensus."[88]

In the structure of the palace episode of *En la vida*, Calderón masterfully intertwines the premises of the wild figure repertoire (mistaken identity, anagnorisis, natural landscapes, political authority), the conventional preoccupation of appearances versus reality along with the ubiquitous obsession with blood. But just as he gestures toward the conventions of these recognizable categories (the wild figure, *desengaño*, *la fuerza de la sangre*, empirical discovery), he swerves from them in a flourish of metatheatrical deconstruction of the certainties that underpin the ideological commitments of each. In a traditional configuration of this *comedia* ending, the revelation of the true identity of Mauricio's heir would be revealed and he takes his rightful place on the imperial throne. The legitimacy of this conclusion would be further justified by primogeniture and evinced through a demonstration of prudence. Dramatically, this is conventionally achieved through the certainty afforded by *la fuerza de la sangre*, which is explicitly confirmed by characters who can speak authoritatively. But Calderón's play points to each of these conventional plot devices only to conspicuously elide them. The metatheatrical structure of the magical palace is appropriate because it mirrors these multifaceted and interworking elements of the play, specifically as they relate to exterior/interior. The external audience peers into the enclosed space of the theatrical spectacle, within which internal characters do the same as they spectate one layer deeper into the metatheatrical keying set up by the conjured castle space. This is where a type of play within a play takes place, a magical laboratory theater within Calderón's theatrical laboratory, Focas's theater of truth within the baroque theater of truth par excellence, the Spanish *comedia*.[89] Focas's epistemological enterprise coincides with this movement in figurative space toward an interior as well; his goal is to peer inside the wild men's appearances to see their true nature, to see their blood, thereby revealing it (i.e., knowledge) to the exterior world or spilling it (literal violence as a requisite outcome of a successful hunt). This spatial organization of interior and exterior, and the inward movement implied in the epistemological metaphor of the hunt, where the hunter travels into the bosom of nature to acquire its secrets, shares this spatiality of Focas's thirst for blood/knowledge just described. This is reflected even further in the visual metaphor of Focas penetrating the Sicilian forest to find his son, and the contrived hunt set up for Eraclio and Leonido to open up the conjured laboratory where their secrets are to be revealed. Each of these observational methodologies promise that the blood will out and nature will open its core to reveal its secret. But neither of these premises are realized, that is, there are no instances of *la fuerza de la sangre* in the play, nor do any of Focas's experiments prove conclusive to establish a matter of fact by this or any other means.[90] The play gestures toward these conventions and devices to set up the expectation that they will serve the purpose for which they are typically relied upon to reveal the Truth and establish Order in the traditional *comedia* ending. The play sets up the plot around traditional conflicts (especially in the wild figure play) and incorporates the devices that would normally reveal the requisite information to produce a satisfying resolution and commitment to the ideologies upon which it hinges. *En la vida* presents the constituent parts to realize Egginton's definition of the "major strategy of the Baroque," but then Calderón's work produces an unconventional swerve when each of those entities withhold their secrets. The multi-faceted spatial coherence of the play—organized around the attempted passage from exterior to interior—hinges on a nuanced conceptualization of theatricality through which it produces meaning. When that passage to the inside of nature is barred access—to the blood, the truth—the play folds back on its own theatricality, acknowledging its own epistemological limitations.

There is a consciousness present in the play of what Egginton calls theater's "founding aporia," that behind each "veil of mediation" is and can only be yet another.[91] In *En la vida* the devices of the major strategy are set in motion, building an expectation that they will lead to an affirmation of dominant ideology through the poetics of discovery and *desengaño* that signify an effort to shut the door of the theatrical mode and replace it with a "renewed promise of presence."[92] But the metatheatrical keying of *En la vida* seems less of an acknowledgment that the door "can always swing both ways," but rather that the door to Reality is locked. The possibility of this type of ideological deconstruction through the illusory space of theater seen in Calderón's play encapsulates the complexities of the Baroque as the unfolding of an aesthetic, philosophical, and cultural milieu. The ideological fervor and sobriety of early *comedias* signals a culture doubling down as it clung to a particular ordering of the universe—the Christian neo-platonic metaphysics of the Renaissance—in an increasingly panicked disavowal of the inaccessibility of the world—of reality—behind the veil of appearances. Calderón's philosophical theater in *La vida es sueño* and *En la vida todo es verdad y todo mentira* is an acknowledgment of that fracturing worldview, and an ideological response that does not require the obsessive reaffirmation of an inaccessible reality, but rather a pragmatic methodology to arrive at the greatest good. The heightened sense of theatricality during the Baroque as it developed over the course of the seventeenth century provides access to this history I have explored in *Wild Theater (que sus faltas perdonéis)*, situated between the Renaissance and the Enlightenment and is critical toward understanding the modern worldview as it emerged between the two.

Conclusion

MY GOAL HAS BEEN to provide a nuanced application of prevailing ideological theory in interpreting the wild figure's function within the *comedia* of the Spanish Baroque. Ideology is not something that one has or rejects, but rather forms a body of subjects. Creative production within a particular context reflects that ideology, and is both incapable of escaping it while also inevitably leaving clues of its own construction. With regards to the Baroque, the wild figure tears at its seams over the course of the seventeenth century. In my analysis, I move past the Maravall/anti-Maravall debate, because I do not see the two positions as mutually exclusive. Not necessarily repressive or subversive (although they could potentially be either) the wild protagonists are creatures of ideology whose existence materializes the push and pull that is always tugging on the completeness ideology works to establish and maintain. They are creatures disavowed by their creator, but can only stay locked up in a tower or hidden in the forest for so long.

Within the greater context of *comedia* studies, and early modern Iberian literary studies more broadly, certain approaches to cultural production that pull out ideologically repressive and subversive messages from the works of baroque Spain are often useful to understand the presiding hegemonic structures of the time, or to view the ways that oppression could be acknowledged, and responded to. My approach reflects an attempt to map the terrain between these two binaries toward a more nuanced perspective on early modern cultural production and the society that incubated it. While I am not the first to chart this terrain, the fact that the debate over Maravall still exists suggests the need for a study such as mine to continue engaging the space where the hegemonic and the oppositional meet, and push the limits of this discussion in productive directions.

While there exists a relatively extensive body of work on the wild figure in early modern Spain that succeeds in cataloguing and theorizing the literary phenomenon well, these studies have left stones unturned to uncover the symbolic depth that wild folk offer toward understanding the ideological parameters of the culture of baroque Spain. As I demonstrate in Chapter 2, from the first wild figure to appear on the commercial stage in *El nacimiento de Ursón y Valentín*, the wild figure belies its own tradition, simultaneously calling our attention to it yet not meeting the expectations of what a wild man or woman "should" be. And the symbolic range of what the baroque wild figure can end up being is one of its defining characteristics. That is, in these plays the wild figure is rarely represented for its own sake; rather, the nature of the figure is to stand in for the myriad cultural anxieties for which it is a vehicle. The acknowledgment of this factor guides the critic to some of the most pressing tensions of the period. As a vehicle for meaning, the wild figure does more than lurk in the woods; it protagonizes thought and ways of thinking about a society's delinquents and its princes, its history and its future, its men and its women, and the value system that underpins it all. By reading the wild figure in this way to further previous interpretations, it opens new doors to peer into the nature of the Baroque. This is what I have found to be the work the wild figure accomplishes for us four hundred years on.

This book analyzes the way ideology manifests itself in the *comedia* without coming to the text with a priori assumptions about what it should do (affirm and prescribe social norms) or could do (subvert those norms). Rather, the present study has explored the complex relationship the wild figure maintains between those two poles. As a result, monsters compel us to look for villainy from within (rather than looking outward), empiricism encounters the limits of its reach (centuries before the rise and fall of positivism), and gender performs radically. By giving the wild figure more space to mean (in these ways), it quickly becomes clear that it is a more complex component of the *comedia* than has previously been described. The fact that it amply illuminates the varied themes of the five chapters herein and holds them in place as an integrated whole demonstrates the extent to which the wild figure pervasively inhabits the Baroque. The wild figure allows us to view the period from a variety of disciplinary perspectives, and within its makeup come together the major ingredients of the Baroque. Existing at the very point where ideology avows itself (and also the site where it is liable to break down), for contemporary scholarship, the wild figure exposes the underlying structure that supports the ideological apparatus of the Baroque.[1] Appropriately, it takes a monster to guide the critic through the web of monstrosities that have always defined the Baroque (and modernity). It takes one, it would seem, to know one.

My approach views social order as that which tries to keep monsters out (or at least at bay), but also the creator of monsters, and a monster itself. Understanding the complex relationship between those realities of culture is useful because it prepares the critic to look for structure and unifying principles but also simultaneously to anticipate aspects of the system under scrutiny to be deformed and with its constituent parts out of place. Hobbes's *Leviathan* imagines the monster as a model illustration for the body politic, which I draw from to define the monster-that-is-culture, in a modified Derridian sense, as anything that has both a commitment to and rejection of a recognizable form. In other words, the monster is not entirely formless, but rather calls upon a particular form that it ultimately defies. That definition can also be applied to baroque society at large. The corpus of works to which I apply it put the Baroque on display in a manner that it maintains enough of its form (as understood by traditional scholarship) to be recognizable, while allowing for the existence of aspects slightly larger than they should be (nonconformity to prescriptive gender performance, for instance), in the wrong place (ideological monsters at court), or missing altogether (a royal heir). As a result, one can comfortably acknowledge and affirm sweeping generalizations traditionally made by scholars of the period, but also examine around the edges of the ideological system for the monstrous bits that have been disavowed. These monstrous entities riddle the exterior of the Baroque, at least from what is observable in the *comedia*, and for which the wild figure corpus is emblematic. Even though monsters are always dealt with in the resolutions of the *comedias* that I analyze, for the 2500 or more verses of each, all we see are monsters. They disappear from view in the end, and we are to understand that their absence is the way things truly are (or ought to be). We are left to infer what something is by what it is not.

In conceiving of the Baroque as a Monster-that-is-culture, on its surface monstrosity is always on display in order to tell us that it—culture—is actually something else. And it is. This monster that I currently describe misdirects our attention from the true monster that has been occluded from view—the monster within. Baroque monsters such as the wild figure are *borrones*, washed away by the conventional *comedia* endings, but the curtain closes before we are able to see much of the order that has actually been restored. However, this study has met this Monster as it lumbers forth, examining how the monsters we see that appear on the surface (that is, those that materialize on the *comedia* stage) point us to the monster within—the repressive realities and anxieties the *comedia* constantly disavows. The culture of the Baroque is a *mise en abîme* of wild things. My approach reveals the sacrificial monsters that culture creates to maintain the illusion of its totalized identity[2] in order to explicate the relationship between the landscape of cultural production, full of monsters, and the society that sustains that landscape's borders (the Monster itself). These monsters and the culture that produced them are both multi-faceted, deformed, yet not completely formless; they maintain enough of their shape for us to give them names: the wild figures of the Baroque.

Consequently, my approach to the Baroque and early modernity also brings into view the modernity the wild figures share with our own cultural context. For example, Calderón offers an early critique of the modern wholesale trust in truth claims arrived at by scientific methods similar to the ones dramatized in prototype form in his *comedia En la vida todo es verdad y todo mentira*. We might ask how Calderón might respond to the fetishizing of scientific objectivity in today's epistemological landscape. We seem to live in the Calderonian now in this regard; his play "debunks" the premise that the blood will out by critiquing the same essential methodological faith in empirical inquiry that remains pervasive today, even if manifested in different ideological commitments. As a core principle, moderns privilege scientific knowledge *über alles*, a commitment that leaves us prone to disavow the scientific worldview as historically contingent and hegemonically reproduced, while disregarding other approaches to knowledge.[3] The status of Lisipo's magical castle as experiment-spectacle resonates in the spectacle culture today (i.e., entertainment industry). Calderón predicts these enduring commitments evinced by recent shows like the Discovery Channel's *MythBusters*, which takes as its premise to debunk "myths" of the past through the abilities of current technology and the scientific method.

This methodology assumes that the folktales under their scrutiny occurred in a time devoid of knowledge (modernity's "fallacy of developmentalism"), and now the tools of technology and empiricism have the historiographical capacity to determine whether or not an event was likely to have occurred. It seems, however, the hosts of the show confound the modes of entertainment and scientific inquiry in a manner that is more complex than is perhaps immediately acknowledged. Their experiments claim that a past event is impossible or plausible through a current experiment in a different time and place. If observation and reproducibility are the key factors to the scientific method, really only reproducibility exists—and tenuously—on *MythBusters*, since knowledge of the original event can only be known in the form that it has been reproduced and disseminated over the course of its textual or oral history. Furthermore, if the early experiments using the air pump are any example, reproducibility is not an accurate measure of whether or not an event took place. For example, natural philosophers with detailed descriptions of seventeenth-century Dutch empiricist Christian Huygens's pump were unable to make it function as well as Huygens contended in his own experiments.[4] Recently, a similar concern has arisen out of a study completed by social psychologists who were unable to reproduce the findings of sixty-one (out of ninety-eight) studies from three well-respected psychology journals.[5] From the dawn of empiricism until now, the question of reproducibility has always been a problematic one within the realm of scientific inquiry. All of that to say, before we are ready to emphatically join the hosts of *MythBusters* in affirming a myth has been busted, a reflection on Calderón's *En la vida* should cause us to pause and ask if we are engaging the subject with the right lines of inquiry in the first place.[6]

And at its base, these dominant modes of knowledge production are born out of an inherent coloniality that organizes the modern order of things, one that wild figures of the *comedia* might chart us a path to decolonize.[7] Dussel asserts that it is only after we unmask the Eurocentrism of Enlightenment reason and "the hegemonic processes of modernization" can we begin to deterritorialize those hegemonies and "liberate the production of knowledge, reflection, and communication from the pitfalls of European rationality/modernity."[8] By studying the wild things of the *comedia* as I have in this study, I have explored questions as varied as pop culture, the history of ideas, gender, political philosophy and history, and more directly literary and performance studies. Furthermore, while addressing these types of issues and answering questions that linger about the *comedia* and the culture of the Baroque, my research seeks to shed light on early modern modes of cultural production and their ideological foundations that continue to prevail in contemporary society.[9]

In the end, this study has explored the depths of what the *comedia* does. Agents of the baroque machine churned out these ideological products as if on a production line. Lope's dramatic production en masse exemplifies this prevailing baroque aesthetic of excess and surplus, and out of this sheer abundance of plays arise repetitions—the assembly line metaphor remains relevant—and the genome of a genre evolves into its own recognizable species of cultural artifact. But then, when Lope decides to draw on the wild figure repertoire as one such monster, he unleashes an ideological force that would be difficult—if not impossible—to impede. As other stock characters were replicated time and time again without significant permutation, the wild figure has a penchant for getting away from its author, causing excesses and deformity that would come to be known as a defining characteristic of the Baroque. For instance, in Lope's second wild figure play, *El animal de Hungría*, the tidy ending is thwarted by Rosaura, who remains in line to become queen of Hungary despite the fact that she is the offspring of the defamed traitor Faustina and her illegitimate relationship with the king. Within the play, ideological anxieties (marital fidelity) that falsely monstrify Teodosia and converted her into a wild woman set in motion the events that would give rise to another wild thing—Rosaura. The resolution never ties up this loose end; the replication of the wild figure creates a surplus that cannot be tidily reinscribed into prevailing hegemonic discourses. This microcosm of replication is mirrored in the trajectory of the wild figure over the course of the sixteenth and seventeenth centuries. Every time it appears, it requires a heavier lift from the conventions of the *comedia* to eliminate or domesticate its wildness. As a result, the dramatic genre *shows* (*mostrare*) more—in more lavish sets and extravagant plots—but *does* less, at least as a vehicle for hegemonic ideology. By the end, the Ismenias and Marfisas replace the Teodosias and Faustinas of nearly a century previous. Not only do they escape their respective containers unpunished, but their domestication is also suggestively absent as well. Caving under the weight of its own conventions, wildness ultimately goes untamed in the later *comedia* to be rebranded in the following century (e.g., the noble savage of the Enlightenment).

EPILOGUE

Framing Bigfoot
*A Genealogy of Savage Misdirection
from Segismundo to Sasquatch*

THE HISTORY OF THE wild figure—the dangerous solitary hairy giant that lives in the forest—has always been illuminating in regard to what it says about the human need to populate the figurative and literal forests with hirsute hominids. This book tells a small slice of that story during the Spanish Renaissance and Baroque as it was harnessed—or rather unleashed—through the spectacular entertainment that was the *comedia*. Although this iteration of the wild figure became less of an obsession as the Baroque gave way to the Enlightenment, vestiges of the type persist today, about which the features of the baroque wild figure maintains explicatory power. There are broad ways that the analysis undertaken here can be applied today, specifically regarding the implications of the notion that the wild figure helps explain the Baroque as theater and theater as a defining characteristic of modernity, but that would be another book (and of which there are already a few excellent examples).[1] To build on these foundational works, I will add some new examples unique to the wild figure, defined narrowly as a forest-dwelling hirsute hominid represented through spectacle. And today, the ideological potency of spectacle has bled out (a different type of bleeding out from the one I described in Chapter 5 of this study) from the stage onto the screen. My methodology for putting in dialogue the wild man of the *comedia* with present-day conceptualizations of the elusive creature of the forests of remote regions like the Pacific Northwest (Sasquatch) and the mountains of Nepal (Yeti) reflects Walter Moser's approach to the neo-Baroque to look "back and forth in historical time in order to identify common baroque features that are shown to be transhisorically reactivated, although in a completely different historical situation, and in a new cultural context in terms of technoscape and mediascape."[2] My concern here is less about the field of cryptozoology and Bigfoot hunters ("Squatchers"), but rather with the ways current representations of the wild figure are transmitted through spectacle, and their implications on our cultural milieu. I will be reading today's spectacular Sasquatch through the lens offered by Castillo and Egginton's *Medialogies*, as well as the *Polemical Companion* to the work, a collection of essays edited by Julio Baena and Bradley Nelson that probes *Medialogies* by putting it into application. If, as the editors note in the introduction to the *Polemical Companion*, their collection of essays is offered in the attitude of "eating a dinner in good company" at the table with *Medialogies*, then I cannot help but offer my concluding remarks here as the wild man bursting into that banquet hall to interrupt the feast for a brief interlude to liven the festivities.[3]

Like with each iteration of the wild figure, certain aesthetic forms prove most suitable. As a response to the foundational shifts in worldview emerging during the Baroque exemplified by the commercial theater—namely a consciousness of a separation between the world as it is and the world as we perceive it—the wild figure became a vehicle within that emblematic medium onto which the resulting fears could be projected and resolved. In *Medialogies*, Egginton and Castillo define this problem of thought as emblematic of the first age of inflationary media, which came into being during the Baroque. They further illuminate this crisis of thought as a consciousness of the fact that "knowledge of self and the world are no longer posed as a search for the truth behind the artifice or, in Platonic terms, the ideal behind the shadows, since for us the true self is unknowable, there is nothing but shadows behind the shadows."[4] The obsession with appearances versus reality that were central to the baroque *comedia* and embodied by representations of wildness (along the lines of the poetics of mistaken identity and the catharsis produced by its revelation) are the hallmark of this first age, and also an undercurrent motivating the hydropic thirst for a marvelous truth that plays a critical role in the twenty-first century Sasquatch documentary genre. Today, documentary film and reality television series (broadly, docu-spectacles) have become the media that best capture the Bigfoot phenomenon in the contemporary cultural imagination. I could draw from what seems like countless "Searching for Bigfoot" documentaries to trace the genealogy of wildness from Segismundo to Sasquatch, but I will focus on one of the most recent examples in the film *Sasquatch* (2021), a documentary that distinguishes itself in ways that are productively explored in juxtaposition with the ideological poetics of wildness in baroque Iberian theater.

As a point of departure, Bigfoot documentaries reflect an emptying out of the Renaissance emblem of science as a *venatio*. Bigfoot researchers are commonly referred to as hunters, literalizing the Renaissance emblem by making the object of their pursuit for knowledge the object itself. But their hunt is equal parts epistemological as it is literal. In the end, the premise is a scientific one, which entails a specific methodology that provides access to a specific type of knowledge. That method is a straightforward one: to establish a matter of fact through observable evidence. It is the answer to the question, does Bigfoot exist? The scope of knowledge privileged by this approach betrays a symptom of modernity's greatest disavowal: the elusive nature of objectivity (a True secret of Nature) in a world that only becomes increasingly subjective and mediated. Bigfoot research must produce a body, the ever-elusive thing itself. To explain a modern semiotics of language, Nelson draws on this illustration to describe the primacy of this "desire for presence": "Just as an empty tomb triggers the desire for the presence of a body, so, too, does the mysterious and reticent signifier spark the desire for the fullness of meaning."[5] One recent documentary, *Bigfoot's Reflections*, reflects the commitment to proving the empirically verifiable existence of Bigfoot (rather than the human need for imagining it). Nevertheless, *Bigfoot's Reflections* opens with an epigraph of a Nietzsche quote shown on a black background: "If you stare for long in the abyss, the abyss also gazes into you."[6] Along with the title, this epigraph evokes the Lacanian mirror; we are defined by our separation from the Other who gazes at us, a meaning maker with whom we can never be unified. Bigfoot's reflection is exactly that, what baroque playwrights would call a shadow, an image, a dream, whose function, along with the wild figure and other mythological creatures of the forest, is to tell us something about ourselves precisely by the stories we tell about him. Yet, finding the body of Sasquatch, which is the actual objective of the film's documentarians, would suggest a markedly different aim, chiefly, to discover a new species that fits into a stable taxonomic classification. Castillo and Egginton describe this as a craving for "the experience of the authentic. This hunger for truth behind 'simulations' has resulted in a fundamentalist search for the original unadulterated word and for the *authentic body*."[7] At the heart of the scientific worldview (and by extension, modernity) is the disavowal that one's access to knowledge of the world the way that it is (i.e., Truth, Nature) is individually limited, inherently mediated, and historically contingent. The hunt for Sasquatch evinces this: beneath the veneer of the objective pursuit of knowledge is a Sasquatch that is always (1) *allusive* (in the absence of a body we imagine the *real* Sasquatch constructed by a network of copies of him that continually construct new composite images as they multiply), (2) through a medium that is *illusive* (it is mediated through a fantasy screen upon which we fetishize objectivity, while disavowing the imperfect copy that plagues mediation, from hearsay accounts to documentary film), and (3) therefore, a Sasquatch that is *elusive*. And it is this absence that also generates our insatiable interest in the thing that always evades our capture.

The 2021 limited docu-series *Sasquatch* directed by Joshua Rofé deploys the conventions of traditional Sasquatch documentaries in the film trailer to create a sense of awe and apprehension that drives (and reflects) the hunt for a mysterious and possibly dangerous giant who lurks the woods of northern California. The trailer begins with a series of landscape shots of the dense and wet forests of the region beneath a thick layer of fog. Backed by a track of suspenseful sound effects, a modulated, disembodied voice speaks about the fear of being alone in the forest, as if something is watching you, "something is going to take you out." This is followed by a voice clip of the investigative journalist *Sasquatch* centers on, who discloses his credentials having worked with a long list of society's most notorious delinquents (with images offering proof to go along with the voice track) from street gangs to neo-Nazis, which serves the rhetorical purpose of setting the bar for what he says next: "I am going to tell you the craziest story you've ever heard." The trailer leads the viewer to expect a Sasquatch docu-spectacle with footage that depicts a series of unexpected (even if conventional) artifacts like plaster molds of giant feet, and allusions to textual references to marvelous creatures found in the historical archive, depicted in rooms with certain resonances to the content of early modern cabinets of curiosities. As established in the pithy title, *Sasquatch*, the series gestures enough toward the genre's conventions by interspersing images of imagined wild men with actual footage from the film, as well as the requisite clips of interviews with Sasquatch researchers and enthusiasts. It turns out, however, this enterprise constitutes a sleight-of-hand, because *Sasquatch* is not ultimately about hunting for a hirsute forest giant at all. Rofé lays the groundwork for this bait-and-switch in the first episode of the three-part limited docu-series, which is dedicated almost entirely to interviews with Sasquatch researchers offering input on the story depicted in the film, which is about a gruesome triple homicide that took place in the fall of 1993. As the first episode ends, the hyper-conventional portrayal of Sasquatch research makes it seem like the Bigfoot enthusiast is the target audience, but it leans into the plausibility of finding a real Bigfoot as a set up for a very different story altogether. In episodes 2 and 3, *Sasquatch* becomes a true-crime narrative about a violent period in the early 1990s in an area of northern California known for cannabis farming. In the end, the documentary follows reporter David Holthouse as he investigates the murders of three migrant farmers who died during that period.

Guiding the viewer's expectations to learn whether a Sasquatch committed these murders is the film's first savage misdirection. *Sasquatch* ultimately presents a convincing explanation for the murder, based on a quasi-confession obtained by Holthouse over the phone with someone who credibly admits to their involvement (under anonymity and speaking through a voice modulator).[8] The person states that a group of white farmers were growing increasingly upset about the emergent influence of migrant growers in the cannabis farming community in the area. So they decided to start spreading rumors about Sasquatch sightings on the edges of their farmland (it is referenced on multiple occasions that Sasquatches would hurl boulders at farmers as they harvested product). Holthouse was undercover investigating the cannabis farming operations in the area in the fall of 1993, and recounts those very rumors earlier in the documentary before learning this information from the voice on the phone. Those rumors were circulated to make it all the more plausible to believe that a Sasquatch was responsible for the gruesome deaths of three migrant farmers. It is indicated that the group of farmers who had been circulating the rumors in fact staged the murder by mangling the corpses, disturbing the area as if a large animal had rampaged through it, made convincing because they didn't take any of the crop, as would be expected of competing farmers motivated to plunder lucrative product. This is the second savage misdirection in the film, the first being the film itself, and now the second the content within its frame, the race-based violence perpetrated by the farmers constituting a grotesque escalation planned and prepared through the mechanisms of monster spectacle inspired by the mythical imagination of Sasquatch.

In the baroque *comedia*, we see a theatricalized image of a type of savage misdirection that displaces blame from the real monsters onto a character. Within the theatrical space, a "real" wild figure (or more than one) is produced because of a crime committed. They are believed to be the violent monster, while the true monster of culture lives on undetected until they are revealed in the play's resolution. The values that underpin this plot structure leverage the particular ideological capacity of modern theater as a representational mode. The emergence of theater reflected a new consciousness thereof, and "when the reality behind appearance is thus removed from immediate perception, it becomes susceptible to manipulation."[9] This is the premise of Maravall's assertion that the *comedia* was an ideological apparatus of a guided culture. In the poetics of baroque monstrosity, the wild man is not a wild man (there is no "actual" wild man), but rather a sign that signifies there is a monster among us.

The horrific events of *Sasquatch* signify a gruesome inversion of baroque theatricality. The violence-made-spectacle reported in the film is made possible when the subjective and objective in the frame of representation are no longer discernably disentangled. According to Castillo and Egginton, the difference between the first and second inflationary ages is the "world, once the transcendent ineffable ground of appearances, has been relegated to the level of copies, just one more, if greater, resource among equals."[10] The subjective violence of horror films "literalizes" the objective destruction of a late-capitalist society careening toward its own destruction, as we, the zombie hordes, are unable to free ourselves from the "economic forces that situate us as agents of our own destruction."[11] This representation of violence points to an objective dehumanization that defines the second inflationary age where humans have lost agency to our own copies (e.g., online avatars), and "copies have turned into things in their own right."[12] The violence in *Sasquatch* as mediated through the documentary mode signals an even more intensified iteration of the flattening out of the subjective and objective, where theater becomes presentational, abject. Monster spectacle and monstrous spectacle are no longer discernable when human bodies are replaced by their theatrical avatars to be mutilated within the frame. In the context of racial and economic disparities that arise as a consequence of illegal drug farming in California during the 1990s, the human and economic flows produced and intensified at the intersection of global neoliberalism and late capitalism, the horror becomes real, intensely literalized through a series of gruesome murders turned into spectacle.

These are the two sides of the coin of true crime media in general; its expressed objective to bring justice to victims and the falsely accused by telling their stories can never fully extricate itself from its status as entertainment; this is made possible by media platforms and funding that directly stand to gain from further entrenching the power wielded by the world's elites. This is not just a question of the rich getting richer, but a neoliberal order responsible for reducing *everything* to the level of *resource* (Castillo and Egginton's term) to be expended or exploited, commodified and turned into profit.[13] *Sasquatch*, as a Hulu original, is a savage misdirection itself, telling us a monster story that raises consciousness about racist violence and the monsters that perpetrate it; meanwhile, another monster exists elsewhere while providing us with this believable *Sasquatch* to divert our gaze, simultaneously collecting the cost of a monthly subscription for the pleasure of turning to look (discounted with a multi-platform bundle).[14] We the People, but increasingly conscious of being the resource that we always were) cannot escape participation in the maintenance of this monstrous social organization of human capital that lumbers forth click-by-click.

Sasquatch is not really about Sasquatch, but if the baroque wild figure tells us anything, *Sasquatch* is *never* about Sasquatch. And that is precisely what makes it such an apt title, a *mise en abyme* of savage misdirections.

NOTES

INTRODUCTION

1. For a study that outlines the transhistorical typology of the Wildman, see Roger Bartra, *The Artificial Savage: Modern Myths of the Wild Man* (Ann Arbor: University of Michigan Press, 1997). The monograph actually begins with chapters on the ancient and medieval iterations of the Wildman, and follows cultural representations through the Romantic period. These figures have often been featured in popular culture (e.g., carnival traditions, the Spanish *comedia*, fairy tales and folklore like *Iron Hans* recorded by the Brothers Grimm, etc.), which, in the time since the Romantic period has flourished across media on page, stage, and over the past century, the screen. A recent representation that can be traced most directly back to the wild figure of the Spanish *comedia* in a western genealogy of wildness would be *Beauty and the Beast*. There are of course typological variations and derivatives produced over time, but like so many of the *comedia*'s wild figures, Beast is presented as a hirsute character ostracized and feared by the townsfolk. He lives in the forest on the outskirts of a "provincial town" (in France, but nameless, which gives the sense that it could be anywhere). Finally, the plot twist is the same as that in the *comedia* corpus analyzed in the present study: Beast is not a beast at all, but in fact a bewitched prince, whose identity is revealed in the conclusion of the numerous versions of the tale ("as old as time"). The story has a long history in European oral traditions (with its own classification in the

Aarne-Thomson-Uther Index, designated as type 425C) and of course is most-well known today to North American audiences thanks to its two Disney adaptations (1991, 2017). In literature and film over the last century, there are too many examples of characters influenced by the wild figure tradition to list them all here. In some cases, the modern variants of the type are directly influenced by the cultural genealogy of the wild figure, either as adaptations of medieval or early modern wild figures or clear allusions to the tradition. These include characters such as the eponymous character in *The Green Knight* (the 2021 feature film of the Arthurian legend of Gawain), Beorn and Radagast the Brown in J. R. R. Tolkien's *Lord of the Rings* universe (each an example of different wild figure types), Hagrid in J. K. Rowling's *Harry Potter* series, and the wildlings that live beyond the wall in George R. R. Martin's *Game of Thrones*. In other cases, they are thematic variants of the marginalized outsider motif: the social outcast living on the fringes of society (literally and figuratively) who receives a humanized portrayal, which becomes a social commentary on the mainstream culture that casts them out. Examples include Mowgli, the feral child protagonist in Kipling's *The Jungle Book* and its sequels (another wild character adapted by Disney), John Merrick in David Lynch's *The Elephant Man* (1980), the civilization of the apes in the *Planet of the Apes* film franchise, and Kya, the youth who raises herself in the marshes of North Carolina in Delia Owen's 2018 novel, *Where the Crawdads Sing* (and film adaptation in 2022). This list is by no means an exhaustive one, the treatment of which merits a book unto itself. Nor am I a modern or contemporary media scholar, but the purpose of this aside is to convey the persisting influence of the wild figure in mainstream popular culture into the present, as well as its diverse manifestations.

2. Peter Brueghel returned to this scene with some frequency, which appears in the background of his famous *The Battle Between Carnival and Lent*. In Bocaccio's *Decameron*, reference to the wild man's role in carnival festivities appears in the second tale of day four of the work's frame tale structure. In the story, a lecherous priest attempts to flee town with an angry mob of cuckolded men on his heels. In as stroke of luck (or so he thinks), he finds quarter in the home of one of the townsfolk, who offers to smuggle him out of town in a wild man costume. The priest fails to escape justice, however. Rather than disguising him, the wild man costume puts him squarely in the townsfolk's crosshairs as part of the carnival festivities. He is duly beaten with sticks in the town square, and his mask is removed to reveal his identity.

3. Arnold G. Reichenberger, "The Uniqueness of the *Comedia*," *Hispanic Review* 27, no. 3 (1959): 307.
4. William Egginton, *How the World Became a Stage: Presence, Theatricality, and the Question of Modernity* (Albany, NY: SUNY Press, 2003), 55.
5. "Todo ello forma parte de una auténtica falacia social, un juego aparente de tensiones, en el que el desenlace supone la vuelta a la realidad primera, anulando así las 'disidencias' que se hayan podido producir por el desacuerdo entre apariencia y realidad." Angel Luis Rubio Moraga, "El teatro barroco, instrumento del poder: Aspectos parateatrales de la fiesta barroca," *Revista Latina de Comunicación Social* 16 (1999): 1.
6. William Egginton, *The Theater of Truth: The Ideology of (Neo)Baroque Aesthetics* (Redwood City, CA: Stanford University Press, 2009), 1–9.
7. "el descubrimiento de los verdaderos orígenes devolverá las cosas a su sitio." Joan Oleza, "La propuesta teatral del primer Lope de Vega," in *Teatro y prácticas escénicas*, ed. J. L. Canet Valles, *La Comedia* (London: Támesis, 1986), 267.
8. David R. Castillo, *Baroque Horrors: Roots of the Fantastic in the Age of Curiosities* (Ann Arbor: University of Michigan Press, 2010), 161.
9. Castillo, *Baroque Horrors*, 31.
10. Castillo, *Baroque Horrors*, 46.
11. Bradley J. Nelson, *The Persistence of Presence: Emblem and Ritual in Baroque Spain* (Toronto: University of Toronto Press, 2010), 10.
12. Castillo, *Baroque Horrors*, xiii.
13. *La lindona de Galicia* has traditionally been attributed either to Juan Pérez de Montalbán or Lope de Vega; however, new digital tools developed by the ETSO Project (Estilometría aplicada al Teatro del Siglo de Oro) have led to advances in stylometric analysis for determining authorship of early modern plays. A stylometric analysis of *La lindona de Galicia* revealed Andrés de Claramonte to be the most likely author of the play. Álvaro Cuéllar and Germán Vega García-Luengos, "Un nuevo repertorio dramático para Andrés de Claramonte," *Hipogrifo: Revista de literatura y cultura del Siglo de Oro* 11, no. 1 (2023): 117–72.
14. See A. D. Deyermond, "El hombre salvaje en la novela sentimental," in *Actas del Segundo Congreso Internacional de Hispanistas*, ed. Jaime Sanchez Romeralo and Norbert Poulussen (Nijmegen: Instituto Español de la Universidad de Nimega, 1967), 265–72. Deyermond examines the prevalence of the wild figure in Iberian sentimental fiction during the late medieval period, highlighting examples in the works of representative writers like Diego de San Pedro (*Cárcel de amor, Arnalte e Lucenda*)

and Juan de Flores (*Grimalte y Gradissa, Grisel y Mirabella*). For Deyermond, the young, lovesick aristocratic protagonists suffer psychological crises as a symptom of their uncontrolled desire. And when in this state, they abscond to the forest where they are portrayed as wild men as a figurative marker for the symptoms of their unmitigated lovesickness. "Madness" is used here as a terminology associated with sentimental romance as a historical literary genre, not as a substitute for a clinical vocabulary or real-world context.

15. "un conjunto de aberraciones pseudoartísticas o literarias impregnadas del mal gusto que el catolicismo contrarreformista había cultivado en los países sujeto a Roma." José Antonio Maravall, *La cultura del barroco: Análisis de una estructura histórica* (Barcelona: Ariel, 1975), 29. For translations of Maravall's *La cultura del barroco*, I have consulted and used Terry Cochran's translation (Minneapolis: University of Minnesota Press, 1983), with minor revisions to maintain normalized orthography, or in some cases to offer what I considered a closer approximation to Maravall's original prose.

16. "en su articulación conjunta sobre una situación política, económica, y social." Maravall, *La cultura del barroco*, 30.

17. Massimo Lollini, "Maravall's Culture of the Baroque: Between Wölfflin, Gramsci, and Benjamin," *Forum: José Antonio Maravall and Baroque Culture, Yearbook of Comparative and General Literature* 45–46 (1996–97): 189.

18. "ofrece con una complejidad de recursos y resultados que hacen de ese período uno de los de más necesaria investigación para entender la historia de la Europa moderna." Maravall, *Cultura del barroco*, 29.

19. Nicholas Spadaccini and Luis Martín-Estudillo, eds., *Hispanic Baroques: Reading Cultures in Context*, Hispanic Issues 31 (Nashville, TN: Vanderbilt University Press, 2005), xii.

20. Egginton, *Theater of Truth*, 1.

21. Egginton, *Theater of Truth*, 2.

22. Mieke Bal, *Quoting Caravaggio: Contemporary Art, Preposterous History* (Chicago: University of Chicago Press, 1999), 16.

23. Angela Ndalianis, *Neo-Baroque Aesthetics and Contemporary Entertainment* (Cambridge, MA: MIT Press, 2004), 5.

24. For more on the neo-Baroque, see Bruce Burningham, *Tilting Cervantes: Baroque Reflections on Postmodern Culture* (Nashville, TN: Vanderbilt University Press, 2008); Walter Moser, Angela Ndalianis, and Peter Krieger, eds., *Neo-Baroques: From Latin America to the Hollywood*

Blockbuster (Boston, MA: BRILL, 2016); Ndalianis, *Neo-Baroque Aesthetics*; Severo Sarduy, *Barroco* (Buenos Aires: Sudamericana, 1974).
25. John H. Elliott, "Concerto Barocco," *New York Review of Books* 34, no. 6 (April 9, 1987).
26. Laura R. Bass, "The Comedia and Cultural Control: The Legacy of José Antonio Maravall," *Bulletin of the Comediantes* 65, no. 1 (2013): 3.
27. Jesús Pérez-Magallón, "The Baroque: The Intellectual and Geopolitical Reasons for a Historiographical Erasure," *Les Dossiers du Grihl* 6, no. 2 (2012): n.p.
28. David R. Castillo, "Maravall on Culture and Historical Discourse: A Question of Methodolgy," *Forum: José Antonio Maravall and Baroque Culture, Yearbook of Comparative and General Literature* 45–46 (1996–1997): 179; Nelson, *Persistence of Presence*, 18–19.
29. Julian Weiss, "Maravall's Materialism," *Forum: José Antonio Maravall and Baroque Culture, Yearbook of Comparative and General Literature* 45–56 (1996–97): 184.
30. Lollini, "Maravall's Culture of the Baroque," 190.
31. Nelson, *Persistence of Presence*, 23.
32. Weiss, "Maravall's Materialism," 183.
33. Wolf Sohlich, "A Frankfurt School Perspective on José Antonio Maravall's Culture of the Baroque," *Forum: José Antonio Maravall and Baroque Culture, Yearbook of Comparative and General Literature* 45–46 (1996–1997): 199.
34. Weiss, "Maravall's Materialism," 184.
35. Stuart Hall, "When Was the 'Post-colonial'? Thinking at the Limit," in *The Postcolonial Question: Common Skies, Divided Horizons*, ed. Iain Chambers and Lidia Curti (London: Routledge, 1996), 259. Hall is speaking about the debates in postcolonial studies over the scope of its critical approach, but it remains applicable to the theme and line of argumentation here, as will become clear in the pages that follow in the discussion of the importance of Latin American postcolonial criticism on my approach to representations of wildness in the Spanish Baroque.
36. Ndalianis, *Neo-Baroque Aesthetics*, 4–5.
37. Ndalianis, *Neo-Baroque Aesthetics*, 25.
38. Spadaccini and Martín-Estudillo, *Hispanic Baroques*, xxviii.
39. Baltasar Gracián, *Oráculo manual y arte de prudencia*, ed. Emilio Blanco, Letras hispánicas 395 (Madrid: Cátedra, 2001). "No hay belleza sin ayuda, ni perfección que no dé en bárbara sin el realce del artificio: a lo malo socorre y lo bueno lo perfecciona."

40. "siempre en oposición dialéctica, siempre a punto de síntesis." Fiorigio Minelli, "Introducción," in *La fingida Arcadia de Tirso de Molina* (Madrid: Edita Revista "Estudios," 1980), 39.
41. On the connection between representations of gardens and ruins in the Baroque, see Emilio Orozco Díaz, "Ruinas y jardines: Su significado y valor en la temática del barroco," in *Temas del barroco de poesía y pintura* (Granada: Universidad de Granada, 1947).
42. It is of course Marx who emphasized primacy of capitalism in the organization of modernity, while Habermas is attributed with identifying the Enlightenment and French Revolution as the "key historical events in establishing the principle of subjectivity," also including the Protestant Reformation in the list. See Jürgen Habermas, *The Philosophical Discourse of Modernity*, trans. Frederick Lawrence (Cambridge: Polity Press, 1998), 17.
43. Aníbal Quijano, "Coloniality of Power, Eurocentrism, and Latin America," trans. Michael Ennis, *Nepantla* 1, no. 3 (2000): 542.
44. Quijano, "Coloniality of Power," 542.
45. Castro-Gómez calls this Marx's "blindspot" in his contention that "what truly constitutes modernity is capitalism, which expands from Europe to the rest of the world, so that to Marx, it seems as if colonialism is an 'effect' related to the consolidation of a global market." Santiago Castro-Gómez, "(Post)Coloniality for Dummies: Latin American Perspectives on Modernity, Coloniality, and the Geopolitics of Knowledge," in *Coloniality at Large: Latin America and the Postcolonial Debate*, ed. Mabel Moraña, Carlos Jauregui, and Enrique Dussel (Durham, NC: Duke University Press, 2008), 264.
46. Castro-Gómez, "(Post)Coloniality," 272.
47. Aníbal Quijano, "Coloniality and Modernity/Rationality," trans. Sonia Therborn, *Cultural Studies* 21, no. 2–3 (2007): 176.
48. Enrique Dussel, "Eurocentrism and Modernity (Introduction to the Frankfurt Lectures)," *boundary 2* 20, no. 3 (1993): 67.
49. Enrique Dussel, "Europe, Modernity, and Eurocentrism," trans. Javier Krauel and Virginia C. Tuma, *Nepantla* 1, no. 3 (2000): 471.
50. Castro-Gómez, "(Post)Coloniality," 280.
51. Castro-Gómez, "(Post)Coloniality," 283.
52. Walter Mignolo, "The Geopolitics of Knowledge and the Colonial Difference," *South Atlantic Quarterly* 101, no. 1 (2002): 84.
53. Mignolo, "The Geopolitics of Knowledge," 84.

54. For an introduction on the garden as political metaphor in the Renaissance and Baroque cultural imagination, see, Alexander Samson, *Locus Amoenus: Gardens and Horticulture in the Renaissance* (Chichester, UK: Wiley & Sons, 2012), 4–8.
55. Two notable examples include the following: Lope de Vega portrays the autobiographical poetic voice in the *jardín de flores* ("garden of flowers") passage in the eighth epistle of *La Filomena*, where he is walking through his garden, pausing to contemplate a series of contemporary poets, as if standing before each of their busts in a garden statuary. In Tirso de Molina's *La fingida Arcadia* (1622), a dramatic parody of Lope's pastoral novel (and play) *La Arcadia*, the playwright explores the metatheatrical depths of the garden metaphor. *La fingida Arcadia* was a commissioned work originally staged for a noble audience in the gardens of one of the Count-Duke of Benavente's estates. The play takes place in a garden setting, much like the one where it was staged, and one of the characters disguises himself as a gardener named Tirso.
56. Mignolo (citing Wallerstein), "The Geopolitics of Knowledge," 79. Francis Bacon was immensely influential in the development of these universalist paradigms in the philosophy of knowledge during the Enlightenment. He helped establish the proscriptive ethos of modern epistemology that assumes a single universal truth that is the natural philosopher's (we would now call this figure a scientist) task to discover and disseminate. His apology for the faculties of the rational mind exemplifies this epistemic ideal: "Wherefore from these three fountains, Memory, Imagination, and Reason flow these three emanations, History, Poesy, and Philosophy, and *there can be no others*." *Di Augmentis Scientiarum*, Book 2.
57. Nelson, *Persistence of Presence*, 10.
58. For the foundational work of scholarship that examines the epistemic impact on the European "discovery" of the New World, see Anthony Pagden, *European Encounters with the New World from Renaissance to Romanticism* (New Haven, CT: Yale University Press, 1993). For a concrete example of the crisis of knowledge in Europe in the context of the New World, see Andrés Prieto's work on the problem of classification in American animal taxonomies. "Classification, Memory, and Subjectivity in Gonzalo Fernández de Oviedo's *Sumario de la natural historia* (1526)," *MLN* 124 (2009): 329–349.
59. Pagden, *European Encounters*, 5.
60. Pagden, *European Encounters*, 10.

61. Pierre Bourdieu, *The Field of Cultural Production* (New York: Columbia University Press, 1993), 110. For Bourdieu, the subject is heavily "disposed" to the values rehearsed and reinforced by all activity in the cultural field. These inherited and rehearsed dispositions are what Bourdieu calls *habitus*, or "the different possible positions in social space . . . bound up with the systems of dispositions (*habitus*) characteristic of the different classes and different class factions." Bourdieu, "From *Distinction: A Social Critique of the Judgment of Taste*," in *The Critical Tradition*, ed. David H. Richter (Boston: Bedford/St. Martin's, 2007), 1402.
62. Nelson, *Persistence of Presence*, 20.
63. Nelson, *Persistence of Presence*, 5–6.
64. Nelson, *Persistence of Presence*, 9–10.
65. David R. Castillo and William Egginton, *Medialogies: Reading Reality in the Age of Inflationary Media* (London: Bloomsbury Academic, 2017), 1.
66. Castillo and Egginton, *Medialogies*, 2.
67. Egginton, *The Theater of Truth*, 40.
68. Castillo and Egginton, *Medialogies*, 120 (my emphasis).
69. As Castillo and Egginton concisely note, "when the reality behind appearance is thus removed from immediate perception, it becomes susceptible to manipulation." *Medialogies*, 4.
70. See Juan Carlos Rodríguez, *Theory and History of Ideological Production: The First Bourgeois Literatures (The 16th Century)* (Newark: University of Delaware Press, 2002). Rodríguez defines *organicism* to describe a medieval model for social organization and subjectivity: "Under organicism, . . . it is supposed that the 'I' is the gift of blood, lineage, the *organic body* (that is, society) in which it is inscribed or born, and which includes or excludes it, as the case may be" (14). The author argues that *organicism* was supplanted by *animism* as the "ideological matrices relevant" to new social formations emerging during early modernity, for which he offers the following definition: "within the context of capitalist freedom it is presumed that the free 'I' is innate, that it is not inscribed by anyone, that it is something given by oneself to oneself. From which it follows that we create our own subjectivity and morality, in every sense of the word 'create'" (14).
71. See Oleh Mazur, *The Wild Man in the Spanish Renaissance and Golden Age Theater: A Comparative Study Including the Indio, the Bárbaro and their Counterparts in European Lores* (Ann Arbor, MI: University Microfilms International, 1980). In his study, he divides the influences

on theatrical wildness on the Iberian Peninsula into the following categories: (1) primitive man, (2) folkloric type, (3) mythological type, (4) faraway places type, (5) exposure type, (6) noble savage type, (7) love madness type, (8) allegorical madness type, and (9) the savage knight. The thrust of Mazur's approach mirrors that of mid-century folkloricists as a type-index to organize wildness into tidy categories (rather than an in-depth analysis). And while the distinctions between Mazur's types and subtypes can become tedious and inevitably break down at points, his study is a useful tool as a catalogue of the many traditions of wild representation in the cultural imagination that precede the Renaissance and Baroque, as well as a broad overview and introduction to the theme of wildness in Iberian dramatic production during the period.

72. This device finds its analogue in pre- and early modern pageantry when a company of wild men would burst into the banquet hall between courses of a noble or royal feast to perform a dramatic interlude. It should also be noted, both in prose fiction and theater, scenes in which eating or singing take place (e.g., pastoral romance, musical theater) mark a pause in the action, a temporal space when narrative time ceases. In Montemayor's *La Diana*, wild folk descend on a group of shepherds singing in a pasture, which serves as an injection of action to advance the narrative.

73. See Raúl A. Galoppe, "Monstruoso Aquiles, aberración y cruce: Las líneas del género y el deseo autorial," *Hecho Teatral: Revista de teoría y práctica del Teatro Hispánico* 2 (2002): 125–45; Jose A. Madrigal, "La transmutación de Aquiles: De salvaje a héroe (Tirso de Molina, *El Aquiles*)," *Hispanófila* 26, no. 2 (1983): 15–26; Alan K. G. Paterson, "Tirso de Molina and the Androgyne: 'El Aquiles' and 'La dama del olivar,'" *Bulletin of Hispanic Studies* 70, no. 1 (1993): 105–14; Anita K. Stoll, "Cross/Dressing in Tirso's *El amor médico* (*Love, the Doctor*) and *El Aquiles* (*Achilles*)," in *Gender, Identity, and Representation in Spain's Golden Age*, ed. Dawn L. Smith and Anita K. Stoll, (Lewisburg, PA: Bucknell University Press, 2000), 86–108.

74. On the representation of race in Vélez de Guevara's play, see Beth Bernstein, "A 'Monstrous' Problem: Examining Issues of Race in *Virtudes vencen señales*," in *Exploring Race, Ethnicity, Gender, and Sexuality in Four Spanish Plays: A Crisis of Identity* (Lanham, MD: Lexington Books, 2021), 53–88; Baltasar Fra-Molinero, "The Play of Race and Gender in Vélez de Guevara's *Virtudes vencen señales*," *Bulletin of the Comediantes* 49, no. 2 (1997); José María Ruano de la Haza, introduction to *Virtudes*

vencen señales by Luis Vélez de Guevara, Ediciones críticas 60 (Newark, DE: Juan de la Cuesta Hispanic Monographs, 2010).
75. Mignolo, "The Geopolitics of Knowledge," 83.
76. Mignolo makes this argument to demonstrate that coloniality is epistemically inextricable from modernity, and that the roots of racism were established and reproduced during the period of Latin Europe's colonial expansion: "Kant's ethno-racial tetragon (Africans are black, Americans are red [Kant was thinking of the United States], Asians are yellow, and Europeans are white) was the eighteenth-century version of early Spanish classifications of Moors, Jews, American Indians, black Africans, and the Chinese." Mignolo, "The Geopolitics of Knowledge," 83.
77. It is unlikely a coincidence that Vélez de Guevara, from Seville, would be the playwright to blur the histrionic conventions between embodying wildness and Blackness on the stage. Scholarship abounds across the disciplines on the sub-Saharan African population of Seville during the early modern period. For scholarship on race and embodied performance of Blackness on the early modern Iberian stage, see John Beusterien, *An Eye on Race: Perspectives from Theater in Imperial Spain* (Lewisburg, PA: Bucknell University Press, 2006); Nicholas R. Jones, *Staging Habla de Negros: Radical Performances of the African Diaspora in Early Modern Spain* (University Park: Pennsylvania State University Press, 2019).

CHAPTER 1

1. Roger Bartra, *The Artificial Savage*, 1.
2. Hayden White, "The Forms of Wildness: Archaeology of an Idea," in *The Wild Man Within: An Image of Western Thought from the Renaissance to Romanticism*, ed. Edward Dudley and Maximillian E. Novak (Pittsburgh, PA: University of Pittsburgh Press, 1972), 4.
3. White, "Forms of Wildness," 4.
4. Georg Wilhelm Friedrich Hegel, *Hegel's Philosophy of Right*, trans. T. M. Knox (Oxford: Clarendon Press, 1958), 13.
5. For example, Roger Bartra's scholarship on the wild man over the course of western history is essential. See *El salvaje en el espejo* (Ediciones Era, 1992, translated and published by the University of Michigan Press in 1995 as *Wild Men in the Looking Glass*) and *The Artificial Savage* (Ann Arbor: University of Michigan Press, 1997).

6. "mucho queda todavía por decir." Fausta Antonucci, *El salvaje en la Comedia del Siglo de Oro: Historia de un tema de Lope a Calderón* (Pamplona, Toulouse: Anejos de RILCE, L.E.S.O., 1995), 12.
7. That isn't to say that representations of wild figures solely belonged to theater in the Spanish sixteenth and seventeenth centuries. A notable literary example is Cervantes's Cardenio, the lovesick wild man in the Sierra Morena episodes of *Don Quijote*. Worth noting, however, is that even Cardenio was reimagined for the stage by Shakespeare in his lost play *The History of Cardenio*. For an in-depth analysis of the sociohistorical backdrop that generated the English translation and adaptation of Spanish cultural production, see Barbara Fuchs, *The Poetics of Piracy* (Philadelphia: University of Pennsylvania Press, 2013).
8. Roger Bartra, *Wild Men in the Looking Glass: The Mythic Origins of European Otherness*, trans. Carl T. Berrisford (Ann Arbor: University of Michigan Press, 1994), 199.
9. Of course, there are exceptions; for example, in the Arthurian cycle, Yvain descends into wildness and takes on the features of both chivalric and sentimental wild figure types. He is portrayed as both the violent unkempt madman that inhabits the peripheral forest, and the lovesick courtier whose madness is precipitated by unrequited love.
10. Bartra argues that these characters mark a decline in the Renaissance portrayals of wildness because they are self-aware and ironic representations of the wild man type that demonstrate a meta-fictional deconstruction of their characteristics on the part of the author of each work. See Bartra, *Wild Men in the Looking Glass*, 171–202.
11. A note on nomenclature: unless otherwise indicated, the terms "paratheatrical" and "prototheatrical" will be used to refer to performance traditions and practices of spectacle in premodern Europe. These terms are not entirely interchangeable, however. "Prototheatrical" implies a linear, historical view of theater as one set of practices that developed into what we now identify as modern theater, whereas "paratheater" can be used transhistorically to describe spectacle that displays the essential elements of theater—an actor and an audience, as defined by Burningham—but not all of the characteristics that have come to define modern commercial theater. Paratheatrical is preferred over prototheatrical in the context of the transitions outlined here, because the latter implies a practice that has yet to become fully theatrical. Burningham persuasively argues against the narrative that "theatricality" is what distinguishes the modern stage from premodern performance practices;

rather, it was the commercial packaging and dissemination of the theater along with theatrical texts that shaped the theater as it became modern. When used in the present study, however imprecise the terms may be and in the absence of a preferred vocabulary, both "paratheatrical" and "prototheatrical" are used to distinguish premodern performance practices from modern ones, not serve as a commentary on the extent of their theatricality. I agree with Burningham on the limitations of this terminology and with his history of theatricality outlined in Bruce Burningham, *Radical Theatricality: Jongleuresque Performance on the Early Spanish Stage* (West Lafayette, IN: Purdue University Press, 2007). My use of the terms here may be idiosyncratic as a result.

12. "A la formación de la figura del salvaje literario contribuyen indudablemente rasgos procedentes del mito y del folclore, así como de las artes figurativas; recíprocamente, elementos literarios pueden influir en la representación del salvaje que se aprecia en las artes figurativas." Antonucci, *Salvaje en la Comedia*, 12.

13. "el núcleo narrativo (mínimo, por lo demás) que sustentaba estas representaciones, era el mismo que tanta parte tenía en la estructura narrativa (e ideológica) de los libros de caballerías." Antonucci, *Salvaje en la Comedia*, 46.

14. Bruce Burningham pushes back against the traditional understanding that the two spheres developed entirely apart from one another. He demonstrates that jongleurs found an audience not only in popular urban spaces, but also performed for the court as well. In crossing the boundary between popular and courtly spaces, jongleuresque performers left an impact on theatrical practice in both that cannot be overlooked. See Burningham, *Radical Theatricality*, especially 61–68.

15. The bibliography on paratheatrical court spectacle is immense, but for a representative list of foundational scholarship, see E. K. Chambers, *The Mediaeval Stage*, vol. IV (Oxford: Oxford University Press, 1903); N. D. Shergold, *A History of the Spanish Stage: From Medieval Times until the End of the Seventeenth Century* (Oxford: Oxford, Clarendon Press, 1967), 113–42; Ronald Surtz, *The Birth of a Theater: Dramatic Convention in the Spanish Theater from Juan del Encina to Lope de Vega* (Princeton, NJ: Princeton University, Dept. of Romance Languages and Literatures; Castalia, 1979), 16–124; Angel Valbuena Prat, *Historia del teatro español* (Barcelona: Noguer, 1956), 27–54. More recently, scholars including Bernardo García García and María Luisa Lobato have published extensively on paratheatrical practices in early modern Iberia. A

representative list of their scholarship includes their co-edited volumes *La fiesta cortesana en la época de los Austrias* (Valladolid: Junta de Castilla y León, Consejería de Educación y Cultura, 2003); and *Dramaturgia festiva y cultura nobiliaria en el siglo de oro* (Madrid: Iberoamericana, 2007). See also Lobato's chapter "El espacio de la fiesta: Máscaras parateatrales y teatrales en el Siglo de Oro," in *Espacios de representación y espacios representados en el teatro áureo español*, ed. Francisco Sáez Raposo (Barcelona: Universitat Autónoma de Barcelona, 2011).

16. Emilio Cotarelo y Mori, *Colección de entremeses, loas, bailes, jácaras y mojigangas desde fines del siglo XVI á mediados del XVIII ordenada* (Madrid: Bailly-Bailliére, 1911), 56. Once the *comedia* takes over as the predominant form of public entertainment in the latter half of the sixteenth century, the term *entremés* (interlude) comes to refer more specifically to the short burlesque interludes that took place between the acts of the three-act *comedia*. In the context of the medieval and Renaissance court, it more generally encompasses a variety of paratheatrical performance entertainments, which usually took place between the courses of a banquet feast.

17. These paratheatrical spectacles did not disappear during the Renaissance and Baroque. In one royal procession in Barcelona, Felipe IV wore lion skins—the unmistakable garb of the wild man—for his entrance into the city. See María de los Ángeles Pérez Samper, "Barcelona, corte: Las fiestas reales en la época de los Austrias," in *La fiesta cortesana en la época de los Austrias*, ed. María Luisa Lobato and Bernardo José García García (Valladolid: Junta de Castilla y León, Consejería de Educación y Cultura, 2003), 142. An avid theater enthusiast, it is reasonable to assume the king would have seen one of the *comedias* treated in this corpus, and however consciously or unconsciously, these sartorial markers are charged with the same theatricality as the many wild figures on the baroque Iberian stage. While there is a spectrum of meanings the lion pelts could signify, in this particular instance it seems clear that the pelts draw a parallel between Felipe and the king of the animal kingdom (a common symbolic gesture of kingship), if not his subjugation of the symbolic beast that hangs upon his shoulders. In the context of the tense relations between the crown and Barcelona during his reign, the metaphor is unlikely to have been mistaken.

18. Research over the past half century has uncovered an abundance of evidence for the existence of burgeoning public spectacle traditions during those events, often appearing in the archive as *representaciones* that were

performed with costumed actors who were also paid. Liturgical drama appears most frequently in the record, but secular plays are present as well, often with pastoral themes and content. For an overview and extensive bibliography on these spectacles, see Ángel Gómez Moreno, "The Challenges of Historiography: The Theatre in Medieval Spain," in *A History of Theatre in Spain*, ed. David T. Gies and Maria M. Delgado (Cambridge: Cambridge University Press, 2012).

19. Bartra curiously submits that "the great absentee at the banquet of civilization is the wild man." *Wild Men in the Looking Glass*, 145. Of course, the anthropologist is speaking metaphorically, and the quote appears in a passage that addresses a topic mostly unrelated to medieval court banquet entertainments, chiefly, the evolution of etiquette in the civilizing process of humankind (citing Norbert Elias); nevertheless, in the context of the present analysis, the irony produced by the comment is a productive one. Indeed, the banquet feast *is* where the wild man always seems to turn up, in precisely the space he should be most absent at the civilized site par excellence: the royal court.

20. Ángel Gómez Moreno, *El teatro medieval castellano en su marco románico* (Madrid: Taurus, 1991), 30.

21. See Teresa Ferrer Valls, *La práctica escénica cortesana: De la época del Emperador a la de Felipe III* (London: Tamesis, en colaboración con la Institució Valenciana d'Estudis i Investigació, 1991), 35–47; María Luisa Lobato, "Nobles como actores: El papel activo de las gentes de palacio en las representaciones cortesanas de la época de los Austrias," in *Dramaturgia festiva y cultura nobiliaria en el Siglo de Oro*, ed. María Luisa Lobato Bernardo J. García García (Madrid: Iberoamericana; Vervuert, 2007), 89–114.

22. This visual metaphor is captured in Leoni's bronze statue of Carlos V, *Carlos V y el Furor*. The statue portrays Carlos standing triumphant over another masculine figure (Fury), depicted as pinned on top of a bed of allegorical objects, the iconic Wildman's club among them (see Figures 1.1–2). Fury and the objects that surround him have traditionally been understood to symbolize Carlos V's enemies and his imperial might (e.g., objects like a trumpet and a bundle of rods [*haz*]—a roman symbol for political authority and in the mid-twentieth century co-opted by fascist movements); however, the statue also is a clear allusion to Virgil's *Aeneid*, in which *furor* runs as a central theme to caution against the dangers of letting unruly emotions run unchecked. This lends itself to a complimentary Neo-stoic reading of the Leoni statue, where Carlos is

depicted as also overcoming the self, conveyed allegorically in the club embedded beneath Fury.
23. Cotarelo y Mori, *Colección de entremeses*, 17.
24. Timothy Husband and Gloria Gilmore-House, *The Wild Man: Medieval Myth and Symbolism* (New York: Metropolitan Museum of Art, 1980), 71.
25. Gerónimo de Blancas, *Coronaciones de los serenísimos reyes de Aragón*, ed. Andrés de Uztarroz (Zaragoza: Diego Dormer, 1641), 75–78.
26. On court entertainments, see Ferrer Valls, *Práctica escénica cortesana*, 19–34; on wild men in royal processions, see Teofilo F. Ruiz, *A King Travels: Festive Traditions in Late Medieval and Early Modern Spain* (Princeton, NJ: Princeton University Press, 2012), 216.
27. Lobato, "Espacio de la fiesta," 259–95. For more on the persistence of paratheatrical activity during the sixteenth and seventeenth centuries, see Lobato and García-García's two edited volumes, *Dramaturgia festiva* (2007) and *La fiesta cortesana* (2003). Teresa Ferrer Valls has also worked extensively on court entertainment under the Habsburgs, including two book-length studies: *Práctica escénica cortesana*, (1991); and *Nobleza y espectáculo teatral (1535–1622): Estudio y Documentos*, ed. Joan Oleza, Textos Teatrales Hispánicos del siglo XVI (Valencia: UNED, Universidad de Sevilla, Universidat de València, 1993), 635–44. Another more recent contribution to this scholarship is Margaret Greer's chapter, "Playing the Palace: Space, Place and Performance in Early Modern Spain," in *A History of Theatre in Spain*, ed. David T. Gies and Maria M. Delgado (Cambridge: Cambridge University Press, 2012), 79–102.
28. "si un tiempo del año fue especialmente proclive para este ambiente lúdico, hay que destacar Carnaval, el cual afectó no solo las celebraciones populares sino también, y muy especialmente, a las fiestas en la corte de los Austrias." Lobato, *La fiesta cortesana*, 261.
29. Javier Huerta Calvo, ed., *Teatro y carnaval*, vol. 12, Cuadernos de Teatro Clásico 12 (Madrid: Compañía Nacional de Teatro Clásico, 1999), 9.
30. The serious tone of the *comedias* in the corpus of wild figure plays, as well as the relative absence of explicit mention of carnival revelry, make the wild figure a distinct phenomenon from the topsy-turvy world of the *comedias burlescas* (burlesque plays) that are often set during the carnival season or Día de San Juan (and staged as part those celebrations). For a dedicated study on the *comedia burlesca* as a subgenre of entertainment almost exclusively put on at court, see Adelaida Cortijo Ocaña and Antonio Cortijo Ocaña, "Carnaval y teatro en los siglos XVI y XVII," *Revista de Filología Española* 84, no. 2 (2004). Importantly,

whereas the wild figure remained a popular figure for both *corral* and court alike, the *comedia burlesca* must be understood "dentro de un contexto cortesano, pues se representan ante la corte y con una audiencia de alta clase social" (within a courtly context, put on for the court with an audience made up of the upper-class elite; 400). That these works were rarely staged for a public audience is telling. The danger in presenting the ludic and subversive nature of the social world depicted in these burlesque plays to a public audience is essentially non-existent in the courtly sphere, where they could be enjoyed by the those that held the power without posing a threat.

31. The foundational study of carnival traditions in Iberia remains Julio Caro Baroja, *El carnaval: Análisis histórico-cultural*, 2nd ed. (Madrid: Taurus, 1979).
32. Mikhail Bakhtin, *Rabelais and His World*, trans. Helene Iswolsky (Bloomington: Indiana University Press, 1984), 11.
33. Bakhtin, *Rabelais and His World*, 7.
34. Bakhtin, *Rabelais and His World*, 10.
35. Bakhtin, *Rabelais and His World*, 24.
36. Bakhtin, *Rabelais and His World*, 19.
37. Rodríguez, *Theory and History of Ideological Production*, 13–14.
38. Paula Findlen, "Between Carnival and Lent: The Scientific Revolution at the Margins of Culture," *Configurations: A Journal of Literature, Science, and Technology* 6, no. 2 (1998): 253.
39. Findlen, "Between Carnival," 256, 60.
40. Findlen, "Between Carnival," 261.
41. Charlotte Stern, "Juan del Encina's Carnival Eclogues and the Spanish Drama of the Renaissance," *Renaissance Drama* 8 (1965): 185.
42. Stern, "Juan del Encina's Carnival Eclogues," 187–91.
43. Bruce W. Wardropper, "Metamorphosis in the Theatre of Juan del Encina," *Studies in Philology* 59 (1962): 45.
44. Egginton, *How the World Became a Stage*, 64–65.
45. Stern, "Juan del Encina's Carnival Eclogues," 193.
46. This is a dominant motif in pastoral literature of the period; the shepherds gathered in the forest to pass the time and sing songs of unrequited love are not actually shepherds, but nobles dressed up as them. Prominent examples include Montemayor's *La Diana* and Lope de Vega's *La Arcadia*, as well as later parodies of the genre in Cervantes's *Don Quijote* (e.g., the Grisóstomo and Marcela episode in chapters 12–14 of Part I, and also chapter 58 in Part II), and Tirso de Molina's *La fingida Arcadia*.

47. Tania de Miguel Magro draws similar conclusions about these transitions in the staging of *mojigangas*, another genre of short theater during the period. See Tania de Miguel Magro, "La mojiganga en el contexto de la fiesta barroca" *Bulletin of the Comediantes* 68, no. 1 (2016).
48. I again draw from Egginton's vocabulary here, in which he unpacks the terms "presence" and "theatricality" as the characteristics that distinguish the medieval and the modern worldviews, respectively. This is in fact his stated purpose in *How the World Became a Stage*, to "propose a new vocabulary through a description of the practices and conventions of spectacle and an analysis of how those practices and conventions change from the Middle Ages to the early modern period." For a dedicated exposition of this vocabulary, see the second and third chapters of the monograph.
49. "y cuando lo hacen con mala intención, y se las ponen por no ser conocidos, agravan su delito, y por esto no se consiente que ninguna máscara lleve armas sin licencia y siendo conocido." Sebastián de Covarrubias, *Tesoro de la lengua castellana* (Madrid: Luis Sánchez, 1611).
50. 3.3000–02: "¿No saben que no pueden en la corte / andar enmascarados por la calle? / Vuesas mercedes vengan a la cárcel." The relevance of this scene was brought to my attention by Debora Vaccari in "*Máscara fue mi locura, / mis mudanzas acabé*: Lás máscaras en el teatro del primer Lope," in *Máscaras y juegos de identidad en el teatro español del Siglo de Oro*, ed. María Luisa Lobato, Biblioteca Filológica Hispana 127 (Madrid: Visor Libros, 2011), 199.
51. "la ubicación del encuentro en el marco de unas fiestas como las del Carnaval, tan ligadas al juego de ocultación de identidades y de la usurpación de papeles diferentes al que uno representa en la vida cotidiana, subraya la vinculación entre este aspecto de la fiesta carnavalesca y la comedia. Como en la fiesta, en la comedia se da rienda suelta a los impulsos más anárquicos de los individuos, a su faceta más instintiva y vital, a aquella que se siente tentada por la exploración de los límites entre lo admitido y lo vedado socialmente." See Teresa Ferrer Valls, "*La viuda valenciana* de Lope de Vega o el arte de nadar y guardar la ropa," in *Doce comedias buscan un tablado*, Cuadernos de teatro clásico 11 (Madrid: Compañía Nacional de Teatro Clasico, 1999). (Accessed using non-paginated copy.)
52. "Llevar máscara le da al personaje la posibilidad de tener 'otra' vida, una vida que coincide con el mundo mismo de la del cambio de identidad y que está en la misma raíz del juego teatral." Vaccari, "*Máscara fue mi locura*," 204–5.
53. "masks were my madness, my inconstancy had to end."

54. "restore the reality of truth." José María Díez Borque, "El disfraz y otras estrategias para el éxito de la comedia," in *Máscaras y juegos de identidad en el teatro español del Siglo de Oro*, ed. María Luisa Lobato, Biblioteca Filológica Hispana (Madrid: Visor Libros, 2011), 32.
55. See Ferrer Vals, *La práctica escénica cortesana*, 11–48; Shergold, *A History of the Spanish Stage*; Charlotte Stern, *The Medieval Theater in Castile* (Binghamton: SUNY Binghamton, 1996), 201–42.
56. Diana Taylor, *The Archive and the Repertoire: Performing Cultural Memory in the Americas* (Durham, NC: Duke University Press, 2003), xix.
57. Taylor, *Archive and the Repertoire*, 16.
58. Terry Castle, *Masquerade and Civilization: The Carnivalesque in Eighteenth-Century English Culture and Fiction* (Redwood City, CA: Stanford University Press, 1986), 71.
59. Cited in Stern, *The Medieval Theater in Castile*, 275.
60. "el teatro popular no fue el producto espontáneo de una fase primitiva de la evolución teatral, que se extendería desde Lope de Rueda hasta la segunda década del XVII, sino todo lo contrario: una conquista. El fruto de la lucha por un modelo teatral capaz de llegar a más amplias capas de la población de las que habían formado el teatro de colegio, el universitario y el cortesano." Oleza, "La propuesta teatral," 297–98.
61. Taylor, *Archive and the Repertoire*, 2.
62. Taylor, *Archive and the Repertoire*, xx.
63. For my explanation and analysis of the baroque spatiality of discovery scenes in Tirso de Molina's playwriting, see Harrison Meadows, "The Figurative Geography of Natural Landscapes in Tirso de Molina," in *Tirso de Molina: Interdisciplinary Perspectives from the Twenty-First Century*, ed. Esther Fernández (Woodbridge, UK: Támesis, 2023), 161–71.
64. William Eamon, *Science and the Secrets of Nature: Books of Secrets in Medieval and Early Modern Culture* (Princeton, NJ: Princeton University Press, 1994), 270. For a preliminary description of the current discussion of the hermetic tradition in Spain, see Miguel López-Pérez, "Ciencia y pensamiento hermético," in *Beyond the Black Legend: Spain and the Scientific Revolution*, ed. Victor Navarro Brotóns and William Eamon (Valencia: Instituto de Historia de la Ciencia y Documentación López Piñero, 2007).
65. See the introduction of the present study for a reading of wilderness space in the baroque through the lens of coloniality.
66. According to Devos's analysis, more than nine hundred plays in Proquest's Teatro Español del Siglo de Oro (TESO) database deploy the mountainside ("monte") set design. Brent Devos, "Evidence Regarding

the 'Monte' Stage Piece in Theatres of the Seventeenth Century," *Bulletin of the Comediantes* 67, no. 2 (2015): 101.
67. Burningham, *Radical Theatricality*, 167.
68. "viene a reflejar el mismo proceso de decadencia que sufrió el espíritu liberador del mundo carnavalesco al ser asimilado y, finalmente, abolido por el mundo autoritario de la cultura oficial." Jorge Luis Castillo, "La lengua del gracioso y el mundo del Carnaval en *El desdén, con el desdén* de Moreto," *Bulletin of the Comediantes* 46, no. 1 (1994): 16.

CHAPTER 2

1. Adriana Gordillo and Nicholas Spadaccini, eds., *Writing Monsters: Essays on Iberian and Latin American Cultures*, vol. 15, Hispanic Issues Online (Minneapolis: University of Minnesota, 2014), 3–4.
2. David R. Castillo and William Egginton, "Dreamboat Vampires and Zombie Capitalists," *New York Times*, October 24, 2014.
3. It is not coincidental that these are also the impulses of colonialism. Colonial expansion was definitory of the early modern nation state in the West as much as a shift toward more centralized and unified governments that relied on institutionalized ideological mechanisms to establish order and guide its citizens into committed compliance. This is the symbolic terrain traversed by the baroque wild figure play: invade the edges of the map to domesticate or conquer its inhabitants so that the new land—ideological or geographical—and its people are inscribed into the established social organization and counted as committed adherents to the dominant cultural milieu. It is important to note that this is the ideological underpinning of modern social organization and colonial expansion that resonates in the symbolic architecture of the cultural production created in this context, which is not to say that *all* cultural activity reproduced this symbolic organization of space or that there were no dissidents that resisted those impulses. Rather, those were the hegemonic impulses against which oppositional or liberatory discourses are resisting. For an anthology of landmark essays in Latin American postcolonial studies that offer a framework for understanding coloniality as an epistemic dimension of the modern world-system and its organization, see Mabel Moraña, Carlos Jáuregui, and Enrique Dussel, eds., *Coloniality at Large: Latin America and the Postcolonial Debate* (Durham, NC: Duke University Press, 2008).

4. Gordillo and Spadaccini, *Writing Monsters*, 2.
5. White, "Forms of Wildness," 6.
6. "Lo monstruo, al final se deja leer como una forma hipostática de la norma, y en él desciframos los enigmas que inquietan el equilibrio siempre precario de la normalidad." Elena del Río Parra, *Una era de monstruos: Representaciones de lo deforme en el Siglo de Oro español*, Colección Áurea Hispánica 27 (Navarra: Iberoamericana-Vervuert, 2003), 114. See del Río Parra's monograph for an extensive analysis of the development of the conceptualization of monsters in the context of early modern Europe. In the work, she synthesizes a formidable corpus of primary materials from a wide array of sources including medical treatises, religious tracts, published *relaciones*, among other literary representations of prodigious abnormality.
7. Michael Uebel, "Unthinking the Monster: Twelfth Century Responses to Saracen Alterity," in *Monster Theory: Reading Culture*, ed. Jeffrey Jerome Cohen (Minneapolis: University of Minnesota Press, 1996), n.p.
8. Julio Baena notes an occurrence akin to this phenomenon in Góngora's famous *Fábula de Polifemo y Galatea*, a poem about one of history's more infamous literary monsters, in which the lone reference to monstrosity is used to describe Galatea, as a "monster of cruelty." For his extended analysis of this aspect of the poem, see Julio Baena, "What Kind of a Monster Are You, Galatea?," in *Writing Monsters: Essays on Iberian and Latin American Cultures*, ed. Adriana Gordillo and Nicholas Spadaccini (Minneapolis: University of Minnesota College of Liberal Arts, 2014).
9. Joan Oleza identifies the mistaken-identity trope as a common vehicle for conflict in the *comedia* and outlines the elements that tend to comprise the conflict and resolution of plays that follow this plot trajectory. For his analysis of representative works in the early career of Lope de Vega, see Oleza, "La propuesta teatral," especially 266–99.
10. Egginton, *How the World Became a Stage*, 7.
11. Quijano, "Coloniality of Power," 541.
12. Egginton, *Theater of Truth*, 40.
13. Egginton, *Theater of Truth*, 6. Parenthetical asides are my own. Egginton's framework of the "major" and "minor" strategies of the Baroque serve as a concise vocabulary throughout this study. The "major strategy," which refers to cultural production that reproduces hegemonic values in the service of maintaining social hierarchies and the status quo, has its counterpart in the "minor" strategy. Whereas, for example, Lope's wild

figures generally legitimize monarchical order, patriarchy, and ethnocentricism (i.e., the "major" strategy), Cervantes attacks Lope through satire by exposing the status of the "reality" behind the veil as just another layer in and of the representation. In so doing, Cervantes uncovers the ideological architecture of the *comedia* to reveal "the limitations and paradoxes of its aesthetics" that are nonetheless deployed by contemporary playwrights to pawn "bogus themes." E. Michael Gerli, "*El retablo de las maravillas*: Cervantes' 'Arte nuevo de deshacer comedias,'" *Hispanic Review* 57, no. 4 (1989): 478.

14. Nelson, *Persistence of Presence*, 10.
15. For further exposition of the broad critical utility of "presence" in explaining the shifts in worldview from the premodern to early modernity in the West, see Nelson, *The Persistence of Presence*, and Egginton, *How the World Became a Stage*, especially 33–59.
16. Nelson, *Persistence of Presence*, 23.
17. The dates of composition provided here are those provided by Morley and Bruerton in their classic study, *The Chronology of Lope de Vega's Comedias, with a Discussion of Doubtful Attributions, the Whole Based on a Study of his Strophic Versification*, MLA Monograph Series XI (New York: Modern Language Association, 1940). They base their chronology on trends found in Lope de Vega's preference for certain verse forms during different stages of his career. For example, the authors surmise that *El animal de Hungría* was written sometime between 1608 and 1612 due to the verse forms—in this case *romances*, *décimas*, and *tercetos*— that are predominant in the text, which characterized Lope's production during that period (280–81).
18. "el itinerario exterior de Ursón del estado de salvaje al de príncipe y, también, su itinerario interior de la animalidad a la humanidad." Antonucci, *Salvaje en la Comedia*, 66. See Fausta Antonucci, *El salvaje en la Comedia*; Roger Bartra, *Wild Men in the Looking Glass*; Bartra, *The Artificial Savage*; José A. Madrigal, "La función del hombre salvaje en el teatro de Lope de Vega, Tirso de Molina, y Calderón de la Barca," (PhD diss., University of Kentucky, 1974); Oleh Mazur, *The Wild Man*.
19. *Nacimiento*, 2.1587–91 (References are to act and line numbers):
 URSÓN: El león suelo yo ver
   con la leona abrazarse,
   y ansí deben de juntarse,
   el hombre con la mujer,
   ¿Qué dudo? A buscarla voy.

English translations of dramatic texts are my own, unless otherwise specified.
20. Mazur, *The Wild Man*, 200.
21. *Nacimiento*, 3.3070: "no tiene cosa alguna de fiereza."
22. *Nacimiento*, 2.1865.
23. *Nacimiento*, 2.1731–35:

> ALCALDE 1: ¡Oh, traidor, qué cara tiene!
> ¡Voto al sol! Al proprio viene,
> y con su palo también.
> ALCALDE 2: ¿Tiene cola este animal?
> ALCALDE 1: Ni es hombre ni garabato.

In contemporaneous sources, the only early modern usage of the term *garabato* that I have found is its meaning as a "meat hook." In this passage, this makes sense as a parallel to the previous mention of the monster with his *palo* ("club"), that is, what they see is not a (hu)man carrying a meat hook. Nevertheless, it is curious that he uses the term *garabato*, which in modern usage signifies a sketch or "scribbles," and would be an appropriate double entendre for this passage. Covarrubias only includes the description of a "meat hook" in the *Tesoro de la lengua castellana*, although it has come to be used to describe a hook in a number of applications, especially as a traditional weeding tool that appears in carnival celebrations in modern-day Atlantic coastal regions of Latin America that are closely related to European processional traditions that include a wild man holding a club. This potential articulation between carnival traditions and comedic representation merits further exploration.

24. *Nacimiento*, 2.1736–37: "¿Que estáis viendo el retrato / donde está el original?" Regarding the orthography of this passage, the question marks do not appear in the original print edition of the work, and are therefore inferred by the modern editor of the text (Tubau). Although not entirely necessary, this orthographical decision on the part of the editor makes the meaning of the passage clearer to guide readers to the interpretation that Ursón is suggesting that they are looking at a representation when the real thing is right in front them. It should also be noted that "donde" bears no diacritic, which would suggest that Ursón is asking the *alcaldes*, either straightforwardly or rhetorically, about the whereabouts of the monster depicted on the page. Ursón seems to be self-aware of his status among the locals, even if, as I argue, it is unmerited.

25. *Nacimiento*, 2.1758: "En verdad que es hombre honrado."

26. "lo que nosotros vemos en escena del comportamiento de Ursón, no se corresponde en nada con lo que cuentan los villanos." Antonucci, *Salvaje en la Comedia*, 69.
27. Mazur, *The Wild Man*, 66.
28. *Nacimiento*, 2.1604–05: "Es del cielo tu hermosura / y de la tierra tu miedo."
29. *Nacimiento*, 2.1558–69:
    VILLANA: Si confiesas que ese es tal
    como se ve en su poder,
    yo soy suya y soy mujer,
    di, ¿por qué me haces mal?
    URSÓN: ¿Yo mal? El cielo me niegue
    el sustento que me ha dado,
    si hacerte mal he pensado
    ni a tanto el alma se atreve.
    No me trates con desdén,
    que por bien me has de obligar,
    y solo pienso tomar
    lo que me dieres por bien.
30. *Nacimiento*, 2.2156–58. "Yo por el monstruo he venido / mas este monstruo es Uberto / muere traidor."
31. Richard F. Glenn, "The Loss of Identity: Towards a Definition of the Dialectic in Lope's Early Drama," *Hispanic Review* 41, no. 4 (1973): 626. Delia Gavela García also identifies this motif running through Lope's corpus. See "Obras hacen linaje o la fuerza de la sangre: identidades ocultas en la producción lopesca," in *Máscaras y juegos de identidad en el teatro español del Siglo de Oro*, ed. María Luisa Lobato, Biblioteca Filológica Hispana (Madrid: Visor Libros, 2011).
32. Of course, *El nacimiento de Ursón y Valentín* is not the only source of intertextuality on which *El animal de Hungría* draws. Simerka compares Shakespeare's *Cymbeline* and *Winter's Tale* to Lope's *comedia* in her *Knowing Subjects*, along with its influence on later works such as Zayas's *La perseguida triunfante*. Each of these works depicts a woman falsely accused of infidelity, and the resultant recuperation of their honor, which serves to "present . . . inadequacies in the cultural models for acquiring and assessing knowledge of honor, gender, and human nature." Barbara Simerka, *Knowing Subjects: Cognitive Cultural Studies and Early Modern Spanish* (West Lafayette, IN: Purdue University Press), 176.

33. Antonucci points out the similarity of this scene with *El nacimiento de Valentín y Ursón*. In this case, Teodosia acts as the she-bear of the earlier play; *Salvaje en la Comedia*, 79. Bernheimer notes the ambiguous connection between the bear and the wild man in folklore. In some medieval Twelfth Night and Carnival festivals, an actor dressed as a wild man would be "hunted" and brought into town to be punished for his misdeeds against the village. Sometimes, the wild figure would be replaced in the farce by a bear, among other figures. For more information, see Richard Bernheimer, *Wild Men in the Middle Ages* (Cambridge, MA: Harvard University Press), especially 49–84. This motif also has resonances with the birth stories of Moses and Amadis of Gaul.

34. This malleable nature is what Roger Bartra tracks in both his foundational works on the Wildman. For an overview of the shifts in the idea of the *homo sylvaticus* over time, see "Sylvan Mutations" and "Wild Men of Demons," in *The Artificial Savage*, 19–92. See also, *Wild Men in the Looking Glass*, 63–126.

35. I by no means intend to imply that this dichotomy between masculine and feminine traits is natural or determined. I only identify the characteristics of these types in a descriptive manner as they appear in the wild folk tradition and how they are juxtaposed in Lope's play.

36. *Animal de Hungría*, 1.525–527: "Ya su retrato anda impreso / y se cantan cada día / las coplas de su traiciones."

37. *Animal de Hungría*, 1.16: "de ver tu rara belleza."

38. Bartolo seems to be alluding to a specific subgenre of crime ballads in the Iberian *romance* tradition, usually recounting the violent deeds of notable bandits, but applied here to the wild figure. For a monograph study on popular representations of crime and outlaws in early modern Spain, see Elena del Río Parra, *Exceptional Crime in Early Modern Spain: Taxonomic and Intellectual Perspectives* (Boston: BRILL, 2019).

39. *Animal de Hungría*, 1.536: "sabe forzar doncellas."

40. *Animal de Hungría*, 1.543–4, 549: "él es como una persona, / poco más o menos / [. . . con] el cuerpo como un gigante." Emphasis is mine.

41. Castro-Gómez succinctly articulates this view, broadly attested by Latin American postcolonial theory: "We face an epistemic strategy of domination, which, as we well know, continues to thrive. Coloniality is not the past of modernity; it is simply its other face." "(Post)Coloniality," 283.

42. *Animal de Hungría*, 1.610–11: "No temas, hombre, confía, / que no vengo a hacerte mal."
43. *Animal de Hungría*, 1.612–14: "¡Ay, señor, por Dios le ruego / que tenga piedad de mí! / Los ojos tiene de fuego."
44. *Animal de Hungría*, 1.627–34:
    > LLORENTE: que de este monte han venido
    > villanos que le han contado
    > lo que ha robado y comido,
    > y darle muerte han jurado.
    > TEODOSIA: Otra vez lo han pretendido,
    > No es aquésta la primera.
    > LLORENTE: En verdad que no es tan fiera
    > como en la villa decían.
45. The wild woman is not the only false appearance that Teodosia takes on. Later in the play, as I mentioned, she disguises herself as a villager after Rosaura has been captured in order to be selected as her tutor. Her ability to play different characters also demonstrates how one should not expect her story to be one of transformation, but rather a series of disguises that keep her identity hidden until the correct moment when she can reveal herself and be who she "really" is, queen Teodosia.
46. *Animal de Hungría*, 2.1143–45: "Eres fiera en ser tratada / como fiera, y donde quiera, / del hombre cruel buscada."
47. *Animal de Hungría*, 2.1136–40, 1196–202:
    > Si a mí me llama animal,
    > ¿para qué dice que el cielo
    > es mi patria natural,
    > y dice que deste velo
    > se cubre un alma inmortal?
    > Si alma tengo y fue crïada
    > para el cielo, no soy fiera.
    >
    > . . .
    >
    > Si soy fiera, a toda fiera
    > veo con su esposo al lado;
    > las ciervas desta ribera
    > de su esposo han engendrado,
    > no, madre, de otra manera.
    > Si es que yo soy animal,
    > ¿con qué animal te juntaste?

48. *Animal de Hungría*, 2.1589–90: "y ansí deben de juntarse / el hombre con la mujer."
49. I thank Bradley Nelson for bringing to my attention that this is a motif found in the *comedia de indios*, in which indigenous characters voice complex political and theological arguments in affirmation of monarchical and Counter-Reformation ideologies. See Moisés R. Castillo, *Indios en escena: La representación del amerindio en el teatro del Siglo de Oro*, Purdue Studies in Romance Literatures 48 (West Lafayette, IN: Purdue University Press, 2009).
50. *Animal de Hungría*, 2.1632–5:
    Desvía bien los cabellos,
    pues no vengo a hacerte daño.
    (Será el rostro desengaño
    de lo que temo por ellos).
51. *Animal de Hungría*, 2.1618–19: "¿Éste llaman en Hungría / animal?"
52. *Animal de Hungría*, 3.2762–64: "Yo firmo lo que es razón, / y el rey, a la imitación / de Dios da premio y castigo."
53. *Animal de Hungría*, 3.2765–6: "Yo no sé leyes, mas digo / que es injusta indignación."
54. Bartra, *Artificial Savage*, 128.
55. *Animal de Hungría*, 3.2262–68:
    Mas fiera y cruel he sido,
    y ansí me castiga
    el cielo, en no me dar sucesión,
    porque en malicia, y traición
    he sido monstruo en el suelo:
    maté mi inocente hermana,
    y también su casto honor.
56. *Animal de Hungría*, 3.3255: "Encierra luego esta fiera."
57. Egginton, *How the World Became a Stage*, 151.
58. Slavoj Žižek, *The Sublime Object of Ideology*, The Essential Žižek, (London: Verso, 2008), 142.
59. Žižek, *Sublime Object of Ideology*, 141. For William Egginton's full explanation of "True Presence" as it relates to the transition of a medieval worldview to one we have come to identify as modern, see "Real Presence, Sympathetic Magic, and Power of Gesture," in *How the World Became a Stage*, 33–66.
60. Žižek, *Sublime Object of Ideology*, 143.
61. Žižek, *Sublime Object of Ideology*, 144.

62. *Hijo de los leones*, f. 104v.: "Dios quisiera algun dia, / que de tus principios sepas." I cite the original published edition of the play in the *Parte diecinueve . . . de las comedias de Lope de Vega Carpio* (1624) due to the discrepancies between this edition and more recent ones by Cotarelo (1930) and Hartzenbusch (1950, orig. 1855). Since the latter texts also do not provide line numbers, they therefore do not provide any mitigating justification for selection for the purposes of citation.
63. Antonucci, *Salvaje en la Comedia*, 95.
64. "el amor obra en él un cambio radical, suavizándolo y transformándolo." Antonucci, *Salvaje en la Comedia*, 94.
65. *Hijo de los leones*, f. 111r.: "rigor / a lágrimas y blandura."
66. *Hijo de los leones*, f. 104v.: "hoy verás / bañarme en lagrimas tiernas."
67. *Hijo de los leones*, f. 103v.:
>
> pues quando me contemplo
> assi rustico, fiero, y espantoso,
> embidio quantos veo,
> y de su imitacion tengo deseo.
> Tal vez aquestas fuentes
> me muestran que soy hombre,
> quando en la yerva duermen sus cristales;
> tal vez los accidentes
> me quitan este nombre,
> que imitan los mas fieros animales,
> viven conmigo iguales,
> y yo sujeto a un viejo,
> que me enseña y corrige,
> que me govierna, y rige,
> si bien yo me resisto a su consejo,
> y pues me riñe en vano,
> fiera devo de ser; no soy humano.

68. Christian Metz, "Instant Self Contradiction" in *On Signs*, ed. Marshall Blonsky (Baltimore: Johns Hopkins University Press, 1985), 260.
69. *Hijo de los leones*, f. 102r.: "Donde vais canalla? / . . . Sin mi licencia passais por el monte?"
70. *Hijo de los leones*, f. 100r.: "que pudiera / embidiar su hazienda el Rey / desde la cabra hasta el buey"; "Si un demonio de un salvage, un monstro, o no sé quien sea, no destruyera la aldea."
71. Faquín's description is not unlike "sightings" of more contemporary iterations of the wild figure such as Bigfoot and Sasquatch, often manifested

in the iconic blurred photographs of the creature. Such photos provide enough information to conclusively identify the figure within the collective and popular imagination, but provide little to no substantial evidence of the object within the frame of the photograph. And, like Faquín's accusatory description, they raise the suspicion of fabrication. For a lengthier analysis of this phenomena, see the epilogue to the present study, "Framing Bigfoot: Savage Misdirection from Segismundo to Sasquatch."

72. *Hijo de los leones*, f. 101v.: "claro está (que gran rigor) / que le sepultaron fieras."
73. Simerka, *Knowing Subjects*, 195. Simerka makes this argument in her analysis of Ruiz de Alarcón's *La verdad sospechosa*. In that play, Simerka makes the case that the gap between the actual and the ideal, as presented in the resolution, is unbridgeable.
74. *Hijo de los leones*, f. 101v.: "tan bello, que bastara a consolar mi honor."
75. Castillo and Egginton, *Medialogies*, 143–44.
76. Weiss, "Maravall's Materialism," 183.
77. Weiss, "Maravall's Materialism," 185.
78. Weiss, "Maravall's Materialism," 185.

CHAPTER 3

1. These are not to be confused with the many plays that drew from Ovid to present classical mythological content, especially the mythological court plays popularized by Calderón which were "a genre unique to Spain," according to Margaret Greer. See Greer, *The Play of Power: Mythological Court Dramas of Calderón de la Barca* (Princeton, NJ: Princeton University Press, 1991), 7. Her research pioneered current trends in scholarship on these court spectaculars. They are concerned with the nature of political power in the context of Habsburg Spain, which cannot be extricated from notions of national identity and therefore relates to the plays examined in the present chapter. The corpus selected for this chapter, however, dramatizes and reconstructs content specifically related to Spanish national mythologies, less directly related to classical mythological narratives found in Ovid.
2. Fuchs, *Poetics of Piracy*, 6.
3. Ian Tyrrell, "The Myth(s) that Will Not Die: American National Exceptionalism," in *National Myths: Constructed Pasts, Contested Presents*, ed. Gérard Bouchard (London: Routledge, 2013), 49.

4. Tyrrell, "The Myth(s) that Will Not Die," 49–50.
5. "radicalmente español." Ignacio Arellano, *Historia del teatro español del siglo XVII*, Crítica y estudios literarios, (Madrid: Cátedra, 1995), 175; Veronika Ryjik, *Lope de Vega en la invención de España: El drama histórico y la formación de la conciencia nacional*, Monografías 292, (Woodbridge: Támesis, 2011), 2. See the introduction of Ryjik's study for a detailed account of the history of this debate and its major interlocutors.
6. Ryjik, *Lope de Vega*, 25.
7. On the history of this folktale that situates Lope's play among its interpretations in other source accounts during the seventeenth century, see María José Vega Ramos, "Las indias interiores: Lope y la invención de *Las Batuecas del Duque de Alba*," *Anuario de Lope de Vega*, no. 2 (1996): 171–96.
8. From this point forward, *Las Batuecas* refers to Lope's *comedia*, and I have chosen to rely on the Spanish term for its inhabitants (*batuecos*) for the sake of brevity.
9. Stuart Hall, *On Postmodernism and Articulation: An Interview with Stuart Hall*, ed. Lawrence Grossberg, Critical Dialogues in Cultural Studies (London: Routledge, 2006), 144.
10. Castillo, *Baroque Horrors*, 139.
11. Moraña, Dussel, and Jáuregui contend that the Reconquista served as a template for the conquest of Latin America: "The prolonged crusades against Islam provided the model of the Holy War that would be implemented, with many variations, in the New World, creating a trade-off in which Indians would occupy the place of Moors within the Christian project of religious dissemination." This premise is the basis for Mignolo's claim that blood purity and ethno-religious hierarchies were precursors to the invention of race, which, according to Quijano then "emerged from colonialism . . . as the pivotal notion that supported the process of world classification. Situated as one of the axes of modernity, the issue of race became the 'rationale' used to support, justify, and perpetuate the practice of imperial domination." Mabel Moraña, Enrique Dussel, and Carlos Jáuregui, "Colonialism and Its Replicants," 6, 8–9.
12. It is moreover starting from an imprecise premise to apply such a binary racial framework. As one would expect, intermarriage was not uncommon, which therefore further highlights the extent to which the identification of the Muslim as other is constructed along ideological lines with little space for nuance.
13. "Que la conquista de América ofrece el modelo histórico, sobre el que se pliega toda esta estructura de ficción que fue *Las Batuecas*, lo evidencia

la sincronía con que se produjeron estos dos fenómenos, ligados entre sí mas de lo que pudiera suponerse." Fernando Rodríguez de la Flor, "El espacio escénico del mito," in *De las Batuecas a las Hurdes: Fragmentos para una historia mítica de Extremadura* (Mérida: Editorial Regional de Mérida, 1989), 133.

14. Although used in a different context, I take this apt juxtaposition of the two terms from Ryjik's analysis of Lope's *El nuevo mundo descubierto de Cristobal Colón*. See Ryjik, *Lope de Vega*, 190.

15. This echoes Nelson's treatment of the same theme in his monograph *The Persistence of Presence*; his analysis "embarks on an excursion of sorts to the frontiers of temporal, geographical, and aesthetic terrain in an analysis of Lope de Vega's *El Nuevo mundo descubierto por Cristóbal Colón*. The baroque concept of fragmentation, emptiness, and estrangement are brought to bear on Lope's staging of the first encounter between Europeans and a peculiar dramatic entity I call the 'emblematic *indio*.' The movement from crisis caused by the appearance of the cross on the shores of *La Deseada* to the eventual acceptance, or recognition, of the *presence* of Christ in the image of the crucifixion by the *indio* displays how Spanish imperialism extends itself in time and space in order to construct and incorporate American Otherness into the symbolic economy and mystical body of Spanish national identity" (25).

16. See S. Griswold Morley, "Notes on the Bibliography of Lope de Vega's Comedias," *Modern Philology* 20, no. 2 (1922): 206n464.

17. Hall, *On Postmodernisn and Articulation*, 141.

18. *Las Batuecas*, 2.188–89: "Y aun otro mundo segundo / que va a descubrir Colón."

19. "todavía en profecía, es coherente intrínsecamente con este catecismo por el derrotero explicativo que lleva la obra, y también porque en toda ella el sentimiento programado de que el descubrimiento de Las Batuecas es semejante—en lo material y aun en lo espiritual—al de América." José Manuel Rozas, "*Las Batuecas del Duque de Alba*, de Lope de Vega," in *Homenaje a Alonso Zamora Vicente* (Madrid: Castalia, 1988), n.p.

20. "*Los guanches de Tenerife* y *El Nuevo Mundo descubierto por Cristóbal Colón*, obras que, sin forzar mucho, podríamos considerar que forman una trilogía en unión con la comedia." Rozas, "*Las Batuecas*," n.p.

21. It should also be noted that the construction of the *batuecos* as the false other relies on a commitment to the existence of another "real" other (i.e., Amerindians) to construct itself as a false one.

22. "se superpondrán aspectos legendarios tradicionales en el país para fijar, en una variante mitologizante de la historia, lo que reside en el inconsciente colectivo y carece, propiamente, de historia. El viejo fantasma nacional de la 'pérdida de España' se da aquí, como en otros lugares de la geografía nacional, como una suerte de origen para toda la fábula." Fernando Rodríguez de la Flor, "Las Batuecas: Fábula barroca; desmitificación ilustrada," *Revista de Dialectología y Tradiciones Populares*, 40 (1985): 138.
23. *Las Batuecas*, 3.915–920:
    Amigos, mi nombre ensalza
    más el ser vuestro señor
    que la gran tierra heredada
    de los claros ascendientes
    que dan principio a mi casa.
    Yo os daré bautismo a todos.
24. *Las Batuecas*, 3.907–914:
    TRISO: Todos gran Duque te abrazan;
        que según este nos cuenta,
        es razón y deuda clara,
        porque eres nuestro señor,
        siendo tuya esta montaña.
    GIROTO: Todos somos venturosos
        en que de sangre tan alta
        vengamos a tener dueño.
25. This evaluation is by no means meant to accuse a seventeenth-century Spanish populace of anything we are not equally culpable of today. Case in point, Thanksgiving.
26. "pero en seguida notamos que esta . . . no es una arcadia, ni una edad de oro, temas tan del gusto de Lope." Rozas, "*Las Batuecas*," n.p.
27. Dussel, "Eurocentrism and Modernity," 67.
28. Moraña, Jáuregui, and Dussel, *Coloniality at Large*, 7.
29. *Las Batuecas*, 2.146–7: "Aunque es bárbaro su talle, / son piadosos sus estremos."
30. *Las Batuecas*, 2.244–46: "¿Cómo habéis vivido aquí, / hombres, sin Dios, y sin Ley, / y habláis castellano así?"
31. *Las Batuecas*, 2.247–251:
    Dicen, que fuyendo un rey
    vino a aportar por aquí,
    y que ciertos labradores

   o soldados de una guerra
   se encerraron en la sierra
   que miras.

32. *Las Batuecas*, 2.474, 480–482: "el cielo / . . . quiere que estos *castellanos* / que desde entonces están / sin saber que son *cristianos*."
33. *Las Batuecas*, 3.885–87.
34. *Las Batuecas*, 3.895: "descendientes de los Reyes Godos"; 3.878–81: "Ese difunto de la cueva estaba, / del Rey Rodrigo dicen que es sobrino; / y que huyendo de los moros africanos / murió entre aquestas peñas."
35. *Las Batuecas*, 3.869: "seiscientos años ha que fue pintado."
36. The space of the cave here where Teodosilo is found is not unique in the corpus of wild folk plays, or the *comedia* more broadly. The space of the cave is often a discovery space, both literally in the early modern stage apparatus, but also as an element of the scenographic repertoire of the period that produces meaning as a spatial metaphor as well. Inside the cave is hidden a "secret of nature," which was a well-wrought epistemological trope during the period that is reflected in baroque art. For natural philosophers, truth was to be uncovered by peering into the bosom of nature to learn its secrets. It is therefore not coincidental that one of the major "truths" or "secrets of nature" conveyed by *Las Batuecas* is revealed in the cave, having been hidden in nature for hundreds of years. I dedicate further attention to the cave as a spatial-epistemological metaphor in my analysis of Bances Candamo's *La piedra filosofal*, later in the present chapter. For an extended analysis of the symbolic spatiality of the cave in *Las Batuecas del Duque de Alba*, see Christopher Kozey, "Las Batuecas, Las Hurdes, and the Spanish Crypt" (PhD diss., Johns Hopkins University, 2015). Kozey reads the Batuecas valley (and more specifically) the cave in Lope's play within Egginton's framework of "the crypt," defined as "a site of inscrutable presence in an epistemologically uncertain world" (ii).
37. *Las Batuecas*, 2.27–30: "La Católica Reina belicosa / acompaña en la guerra a su Fernando, / y con esto se anima tanta gente."
38. This of course is not the only example in Lope's corpus for which the secondary plot is not only of historical significance but also provides context essential to understanding the message presented in the primary plot. The most notable is *Fuenteovejuna*, which also features the Catholic Monarchs in the secondary plot.
39. *Las Batuecas*, 3.892.
40. The trilogy comprises the following *comedias*: *Todo es dar en una cosa*, *Amazonas en las Indias*, and *La lealtad contra la envidia*. For an overview,

see Zugasti's critical introduction and annotated editions of the trilogy, *La "trilogía de los Pizarros" de Tirso de Molina*, vols. 1–4 (Kassel: Reichenberger, 1993).

41. "la verdadera circunstancia que motivó la escritura de la trilogía fueron sus años vividos en Trujillo (Cáceres) y su contacto directo con los descendientes de los Pizarros conquistadores." Zugasti, *La "trilogía de los Pizarros,"* 1:8.

42. Zugasti does not attend to the question of Egginton's notion of theatrical keying here, however. The critic takes the characters words at face value as the stand-ins for the playwright's poetics. The production of meaning in dramatic space is rather more complicated, which includes each of the characters' often competing and conflicting viewpoints, their expectations, interpretations, misinterpretations, as well as the contingencies these elements (to name but a few) create in relation to one another, as well as the context that conditioned their reception by the audience. Even more plainly, taking a comic character's word at face value evades dealing with the possibility of irony—that is, the space between what is said and what is meant—which is part of the essential nature of theatricality, and even more so during the Baroque, an aesthetic obsessed with the ironic space between reality and its representation put on display with great rhetorical and spatial intensity.

43. "¡Como si la licencia de Apolo se estrechase a la recolección histórica y no pudiese fabricar, sobre cimientos de personas verdaderas, arquitecturas del ingenio fingidas!" Zugasti, *La "trilogía de los Pizarros,"* 1:57.

44. Nancy Mayberry, "The Role of the Warrior Women in *Amazonas en las Indias*," *Bulletin of the Comediantes* 29 (1977): fn. 12.

45. See Zugasti, *La "trilogía de los Pizarros,"* 1:110.

46. The Greek names of the Amazons, Martesia and Menalipe, further this notion that any appearance of these characters as indigenous Americans is mitigated by the European origins that underpin every aspect of their representation.

47. Otis Green is the first to put forward this reading of *Amazonas* in "Notes on the Pizarro Trilogy of Tirso de Molina," *Hispanic Review* 4, no. 3 (1936). His article served as the foundation for subsequent articles by Mayberry. See Nancy Mayberry, "Tirso's Use of Myths and Symbols in Part I of the Pizarro Trilogy," *Kentucky Romance Quarterly* 22 (1975); Mayberry, "Role of the Warrior Women."

48. "El objetivo de Tirso es la reivindicación política de Gonzalo Pizarro, y para ello era necesario combatir su fama de rebelde con la imagen

opuesta: él se mantuvo leal a la corona, pero sus amigos le traicionaron y quedó como chivo expiatorio de un movimiento que nunca secundó." Zugasti, La "trilogía de los Pizarros," 1:79.

49. Mayberry, "Role of the Warrior Women," 38.
50. Green, "Notes on the Pizarro Trilogy," 209. See Melveena McKendrick, "The Amazon, the Leader, the Warrior" in *Woman and Society in the Spanish Drama of the Golden Age: A Study of the mujer varonil* (Cambridge: Cambridge University Press, 1974), 174–21; Antonio Miró Quesada Sosa, "Gonzalo Pizarro en el teatro de Tirso de Molina," *Revista de las Indias* 5, no. 14 (1940), 65.
51. Mayberry, "Role of the Warrior Women," 40, 42.
52. Mayberry, "Role of the Warrior Women," 40.
53. Rebecca W. Bushnell, *Tragedies of Tyrants: Political Thought and Theater in the English Renaissance* (Ithaca, NY: Cornell University Press, 1990), 2.
54. Green, "Notes on the Pizarro Trilogy," 201–2.
55. He is also the grandson of Hernando Pizarro, which may initially sound confusing, and understandably so. Francisco Pizarro's relationship with an Incan princess bore them a daughter, Francisca, who was legitimized by Carlos V. Francisca later marries her uncle Hernando, thereby establishing the family line.
56. Hugh Grady, "Tragedy and Materialist Thought," in *A Companion to Tragedy*, ed. Rebecca Bushnell (Malden, MA: Blackwell, 2005), 135.
57. Grady, "Tragedy and Materialist Thought," 135.
58. Grady, "Tragedy and Materialist Thought," 135.
59. *Amazonas*, 3.3169–3173: "prevenirle venganzas / contra todos que intenten / de su nación inhumana/ conquistar nuestras provincias, / tiranizar nuestra patria."
60. See Nicholas R. Jones's monograph *Staging Habla de Negros: Radical Performances of the African Diaspora in Early Modern Spain*, Iberian Encounter and Exchange 1475–1755 3 (University Park: Pennsylvania State Univesity Press, 2019). I am indebted to Jones' articulation of the destabilizing ideological resistance that can be embodied by the representation of the Other, found at 18–25. See the opening section of Chapter 4 of the present study for a dedicated discussion of Jones's work.
61. "Tal profusión de noticias indica que en los siglos XVI y XVII para muchas personas era realidad lo que hoy sabemos que es fábula. Había pareceres opuestos respecto a la veracidad o no del mito: las Casas, López de Gómara, o Fernández de Oviedo no creían en él, pero ya hemos visto cómo Colón, Cortés, Orellana y otros muchos sí. Todavía

en 1641 Cristóbal de Acuña (autor del *Nuevo descubrimiento del gran río de las Amazonas*) creía firmemente en su existencia. Tirso de Molina no entra en la dialéctica, pero parece evidente que para él todo era un mito: las trata como en broma, las dotes mágicas que les atribuye apuntan hacia visión literaria, nunca realista." Zugasti, La *"trilogía de los Pizarros,"* 1:110.

62. My contribution here is not to say that the specific references to the figurative or literal existence of the Amazons were not influential, just that many of the conventions of wild representation so popular in dramatic practice during the period are reproduced in *Amazonas en las Indias* and cannot be overlooked.

63. *Amazonas*, 1.145: "¿cómo no sois vieja siendo bruja?"

64. This motif—how to resolve the problem of mutual incomprehensibility—has become more characteristic of science fiction in modern literature, television and film. The problem is produced by the same mechanisms as in *Amazonas en las Indias*; technological advancements make it possible to travel to previously inaccessible locations, either geographically, chronologically, or dimensionally. One example is *Dr. Who*, who takes their modern-day British companions on intergalactic adventures in time and space thanks to the sophisticated technology of the TARDIS, a police call box that can travel to any location in the past, present, or future. The TARDIS is also equipped to transmit a translation circuit to its passengers, so that they can communicate in any language during their travels, even though to them (and to English-speaking audiences) it still sounds like English when they speak and are spoken to. This type of technique has been historically conventional in genres as disparate as the Spanish *comedia* and contemporary science fiction: in order to make a novel, play, television series, or film comprehensible to a largely monolingual audience, part of the writer's innovation and world building includes creating a mechanism so that all of the characters speak the same language (although the number of exceptions is on the rise thanks to current trends in the culture industry that are more attuned to cultural plurality and as such embrace multilingualism as an aspect of their aesthetic).

65. *Amazonas*, 1.106–9:
 ¿Cómo hablas el idioma
 que España por sus minas ferió a Roma?
 ¿Quién te enseñó el estilo
 de la elocuente lengua castellana?

66. *Amazonas*, 1.115–23, 134–43:
> Dudas discreto, pero no te espantes,
> que tal divinidad mi pecho encierra
> que oráculo soy, pasmo desta tierra.
> Los hombres y los brutos
> veneran mis preceptos absolutos;
> los tigres, los leones,
> sierpes y basiliscos,
> habitadores desos arduos riscos,
> vendrán, si los convoco, en escuadrones;
>
> ...
>
> Escalas pongo al cielo,
> sobre los vientos vuelo
> y a imitación del sol que al indio admira,
> mi agilidad, como él, los orbes gira.
> ¿Espantaráste agora
> (si esto te certifica la experiencia)
> que quien registra cuanto su luz dora
> tenga noticia de cualquiera ciencia
> y hablando en todas lenguas tus vocablos
> pronuncie?

67. Green, "Notes on the Pizarro Trilogy," 209.
68. Another play, *La piedra filosofal* (1693), analyzed later in the current chapter presents the mage as a wild figure, which further demonstrates the utility of thinking of these individual iterations as pulling from available repertoires. Identifying where they overlap with other examples reveals an increasingly complex intertextual network of repertoires that illuminate one another even more than approaches that focus on transhistorical examples of whatever the specific dominant character identification may be in a given instance (Amazons or court magicians, for example).
69. *Amazonas*, 1.120–23: "los tigres, los leones, / sierpes y basiliscos, / habitadores desos arduos riscos, / vendrán, si los convoco, en escuadrones."
70. Eamon, *Science and the Secrets*, 229.
71. *Amazonas*, 1.115–17: "pero no te espantes; / que tal divinidad que mi pecho encierra / que oráculo soy."
72. *Amazonas*, 3.3279–80: "Ábrese el monte y encúbrense las dos."
73. This is the convention I will examine at greater length below in my analysis of Bances Candamo's *La piedra filosofal* (1693). Briefly, Rocas

is the magus figure and quasi-Wildman, who the king finds and asks to create a means by which he can pick the correct suitor of the three vying for the hand of his daughter. Bances's play is heavily influenced by *En la vida todo es verdad y todo mentira* by Calderón de la Barca (see Chapter 5), in which a similar scenario plays out. The emperor Focas wants to determine which of two characters is possibly his son, and entreats the magus Lisipo to set up an experiment that will allow him to observe them in certain scenarios, a methodology that is supposed to produce the information for him to identify which one is his son and heir. In both plays, the magicians' "experiments" rely on natural magic to create alternative realities in which observational data can be collected on their subjects. (Well before the days of the IRB, the human subjects in the plays are unaware they are being observed, which becomes a motor of the plot conflict and character development—or psychological breakdown—thereafter.)

74. *Amazonas*, 3.3171–73: "intenten / de su nación inhumana / conquistar nuestras provincias, / tiranizar nuestra patria."
75. Castillo, *Indios en escena*, 1–10.
76. Michel Foucault, *The Archaeology of Knowledge: The Discourse on Language*, trans. Alan Sheridan (New York: Pantheon Books, 1972), 217 (emphasis mine).
77. Alfonso D'Agostino, "Introducción," in *La piedra filosofal de Francisco Antonio de Bances Candamo* (Rome: Bulzoni, 1988), 15–19.
78. Chad Gasta situates the play within the contexts of the *novatores*, exploring its position on astrology specifically. For more on astrology in the work and a detailed exposition of the *novatores* active in Spain that further situates the play within contemporary epistemological trends, see Gasta, "La visión de los novatores en Bances Candamo: La astrología como experimento teatral," in *Atardece el Barroco: Ficción experimental en la España de Carlos II (1665–1700)*, ed. Jorge García López and Enrique García Santo-Tomás (Madrid: Iberoamericana/Vervuert, 2021).
79. "A un lado suena como a lo lejos la música, a otro las voces, cajas y trompetas y se descubre medio en una gruta Rocas, filósofo anciano, en traje montaraz, entre libros, esferas, cuadrantes y otros instrumentos matemáticos."
80. The opening stage directions in Calderón's *En la vida* read as follows: "Offstage coming from one direction are the sounds of martial drums and trumpets, and coming from the other direction offstage are musical instruments, and entering from one side of the stage are soldiers

and Focas, and from the other, enter women and Cintia behind them" ("Dentro a una parte cajas y trompetas, y a otra parte instrumentos músicos, y salen por una parte soldados y Focas, y por otra parte damas y detrás Cintia"). It is not until halfway through the first act that Focas finds the cave where Eraclio and Leonido (the two protagonistas) are hiding; nevertheless, in *La piedra filosofal*, Bances directly replicates the structure of the opening scene and the later one when they are found, just condensed into one scene to begin the play.

81. Teofilo F. Ruiz, *Spanish Society, 1348–1700* (London: Routledge, 2017), 292. For a focused examination on the important influence of hermeticism on early modern science, see López-Pérez, "Ciencia y pensamiento hermético."

82. The influence of hermeticism in works by early modern Spanish authors has received scholarly attention. See Frederick A. De Armas, "Lope de Vega and the Hermetic Tradition: The Case of Dardanio in *La Arcadia*," *Revista canadiense de estudios hispánicos* 7, no. 3 (1983); Catherine Connor (Swietlicki), "The Occult/Hermetic *Burlador de Sevilla*," *Crítica Hispánica* 15, no. 1 (1993). And of course, astrology plays a prominent role in Calderón's *La vida es sueño* and throughout his dramaturgy. See Frederick A. de Armas, "Segismundo/Philip IV: The Politics of Astrology in *La vida es sueño*," *Bulletin of the Comediantes* 53, no. 1 (2001); Antonio Hurtado Torres, "La astrología en el teatro de Calderón de la Barca," in *Calderón: Actas del Congreso internacional sobre Calderón y el teatro español del Siglo de Oro*, ed. Luciano García Lorenzo, Anejos de la Revista Segismundo 6 (Madrid: Consejo Superior de Investigaciones Científicas, 1983).

83. The play draws inspiration from Calderón's *La vida es sueño* here as well, specifically the scene in act 2 where Basilio and Clotaldo decide to release Segismundo so they can observe how he behaves as a prince at court. Calderón reprises this premise in a similar scene in *En la vida todo es verdad y todo mentira*; I offer extended analyses of both plays in Chapter 5 of the present study.

84. *Piedra filosofal*, 1.931–41:
>
> Con príncipes estranjeros
> quiero escusar alianzas
> que al límite de mi imperio
> término mayor añadan;
> que tienen monarquías
> cierto coto y cierta raya,

hasta donde a mantenerlas
de un rey la prudencia basta
y de un poder el dominio;
pero si esta línea pasan,
luego a declinar empiezan.

85. During antiquity (and as represented in mythology), the peninsula where Cádiz is located was comprised of three distinct islands. The island that was first populated was Erytheia (the northern end of the modern city center), which is the island first fortified by the Phoenicians that came to be known as Gades ("walled compound" or "stronghold"). This is the geography of Cádiz as depicted in Alfonso's *Estoria* and Bances's *comedia*, both of which mythologize its fortification. Erytheia is of mythological relevance as the island in the tenth labor of Hercules where he slays the monster Geryon.

86. Rocas's wildness is not a developed aspect of *La piedra filosofal*. However, his status as Wildman at the beginning of the work inaugurates the obsession with limits that pervade the play, and is therefore significant, both in the literary history of the figure and within Bances's allegorical drama.

87. Victor Navarro Brotóns and William Eamon, eds., *Beyond the Black Legend: Spain and the Scientific Revolution* (Valencia: Instituto de Historia de la Ciencia y Documentación López Piñero, 2007), 34. Cañizares-Esguerra notes the likelihood that "Bacon purposefully sought to imitate García de Céspedes" in copying the frontispiece of Spanish cosmographer's *Regimiento de navegación*. Jorge Cañizares-Esguerra, "The Colonial Iberian Roots of the Scientific Revolution," in *Nature, Empire, and Nation: Explorations of the History of Science in the Iberian World* (Redwood City, CA: Stanford University Press, 2006), 18.

88. *Piedra filosofal*, 3.3912–17:
    pues yo tengo acá en mí mismo
    la piedra filosofal;
    contento estaré conmigo,
    puesto que el entendimiento
    del hombre bien instruido
    convierte en bienes los males
    y lo trágico en festivo.

89. *Piedra filosofal*, 3.3861–70:
    Pues ha sido
    fingir Rocas, conjurando

> negras sombras del abismo,
> que yo a Hispalo (¡qué pena!)
> cariñosa (¡qué martirio!)
> favorecí; a cuya causa,
> viendo en efectos distintos
> confundido su dictamen,
> entre lo cierto y fingido
> a todos pareció loco.

90. *Piedra filosofal*, 3.3884–86: "que des a Hispalo la muerte, / o sea él el elegido / por tu sucesor."
91. It bears mentioning that "grotesque" and "grotto" are etymologically linked. The fascination with the grotesque in the Baroque is well-known; grottos are also a common, if not one of the essential architectural features of the royal and noble gardens across Europe in the sixteenth and seventeenth centuries. The link between the grotto and grotesque are more than coincidental. For more on the baroque aesthetic of the grotto in early modern landscape design, see Luke Morgan, *The Monster in the Garden: Reframing Renaissance Landscape Design* (Philadelphia: University of Pennsylvania Press, 2015), especially chapter 2, "The Grotesque and the Monstrous," 48–81.
92. *Piedra filosofal*, 3.3916–17: "convierte . . . lo trágico en festivo."

CHAPTER 4

1. Castillo, *Indios en escena*, 5.
2. Castillo, *Indios en escena*, 5.
3. Castillo, *Indios en escena*, 5.
4. Dussel, "Europe, Modernity, and Eurocentrism," 473.
5. Dussel, "Europe, Modernity, and Eurocentrism," 473.
6. Jones, *Staging Habla de Negros*, xiii.
7. Jones, *Staging Habla de Negros*, 121.
8. Jones, *Staging Habla de Negros*, 5.
9. To reiterate a discussion outlined at length in the introduction, it should be reminded that there is a long-standing debate in Hispanic theater studies on the extent to which artistic production during the Spanish Baroque served as a primarily repressive or subversive apparatus. José Antonio Maravall's claim in *La cultura del barroco* that the Baroque was a "guided culture" in which cultural production served to maintain

the interests of the ruling class prevailed in approaches to the *comedia* until scholars like Dian Fox, Melveena McKendrick, and Margaret Greer came to question the all-encompassing applicability of Iberian theater as a repressive apparatus. Nuanced approaches in both camps have developed in scholarship over recent decades.

10. Egginton, *Theater of Truth*, 40. For Egginton's extended exploration of the implications of the claim that the "Baroque is theater and theater is Baroque," see 39–55. He builds on this modern theory of theatricality with David R. Castillo in the co-authored *Medialogies*, especially "Part I," 9–58.
11. Reichenberger, "The Uniqueness of the *Comedia*."
12. Dale Pratt, "*Felix Culpa*: Allegory and Play in Calderón's *Autos*," *Bulletin of the Comediantes* 51, no. 1–2 (1999): 39.
13. *Lindona de Galicia*, 6. "borrón es la Lindona." The early modern edition consulted does not include line numbers. References are to page numbers, which are numbered consecutively front and back, designated explicitly as pages, rather than following *recto* and *verso* folio numbering conventions.
14. Hélène Cixous, "The Laugh of the Medusa," *Signs* 1, no. 4 (1976): 893.
15. This language reminds of act 5 of *Macbeth*, when Lady Macbeth, whilst sleepwalking, yells, "Out, damn spot!" Referring to her blood-stained clothes, she is incapable of covering up her transgression—driving her husband to murder the king—which is the very thing she most wants to keep silent. I thank John Slater for pointing out that in the case of the wild figure of the Spanish *comedia*, it is more appropriately, "Out, darned spot!"
16. She both is the third member of a pair (n+1) and her portrayal emphasizes her marginality, as peripheral of a culturally charged center positioned by the *comedia* (the geographical periphery of Galicia, the linguistic distinction of speaking gallego-portugués, and ostracized for transgressing repressive codes regulating sexuality).
17. Pratt, "*Felix Culpa*," 50–51.
18. Gilles Deleuze, "The Fold," *Yale French Studies*, no. 80 (1991): 246.
19. The play interchanges the names of Sancho III El Mayor (The Elder, r. 1000–1035) for Fernando I El Magno (The Great, r. 1035–1065), making Fernando the father and Sancho García's brother. For further background on the historical context of Fernando I of León and the breaking up of his kingdom among his successors, see Joseph F. O'Callaghan, *A History of Medieval Spain* (Ithaca, NY: Cornell University Press, 1983).

For a study that focuses García within that context, see S. Griswold Morley, "The Imprisonment of King García," *Modern Philology* 17, no. 7 (1919).
20. Jeremy Robbins, *Arts of Perception: The Epistemological Mentality of the Spanish Baroque, 1580–1720* (Abingdon: Routledge, 2007), 98.
21. The representation of Linda's inability to communicate is as close as the *comedia* comes to an "accurate" portrayal of what happens in the circumstances of a child who is deprived of language; however, she picks it up rather quickly with instruction, unlike known cases of feral children that experience language deprivation beyond the critical period of language learning. In the exploration of linguistic aspects of wildness, Claramonte appears to be drawing from Lope de Vega's *El animal de Hungría* for inspiration. In that play, Teodosia raises Rosaura in the woods away from all other human contact, which serves as the basis for moments in the dialogue when she encounters unfamiliar vocabulary due to never having had context to learn certain words. There is one passage in which her misunderstanding of the word *otro* (other) serves as the basis for an extended conversation on the nature of the self and other as a result of her misunderstandings and the attempts by another young character, Felipe, to explain the concept to her.
22. Scholarship on the play has focused on other aspects than the ones emphasized here, and this work has only been analyzed briefly in studies on a larger sub-set of Pérez de Montalbán's dramatic corpus, whose authorship of the play has been questioned in favor of Andrés de Claramonte.
23. Even within the corpus of wild figure plays there exists a substantial selection of such plays. In Lope de Vega's works, women that are scorned and banished include Margarita in *El nacimiento de Ursón y Valentín*, Teodosia in *El animal de Hungría*, and Fenisa in *El hijo de los leones*. Rosaura is another notable example in *La vida es sueño*, and while a list of other examples would be extensive, two works from the period that exemplify the inequitable treatment of women as a result of extramarital affairs (whether actual or imagined) are Cervantes's novella *La fuerza de la sangre* (Compelled by Blood) and Calderón de la Barca's *comedia El médico de su honra* (1637).
24. José A. Fernández-Santamaria, "Reason of State and Statecraft in Spain (1595–1640)." *Journal of the History of Ideas* 41, no. 3 (1980): 355.
25. Robert Bireley, *The Counter-Reformation Prince: Anti-Machiavellianism or Catholic Statecraft in Early Modern Europe* (Chapel Hill: University of North Carolina Press, 1990), 81. In the *Criticón* (1651), Balthasar Gracián would be the prominent exception to this general principal of

the Spanish response to Machiavelli. For a bibliography on the development of political philosophy on reason of state in the wake of Machiavelli, see Robbins, *The Arts of Perception*, 102n16.
26. Robbins, *Arts of Perception*, 98.
27. "No ha de ser Reyna la que fue manceba del Rey."
28. *Lindona*, 6: "¡O fiera embidia! ¡O máscara engañosa!"
29. Diego de Saavedra Fajardo, *Empresas políticas*, ed. Francisco Javier Díez de Revenga, Clásicos universales (Madrid: Planeta, 1988), 291. For his extended explanation of deception, prudence and reason of state, see *Empresas políticas*, "Empresa 46," 290–98.
30. See Egginton, *Theater of Truth*, 40.
31. *Lindona*, 7: "no es ser Rey, es ser tirano."
32. Robbins, *Arts of Perception*, 102.
33. Arriving at an early modern definition of tyranny is complicated because this is the period when historical uses of the term are still being used (tyranny defined more narrowly as usurpation) and had yet to be supplanted by emerging uses that define tyranny as we do today as the abuse of political power. The implication of archaic definitions that conceived of the tyrant as a usurper was that a tyrant would mismanage public authority, and abuse of power flowed naturally—necessarily even—out of the tyrant's false claim to the power afforded the position, rather than the other way around (i.e., the tyrant's legitimacy negated a result of their abuse of power). What both definitions share is the notion that the tyrant's claim to power is illegitimate, which is the important element of the dramatic irony produced when García identifies himself as a tyrant for one reason, but also applies more directly to the status of his political authority as well. For an examination of the historical development of the concept of tyranny, see Shannon K. Brincat, "'Death to Tyrants': The Political Philosophy of Tyrannicide—Part I," *Journal of International Political Theory* 4, no. 2 (2008).
34. *Lindona*, 7: "Mira, señor, que la pasión te ciega."
35. Saavedra Fajardo, *Empresas políticas*, 291.
36. *Lindona*, 8:
>   razon de estado son
>   las paces con Reyno tal,
>   mintamos lo desleal
>   con las razones de estado,
>   y ocupe el puesto el traslado
>   que pierde el original.

>   Leonor, y el Reyno han podido
>   dexarte, Linda,* burlada.

*Especially in act 1, Lindona and Linda are both names used to address and identify the character abandoned by García. It is clear here that the reference is to Lindona, but it is not inconsequential that Linda becomes the name of their daughter as well. The play makes takes advantage of the symbolic affiliation implied by their names. They are of the same substance defined by their wildness, which is defined by the supplementary nature of wildness through replication (wildness not only resists domestication but also begets more wildness in the process).

37. "Peligran también los reinos hereditarios cuando el sucesor, olvidado de los institutos de sus mayores, tiene por natural la servidumbre de los vasallos; y no reconociendo dellos su grandeza, los desama y gobierna como á esclavos, atendiendo mas a sus fines propios y al cumplimiento de sus apetitos que al beneficio público, *convertida en tiranía la dominación*; de donde concibe el pueblo una desestimación del príncipe y un odio y aborrecimiento á su persona y acciones, con que se deshace aquella unión recíproca que hay entre el rey y el reino donde este obedece y aquel manda, por el beneficio que reciben, el uno en el esplendor y superioridad de gobernar, y el otro en la felicidad de ser bien gobernado." Saavedra Fajardo, *Empresas políticas*, 426.
38. *Lindona*, 8.
39. The motive and emotional charge of this scene shares affinities with Laurencia's passionate plea to the town council, a group of men that includes her father, to stop deliberating and take action against the Comendador in Lope's *Fuenteovejuna* (3.1723–93).
40. *Lindona*, 8: "Está su silla ocupada."
41. *Lindona*, 8: "Eu so la vosa muller, / dexay essas zumberías."
42. *Lindona*, 9:
>   Y la palabra, y la mao?
>   ... Y el meu honor, y esta filla?
>   ... En mi, escarmentad, mulleres;
>   catay quein los homes son:
>   para esto venir me has feyto
>   á ò Coruña?
43. *Lindona*, 8:
>   Un borrón, que todo es vida,
>   y un ser, que todo es sentido;
>   un assombro reducido

> à la belleza mas rara
> que soberaba, y avàra,
> peregrina* y singular,
> està hablando, sin hablar
> con mas fuerza que si hablàra.

*The term *peregrina* is difficult to translate in a single word, and by translating it to "incredible" I have also selected a less common usage. As a noun, *peregrino* refers to a "pilgrim," while the adjective captures the action that describes a pilgrimage; it implies the act of making a purposeful journey, usually toward an intended or important destination. In Basco's description of Leonor's beauty, the term can also be used to serve as a beauty that is absent (e.g., on a pilgrimage), a version of the poetic trope of the unattainability of the desired object. This is a plausible (but again difficult to translate without breaking the poetic verse) translation here provided the scene foregrounds Leonor's absence.

44. *Lindona*, 8: "las paces en Reyno tal."
45. *Lindona*, 9: "Castellano, que es peor que ser Gallego."
46. *Lindona*, 9:
    > engaña,
    > sin cara segura;
    > si promete á Deus,
    > y home despúes burla
    > [he] deceives,
    > two-faced;
    > if he makes a promise to God,
    > he will just as soon break his word.
47. "la despechada Lindona ha abandonado a la hija recién nacida." Antonucci, *Salvaje en la Comedia*, 166.
48. "una salvaje muy verosímil." Antonucci, *Salvaje en la Comedia*, 169. While Antonucci points out a true characteristic of feral children who have never come into contact with other humans, verisimilitude never really seems to be the function of the wild figure throughout the trajectory of the subgenre in sixteenth- and seventeenth-century Spain. Even here, the nature of the wild figure is so intertwined with its mythological and folkloric forebears that the fact that Linda cannot speak has less to do with the veracity of her portrayal than a commitment to a mythological precedent.
49. I use this term *swerve*, drawing from Harold Bloom's critical vocabulary on authorship and artistic creation in *The Anxiety of Influence: A Theory of Poetry* (New York: Oxford University Press, 1973).

50. Ovid, *Metamorphoses*, 68.
51. *Lindona*, p. 21: "No llegues / á abrazar los hombres / . . . que no es amar decente."
52. This and other talismans commonly serve to identify the wild characters in the works within the wild figure corpus. Mazur calls these items "tokens of identification." For example, it is a ring that reveals Heraclio's identity in Mira de Amescua's *La rueda de la fortuna* and a garment worn by Leonido when he is found in the forest in Lope de Vega's *El hijo de los leones*. Ismenia's gemstone reveals her identity to Alberto in Figueroa's *La sirena de Tinacria*. A *lámina* identifies Leonido and Marfisa in the Calderón play staged at court in 1680 that bears their name, while the same playwright frustrates the reliability of this type of object in *En la vida todo es verdad y todo mentira* when Astolfo produces a *lámina de oro* (etched golden leaf), which does not provide enough information to distinguish between Eraclio and Leonido.
53. *Lindona*, 28:

> FERNANDO: Tú, Linda, dame esa mano.
> LINDA: ¿Para qué?
> FERNANDO: Para ser dueño de mi alma.
> LINDA: ¿Eso es amor?
> FERNANDO: Amor en vínculo eterno,
>   siendo mi esposa.
> LINDA: Pues yo,
>   por los celos, amor tengo
>   al Infante; y este amor
>   en el ilustrarlo quiero:
>   por él dejo de ser fiera,
>   por él de ser monstruo dejo,
>   a él le debo esta razón
>   a su amor mi entendimiento.

54. *Lindona*, 28: "Dayme essa mao."
55. *La sirena de Tinacria*, 383: "ciego y loco." References are to page numbers, as indicated in the 1678 edition consulted, which does not provide scene divisions or line numbering.
56. Ann Rosalind Jones and Peter Stallybrass, *Renaissance Clothing and the Materials of Memory*, Cambridge Studies in Renaissance Literature and Culture (Cambridge: Cambridge University Press, 2000), 1.
57. Jones and Stallybrass, *Renaissance Clothing*, 2.
58. Jones and Stallybrass, *Renaissance Clothing*, 4.

59. Jones and Stallybrass, *Renaissance Clothing*, 4.
60. In the third episode of *Lazarillo*, the protagonist joins his third master, the squire. His fine clothes and noble manner lead Lázaro to believe he has improved his lot, but quickly learns the squire is "all show," and in fact is so poor he does not have enough money to buy food, or even furniture for his house. Upon arriving to the apartment for the first time, Lázaro notes, "The walls were the only things there were to look at" ("Todo lo que yo había visto eran paredes").
61. *Sirena*, 389.
62. *Sirena*, 389: "Conmigo os burlais villanos / quitadme aquestos vestidos."
63. I am thankful to Kathleen Jeffs for noting the similarities between this scene and one with striking similarities where Hipólita wears female noble dress for the first time in Guillén de Castro's *La fuerza de la costumbre* (*The Force of Habit*). I also appreciate Kathleen Jeffs for generously sharing a galley copy of her chapter on the play, "Gender Politics in Guillén de Castro's *La fuerza de la costumbre*" in the then-forthcoming volume, *The Unsafe Stage: Daring Adaptations, Creative Failures and Experimental Performances in Iberian and Transnational Contexts*, ed. Esther Fernández, María Chouza-Calo, and Jonathan Thacker (Liverpool: Liverpool University Press, 2023). Jeffs' analysis leads me to find a compelling argument that the connection between Figueroa y Córdoba's *La sirena de Tinacria* and Guillén de Castro's *La fuerza de la costumbre* is more than fortuitous; Figueroa appears to be clearly reproducing elements from Guillén de Castro's original.
64. *Sirena*, 389: "que desta manera / andan todas en palacio." Chopines are high-platformed shoes (usually open-toe) that were in style over the Renaissance and Baroque. They grew increasingly lavish in their constructions and adornments, but more importantly here, could also be more than eight inches in height (21 cm) and were notoriously difficult to walk in. Noelia S. Cirnigliaro, "Touching the Ground: Women's Footwear in the Early Modern Hispanic World. An Introduction," *Journal of Spanish Cultural Studies* 14, no. 2 (2013), 109–10.
65. *Sirena*, 389:
    Aquesso es falso
    . . . porque si se cae
    una muger de su estado
    con ellos, estando en tierra
    harán los cuerpos mas baxos.
66. Cirnigliaro, "Touching the Ground," 107, 109.

67. *Sirena*, 389: "tormento más estraño."
68. The literal translation of the Spanish term *guardainfante* (farthingale, but literally "child hider") more aptly reflects the sartorial illustration I am elaborating here. The explicit connection to the farthingale's ability to hide a pregnancy points to the cultural ideologies that condition female subjectivities to have a reason to keep a pregnancy secret for fear of social consequences. Over the course of the seventeenth century, increasingly large farthingales came into vogue (see depicted in Velazquez's paintings of the royal family); even if only a coincidence, it is a profitable one for this illustration in so far as the larger farthingales betray the social conservatism of a culture in crisis like the Spanish Baroque. In times marked by imperial decline and fracturing social cohesion, the response to increasingly tenuous values is to double down on them, enforcing them ever more fervently. This exacerbates narrow subjectivities and with more at stake, conditions one's need to disavow (or hide) transgressive aspects of the self.
69. *Sirena*, p. 139: "con el tiempo, y la experiencia / te vayas haziendo a el uso"
70. Judith Butler, *Gender Trouble: Feminism and the Subversion of Identity* (New York: Routledge, 1999), 191.
71. *Sirena*, 399:
    >Ismenia, que altiva, y vana,
    >se ha buelto ya cortesana:
    >y olvidando los estremos
    >rusticos, vive sujeta
    >a la razon.
72. *Sirena*, 395: "su opinion agraviada, / siendo un hombre que no sufre / escrupulos en la fama."
73. *Sirena*, 397:
    >Que esto sufra!
    >Ya la paciencia me falta!
    >Atrevido Embaxador,
    >que con sobervia arrogancia
    >mañosamente reduces
    >las obras á las palabras!
    >...
    >Agradece que se halla
    >presente su Alteza aquí.
74. *Sirena*, 397: "Ya Ismenia ha respondido."

75. *Sirena*, 401:
    > que en vuestros labios he visto
    > tantas vezes, pues no siendo
    > yo vuestro igual, fuera indigno
    > blason de vuestra grandeza
    > ofenderos á vos mismo,
    > engañando á una muger.
76. *Sirena*, 400:
    > si mi fee no ha de poder
    > conseguir, ni merecer,
    > engañar á quien adoro.
    > Salga del pecho, y mi amor,
    > busque en Matilde su igual.
77. This is a possible reaction that Fernando, the king who proposes to Linda at the end of *La lindona de Galicia*, could have had. Enrique's response, juxtaposed with Fernando's, further demonstrates the posture that these two *comedias* take regarding the obsession with honor. Fernando's gracious attitude resolves conflict, whereas Enrique's defeat is just rewards for his lack of prudence in the administration of monarchical authority.
78. *Sirena*, 412:
    > Y yo Ismenia,
    > pues no tuve en tu desgracia
    > culpa alguna, con los braços
    > te vuelvo el cetro.
79. *Sirena*, 412: "y su Autor os pide / perdoneis sus muchas faltas."
80. Matilde's father had contracted her marriage to Enrique before his death, years prior to the action of the play, when she was a child.
81. Catherine Connor (Swietlicki), "Marriage and Subversion in Comedia Endings: Problems in Art and Society," in Smith and Stoll, *Gender, Identity, and Representation*, 27.
82. Ovid, *Metamorphoses*, 64. There is a marked linguistic element to his death, just as there is in the myth narratives of Echo and Callisto. Actaeon's impulse is to identify himself by calling to his hounds, but he is unable to speak, and his own dogs rip him apart. Similarly, Callisto, as a she-bear, cannot call out to her son to identify herself when they meet in the forest. Echo's demise occurs due to her inability to communicate with Narcissus, not unrelated from the previous two instances. One's human death and passage into wildness nearly always seems to be associated with the use of language. This element is most clearly dramatized

in *La lindona de Galicia*, but in a more metaphorical sense, these plays treat the wild women recuperating the voice lost by their mythological inspirations.

83. Margaret E. Boyle, *Unruly Women: Performance, Penitence, and Punishment in Early Modern Spain* (Toronto: University of Toronto Press, 2014): 12.
84. Castillo and Egginton, *Medialogies*, 143–44.
85. Matthew D. Stroud, "Performativity and Sexual Identity in Calderón's *Las manos blancos no ofenden* (*White Hands Don't Offend*)," in Smith and Stoll, *Gender, Identity, and Representation*, 120.
86. Butler, *Gender Trouble*, 185.
87. The "minor strategy of the Baroque" compliments Egginton's "major strategy" terminology I have deployed throughout the study. He defines the minor strategy of the Baroque as the focus "on the concrete reality of mediation itself and hence produces a thought, an art, a literature, or a politics that does not deny the real, but focuses on how the media are themselves real even while they try to make us believe that their reality, the reality in which we live, is always somewhere else." Egginton, *Theater of Truth*, 8.
88. See Margaret Greer, "Art and Power in the Spectacle Plays of Calderón de la Barca," *PMLA* 104, no. 3 (1989). In the article, she focuses on a number of plays, but in her discussion of *Hado y divisa de Leonido y Marfisa*, the critic primarily analyzes the *loa* that accompanied the play upon its first performance, and that directly addressed Carlos II and Marie Louise d'Orléans. She contends that the shorter theatrical performances that took place before and between the acts of *comedias* "foreground the critical content of the Calderonian court spectacle," and influence the way that the play should be interpreted, however delicate the balance between "royal pomp" and "a reasonable degree of credibility" (334–35).
89. See Maria Cristina Quintero, *Gendering the Crown in the Spanish Baroque Comedia*, New Hispanisms: Cultural and Literary Studies 2 (Farnham, UK: Ashgate, 2012), 91–99.

CHAPTER 5

1. See Albert E. Sloman, *The Dramatic Craftsmanship of Calderón: His Use of Earlier Plays* (Oxford: Dolphin Book Co., 1958). The author convincingly argues the indebtedness of *La vida es sueño* to a work Calderón

co-authored with Coello, *Yerros de naturaleza y aciertos de fortuna*, which he provides the date of composition as 1634. More recent research indicates that *La vida es sueño* may have been written as early as the late 1620s, which undermines Sloman's thesis that *La vida es sueño* improves upon the major themes developed in *Yerros*. Nevertheless, this chapter demonstrates other influences on Calderón's masterpiece—the wild figure tradition—and affirms Sloman's overall assertion that Calderón productively manipulated previous iterations of a story, character or theme to masterful dramatic effect. Sloman, *The Dramatic Craftmanship*, 15–17. For more on the earlier date of composition of *La vida es sueño*, see Don William Cruickshank, *Don Pedro Calderon* (Cambridge: Cambridge University Press, 2009).

2. The topic is glossed extensively if not treated explicitly in many publications of the dramaturg. For a brief list, see Antonucci, *Salvaje en la Comedia*; Sloman, *The Dramatic Craftsmanship*; A. D. Deyermond, "Segismundo the Wild Man," in *Golden Age Spanish Literature: Studies in Honor of John Varey by his Colleagues and Pupils*, ed. Charles Davis and Alan Deyermond (Westfield: Westfield College, 1991); Aurora Egido, "El vestido del salvaje en los autos sacramentales de Pedro de Calderón," in *Serta philologica F. Lázaro Carreter: natalem diem sexagesimum celebranti dicata.*, ed. Emilio Alarcos Llorach (Madrid: Cátedra, 1983); Mazur, *The Wild Man*.

3. Deyermond, "Segismundo the Wild Man," 85–86.

4. Deyermond, "Segismundo the Wild Man," 86. Ismenia of Figueroa y Córdoba's *La sirena de Tinacria* and Marfisa of Calderón's own *Hado y divisa de Leonido y Marfisa* also exhibit resentment against the hermit figure who raises them and keeps them secluded. Since both of these plays were written in the latter half of the seventeenth century but absent from earlier instances of the type, this characteristic of the wild figure seems to be a development that takes place during the arc currently under analysis.

5. "en el sentido de que su personaje y su trayectoria en *La vida es sueño* se construyen con piezas de montaje que derivan de la tradición teatral del salvaje." Antonucci, *Salvaje en la Comedia*, 172.

6. Antonucci, *Salvaje en la Comedia*, 171–72.

7. Antonucci, *Salvaje en la Comedia*, 173.

8. Of the works included in Antonucci's study that are not highlighted here include a brief but compelling analysis of the wild protagonist Irífile in *La fiera, el rayo y la piedra* (1652). Antonucci also provides a catalog

of Calderón's "static wild men," which they define as characters who usually have minor roles and play the same limited function as their counterparts in paratheatrical court pageantry. Antonucci attributes this as possibly stemming from the fact that Calderón wrote for the court more frequently during celebrations in which wild figures would have appeared. I concur with this claim, which is not mutually exclusive with my argument in the introduction of this book that the wild figures that feature as protagonists are also direct heirs of those that appear in paradramatic court spectacle, even if more developed. See Antonucci, *El salvaje en la Comedia*, 173–74.

9. Castillo sees the hyperattention to artifice and abundance that defines the baroque aesthetic as "a wall that has been completely covered over might call attention to what is hidden possible to think of the Baroque as a period concept (a la Maravall), and also as an ongoing 'condition' of modernity triggered by a pervasive sense of loss of meaning and a paradoxical longing for the Absolute." For more on this view of the Baroque and the modern condition, see David R. Castillo, "Horror (vacui): The Baroque Condition," in *Hispanic Baroques*, ed. Nicholas Spadaccini and Luis Martín-Estudillo (Nashville, TN: Vanderbilt University Press, 2005), 87–88.

10. On this question central to *La vida es sueño* (is this life I perceive real or only a dream?), readers will be familiar with recent manifestations on the probability that we are living in a simulation. That Calderón imagined this question in the seventeenth century and it remains exigent today points to something shared between then and now, which Egginton argues is our modernity. For more on the modernity of Calderón's ideology of space in *La vida es sueño*, see Egginton, *Theater of Truth*, 86–106. For a dialogue on the current fascination with the possibility of our simulated existence as imagined in contemporary culture, find "Living in a Simulation," podcast audio, *Imaginary Worlds*, June 12, 2021, https://www.imaginaryworldspodcast.org/episodes/living-in-a-simulation.

11. "hijos todos y confrontados todos . . . con el silencio, la abdicación o la agresión de los padres, estos héroes del crepúsculo de la Divinidad formulan para nosotros la primera contestación a nuestra tragedia moderna de hombres cortados de Dios." Marc Vitse, "Concepto del teatro en la época," in *Historia del teatro en España*, ed. José María Díez Borque (Madrid: Taurus Ediciones, 1983), 569.

12. This term and framing is offered by Vitse, who states: "as a result of parents' failure, faced with the silence of God . . . and an order affirmed

but never perceived, *aristocratic heroism* is born" (562). As a response, in order for the hero to succeed, they cannot solely rely on their noble birth, but must create their own destiny. My contention is that "success" is more equivocal in Calderón than this term and definition imply. For a longer explanation with analysis of examples viewed through this lens, see Vitse, "Concepto del teatro," 560–76.

13. *La vida es sueño*, 1.111–12. But that is the human predicament after all, being born into sin (in the broadest philosophical sense—suffering, desire, mortality, etc.). Also, I do not mean to imply a reading that Calderón's tower is so specifically designed as a critique of modern state control vis-à-vis the prison. But it is curious the extent to which the tower prefigures the logic of the modern penal system in terms of the institutionalized exertion of social control over a body of subjects (or in this case the body of one subject), even if not for the purpose of deterrence or rehabilitation. On the birth of the modern penal system, see Michel Foucault, *Discipline and Punish: The Birth of the Prison*, trans. Alan Sheridan (New York: Vintage Books, 1995), especially 231–92.

14. Ciriaco Morón identifies the motif of hybrid contradictions in the introduction to his edition of *La vida es sueño* cited in this study. Dussel contends this is the contradiction epistemic to modernity, born out of the colonial world-system: "modernity implicitly contains a strong rational core . . . [but] this same modernity carries out an irrational process that remains concealed even to itself. That is to say, given its secondary and mythical negative content, modernity can be read as the justification of an irrational praxis of violence." "Europe, Eurocentrism, and Modernity," 472.

15. *La vida es sueño*, 1.56–57: "Rústico yace entre desnudas peñas un palacio." The verb *yacer* ("to lie") is of note for two reasons. First, it is a peculiar predicate for a tower, a structure defined by its height relative to its width. Also, *yacer* is a term with connotations to death, frequently used idiomatically in phrases associated with lying on one's deathbed or in a coffin. This marks yet another contradiction in the increasingly complex visual-poetic conceit Calderón develops in the image of the tower.

16. *La vida es sueño*, 1.195: "cuna y sepulcro"; 1.665: "le diese ese sepulcro vivo de su vientre."

17. *La vida es sueño*, 1.672: "monstruo en forma de hombre."

18. Barbara Mujica, "Stuff of Dreams," in *A New Anthology of Early Modern Spanish Theater: Play and Playtext* (New Haven, CT: Yale University Press, 2014), 407.

19. *La vida es sueño*, 1.69–71: "La puerta / —mejor diré funesta boca— abierta / está." In Luis de Góngora's *Fábula de Polifemo y Galatea*, the cavernous home of the titular cyclops is described in stanzas 4–6. "4. Where foamily the sea of Sicily silvers the foot of My. Lilybaeum (either the vault of Vulcan's forges, or the tomb of Typhaeus' bones), an ashy plain gives pale indications—if not of the sacrilegious desire [of the giant Typhaeus]—of the difficult occupation [of the blacksmith]. There a high rock serves as gag to a grotto's mouth. 5. A crude adornment [or fortification] for this harsh crag are robust trunks, to whose matted hair the deep cavern owes less light and fresh air than to the cliff itself; that the obscure recess is black night's caliginous be is demonstrated to us by an infamous mob of nocturnal fowls, moaning sadly and flying heavily. 6. The melancholy emptiness, then, of this formidable yawning of the earth serves Polyphemus, the terror of the mountain, as a barbaric hut, a shadowy, and a spacious fold." Luis de Góngora y Argote, *Fábula de Polifemo y Galatea*, in *Renaissance and Baroque Poetry of Spain*, edited by Elias Rivers (Long Grove, IL: Waveland Press, 1988), 165–66.
20. La vida es sueño, 1.1–8:
    Hipogrifo violento
    que corriste parejas con el viento,
    ¿dónde, rayo sin llama,
    pájaro sin matiz, pez sin escama,
    y bruto sin instinto
    natural, al confuso laberinto
    de estas peñas
    te desbocas, arrastras y despeñas?
    The in-text translation has been amended from Eric Bentley's translation of Calderón's work in Eric Bentley, *The Classic Theatre* (Garden City, NJ: Doubleday, 1958), 409.
21. Frederick A. de Armas, "Papeles de zafiro: Signos político-mitológicos en *La vida es sueño*," *Anuario calderoniano* 2 (2009): 81.
22. "arte monstroso." Roberto González-Echevarría, "El 'monstruo de una especie y otra': *La vida es sueño*," in *Calderón: Códigos, Monstruos, Icones* (Montpellier: Centre d'études et recherches sociocritiques, 1982), 52.
23. Joachim Küpper, "The Case of Rosaura's Honor, and the Problem of Modernity (*La vida es sueño*)," *Modern Language Notes* 124, no. 2 (2009): 514. Küpper concludes that "Rosaura's project, although it might win her spontaneous sympathy from a modern standpoint, confers upon her the status of a character steeped in sin from the standpoint of the dominant

Golden Age discourse. She transgresses the boundaries of natural order" (517). This interpretation demonizes Rosaura in a way that is inconsistent both with the question of honor in the Spanish Baroque, and also in the corpus of wild character plays under analysis here. Küpper misconceives her role as what I call the perceived monster for being a "true" baroque monster, worthy of punishment.

24. *La vida es sueño*, 1.445–54:
    Pero si ya ha sucedido
    un peligro, de quien nadie
    se libró, porque el honor
    es de materia tan frágil
    que con una acción se quiebra
    o se mancha con un aire
    ¿qué más puede hacer, qué más
    el que es noble, de su parte,
    que a costa de tantos riesgos
    haber venido a buscarle?
    At this point in the play, Clotaldo is speaking in general terms, as he is unaware that the figure before him is his daughter Rosaura. In this moment of dramatic irony, he unwittingly approves of his daughter's behavior and laments her situation, for which he is partially responsible.
25. Michel Foucault, *Abnormal: Lectures at the Collège de France 1974–1975*, trans. Graham Burchell, ed. Arnold I. Davidson (London: Verso, 2003), 63.
26. See de Armas, "Papeles de zafiro" for a discussion of the mythological implications of each of those creatures in Calderón's play. Also, Küpper outlines the argument that Rosaura's horse is a projection of her character. While I agree that this is true, our views diverge on the exact nature of her character.
27. *La vida es sueño*, 3.2724–83: "siendo / monstruo de una especie y otra, entre galas de mujer/ armas de varón me adornan." Hermaphrodism was also a commonly held distinctive of monstrosity in the early modern period. See Río Parra's discussion of this monstrous trait in *Una era de monstruos*, 86–95.
28. *La vida es sueño*, 1.74: "Inmóvil bulto soy de fuego y hielo."
29. *La vida es sueño*, 1.277: "Yo soy . . ."
30. On the significance of this line in the *comedia*, see Leo Spitzer, "Soy quien soy," *Nueva Revista de Filología Hispánica* 1, no. 2 (1947). Also, more recently, Jonathan Thacker, "Maravall and the Self in the *Comedia Nueva*," *Bulletin of the Comediantes* 65, no. 1 (2013).

31. *La vida es sueño*, 2.1553–55: "y de Clotaldo fío / su efeto, pues le debo agradecida / aquí el amparo de mi honor y vida."
32. *La vida es sueño*, 1.944–5.
33. *La vida es sueño*, 1.945–54.
34. Dian Fox, *Kings in Calderón: A Study in Characterization and Political Theory*, Monografías 121 (London: Támesis, 1986), 108–9.
35. *La vida es sueño*, 3.3298: "Tu ingenio a todos admira."
36. *La vida es sueño*, 3.3299–300: "ASTOLFO: ¡Qué condición tan mudada!, ROSAURA: ¡Qué discreto y qué prudente!"
37. *La vida es sueño*, 3.3301: "¿Qué os admira? ¿Qué os espanta?" I follow Nelson's methodology for reception in this passage. As a means to get at reception in the absence of data about actual audiences' response to these plays when they were originally staged, Nelson looks for clues that point to the possibilities of reception "realized within literary texts themselves; which is to say, that the emblematic moment includes both actors and spectators in the diegetical medium of the texts." *Persistence of Presence*, 20.
38. Ruth El Saffar, "Reason's Unreason in *La vida es sueño*," in *Plays and Playhouses in Imperial Decadence*, edited by Anthony Zahareas, Ideologies & Literature (Madison: University of Wisconsin Press, 1986), 103–18.
39. Margaret Greer, "An (In)convenient Marriage? Justice and Power in *La vida es sueño, Comedia* and *Auto Sacramental*," *Bulletin of Spanish Studies* 85, no. 6 (2008): 58.
40. Mujica, "Stuff of Dreams," 406–8.
41. Deyermond, "Segismundo the Wild Man," 86. A great many wild characters do choose such a life, particularly in the sources that Deyermond considers. The "hairy anchorite" described in Bernheimer's classic work on the wild man most closely resembles the figure that Deyermond describes, but is just one of many types in the shared lineage of the wild character.
42. *La vida es sueño*, 1.277.
43. *La vida es sueño*, 1.1512–18, 1546–47:
    > Luego aunque esté en tal estado,
    > obligado no te quedo,
    > y pedirte cuentas puedo
    > del tiempo que me has quitado
    > libertad, vida y honor;
    > . . .

>   y sé quien soy
>   un compuesto de hombre y fiera.

44. *La vida es sueño*, 1.193–196, 198–201:
    >   que yo aquí
    >   tan poco del mundo sé
    >   que cuna y sepulcro fué
    >   esta torre para mi
    >   ...
    >   solo advierto
    >   este rústico desierto
    >   donde miserable vivo,
    >   siendo un esqueleto vivo
    >   siendo un animado muerto.

45. "debe ser rey, pero reprimir, como ser humano, los excesos del león." De Armas, "Papeles de zafiro," 85.
46. de Armas, "Papeles de zafiro," 82–83.
47. "Lo monstruo, al final se deja leer como una forma hipostática de la norma, y en él desciframos los enigmas que inquietan el equilibrio siempre precario de la normalidad." Río Parra, *Una era de monstruos*, 114.
48. Alexander A. Parker, "Segismundo's Tower: A Calderonian Myth," *Bulletin of Hispanic Studies* 59, no. 3 (1982): 248.
49. Like in many examples of the horror genre, the monster is killed, or at least thought to be dead, only to return in the sequel. In symbolic terms, overcoming whatever fear for which the monster served as a placeholder inevitably comes back to "haunt" the subject. The monster dies, but he is never really dead. Carroll explains this phenomenon as an indication of the malleability of the horror genre as both a repressive and subversive genre. On the one hand, the death of the monster signifies the triumph over evil (as defined within a particular socio-cultural context), while on the other, it dramatizes the inevitable failure to completely blot out the danger of transgression. Other instances, such as the zombie genre, go even further to criticize the cultural and economic milieu of their own production. See Noel Carroll, "The Ideology of Horror," in *The Philosophy of Horror, or, The Paradoxes of the Heart* (New York: Routledge, 1990), 196–99. As has been emphasized throughout this study, I contend that built into the *comedia* is a similar ambiguity, one that is difficult—actually impossible—to resolve. But the wild figure is not just any monster; it is a particular type that exists on the other side of

imagined borders, where Butler states "all social systems are vulnerable." *Gender Trouble*, 180.
50. Parker, "Segismundo's Tower," 249; *La vida es sueño*, 1.109–12.
51. Anthony Cascardi, "Allegories of Power," in *The Prince in the Tower: Perceptions of the La vida es sueño*, ed. Frederick de Armas (Lewisburg, PA: Bucknell University Press, 1993), 24.
52. Greer, "An (In)convenient Marriage?," 55.
53. Greer, "An (In)convenient Marriage?," 58.
54. Greer, "An (In)convenient Marriage?," 68.
55. See Emilio Cotarelo y Mori, "Mira de Amescua y su teatro," *Boletín de la Real Academia Española* 17, no. 84 (1930): 476–505; Angel Valbuena Prat, "Prólogo," in *Mira de Amescua: Teatro* (Clásicos Castellanos, 1961).
56. Salic Law is the political ideology that relies on the model of primogeniture in determining monarchical succession. Also, a brief note on orthography: Calderón spells his character's name "Eraclio"; Mira de Amescua's is spelled "Heraclio."
57. *La rueda de la fortuna*, 1.873–882.
58. The nature of dreams begins to reach a turning point during early modernity. Their capacity to predict the future remained a popular belief, and dream interpreters were prevalent throughout the period. However, as de Armas Wilson demonstrates in her analysis of don Quixote's vision in the Cave of Montesinos, Cervantes "introduces the desire to *give* meaning to dreams rather than to *find* it there." Diana de Armas Wilson, "Cervantes and the Night Visitors: Dream Work in the Cave of Montesinos," in *Quixotic Desire: Psychoanalytic Perspectives on Cervantes*, ed. Ruth El Saffar and Diana de Armas Wilson (Ithaca, NY: Cornell University Press, 1993), 79, emphasis original. Heraclio's dream exemplifies the understanding that meaning is found in dreams, and that they predict the future, whereas Cervantes problematizes the notion of dream-as-sign by encouraging multiple interpretations. As would be expected, Cervantes is more innovative in this regard, but that is not meant to imply that Mira's work is devoid of pleasure and entertainment; what it lacks in innovation, it makes up for in winsome and extravagant plot twists. However unbelievable they may be, they do not fail to entertain.
59. *La rueda de la fortuna*, 3.2812–16:
    Viendo su sangre vertida,
    y con lastimosas penas,
    la que a mi cuerpo da vida

siento alteradas las venas,
   aunque no soy su homicida.
60. For more details on the events that serve as the historical background of these *comedias*, see A. A. Vasil′ev and Sarra Mironovna Ragozina, *History of the Byzantine Empire* (Madison: University of Wisconsin Press, 1928), 169–99; Jonathan Shepard, *The Cambridge History of the Byzantine Empire c. 500–1492* (Cambridge: Cambridge University Press, 2008), 221–30. For a discussion of the similarities between Mira de Amescua's work and Calderón's *En la vida*, see Miguel Gallego Roca, "La rueda de la fortuna de Mira de Amescua y la polémica sobre el Heraclio español," *RILCE: Revista de Filologia Hispanica* 7, no. 2 (1991). It has also been argued that Corneille serves as Calderón's primary influence for the work, which is convincingly refuted in Cruickshank's introduction to his edition of *En la vida*, lxxii–xcvii. It is noteworthy that Amescua and Calderón collaborated in the composition of the *comedia Polifemo y Circe*, which further points to the likelihood that the affinities between *La rueda de la fortuna* and *En la vida* are "more than random chance." Edward William Hopper, "A Critical and Annotated Edition of Mira de Amescua's *La rueda de la fortuna*" (PhD diss., University of Missouri, 1972), 63.
61. *En la vida todo es verdad y todo mentira*, 1.83–4: "leche de lovas, ynfante, / me alimentó allí en mi tierna hedad." In Amescua's play, it reads: "como a mí me crió /con palmas y verdes ovas / y leche de mansas lobas" (as I was raised among palms and wetland and drank milk from wolves) (2.2159–61).
62. *En la vida*, 1.61: "ydrópica sed de sangre"; *La rueda de la fortuna*, 2.1178–79: "Hidrópico soy. Mi sed / es beber la sangre humana."
63. I am indebted to the vocabulary of psychoanalysis, specifically Lacan, in my explanation of desire here, specifically the fetishization of an object of desire produced out of a lack (in this case, blood).
64. Tyranny, and therefore monarchical legitimacy, is a primary concern of the play. Variations of the term "tyranny" are explicitly referenced sixteen times over the course of *En la vida*. For a dedicated study the nature of Focas's tyrannical rule, see Harrison Meadows, "On Tyranny and Succession: Rethinking Monarchical Legitimacy in Calderón's *En la vida todo es verdad y todo mentira* (1659)," *MLN* 133, no. 2 (2018). Portions of the analysis presented here, chiefly those related to the Focas's pseudo-empiricism, appear here as an abbreviated version of my argument in that article in so far as they are relevant to contextualize *En la*

vida in Calderón's dramatic corpus and the larger repertoire of baroque theatrical wildness.

65. The island of Sicily/Trinacria is notably also a location closely connected to mythology as the backdrop for numerous classical narratives and their wild inhabitants. Readers may notice the spelling variants Trinacria/Tinacria, as in the title of Figueroa y Córdoba's play, *La sirena de Tinacria*. On the influence of natural landscapes found in classical literature on western cultural traditions, see Ernst Robert Curtius, "The Ideal Landscape," in *European Literature and the Latin Middle Ages* (New York: Routledge & Kegan Paul, 1953).

66. *En la vida*, 2.372–75:
    ¿No me dirás, pensamiento,
    cuál experiencia con los dos
    hiciera, que fuera medio
    de dar luz al desengaño?

    Cruickshank's edition of the play has been consulted for citations and lineation in the original Spanish. Note that Cruickshank restarts the line numbers at the beginning of each act. See Pedro Calderón de la Barca, *En la vida todo es verdad y todo mentira*, ed. Don William Cruickshank (London: Támesis, 1973). For the English translations, line glosses and footnotes were consulted from the edition by Slater and Meadows, which I followed where available. See Pedro Calderón de la Barca, *En la vida todo es verdad y todo mentira and Sueños hay que verdad son*, ed. John Slater and Harrison Meadows, Cervantes & Co. European Masterpieces 78 (Newark, NJ: Juan de la Cuesta, 2016).

67. This scene clearly echoes the scene in act 2 of *La vida es sueño* when Basilio and Clotaldo remove Segismundo from the tower and observe his behavior at court to test the hypothesis that he is, in fact, the monster they thought he would be. While the nature of the flaws in their respective experimental designs are different in each of the plays, they share important similarities, chiefly, that absent fathers who rely on misguided premises to set up tests to learn something about their children by observing them from afar are destined to fail.

68. *En la vida*, 1.1192–94: "que la natural pasión / con esperiencias dirá / quál es mi hijo y quál no."

69. *En la vida*, 1.1197–98: "No te creas de esperiencias / de hijo a quien otro crïó."

70. He states this as his explicit objective: "coronar / . . . a quien con mis señas halle, / y dar muerte a quien sin ellas halle" (crown the one in

whom I find signs of myself and put to death the one whom I find without them; 1.321, 323–25).

71. Note that the inverse occurs in Lope de Vega's *El animal de Hungría*. It is while the king and his entourage is on a hunt that his daughter and heir, Rosaura, is lost, whereas in *En la vida* the hunt serves as a dramatic metaphor, in all its complexity, for the search to find the heir.
72. Eamon, *Science and the Secrets*, 299.
73. Eamon, *Science and the Secrets*, 299.
74. Eamon, *Science and the Secrets*, 299.
75. *En la vida*, 3.15–17: "para descrubir / lo ynterior, la que Lisipo traçando está."
76. Examples of notable professors of secrets are Leonardo Fioravanti and Giambattista Della Porta who acquired fame throughout Europe, including Spain. Fioravanti, a renowned alchemist, spent a period in the court of Philip II during 1575 and 1576, and both he and della Porta carried out the majority of their work in Spanish Naples. Philip II's interest in alchemy, contrary the notion that his religious fanaticism stifled intellectual curiosity, is well documented. Mar Rey Bueno's extensive research on the topic concludes that Philip II was "a forward-thinking monarch who promoted the development of new medicines elaborated by alchemical practices and the search for the Llulian essence." Mar Rey Bueno, "La Mayson pour Distiller des Eaües at El Escorial: Alchemy and Medicine at the Court of Philip II, 1556—1598," *Medical History* 52, no. 29 (2009): 27. His nephew, Rudolph II, whose court has been described as "a metropolis of alchemy," spent time during his youth at Philip's court where "it seems reasonable to conjecture that [his] scientific education began not in Vienna or Prague, but during his eight-year sojourn in Spain." William Eamon, "The Scientific Education of a Renaissance Prince: Archduke Rudolph in the Spanish Court," in *Alchemy and Rudolph II: Exploring the Secrets of Nature in Central Europe in the 16th and 17th Centuries*, ed. Ivo Purš and Vladimír Karpenko (Prague: artefactum, 2017).
77. William Eamon, *The Professor of Secrets: Mystery, Medicine, and Alchemy in Renaissance Italy* (Washington, DC: National Geographic, 2010), 11.
78. Eamon, *Science and the Secrets of Nature*, 235.
79. *En la vida*, 2.398–99. Focas's line reads: "Siendo ansí, que en mí no habrá /minuto, instante, momento / que no sea siglo, hasta que / aquilatados los pechos / en la forja de las horas, / que son cristales del tiempo, / muestren el oro y la liga, / amor y aborrecimiento." (2.398–405)

80. Antonio Regalado, *Calderón: Los orígenes de la modernidad en la España del Siglo de Oro*, vol. 1 (Barcelona: Ediciones Destino, 1995), 641.
81. Steven Shapin and Simon Schaffer, *Leviathan and the Air-Pump: Hobbes, Boyle, and the Experimental Life* (Princeton, NJ: Princeton University Press, 1985), 36.
82. John Slater, "Sacramental Instrumentality: Representation, Demonstration, and the Calderonian Auto," *Bulletin of the Comediantes* 58, no. 2 (2006): 483.
83. See William R. Blue, *The Development of Imagery in Calderón's Comedias* (York: Spanish Literature Publications Co., 1983); Don William Cruickshank, "Introducción," in *En la vida todo es verdad y todo mentira* (London: Támesis, 1973); Anthony Cascardi, *The Limits of Illusion: A Critical Study of Calderón* (Cambridge: Cambridge University Press, 1984), 121–29; David J. Hildner, *Reason and the Passions in the Comedias of Calderón* (Amsterdam: J. Benjamins, 1982); Barbara Mujica, "The Skeptical Premises of Calderón's *En esta vida todo es verdad y todo mentira*" (paper presented at the Texto y espectátculo: Selected Proceedings of the Symposium on Spanish Golden Age Theater, Lanham, 1989); Regalado, *Calderón*, 1.
84. Mujica, "Skeptical Premises," 125.
85. "las evidencias averiguables acerca de la identidad de los jóvenes no son tan concluyentes como parecen. En primer lugar el examen de su conducta que lleva a cabo Focas no da un resultado incuestionable. Cada uno exhibe rasgos contradictorios que no pueden vincularse exclusivamente ni con Focas ni con el difunto Mauricio." David J. Hildner, "Conocimiento, escepticismo y poder en En la vida todo es verdad y todo mentira de Calderón," *Neophilologus*, no. 102 (2018): 32.
86. *En la vida*, 3.140–41: "Sí diré, pues que te asisto / para ovedeçerte."
87. Focas's lines in 2.1307–11 read: "Mucho, y nada. / Pues que quedo con mis dudas / al ver que iguales me/ agradan en el uno la soberbia / y en el otro la templanza" (Much, and nothing. I still have my doubts in seeing that I equally appreciate the arrogance in one and temperance in the other).
88. Castillo and Egginton, *Medialogies*, 3; John Slater, and Harrison Meadows, introduction in *En la vida todo es verdad y todo mentira & Sueños hay que verdad son by Pedro Calderón de la Barca*, Cervantes & Co. Spanish Classics 78 (Newark, NJ: Juan de la Cuesta, 2016), 27.
89. I draw directly here from William Egginton's critical vocabulary. See Egginton, *Theater of Truth*, 39–55.

90. Other wild man plays rely on characters like Astolfo and revelatory objects to corroborate the identity of the character in question. For instance, in *La rueda de la fortuna*, Aureliana gives Mauricio's ring to Heraclio, which confirms his identity to the wounded king when he sees him wearing it. In *El hijo de los leones*, Fenisa confirms that Leonido is her son when Fileno, who had raised him in the forest, produces the clothes he was wearing when she left him at the base of a tree as an infant. Margarita reveals herself as the queen and identifies Uberto and Valentín as her sons (and therefore royal blood) in Lope's *El nacimiento de Ursón y Valentín*.
91. Egginton, *Theater of Truth*, 40.
92. Egginton, *Theater of Truth*, 40.

CONCLUSION

1. Although I have not explicitly referenced Althusser, I draw from his theory of ideological apparatuses and modern subjectivity found in *Lenin and Philosophy and Other Essays* throughout. See Louis Althusser, *Lenin and Philosophy, and Other Essays*, trans. Ben Brewster (New York: Monthly Review, 1972), especially 134–48.
2. This idea comes from Girard's scapegoat mechanism. See René Girard, *Violence and the Sacred* (Baltimore, MD: Johns Hopkins University Press, 1977). The wild things in the corpus analyzed in the present study point to the pervasiveness of its application. The villagers, for instance, are happy to blame their problems on the wild figure, until they learn that the culpable party is actually someone else. Blame for social ills is immediately redirected, and dealt with in the death, punishment, or domestication of the ideological monster of the work. Once sacrificed, society may proceed.
3. This is the unquestioned faith in scientific inquiry and objectivity that is the target of the author's critique in Bruno Latour, *We Have Never Been Modern* (New York: Harvester Wheatsheaf, 1993).
4. Shapin and Schaffer, *Leviathan and the Air-Pump*. See chapter 6, "Replication and Its Troubles: Air Pumps in the 1660s."
5. Monya Baker, "Over Half of Psychology Studies Fail Reproducibility Test," *Nature*, August 27, 2015. I thank John Slater for directing me to this article.
6. I do not intend to negate the function and purpose of scientific research, only to highlight examples where its application is only one approach

that overshadows other modes of inquiry with perhaps greater explanatory power for a given phenomenon.
7. Moraña, Dussel, and Jáuregui offer a concise summary of this view: "The critique of Occidentalism—that is, the philosophical, political, and cultural paradigms that emerge from and are imbedded in the historical phenomenon of European colonialism" of modernity and that drove European colonization—is essential to the understanding of the aggressive strategies used in imposing material and symbolic domination on vast territories in the name of *universal reason*." *Postcoloniality at Large*, 2.
8. Dussel, "Europe, Modernity, and Eurocentrism," 473; Quijano, "Coloniality and Modernity," 177.
9. Traditional folk iterations of the wild figure remain popular in Carnival and other festive traditions into the present. See for instance, Charles Fréger's photography series titled *Wilder Mann* that took him to eighteen European countries to find the lingering masquerade tradition of the wild figure. This collection has enjoyed numerous exhibitions in galleries throughout Europe, including the Pôle International de la Préhistoire to initiate a conversation about the possible connection between the dramatic history of the wild figure and early *sapien* representations of Cro-magnon. The photographer aptly notes the complexity of making such a claim and its consequences, even if he is unable to resist the temptation to "stay dry and objective and leave these discussions to scientists." Charles Fréger, *Wilder Mann: The Image of the Savage* (Stockport, UK: Dewi Lewis, 2012).

EPILOGUE

1. See Gordillo and Spadaccini's edited collection *Hispanic Baroques*, David Castillo's *Baroque Horrors*, Egginton's *Theater of Truth*, and Castillo and Egginton's *Medialogies*, as well as the essays that comprise its *Polemical Companion*. Each of these are cited elsewhere in *Wild Theater*.
2. Walter Moser, "Introduction to Part 1," in *Neo-Baroques: From Latin America to the Hollywood Blockbuster*, eds. Walter Moser, Angela Ndalianis and Peter Krieger (Leiden: BRILL, 2016), 29.
3. Julio Baena and Bradley Nelson, ed., *A Polemical Companion to Medialogies: Reading Reality in the Age of Inflationary Media*, Hispanic Issues Online Debates 8 (Minneapolis: University of Minnesota College of Liberal Arts, 2017).

4. Castillo and Egginton, *Medialogies*, 4.
5. Nelson, *Persistence of Presence*, 13.
6. Evan Beloff, "Bigfoot's Reflections" (Bunbury Films, 2007).
7. Castillo and Egginton, *Medialogies*, 3, my emphasis.
8. Important to note however, at the beginning of each episode a disclaimer reads "Some phone calls with sources and suspects have been reconstructed and some of their identifying details have been changed." It appears to be clear which calls are dramatized, having taken place before filming or when the cameras were not rolling, but in a series already capable of masterful misdirections, it would undermine my current approach to be focusing on whether a phone call was accurately portrayed and how that affects the veracity of the information conveyed. *Sasquatch* is constantly circling back to a portrayal of the world on the razor's edge between giants and windmills.
9. Castillo and Egginton, *Medialogies*, 4.
10. Castillo and Egginton, *Medialogies*, 159.
11. Castillo and Egginton, *Medialogies*, 153.
12. Castillo and Egginton, *Medialogies*, 160.
13. The articulation of race and labor to justify the exploitation of people/groups in the neoliberal world order is just a twentieth-century reformulation of the coloniality of power that has been dominant in the modern world-system since 1492. According to Quijano, in the conquest and colonization of Latin America, "a new technology of domination/exploitation, in this case race/labor, was articulated in such a way that the two elements appeared naturally associated. Until now, this strategy has been exceptionally successful." "Coloniality of Power," 537.
14. Castillo and Egginton use a different metaphor: "the world blissfully goes on spinning the rope it will hang itself with, while the same elites bunker down in estates paid for by profits they make selling that rope." *Medialogies*, 158.

BIBLIOGRAPHY

Alfonso X. *General estoria*. Edited by Antonio García. Madrid: Centro de estudios históricos, 1930.

Althusser, Louis. *Lenin and Philosophy, and Other Essays*. Translated by Ben Brewster. New York: Monthly Review, 1972.

Antonucci, Fausta. *El salvaje en la Comedia del Siglo de Oro: Historia de un tema de Lope a Calderón*. Pamplona, Toulouse: Anejos de RILCE, L.E.S.O., 1995.

Arellano, Ignacio. *Historia del teatro español del siglo XVII*. Crítica y estudios literarios. Madrid: Cátedra, 1995.

Ariosto, Ludovico. *Orlando furioso*. Edited by Cesare Segre, María de las Nieves Muñiz Muñiz, and Jerónimo de Urrea. Letras universales 333/334. Madrid: Cátedra, 2002.

Aristotle. *Poetics*. Edited by Michelle Zerba and David Gorman. Translated by James Hutton. New York: Norton, 2018.

Armas, Frederick A. de. "Lope de Vega and the Hermetic Tradition: The Case of Dardanio in *La Arcadia*." *Revista canadiense de estudios hispánicos* 7, no. 3 (1983): 345–62.

———. "Papeles de zafiro: Signos político-mitológicos en *La vida es sueño*." *Anuario calderoniano* 2 (2009): 75–96.

———. "Segismundo/Philip IV: The Politics of Astrology in *La vida es sueño*." *Bulletin of the Comediantes* 53, no. 1 (2001): 83–100.

Armas Wilson, Diana de. "Cervantes and the Night Visitors: Dream Work in the Cave of Montesinos." In *Quixotic Desire: Psychoanalytic Perspectives on Cervantes*, edited by Ruth El Saffar and Diana de Armas Wilson. Ithaca, NY: Cornell University Press, 1993.

Bacon, Francis. *The Instauratio Part II: Novum Organum and Associated Texts*. Edited by Graham Rees and Maria Wakely. Oxford: Clarendon Press, 2004.

Baena, Julio. "What Kind of a Monster Are You, Galatea?" In *Writing Monsters: Essays on Iberian and Latin American Cultures*, edited by Adriana Gordillo and Nicholas Spadaccini, 26–41. Minneapolis: University of Minnesota College of Liberal Arts, 2014.

Baena, Julio, and Bradley Nelson, eds. *A Polemical Companion to Medialogies: Reading Reality in the Age of Inflationary Media*, Hispanic Issues Online Debates 8. Minneapolis: University of Minnesota College of Liberal Arts, 2017.

Baker, Monya. "Over Half of Psychology Studies Fail Reproducibility Test." *Nature*, August 27, 2015.

Bakhtin, Mikhail. *Rabelais and His World*. Translated by Helene Iswolsky. Bloomington: Indiana University Press, 1984.

Bal, Mieke. *Quoting Caravaggio: Contemporary Art, Preposterous History*. Chicago: University of Chicago Press, 1999.

Bances Candamo, José Antonio. *La piedra filosofal*. Edited by Alfonso D'Agostino. Rome: Bulzoni, 1988.

———. *Theatro de los theatros de los passados y presentes siglos*. Edited by Duncan Moir. Textos 3. London: Támesis, 1970

Bartra, Roger. *The Artificial Savage: Modern Myths of the Wild Man*. Ann Arbor: University of Michgan Press, 1997.

———. *Wild Men in the Looking Glass: The Mythic Origins of European Otherness*. Translated by Carl T. Berrisford. Ann Arbor: University of Michigan Press, 1994.

Bass, Laura R. "The *Comedia* and Cultural Control: The Legacy of José Antonio Maravall." *Bulletin of the Comediantes* 65, no. 1 (2013): 1–13.

Beloff, Evan. *Bigfoot's Reflection*. Vancouver, BC: Bunbury Films, 2007.

Bentley, Eric. *The Classic Theatre*. Garden City, NJ: Doubleday, 1958.

Bernheimer, Richard. *Wild Men in the Middle Ages*. Cambridge, MA: Harvard University Press, 1952.

Bernstein, Beth. "A 'Monstrous' Problem: Examining Issues of Race in *Virtudes vencen señales*." In *Exploring Race, Ethnicity, Gender, and Sexuality in Four Spanish Plays: A Crisis of Identity*. Lanham, MD: Lexington Books, 2021.

Beusterien, John. *An Eye on Race: Perspectives from Theater in Imperial Spain*. Lewisburg, PA: Bucknell University Press, 2006.

Bireley, Robert. *The Counter-Reformation Prince: Anti-Machiavellianism or Catholic Statecraft in Early Modern Europe*. Chapel Hill: University of North Carolina Press, 1990.

Blancas, Gerónimo de. *Coronaciones de los sereníssimos reyes de Aragón*. Edited by Andrés de Uztarroz. Zaragoza: Diego Dormer, 1641.

Bloom, Harold. *The Anxiety of Influence: A Theory of Poetry*. Oxford: Oxford University Press, 1973.

Blue, William R. *The Development of Imagery in Calderón's Comedias*. York: Spanish Literature Publications, 1983.

Boadas, Sònia. "Lope ante la puesta en escena: Las acotaciones en las comedias autógrafas." In *"Entra el editor y dice": Ecdótica y acotaciones teatrales (siglos XVI y XVII)*, edited by Luigi Giuliani and Victoria Pineda. Venice: Edizioni Ca'Foscari (Venice University Press), 2018.

Boccaccio, Giovanni. *The Decameron*. Edited by Mark Musa and Peter Bondanella. Norton Critical Editions. New York: Norton, 1977.

Bourdieu, Pierre. *The Field of Cultural Production*. New York: Columbia University Press, 1993.

———. "From *Distinction: A Social Critique of the Judgment of Taste*." In *The Critical Tradition*, edited by David H. Richter. Boston: Bedford/St. Martin's, 2007.

Boyle, Margaret E. *Unruly Women: Performance, Penitence, and Punishment in Early Modern Spain*. Toronto: University of Toronto Press, 2014.

Brincat, Shannon K. "'Death to Tyrants': The Political Philosophy of Tyrannicide—Part I." *Journal of International Political Theory* 4, no. 2 (2008): 212–40.

Burningham, Bruce. *Radical Theatricality: Jongleuresque Performance on the Early Spanish Stage*. Purdue Studies in Romance Literature 39. West Lafayette, IN: Purdue University Press, 2007.

———. *Tilting Cervantes: Baroque Reflections on Postmodern Culture*. Nashville, TN: Vanderbilt University Press, 2008.

Bushnell, Rebecca W. *Tragedies of Tyrants: Political Thought and Theater in the English Renaissance*. Ithaca, NY: Cornell University Press, 1990.

Butler, Judith. *Gender Trouble: Feminism and the Subversion of Identity*. New York: Routledge, 1999.

Calderón de la Barca, Pedro. *El médico de su honra*. Edited by Don William Cruickshank. Madrid: Castalia, 1989. 1637.

———. *En la vida todo es verdad y todo mentira*. Edited by Don William Cruickshank. London: Támesis, 1973.

———. *En la vida todo es verdad y todo mentira and Sueños hay que verdad son*. Edited by John Slater and Harrison Meadows. Cervantes & Co. European Masterpieces 78. Newark: Juan de la Cuesta, 2016.

———. "Hado y divisa de Leonido y Marfisa. Comedias." In *Comedias*, edited by Luis Iglesias Feijoo. Madrid: Fundación José Antonio de Castro, 2010.

———. *La fiera, el rayo y la Piedra*. Edited by Aurora Egido. Letras hispánicas 299. Madrid: Cátedra, 1989.

———. *La vida es sueño*, 27th ed. Edited by Ciriaco Morón Arroyo. Letras hispánicas 57. Madrid: Cátedra, 2001.

Cañizares-Esguerra, Jorge. "The Colonial Iberian Roots of the Scientific Revolution." In *Nature, Empire, and Nation: Explorations of the History of Science in the Iberian World*. Redwood City, CA: Stanford University Press, 2006.

Caro Baroja, Julio. *El carnaval: Análisis histórico-cultural*, 2nd ed. Madrid: Taurus, 1979.

Carroll, Noel. "The Ideology of Horror." In *The Philosophy of Horror, or, The Paradoxes of the Heart*. New York: Routledge, 1990.

Cascardi, Anthony. "Allegories of Power." In *The Prince in the Tower: Perceptions of the La vida es sueño*, edited by Frederick A. de Armas. Lewisburg, PA: Bucknell University Press, 1993.

———. *The Limits of Illusion: A Critical Study of Calderón*. Cambridge: Cambridge University Press, 1984.

Castillo, David R. *Baroque Horrors: Roots of the Fantastic in the Age of Curiosities*. Ann Arbor: University of Michigan Press, 2010.

———. "Horror (vacui): The Baroque Condition." In *Hispanic Baroques*, edited by Nicholas Spadaccini and Luis Martín-Estudillo. Nashville, TN: Vanderbilt University Press, 2005.

———. "Maravall on Culture and Historical Discourse: A Question of Methodolgy." *Forum: José Antonio Maravall and Baroque Culture, Yearbook of Comparative and General Literature* 45–46 (1996–1997): 177–81.

Castillo, David R., and William Egginton, "Dreamboat Vampires and Zombie Capitalists." *New York Times*, 24 October, 2014.

———. *Medialogies: Reading Reality in the Age of Inflationary Media*. Poltical Theory and Contemporary Philosophy. London: Bloomsbury Academic, 2017.

Castillo, Jorge Luis. "La lengua del gracioso y el mundo del Carnaval en *El desdén, con el desdén* de Moreto." *Bulletin of the Comediantes* 46, no. 1 (1994): 7–20.

Castillo, Moisés R. *Indios en escena: La representación del amerindio en el teatro del Siglo de Oro*. Purdue Studies in Romance Literatures 48. West Lafayette, IN: Purdue University Press, 2009.

Castle, Terry. *Masquerade and Civilization: The Carnivalesque in Eighteenth-Century English Culture and Fiction*. Redwood City, CA: Stanford University Press, 1986.

Castro-Gómez, Santiago. "(Post)Coloniality for Dummies: Latin American Perspectives on Modernity, Coloniality, and the Geopolitics of Knowledge." In *Coloniality at Large: Latin America and the Postcolonial Debate*, edited by Mabel Moraña, Carlos Jáuregui, and Enrique Dussel. Durham, NC: Duke University Press, 2008.

Cervantes Saavedra, Miguel de. *La fuerza de la sangre*. In *Novelas ejemplares*, II, 20th ed., edited by Harry Sieber. Letras hispánicas. Madrid: Cátedra, 2001.

———. *El ingenioso hidalgo Don Quixote de la Mancha*. Edited by Martín de Riquer. 2 vols. Madrid: Real Academia Española, 1950.

Chambers, E. K. *The Mediaeval Stage*, vol. 4. Oxford: Oxford University Press, 1903.

Cirnigliaro, Noelia S. "Touching the Ground: Women's Footwear in the Early Modern Hispanic World. An Introduction." *Journal of Spanish Cultural Studies* 14, no. 2 (2013): 107–19.

Cixous, Hélène. "The Laugh of the Medusa." *Signs* 1, no. 4 (1976): 875–93.

Claramonte, Andrés de. "Comedia famosa, *La lindona de Galicia*." In *3a. parte de las comedias del doctor J. de Montalván*. Valencia: Viuda de José de Orga, 1762.

Cohen, Jeffrey Jerome, ed. *Monster Theory: Reading Culture*. Minneapolis: University of Minnesota Press, 1996.

Connor (Swietlicki), Catherine. "Marriage and Subversion in *Comedia* Endings: Problems in Art and Society." In Smith and Stoll, *Gender, Identity, and Representation in Spain's Golden Age*.

———. "The Occult/Hermetic *Burlador de Sevilla*." *Crítica Hispánica* 15, no. 1 (1993): 97–104.

Cortijo Ocaña, Adelaida, and Antonio Cortijo Ocaña. "Carnaval y teatro en los siglos XVI y XVII." *Revista de Filología Española* 84, no. 2 (2004): 399–412.

Cotarelo y Mori, Emilio. *Colección de entremeses, loas, bailes, jácaras y mojigangas desde fines del siglo XVI á mediados del XVIII ordenada*. Madrid: Bailly-Bailliére, 1911.

———. "Mira de Amescua y su teatro." *Boletín de la Real Academia Española* 17, no. 84 (1930): 467–505.
Covarrubias, Sebastián de. *Tesoro de la lengua castellana*. Madrid: Luis Sánchez, 1611.
Cruickshank, Don William. *Don Pedro Calderon*. Cambridge: Cambridge University Press, 2009.
———. Introduction to *En la vida todo es verdad y todo mentira de Pedro Calderón de la Barca*. London: Támesis, 1973.
Cuéllar, Álvaro, and Germán Vega García-Luengos. "Un nuevo repertorio dramático para Andrés de Claramonte." *Hipogrifo: Revista de literatura y cultura del Siglo de Oro* 11, no. 1 (2023): 117–72.
Curtius, Ernst Robert. "The Ideal Landscape." Translated by Willard R. Trask. In *European Literature and the Latin Middle Ages*. New York: Routledge & Kegan Paul, 1953.
D'Agostino, Alfonso. Introduction to *La piedra filosofal de Francisco Antonio de Bances Candamo*. Rome: Bulzoni, 1988.
Deleuze, Gilles. "The Fold." *Yale French Studies*, no. 80 (1991): 227–47.
della Porta, Giambattista. *Magia Naturalis*. New York: Basic Books, 1957.
Dendle, Peter. "Cryptozoology in the Medieval and Modern Worlds." *Folklore* 117, no. 2 (2006): 190–206.
Devos, Brent. "Evidence Regarding the 'Monte' Stage Piece in 'Corral' Theatres of the Seventeenth Century." *Bulletin of the Comediantes* 67, no. 2 (2015): 101–12.
Deyermond, A. D. "El hombre salvaje en la novela sentimental." In *Actas del Segundo Congreso Internacional de Hispanistas*, edited by Jaime Sanchez Romeralo and Norbert Poulussen. Nijmegen: Instituto Español de la Universidad de Nimega, 1967.
———. "Segismundo the Wild Man." In *Golden Age Spanish Literature: Studies in Honor of John Varey by his Colleagues and Pupils*, edited by Charles Davis and Alan Deyermond. London: Westfield College, 1991.
Díez Borque, José María. "El disfraz y otras estrategias para el éxito de la comedia." In *Máscaras y juegos de identidad en el teatro español del Siglo de Oro*, edited by María Luisa Lobato. Biblioteca Filológica Hispana. Madrid: Visor Libros, 2011.
Dussel, Enrique. "Eurocentrism and Modernity (Introduction to the Frankfurt Lectures)." *boundary 2* 20, no. 3 (1993): 65–76.
———. "Europe, Modernity, and Eurocentrism." *Nepantla* 1, no. 3 (2000): 465–78.

Eamon, William. *The Professor of Secrets: Mystery, Medicine, and Alchemy in Renaissance Italy.* Washington, DC: National Geographic, 2010.

———. *Science and the Secrets of Nature: Books of Secrets in Medieval and Early Modern Culture.* Princeton, NJ: Princeton University Press, 1994.

———. "The Scientific Education of a Renaissance Prince: Archduke Rudolph in the Spanish Court." In *Alchemy and Rudolph II: Exploring the Secrets of Nature in Central Europe in the 16th and 17th Centuries*, edited by Ivo Purš and Vladimír Karpenko. Prague: artefactum, 2017.

Egginton, William. *How the World Became a Stage: Presence, Theatricality, and the Question of Modernity.* Albany, NY: SUNY Press, 2003.

———. *The Theater of Truth: The Ideology of (Neo)Baroque Aesthetics.* Redwood City, CA: Stanford University Press, 2009.

Egido, Aurora. "El vestido del salvaje en los autos sacramentales de Pedro de Calderón." In *Serta philologica F. Lázaro Carreter: Natalem diem sexagesimum celebranti dicata*, edited by Emilio Alarcos Llorach. Madrid: Cátedra, 1983.

Elliott, John H. "Concerto Barocco." *New York Review of Books* 34, no. 6 (April 9, 1987).

El Saffar, Ruth. "Reason's Unreason in *La vida es sueño*." In *Plays and Playhouses in Imperial Decadence*, edited by Anthony Zahareas. Ideologies & Literature. Madison: University of Wisconsin Press, 1986.

Fernández-Santamaria, José A. "Reason of State and Statecraft in Spain (1595–1640)." *Journal of the History of Ideas* 41, no. 3 (July–Sept. 1980): 355–79.

Ferrer Valls, Teresa. *La práctica escénica cortesana: De la época del Emperador a la de Felipe III.* London: Támesis, en colaboración con la Institució Valenciana d'Estudis i Investigació, 1991.

———. *Nobleza y espectáculo teatral (1535–1622): Estudio y Documentos.* Edited by Joan Oleza.Textos Teatrales Hispánicos del siglo XVI. Valencia: UNED, Universidad de Sevilla, Universidat de València, 1993.

———. "*La viuda valenciana* de Lope de Vega o el arte de nadar y guardar la ropa." In *Doce comedias buscan un tablado*. Cuadernos de teatro clásico 11. Madrid: Compañía Nacional de Teatro Clasico, 1999.

Findlen, Paula. "Between Carnival and Lent: The Scientific Revolution at the Margins of Culture." *Configurations: A Journal of Literature, Science, and Technology* 6, no. 2 (1998): 243–67.

Foucault, Michel. *Abnormal: Lectures at the Collège de France 1974–1975.* Edited by Arnold I. Davidson. Translated by Graham Burchell. London: Verso, 2003.

———. *The Archaeology of Knowledge: The Discourse on Language*. Translated by Alan Sheridan. New York: Pantheon Books, 1972.

———. *Discipline and Punish: The Birth of the Prison*. Translated by Alan Sheridan. New York: Vintage Books, 1995.

Fox, Dian. *Kings in Calderón: A Study in Characterization and Political Theory*. Monografías 121. London: Támesis, 1986.

Fra-Molinero, Baltasar. "The Play of Race and Gender in Vélez de Guevara's *Virtudes vencen señales*." *Bulletin of the Comediantes* 49, no. 2 (1997): 337–55.

Fréger, Charles. *Wilder Mann: The Image of the Savage*. Stockport, UK: Dewi Lewis, 2012.

Fuchs, Barbara. *The Poetics of Piracy: Emulating Spain in English Literature*. Haney Foundation Series. Philadelphia: University of Pennsylvania Press, 2013.

Gallego Roca, Miguel. "*La rueda de la fortuna* de Mira de Amescua y la polémica sobre el Heraclio español." *RILCE: Revista de Filologia Hispanica* 7, no. 2 (1991): 311–24.

Galoppe, Raúl A. "Monstruoso Aquiles, aberración y cruce: Las líneas del género y el deseo autorial." *Hecho Teatral: Revista de teoría y práctica del Teatro Hispánico* 2 (2002): 125–45.

García de Céspedes, Andrés. *Regimiento de navegación*. Madrid: Juan de la Cuesta, 1606.

Gasta, Chad. "La visión de los novatores en Bances Candamo: La astrología como experimento teatral." In *Atardece el Barroco: Ficción experimental en la España de Carlos II (1665–1700)*, edited by Jorge García López and Enrique García Santo-Tomás. Madrid: Iberoamericana/Vervuert, 2021.

Gavela García, Delia. "Obras hacen linaje o la fuerza de la sangre: Identidades ocultas en la producción lopesca." In *Máscaras y juegos de identidad en el teatro español del Siglo de Oro*, edited by María Luisa Lobato. Biblioteca Filológica Hispana. Madrid: Visor Libros, 2011.

Gerli, E. Michael. "*El retablo de las maravillas*: Cervantes' 'Arte nuevo de deshacer comedias.'" *Hispanic Review* 57, no. 4 (1989): 477–92.

Girard, René. *Violence and the Sacred*. Baltimore, MD: Johns Hopkins University Press, 1977.

Glenn, Richard F. "The Loss of Identity: Towards a Definition of the Dialectic in Lope's Early Drama." *Hispanic Review* 41, no. 4 (1973): 609–26.

Gómez Moreno, Ángel. "The Challenges of Historiography: The Theatre in Medieval Spain." In *A History of Theatre in Spain*, edited by David T. Gies and Maria M. Delgado. Cambridge: Cambridge University Press, 2012.

———. *El teatro medieval castellano en su marco románico*. Madrid: Taurus, 1991.
Góngora y Argote, Luis de. *Fábula de Polifemo y Galatea*. In *Renaissance and Baroque Poetry of Spain*. Translated and edited by Elias Rivers. Long Grove, IL: Waveland, 1988.
———. *Fábula de Polifemo y Galatea*, 7th ed. Edited by Alexander A. Parker. Letras hispánicas 171. Madrid: Cátedra, 2000.
González-Echevarría, Roberto. "El 'monstruo de una especie y otra': *La vida es sueño*, iii, 2, 725." In *Calderón: Códigos, Monstruos, Icones*, edited by Javier Herrero. Co-textes no. 3. Montpellier: Centre d'études et recherches sociocritiques, 1982.
Gordillo, Adriana, and Nicholas Spadaccini, eds. *Writing Monsters: Essays on Iberian and Latin American Cultures*, vol. 15. Hispanic Issues Online. Minneapolis: University of Minnesota, 2014.
Gracián, Baltasar. *El criticón*, 8th ed. Letras hispánicas. Madrid: Cátedra, 2001.
———. *Oráculo manual y arte de prudencia*. Edited by Emilio Blanco. Letras hispánicas 395. Madrid: Cátedra, 2001.
Grady, Hugh. "Tragedy and Materialist Thought." In *A Companion to Tragedy*, edited by Rebecca Bushnell. Malden, MA: Blackwell, 2005.
Green, Otis H. "Notes on the Pizarro Trilogy of Tirso de Molina." *Hispanic Review* 4, no. 3 (1936): 201–25.
Greer, Margaret R. "Art and Power in the Spectacle Plays of Calderón de la Barca." *PMLA* 104, no. 3 (1989): 329–39.
———. "An (In)convenient Marriage? Justice and Power in *La vida es sueño, Comedia and Auto Sacramental*." *Bulletin of Spanish Studies* 85, no. 6 (2008): 55–68.
———. "Playing the Palace: Space, Place and Performance in Early Modern Spain." In *A History of Theatre in Spain*, edited by David T. Gies and Maria M. Delgado. Cambridge: Cambridge University Press, 2012.
———. *The Play of Power: Mythological Court Dramas of Calderón de la Barca*. Princeton, NJ: Princeton University Press, 1991.
Habermas, Jürgen. *The Philosophical Discourse of Modernity*. Translated by Frederick Lawrence. Cambridge: Polity Press, 1998.
Hall, Stuart. *On Postmodernism and Articulation: An Interview with Stuart Hall*. Critical Dialogues in Cultural Studies. London: Routledge, 2006.
———. "When Was the 'Post-Colonial'? Thinking at the Limit." In *The Postcolonial Question: Common Skies, Divided Horizons*, edited by Iain Chambers and Lidia Curti. London: Routledge, 1996.

Hegel, Georg Wilhelm Friedrich. *Hegel's Philosophy of Right*. Translated by T. M. Knox. Oxford: Clarendon Press, 1958.

Hildner, David J. "Conocimiento, escepticismo y poder en En la vida todo es verdad y todo mentira de Calderón." *Neophilologus*, no. 102 (2018): 25–37.

———. *Reason and the Passions in the Comedias of Calderón*. Amsterdam: J. Benjamins, 1982.

Hobbes, Thomas. *Leviathan*. Edited by Karl Schuhmann and G. A. J. Rogers. London: Bloomsbury, 2006.

Hopper, Edward William. "A Critical and Annotated Edition of Mira de Amescua's *La rueda de la fortuna*." PhD diss., University of Missouri, 1972.

Hoz y Mota, Juan Claudio de la. *Descubrimiento de las Batuecas del Duque de Alba*. Biblioteca Nacional de España, MSS. 2504, 1710.

Huerta Calvo, Javier, ed. *Teatro y carnaval*. Cuadernos de Teatro Clásico 12. Madrid: Compañía Nacional de Teatro Clásico, 1999.

Hurtado Torres, Antonio. "La astrología en el teatro de Calderón de la Barca." In *Calderón: Actas del Congreso internacional sobre Calderón y el teatro español del Siglo de Oro*, edited by Luciano García Lorenzo. Anejos de la Revista Segismundo 6, Madrid: Consejo Superior de Investigaciones Científicas, 1983.

Husband, Timothy, and Gloria Gilmore-House. *The Wild Man: Medieval Myth and Symbolism*. New York: Metropolitan Museum of Art, 1980.

Jeffs, Kathleen. "Gender Politics in Guillén de Castro's *La fuerza de la costumbre*." In *The Unsafe Stage: Daring Adaptations, Creative Failures and Experimental Performances in Iberian and Transnational Contexts*, edited by María Chouza-Calo and Jonathan Thacker. Liverpool: Liverpool University Press, 2023.

Jones, Ann Rosalind, and Peter Stallybrass. *Renaissance Clothing and the Materials of Memory*. Cambridge Studies in Renaissance Literature and Culture. Cambridge: Cambridge University Press, 2000.

Jones, Nicholas R. *Staging Habla de Negros: Radical Performances of the African Diaspora in Early Modern Spain*. Iberian Encounter and Exchange 1475–1755 3. University Park: Pennsylvania State University Press, 2019.

Kozey, Christopher. "Las Batuecas, Las Hurdes, and the Spanish Crypt." PhD diss., Johns Hopkins University, 2015.

Küpper, Joachim. "The Case of Rosaura's Honor, and the Problem of Modernity (*La vida es sueño*)." *Modern Language Notes* 124, no. 2 (2009): 509–17.

La vida de Lazarillo de Tormes, y de sus fortunas y adversidades. Edited by Everett W. Hesse. Madison: University of Wisconsin Press, 1961.

Latour, Bruno. *We Have Never Been Modern*. New York: Harvester Wheatsheaf, 1993.

"Living in a Simulation." Podcast audio. *Imaginary Worlds*, June 12, 2021. https://www.imaginaryworldspodcast.org/episodes/living-in-a-simulation.

Lobato, María Luisa. "El espacio de la fiesta: Máscaras parateatrales y teatrales en el Siglo de Oro." In *Espacios de representación y espacios representados en el teatro áureo español*, edited by Francisco Sáez Raposo. Barcelona: Universitat Autónoma de Barcelona, 2011.

———. "Nobles como actores: El papel activo de las gentes de palacio en las representaciones cortesanas de la época de los Austrias." In *Dramaturgia festiva y cultura nobiliaria en el Siglo de Oro*, edited by Bernardo J. García García and María Luisa Lobato. Madrid: Iberoamericana, Vervuert, 2007.

Lobato, María Luisa, and Bernardo José García García, ed. *La fiesta cortesana en la época de los Austrias*. Valladolid: Junta de Castilla y León, Consejería de Educación y Cultura, 2003.

Lollini, Massimo. "Maravall's Culture of the Baroque: Between Wölfflin, Gramsci, and Benjamin." *Forum: José Antonio Maravall and Baroque Culture, Yearbook of Comparative and General Literature* 45–46 (1996–97): 187–96.

López-Pérez, Miguel. "Ciencia y pensamiento hermético." In *Beyond the Black Legend: Spain and the Scientific Revolution*, edited by Victor Navarro Brotóns and William Eamon. Valencia: Instituto de Historia de la Ciencia y Documentación López Piñero, 2007.

López Pinciano, Alonso. *Philosophia antigua poética*. Edited by Alfredo Carballo Picazo. Biblioteca de antiguos libros hispánicos, 19–21. Madrid: Consejo Superior de Investigaciones Científicas, Instituto "Miguel de Cervantes," 1953.

Machiavelli, Niccolo. *The Prince*. Edited by Peter E. Bondanella. Oxford's World Classics. Oxford: Oxford University Press, 2005.

Madrigal, José A. "La función del hombre salvaje en el teatro de Lope de Vega, Tirso de Molina, y Calderón de la Barca." PhD diss., University of Kentucky, 1974.

———. Madrigal, José A. "La transmutación de Aquiles: De salvaje a héroe (Tirso de Molina, *El Aquiles*)." *Hispanófila* 26, no. 2 (1983): 15–26.

Manuel, Juan. *El Conde Lucanor*, 6th ed. Edited by Enrique Moreno Báez. Madrid: Castalia, 1970.

Maravall, José Antonio. *La cultura del barroco: Análisis de una estructura histórica*. Letras e ideas 7. Barcelona: Ariel, 1975.

———. *The Culture of the Baroque: Analysis of a Historical Structure*. Edited by Wlad Godzich and Nicholas Spadaccini. Translated by Terry Cochran. Theory and History of Literature 25. Minneapolis: University of Minnesota Press, 1983.

———. *Teoría del saber histórico*, 2nd ed. Madrid: Revista de Occidente, 1961.
Mariana, Juan de. *Del Rey, y de la institución de la dignidad real*. Madrid: Imprenta de la sociedad literaria y tipográfica, 1845. Original publication 1640.
Matos Fragoso, Juan de. *El nuevo mundo en Castilla*. In *Parte treinta y siete de Comedias nuevas escritas por los mejores ingenios de España*. Madrid: Melchor Alegre, 1671.
Mayberry, Nancy. "The Role of the Warrior Women in *Amazonas en las Indias*." *Bulletin of the Comediantes* 29, no. 1 (1977): 38–44.
———. "Tirso's Use of Myths and Symbols in Part I of the Pizarro Trilogy." *Kentucky Romance Quarterly* 22, no. 2 (1975): 235–45.
Mazur, Oleh. *The Wild Man in the Spanish Renaissance and Golden Age Theater: A Comparative Study Including the Indio, the Bárbaro and their Counterparts in European Lores*. Ann Arbor, MI: University Microfilms International, 1980.
McKendrick, Melveena. "The Amazon, the Leader, the Warrior." In *Woman and Society in the Spanish Drama of the Golden Age: A Study of the mujer varonil*. Cambridge: Cambridge University Press, 1974.
Meadows, Harrison. "On Tyranny and Succession: Rethinking Monarchical Legitimacy in Calderón's *En la vida todo es verdad y todo mentira* (1659)." *MLN* 133, no. 2 (2018): 257–76.
———. "The Figurative Geography of Natural Landscapes in Tirso de Molina." In *Tirso de Molina: Interdisciplinary Perspectives from the Twenty-First Century*, edited by Esther Fernández. Monografías. Woodbridge, UK: Támesis, 2023.
Metz, Christian. "Instant Self Contradiction." In *On Signs*, edited by Marshall Blonsky. Baltimore: Johns Hopkins University Press, 1985.
Mignolo, Walter D. "The Geopolitics of Knowledge and the Colonial Difference." *South Atlantic Quarterly* 101, no. 1 (2002): 57–96.
Miguel Magro, Tania de. "La mojiganga dramática en el contexto de la fiesta barroca." *Bulletin of the Comediantes* 68, no. 1 (2016): 179–95.
Minelli, Fiorigio. Introduction to *La fingida Arcadia de Tirso de Molina*. Madrid: Edita Revista "Estudios," 1980.
Mira de Amescua, Antonio. *La rueda de la fortuna*. In *Teatro completo*, 489–630. Granada: Universidad de Granada-Diputación de Granada, 2012.
Miró Quesada Sosa, Antonio. "Gonzalo Pizarro en el teatro de Tirso de Molina." *Revista de las Indias* 5, no. 14 (1940).
Molina, Tirso de. *Amazonas en las indias*. Teatro del Siglo de Oro. Ediciones críticas 38. Kassel: Edition Reichenberger, 1993.

———. *Cigarrales de Toledo*. Edited by Luis Vázquez. Madrid: Castalia, 1996.
———. *El vergonzoso en palacio*. Edited by Francisco Florit. Madrid: Taurus, 1987.
———. *La fingida Arcadia*. Edited by Victoriano Roncero López. Pamplona: Auriseculares, Instituto de Estudios Tirsianos, 2016.
Montemayor, Jorge de. *Los siete libros de La Diana*, 3rd ed. Edited by Asunción Rallo Gruss. Letras hispánicas 332. Madrid: Cátedra, 1999.
Moraña, Mabel, Enrique Dussel, and Carlos A. Jáuregui. "Colonialism and Its Replicants." In *Coloniality at Large: Latin America and the Postcolonial Debate*. Durham, NC: Duke University Press, 2008.
Morgan, Luke. *The Monster in the Garden: Reframing Renaissance Landscape Design*. Philadelphia: University of Pennsylvania Press, 2015.
Morley, S. Griswold. "Notes on the Bibliography of Lope de Vega's *Comedias*." *Modern Philology* 20, no. 2 (1922): 201–17.
———. "The Imprisonment of King García." *Modern Philology* 17, no. 7 (1919): 393–413.
Morley, S. Griswold, and Courtney Bruerton. *The Chronology of Lope de Vega's Comedias, with a Discussion of Doubtful Attributions, the Whole Based on a Study of his Strophic Versification*. MLA Monograph Series XI. New York: Modern Language Association, 1940.
Moser, Walter. "Introduction to Part 1." In *Neo-Baroques: From Latin America to the Hollywood Blockbuster*, edited by Walter Moser, Angela Ndalianis, and Peter Krieger. Leiden: BRILL, 2016.
Moser, Walter, Angela Ndalianis, and Peter Krieger, eds. *Neo-Baroques: From Latin America to the Hollywood Blockbuster*. Boston: BRILL, 2016.
Mujica, Barbara. "The Skeptical Premises of Calderón's *En esta vida todo es verdad y todo mentira*." Paper presented at the Texto y espectátculo: Selected Proceedings of the Symposium on Spanish Golden Age Theater, Lanham, MD, 1989.
———. "Stuff of Dreams." In *A New Anthology of Early Modern Spanish Theater: Play and Playtext*. New Haven, CT: Yale University Press, 2014.
Navarro Brotóns, Victor, and William Eamon, eds. *Beyond the Black Legend: Spain and the Scientific Revolution*. Valencia: Instituto de Historia de la Ciencia y Documentación López Piñero, 2007.
Ndalianis, Angela. *Neo-Baroque Aesthetics and Contemporary Entertainment*. Media in Transition. Cambridge, MA: MIT Press, 2004.
Nelson, Bradley J. *The Persistence of Presence: Emblem and Ritual in Baroque Spain*. University of Toronto Romance Series. Toronto: University of Toronto Press, 2010.

O'Callaghan, Joseph F. *A History of Medieval Spain*. Ithaca, NY: Cornell University Press, 1983.
Oleza, Joan. "La propuesta teatral del primer Lope de Vega." In *Teatro y prácticas escénicas*, edited by J. L. Canet Valles. London: Támesis, 1986.
Orozco Díaz, Emilio. "Ruinas y jardines: Su significado y valor en la temática del barroco." In *Temas del barroco de poesía y pintura*. Granada: Universidad de Granada, 1947.
Ovid. *Metamorphoses*. Translated by Rolphe Humphries. Bloomington: Indiana University Press, 1983.
Pagden, Anthony. *European Encounters with the New World from Renaissance to Romanticism*. New Haven, CT: Yale University Press, 1993.
Parker, Alexander A. "Segismundo's Tower: A Calderonian Myth." *Bulletin of Hispanic Studies* 59, no. 3 (1982): 247–56.
Paterson, Alan K. G. "Tirso de Molina and the Androgyne: 'El Aquiles' and 'La dama del olivar.'" *Bulletin of Hispanic Studies* 70, no. 1 (1993): 105–14.
Pérez-Magallón, Jesús. "The Baroque: The Intellectual and Geopolitical Reasons for a Historiographical Erasure." *Les Dossiers du Grihl* 6, no. 2 (2012).
Pérez Samper, María de los Ángeles. "Barcelona, corte: Las fiestas reales en la época de los Austrias." In *La fiesta cortesana en la época de los Austrias*, edited by María Luisa Lobato and Bernardo José García García. Valladolid: Junta de Castilla y León, Consejería de Educación y Cultura, 2003.
Poema de mío Cid. Edited by Colin Smith. Letras hispánicas 35. Madrid: Cátedra, 2001.
Pratt, Dale. "*Felix Culpa*: Allegory and Play in Calderón's *Autos*." *Bulletin of the Comediantes* 51, no. 1–2 (1999): 37–53.
Prieto, Andrés I. "Classification, Memory, and Subjectivity in Gonzalo Fernández de Oviedo's *Sumario de la natural historia* (1526). *MLN* 124 (2009): 329–49.
Quijano, Aníbal. "Coloniality of Power, Eurocentrism, and Latin America." *Nepantla* 1, no. 3 (2000): 533–80.
———. "Coloniality and Modernity/Rationality." *Cultural Studies* 21, no. 2–3 (2007): 168–78.
Quintero, Maria Cristina. *Gendering the Crown in the Spanish Baroque Comedia*. New Hispanisms: Cultural and Literary Studies 2. Farnham, UK: Ashgate, 2012.
Regalado, Antonio. *Calderón: Los orígenes de la modernidad en la España del Siglo de Oro*, vol. 1. Barcelona: Ediciones Destino, 1995.
Reichenberger, Arnold G. "The Uniqueness of the *Comedia*." *Hispanic Review* 27, no. 3 (1959): 303–16.

Rey Bueno, Mar. "La Mayson pour Distiller des Eaües at El Escorial: Alchemy and Medicine at the Court of Philip II, 1556–1598." *Medical History* 52, no. 29 (2009): 26–39.
Ribadeneyra, Pedro de, and Vicente de la Fuente. *Obras escogidas del padre Pedro de Rivadeneira: Con una noticia de sus vida y juicio critico de sus escritos*. Biblioteca de autores españoles 60. Madrid: Ediciones Atlas, 1952.
Río Parra, Elena del. *Exceptional Crime in Early Modern Spain: Taxonomic and Intellectual Perspectives*. Boston, MA: BRILL, 2019.
———. *Una era de monstruos: Representaciones de lo deforme en el Siglo de Oro español*. Colección Áurea Hispánica 27. Navarra: Iberoamericana-Vervuert, 2003.
Robbins, Jeremy. *Arts of Perception: The Epistemological Mentality of the Spanish Baroque, 1580–1720*. Abingdon, UK: Routledge, 2007.
Rodríguez de la Flor, Fernando. "Las Batuecas: Fábula barroca; desmitificación ilustrada." *Revista de Dialectología y Tradiciones Populares*, no. 40 (1985): 133–48.
———. "El espacio escénico del mito." In *De las Batuecas a las Hurdes: Fragmentos para una historia mítica de Extremadura*. Mérida: Editorial Regional de Mérida, 1989.
Rodríguez, Juan Carlos. *Theory and History of Ideological Production: The First Bourgeois Literatures (The 16th Century)*. Monash Romance Studies. Newark, NJ: University of Delaware Press, 2002.
Rofé, Joshua, dir. *Sasquatch*. Hulu Originals, 2021. https://press.hulu.com/shows/sasquatch.
Rozas, José Manuel. "*Las Batuecas del Duque de Alba*, de Lope de Vega." In *Homenaje a Alonso Zamora Vicente*. Madrid: Castalia, 1988.
Ruano de la Haza, José María "Introducción." In *Virtudes vencen señales by Luis Vélez de Guevara*, edited by William R. Manson and C. George Peale. Hispanic Monographs, Ediciones críticas 60. Newark, DE: Juan de la Cuesta, 2010.
Rubio Moraga, Angel Luis. "El teatro barroco, instrumento del poder: Aspectos parateatrales de la fiesta barroca." *Revista Latina de Comunicación Social*, no. 16 (1999).
Ruiz, Teofilo F. *A King Travels: Festive Traditions in Late Medieval and Early Modern Spain*. Princeton, NJ: Princeton University Press, 2012.
———. *Spanish Society, 1348–1700*. London: Routledge, 2017.
Ryjik, Veronika. *Lope de Vega en la invención de España: El drama histórico y la formación de la conciencia nacional*. Monografías 292. Woodbridge: Támesis, 2011.

Saavedra Fajardo, Diego de. *Empresas políticas*. Edited by Francisco Javier Díez de Revenga. Clásicos universales. Madrid: Planeta, 1988.

Samson, Alexander. *Locus Amoenus: Gardens and Horticulture in the Renaissance*. Chichester, UK: Wiley & Sons, 2012.

Sarduy, Severo. *Barroco*. Colección perspectivas. Buenos Aires: Sudamericana, 1974.

Shakespeare, William. *Macbeth*. Edited by Sandra Clark and Pamela Mason. The Arden Shakespeare. Third series. London: Bloomsbury Arden Shakespeare, 2015.

Shapin, Steven, and Simon Schaffer. *Leviathan and the Air-Pump: Hobbes, Boyle, and the Experimental Life*. Princeton, NJ: Princeton University Press, 1985.

Shepard, Jonathan. *The Cambridge History of the Byzantine Empire c. 500–1492*. Cambridge: Cambridge University Press, 2008.

Shergold, N. D. *A History of the Spanish Stage: From Medieval Times until the End of the Seventeenth Century*. Oxford: Clarendon Press, 1967.

Simerka, Barbara. *Knowing Subjects: Cognitive Cultural Studies and Early Modern Spanish*. Purdue Studies in Romance Literatures 57. West Lafayette, IN: Purdue University Press, 2013.

Slater, John. "Sacramental Instrumentality: Representation, Demonstration, and the Calderonian Auto." *Bulletin of the Comediantes* 58, no. 2 (2006): 479–500.

Slater, John, and Harrison Meadows. Introduction to *En la vida todo es verdad y todo mentira & Sueños hay que verdad son* by Pedro Calderón de la Barca. Cervantes & Co. Spanish Classics 78. Newark, DE: Juan de la Cuesta, 2016.

Sloman, Albert E. *The Dramatic Craftsmanship of Calderón: His Use of Earlier Plays*. Oxford: Dolphin Book Co., 1958.

Smith, Dawn L., and Anita K. Stoll, eds. *Gender, Identity, and Representation in Spain's Golden Age*. Lewisburg, PA: Bucknell University Press, 2000.

Sohlich, Wolf. "A Frankfurt School Perspective on José Antonio Maravall's Culture of the Baroque." *Forum: José Antonio Maravall and Baroque Culture, Yearbook of Comparative and General Literature* 45–46 (1996–1997): 196–200.

Spadaccini, Nicholas, and Luis Martín-Estudillo, eds. *Hispanic Baroques: Reading Cultures in Context*, Hispanic Issues 31. Nashville, TN: Vanderbilt University Press, 2005.

Spitzer, Leo. "Soy quien soy." *Nueva Revista de Filología Hispánica* 1, no. 2 (1947): 113–27.

Stern, Charlotte. "Juan del Encina's Carnival Eclogues and the Spanish Drama of the Renaissance." *Renaissance Drama* 8 (1965): 181–95.
———. *The Medieval Theater in Castile*. Medieval & Renaissance Texts & Studies 156. Binghamton: SUNY Binghamton, 1996.
Stoll, Anita K. "Cross/Dressing in Tirso's *El amor médico* (*Love, the Doctor*) and *El Aquiles* (*Achilles*)." In Smith and Stoll, *Gender, Identity, and Representation in Spain's Golden Age*.
Stroud, Matthew D. "Performativity and Sexual Identity in Calderón's *Las manos blancos no ofenden* (*White Hands Don't Offend*)." In Smith and Stoll, *Gender, Identity, and Representation in Spain's Golden Age*.
Surtz, Ronald. *The Birth of a Theater: Dramatic Convention in the Spanish Theater from Juan del Encina to Lope de Vega*. Princeton, NJ: Princeton University, Dept. of Romance Languages and Literatures; Castalia, 1979.
Taylor, Diana. *The Archive and the Repertoire: Performing Cultural Memory in the Americas*. Durham, NC: Duke University Press, 2003.
Thacker, Jonathan. "Maravall and the Self in the *Comedia Nueva*." *Bulletin of the Comediantes* 65, no. 1 (2013): 155–73.
Tyrrell, Ian. "The Myth(s) that Will Not Die: American National Exceptionalism." In *National Myths: Constructed Pasts, Contested Presents*, edited by Gérard Bouchard. London: Routledge, 2013.
Uebel, Michael. "Unthinking the Monster: Twelfth Century Responses to Saracen Alterity." In *Monster Theory: Reading Culture*, edited by Jeffrey Jerome Cohen. Minneapolis: University of Minnesota Press, 1996.
Uther, Hans-Jörg. "425C: Beauty and the Beast." *The Types of International Folktales: A Classification and Bibliography, Based on the System of Antti Aarne and Stith Thompson*. FF Communications 284–286. Helsinki: Suomalainen Tiedeakatemia, Academia Scientiarum Fennica, 2011.
Vaccari, Debora. "*Máscara fue mi locura, / mis mudanzas acabé*: Lás máscaras en el teatro del primer Lope." In *Máscaras y juegos de identidad en el teatro español del Siglo de Oro*, edited by María Luisa Lobato. Biblioteca Filológica Hispana 127. Madrid: Visor Libros, 2011.
Valbuena Prat, Angel. *Historia del teatro español*. Barcelona: Noguer, 1956.
———. "Prólogo." In *Mira de Amescua: Teatro*. Clásicos Castellanos, 1961.
Vasil'ev, A. A., and Sarra Mironovna Ragozina. *History of the Byzantine Empire*. Studies in the Social Sciences and History. Madison: University of Wisconsin Press, 1928.
Vega, Lope de. *El animal de Hungría*. In *Comedias de Lope de Vega: Parte IX*, edited by Xavier Tubau, 679–816. Barcelona: Milenio/Universitat Autònoma de Barcelona, 2007.

———. *Las Batuecas del Duque de Alba*. In *Parte veinte y tres del Lope Felix de Vega y Carpio*. Madrid: María de Quiñones, 1638.

———. *Comedia famosa de Las ferias de Madrid*. Valencia: ARTELOPE, 2016. http://artelope.uv.es/biblioteca/textosAL/AL0632_LasFeriasDeMadrid.

———. *El hijo de los leones: Parte diecinueue y la meior parte de las comedias de Lope de Vega Carpio*. Madrid: Juan Gonçalez, 1624.

———. *El nacimiento de Ursón y Valentín*. In *Comedias de Lope de Vega*, edited by Patrizia Campana and Juan-Ramón Mayol Ferrer. Lleida: Editorial Mileno, 1997.

———. *Fuenteovejuna*. In *A New Anthology of Early Modern Spanish Theater: Play and Playtext*, edited by Bárbara Mujica. New Haven, CT: Yale University Press, 2014.

———. *El Nuevo Mundo descubierto por Cristóbal Colón*. Edited by J. Lemartinel and Veronika Ryjik. Lille: Presses Universitaires de Lille, 1980.

Vega Ramos, María José. "Las indias interiores: Lope y la invención de *Las Batuecas del duque de Alba*." *Anuario Lope de Vega*, no. 2 (1996): 171–96.

Vitse, Marc. "Concepto del teatro en la época." In *Historia del teatro en España*, edited by José María Díez Borque. Madrid: Taurus Ediciones, 1983.

Wardropper, Bruce W. "Metamorphosis in the Theatre of Juan del Encina." *Studies in Philology* 59 (1962): 41–51.

Weiss, Julian. "Maravall's Materialism." *Forum: José Antonio Maravall and Baroque Culture, Yearbook of Comparative and General Literature* 45–56 (1996–97): 181–87.

White, Hayden. "The Forms of Wildness: Archaeology of an Idea." In *The Wild Man Within: An Image of Western Thought from the Renaissance to Romanticism*, edited by Edward Dudley and Maximillian E. Novak. Pittsburgh, PA: University of Pittsburgh Press, 1972.

Wölfflin, Heinrich. *Renaissance and Baroque*. Translated by Kathrin Simon. Ithaca, NY: Cornell University Press, 1967.

Žižek, Slavoj. *The Sublime Object of Ideology*. The Essential Žižek. London: Verso, 2008.

Zugasti, Miguel. *La "trilogía de los Pizarros" de Tirso de Molina, Estudio crítico*, vol. 1. Teatro del Siglo de Oro. Ediciones críticas 38. Kassel: Edition Reichenberger, 1993.

INDEX

Page numbers in *italic* refer to figures.

Accademia dei Lincei (Lincean Academy), 114, 188
Actaeon, 160
alchemy, 120–21, 126, 189, 269n76
Alfonso X of Castile, 117–20, 121
Amazonas en las Indias, Las (Molina)
  cave in, 92
  coloniality of power and, 104–6, 109
  as national mythological drama, 89–93
  tragedy and, 106–8
  wild figure in, 91–93, 106–17
Amescua, Mira de, 167, 182–85, 254n52, 271n90
Amor es naturaleza (Love Is Nature) (Vélez de Guevara), 31
anagnorisis
  in *El animal de Hungría* (Vega), 72, 74, 78–80
  in *En la vida todo es verdad y todo mentira* (Calderón de la Barca), 182, 186
  as missing in *La vida es sueño* (Calderón de la Barca), 180
  in *El nacimiento de Ursón y Valentín* (Vega), 64–65

animal de Hungría, El (Vega)
  allusions to Callisto in, 148
  Amor es naturaleza (Vélez de Guevara) and, 31
  anagnorisis in, 72, 74, 78–80
  animal pelts in, 76, 78, 163
  forest in, 55, 69–81
  inequitable treatment of women in, 250n23
  language in, 250n21
  El nacimiento de Ursón y Valentín (Vega) and, 69–70, 72–74, 77, 78–79, 80–81, 232n33
  wild figure as monster in, 63, 69–81, 200
  wild man tradition and, 69–71, *70–71*
animal pelts
  in *El animal de Hungría* (Vega), 76, 78, 163
  gendered performance of wildness and, 130–31, 145, 152–55, 160–64
  in *La lindona de Galicia* (Claramonte), 130–31, 145
  in *La sirena de Tinacria* (Figueroa y Córdoba), 152–55

animal pelts (*cont'd.*)
    in *La vida es sueño* (Calderón de la
        Barca), 165–68, 169–70, 177
    wild man tradition and, 8, 167–68
animism, 44
Antonucci, Fausta
    on *El hijo de los leones* (Vega), 83, 84
    on *La lindona de Galicia* (Claramonte), 144, 145
    on *El nacimiento de Ursón y Valentín* (Vega), 64–65, 67, 68, 232n33
    on *La vida es sueño* (Calderón de la Barca), 167–68
    on wild man, 36, 37–38
Aquiles, El (Achilles) (Molina), 31–32
Arcadia, 17, 19, 51, 148, 151, 160
Arcadia, La (Vega), 215n55, 224n46
Arellano, Ignacio, 92
Ariosto, Ludovico, 36–37
Armas, Frederick A. de, 172, 178–79
Armas Wilson, Diana de, 266n58
articulation, 95, 103–4
Attack on the Castle of Love (ivory carving), 41
autos sacramentales (eucharist plays), 131, 189

Bacon, Francis, 45–46, 119, *119*, 124, 188–89, 215n56
Baena, Julio, 202, 228n8
Bakhtin, Mikhail, 43–44, 45, 47–48
Bal des Ardents, 52
Baroque, 12–18, 21–26. *See also* wild man in Baroque *comedia*
Bartra, Roger, 35–38, 64, 78, 222n19, 232n34
bastón (club), 78
Battle Between Carnival and Lent, The (Brueghel), 3, 4–5, 43
Batuecas del Duque de Alba, Las (Vega)
    Las Amazonas en las Indias (Molina) and, 111
    cave in, 91–92, 102–3
    coloniality of power and, 95–104
    folkloric source material for, 91–92, 93–95
    as national mythological drama, 89–93
    rewritings of, 97–98
    wild figure in, 91–95, 99–104
Beauty and the Beast (fairy tale), 209–10n1
Benjamin, Walter, 17
Bernheimer, Richard, 43, 232n33
Bigfoot (Sasquatch), 33–34, 202–8, 235–36n71
Bigfoot's Reflections (documentary), 203–4
blood, 95. *See also fuerza de la sangre* (power of blood)
Bloom, Harold, 253n49
Boccaccio, Giovanni, 3
Bourdieu, Pierre, 216n61
Boyle, Margaret E., 161
Boyle, Robert, 114, 188–89
Brueghel, Peter, 3, 43
Bruerton, Courtney, 229n17
Bruno, Giordano, 45
Burningham, Bruce, 57, 219–20n11, 220n14
Bushnell, Rebecca W., 107
Butler, Judith, 155, 161–62, 265–66n49

Calderón de la Barca, Pedro
    anagnorisis and, 180, 182, 186
    desengaño (disillusionment) and, 162–63, 172, 194
    gendered performance of wildness and, 162–64, 170–71, 172–77
    Ovid and, 236n1
    wild man tradition and, 53, 166–68
    See also *En la vida todo es verdad y todo mentira* (Calderón de la Barca); *vida es sueño, La* (Calderón de la Barca); *specific works*
Callisto, 146, 148–51, 257n82
Candamo, Bances. See *piedra filosofal, La* (Candamo)

Cañizares-Esguerra, Jorge, 247n87
Cantar de mío Cid (Castilian epic poem), 120–21
capitalism, 44–45
Cárcel de amor (Prison of Love) (San Pedro), 126
cardenal de Belén, El (Vega), 55, *55*–56
Carlos II of Spain, 126
Carlos V y el Furor (Leoni and Leoni), *40*, 222–23n22
Carnival
   baroque monster and, 59
   Encina's eclogues and, 46–48, 53
   modernity and, 44–46
   wild man tradition and, 3–7, 42–51, 56–57, *70*, 272n9
Carroll, Noel, 265n49
Cascardi, Anthony, 180
Castillo, David R.
   on baroque aesthetic, 260n9
   Bigfoot research and, 202–8
   on Maravall, 14–15
   on modernity, 24, 33–34
   on monsters, 9–10, 58
   on national identity, 95
Castillo, Jorge Luis, 57
Castillo, Moisés, 127
Castle, Terry, 51–52
Castro, Guillén de, 255n63
Castro-Gómez, Santiago, 19–20, 232n41
cave
   in *Las Amazonas en las Indias* (Molina), 92
   in *Las Batuecas del Duque de Alba* (Vega), 91–92, 102–3
   as discovery space, 54, 240n36
   in *En la vida todo es verdad y todo mentira* (Calderón de la Barca), 120, 181, 186
   as feminine space, 170–71
   in *Hado y divisa de Leonido y Marfisa* (Calderón de la Barca), 164
   in *La piedra filosofal* (Candamo), 92, 120, 126

Cervantes Saavedra, Miguel de
   minor strategy and, 162
   pastoral literature and, 224n46
   Vega and, 228–29n13
   wild man tradition and, 36–37, 219n7
   on women, 250n23
   See also specific works
Charles VI of France, 52
chivalric romance, 2, 36–40
cigarrales de Toledo, Los (The Country Estates of Toledo) (Molina), 104
Cirnigliaro, Noelia S., 154
Cixious, Hélène, 133
Claramonte, Andrés de. *See lindona de Galicia, La* (The Belle of Galicia) (Claramonte)
Cohen, Jeffrey, 58, 59
colonialism, 18–26, 33, 227n3
coloniality of power
   Las Amazonas en las Indias (Molina) and, 104–6, 109
   Las Batuecas del Duque de Alba (Vega) and, 95–104
   modernity and, 19, 33, 199–200
   La piedra filosofal (Candamo) and, 126
   Virtudes vencen señales (Vélez de Guevara) and, 32–33
Comedia salvaje (A Savage Comedy) (Romero de Cepeda), 30
comedias burlescas (burlesque plays), 223n30
comedias de indios, 99, 109, 115–16, 234n49
comedias de magia, 54, 111–13
Conde Lucanor, El (Juan Manuel), 123
Corneille, Pierre, 267n60
corrales, 50–57
corralling, 57
Cotarelo y Mori, Emilio, 182–83
Covarrubias, Sebastián de, 49, 230n23
cross-dressing, 160–61, 163
Cruickshank, Don William, 190, 267n60, 268n66
Cymbeline (Shakespeare), 231n32

dances (*bailes*), 39–42
Decameron (Boccaccio), 3
Deleuze, Gilles, 133
Della Porta, Giambattista, 114, 187–88, 269n76
Derrida, Jacques, 174, 179
descubrimiento de las Batuecas del Duque de Alba, El (The Discovery of the Duke of Alba's Batuecas) (Hoz y Mota), 97–98
desengaño (disillusionment)
　in *El animal de Hungría* (Vega), 76, 79
　Calderón de la Barca and, 162–63, 172, 194
　cave and, 54, 240n36
　gendered performance of wildness and, 130–31
　in *La lindona de Galicia* (Claramonte), 162
　as missing in *La piedra filosofal* (Candamo), 124–25
　"true" identity of wild man and, 6, 8–10, 22–26. *See also* identity
　wild figure as monster and, 61–62
Devos, Brent, 226n66
Deyermond, A. D., 167, 177, 211–12n14
Diana, La (Montemayor), 30, 224n46
Don Quixote (Cervantes), 36–37, 219n7, 224n46, 266n58
Dr. Who (television series), 243n64
Dussel, Enrique, 18–20, 128, 199, 237n11, 261n14, 272n7

Eamon, William, 114, 187–88
Echo, 146–48, 150, 257n82
Egginton, William
　on baroque aesthetics, 61–62
　Bigfoot research and, 202–8
　on Encina, 47
　on major and minor strategies of Baroque, 8–9, 194, 228–29n13, 258n87
　on modernity, 13, 24, 33–34
　on monsters, 58
　on presence, 79, 225n48
　on theatricality, 6, 225n48
　on *La vida es sueño* (Calderón de la Barca), 260n10
El Saffar, Ruth, 177
Elephant Man, The (1980 film), 209–10n1
Elliot, J.H., 14
Elsner, Jacob, 71
emblem culture, 23–24, 62
embodied practices, 53–54
empiricism
　modernity and, 18, 21, 198–99
　natural magic and, 114, 121, 187–89
　La piedra filosofal (Candamo) and, 117–19, 124
　pillars of Hercules and, 124
En la vida todo es verdad y todo mentira (Calderón de la Barca)
　fuerza de la sangre (power of blood) in, 184–94
　Hado y divisa de Leonido y Marfisa (Calderón de la Barca) and, 163
　modernity in, 198–99
　natural magic in, 120, 186–89
　La piedra filosofal (Candamo) and, 120, 124, 244–45n73
　La rueda de la fortuna (Amescua) and, 182–85
　talismans in, 254n52
　La vida es sueño (Calderón de la Barca) and, 167, 181–82, 185–86
　wild figures in, 167, 179, 181–82
Encina, Juan del, 46–48, 53
entremeses (interludes), 39–42
Epic of Gilgamesh (epic poem), 1, 2
Eraclio (Heraclius), Byzantine emperor, 124–25, 181–93
españolidad, 95–97. *See also* national identity
Estoria de España (History of Spain) (Alfonso X), 117–20
Et in Arcadia ego (Poussin), 17, 19
ethnography, 2
Eurocentrism, 19–21, 23, 104, 199

Index [297]

Fábula de Polifemo y Galatea (Góngora), 171, 228n8
Felipe IV of Spain, 221n17
femininity. *See* gender
ferias de Madrid, Las (Vega), 49
Ferrer Valls, Teresa, 49
Figueroa y Córdoba, Diego de. *See sirena de Tinacria, La* (Figueroa y Córdoba)
Filomena, La (Vega), 215n55
Findlen, Paula, 45
fingida Arcadia, La (Molina), 215n55, 224n46
Fioravanti, Leonardo, 269n76
Focas (Phocas), Byzantine emperor, 181–93
forests
  in *Las Amazonas en las Indias* (Molina), 111, 116–17
  in *El animal de Hungría* (Vega), 55, 69–81
  in *El hijo de los leones* (Vega), 55, 82–87
  in *La lindona de Galicia* (Claramonte), 142–43, 145–50
  in *El nacimiento de Ursón y Valentín* (Vega), 55, 64–69
  in pre-modern spectacle, 51–57
  in *La sirena de Tinacria* (Figueroa y Córdoba), 151
  See also cave
Foucault, Michel, 116, 174, 179
Fox, Dian, 176, 248–49n9
Fréger, Charles, 7, 272n9
Fuchs, Barbara, 92
Fuenteovejuna (Vega), 252n39
fuerza de la costumbre, La (*The Force of Habit*) (Castro), 255n63
fuerza de la sangre (power of blood)
  in *En la vida todo es verdad y todo mentira* (Calderón de la Barca), 184–94
  in *El hijo de los leones* (Vega), 83–84
  in *El nacimiento de Ursón y Valentín* (Vega), 64–65
  La rueda de la fortuna (Amescua) and, 183–85
  in *La sirena de Tinacria* (Figueroa y Córdoba), 157–58
fuerza de la sangre, La (*Compelled by Blood*) (Cervantes), 176, 250n23

Galilei, Galileo, 114
Game of Thrones (Martin), 209–10n1
ganso de oro, El (The Golden Goose) (Vega), 30
García de Céspedes, Andrés, 118, 124
gardens, 21
Gasta, Chad, 245n78
Geese Book (*Gradual*), 71
gender
  in *El animal de Hungría* (Vega), 69–81
  in *Hado y divisa de Leonido y Marfisa* (The Tokens of Fate of Leonido and Marfisa) (Calderón de la Barca), 162–64
  in *La lindona de Galicia* (Claramonte), 10, 131–35, 137–51
  in *La sirena de Tinacria* (Figueroa y Córdoba), 151–60
  in *La vida es sueño* (Calderón de la Barca), 170–71, 172–77
  wildness and, 31–32, 127–31
Girard, René, 271n2
Glenn, Richard, 68–69
Góngora, Luis de, 16–17, 171, 228n8
González Echeverría, Roberto, 172
Gordillo, Adriana, 59
Gracián, Baltasar, 17
Gracián, Balthasar, 250–51n25
gracioso, 115–16
Gradual (*Geese Book*), 71
Grady, Hugh, 108
Gramsci, Antonio, 15
Green, Otis, 106, 241n47
Green Knight, The (2001 film), 1, 3, 209–10n1
Greer, Margaret, 180, 236n1, 248–49n9, 258n88
grotesque, 126
grottos, 126, 171

guanches de Tenerife, Los (The Guanches of Tenerife) (Vega), 96–97, 99
Gurevich, Aron, 52

Habermas, Jürgen, 214n42
Hado y divisa de Leonido y Marfisa (The Tokens of Fate of Leonido and Marfisa) (Calderón de la Barca), 162–64, 179, 259n4
Hall, Stuart, 15, 95, 103–4
Harry Potter series (Rowling), 209–10n1
Hegel, Georg Wilhelm Friedrich, 36
Heraclius (Eraclio), Byzantine emperor, 124–25, 181–93
Hercules, 10–11, *11*
Hércules lucha con la hidra de Lerna (Zurbarán), *11*
hijo de los leones, El (Vega)
  Las Amazonas en las Indias (Molina) and, 113
  forest in, 55, 82–87
  inequitable treatment of women in, 250n23
  La piedra filosofal (Candamo) and, 121
  proof of identity in, 271n90
  talismans in, 254n52
  wild figure as monster in, 63, 81–87
Hildner, David J., 190
History of Cardenio, The (Shakespeare), 219n7
Hobbes, Thomas, 197
Holthouse, David, 205
horror films, 9, 206–7, 245n69
Hoz y Mota, Juan Claudio de la, 97–98
Huygens, Christian, 114, 188–89, 199

identity
  blood and. See *fuerza de la sangre* (power of blood)
  forests and, 54–57
  wild figure as monster and, 60–63
  See also anagnorisis; masks; national identity

Jáuregui, Carlos, 237n11, 272n7
Jeffs, Kathleen, 255n63
Jones, Nicholas R., 128–29
Jones, Rosalind, 152
Juan Manuel, 123
Jungle Book, The (Kipling), 209–10n1

Kepler, Johannes, 45
Kipling, Rudyard, 209–10n1
Küpper, Joachim, 172

Lacan, Jacques, 267n63
language
  in *El animal de Hungría* (Vega), 250n21
  in *La lindona de Galicia* (Claramonte), 134, 142–43, 145, 146–47
Lazarillo de Tormes (novella), 153
Lent, 4–6, 43, 45
Leoni, Leone, 40, 222–23n22
Leoni, Pompeo, 40, 222–23n22
Leviathan (Hobbes), 197
Lincean Academy (Accademia dei Lincei), 114, 188
lindona de Galicia, La (The Belle of Galicia) (Claramonte)
  allusions to Echo and Callisto in, 146–51
  animal pelts in, 130–31, 145
  gendered performance of wildness and, 10, 131–35, 137–51
  language in, 134, 142–43, 145, 146–47
  reason of state in, 135–44, 150–51
  La sirena de Tinacria (Figueroa y Córdoba) and, 257n77
Lobato, María Luisa, 5, 41–42
locus amoenus, 17, 21, 30
Lord of the Rings (Tolkien), 209–10n1
Lynch, David, 209–10n1

Macbeth (Shakespeare), 249n15
Machiavelli, Niccolò, 135–44
Mackay, Ruth, 14
madmen, 116
Madrigal, José, 64
Magiae naturalis (Della Porta), 187–88

Manrique, Gómez, 39
Maravall, José Antonio, 12–15, 62, 87, 195–96, 206, 248–49n9
Mariana, Juan de, 136
Martí I of Aragon, 40–41
Martin, George R. R., 209–10n1
Martín-Estudillo, Luis, 15
Marx, Karl, 214n42, 214n45
masculinity. *See* gender
masks, 39, 49–50. *See also* animal pelts
Masquerade of Orson and Valentine, The (1566 woodcut), 5
masques (*máscaras*), 39–42
Matos Fragoso, Juan de, 97–98
Maurice (Mauricio), Byzantine emperor, 182–93
Mayberry, Nancy, 104–5, 106–7
mayor encanto, amor, El (*Love, the Greatest Enchantment*) (Calderón de la Barca), 30
Mazur, Oleh, 30, 64, 65, 67, 254n52
McKendrick, Melveena, 106, 248–49n9
Medialogies (Castillo and Egginton), 33–34, 202–8
médico de su honra, El (Calderón de la Barca), 250n23
Metamorphoses (Ovid), 146–51, 160
Metz, Christian, 85
Mignolo, Walter, 18–19, 21, 237n11
Miguel Magro, Tania de, 225n47
Miró Quesada Sosa, Aurelio, 106
modernity
   Bigfoot research and, 203
   Carnival and, 44–46
   colonialism and, 18–26, 33, 199–200
   concept of, 12–18
   empiricism and, 18, 21, 198–99
   founding moment of, 62
   gender norms and, 128
   in *La vida es sueño* (Calderón de la Barca), 170
Molina, Tirso de. *See Amazonas en las Indias, Las* (Molina); *fingida Arcadia, La* (Molina)

monsters and monstrosity
   Las Amazonas en las Indias (Molina) and, 110–11
   El animal de Hungría (Vega) and, 63, 69–81, 200
   El hijo de los leones (Vega) and, 63, 81–87
   El nacimiento de Ursón y Valentín (Vega) and, 63–70, 72–74, 77, 78–79, 80–81, 232n33
   in *La vida es sueño* (Calderón de la Barca), 172–81
   wild man and, 8–10, 32, 58–63
Montemayor, Jorge de, 30, 224n46
Moraña, Mabel, 237n11, 272n7
Morley, S. Griswold, 229n17
Moser, Walter, 202
mountainsides, 51. *See also* forests
Mujica, Bárbara, 170, 177, 190
mummeries (*momos*), 39–42
mysteries, 39–42
MythBusters (television series), 198–99

nacimiento de Ursón y Valentín, El (*The Birth of Orson and Valentine*) (Vega)
   allusions to Callisto in, 148
   anagnorisis in, 64–65
   El animal de Hungría (Vega) and, 69–70, 72–74, 77, 78–79, 80–81, 232n33
   forest in, 55, 64–69
   El hijo de los leones (Vega) and, 83, 87
   inequitable treatment of women in, 250n23
   La lindona de Galicia (Claramonte) and, 145–46
   proof of identity in, 271n90
   Virtudes vencen señales (Vélez de Guevara) and, 32–33
   wild figure as monster in, 1, 63–70, 72–74, 77, 78–79, 80–81, 232n33
national identity
   in *La lindona de Galicia* (Claramonte), 143

national identity (cont'd.)
  mythologized histories and, 89–93. See also *Amazonas en las Indias, Las* (Molina); *Batuecas del Duque de Alba, Las* (Vega); *piedra filosofal, La* (Candamo)
  wild man in Baroque *comedia* and, 81–82
natural philosophy and natural magic
  Las Amazonas en las Indias (Molina) and, 110–15
  in *En la vida todo es verdad y todo mentira* (Calderón de la Barca), 120, 186–89
  En la vida todo es verdad y todo mentira (Calderón de la Barca) and, 120
  modern scientic worldview and, 45–46, 114, 121, 187–89
  La piedra filosofal (Candamo) and, 120–26
  See also alchemy
natural science, 54. See also empiricism
Ndalianis, Angela, 16
Nelson, Bradley J.
  Bigfoot research and, 202, 203
  on *comedias de indios*, 234n49
  on emblem culture, 23–24, 62
  on Maravall, 14–15
  on presence, 79, 238n15
  on *La vida es sueño* (Calderón de la Barca), 264n37
Neoclassicism, 162
Nietzsche, Friedrich, 203
Novum Organum (Bacon), 119, *119*, 124
Nuevo Mundo descubierto por Cristóbal Colón, El (The New World Discovered by Christopher Columbus) (Vega), 96–97, 99
nuevo mundo en España, El (Thee New World in Spain) (Matos Fragoso), 97–98

O'Brien, Eavan, 231n32
Oleza, Joan, 9, 53, 228n9

organicism, 44
Orlando furioso (Ariosto), 36–37
Ovid, 146–51, 160, 236n1
Owen, Delia, 209–10n1

Pagden, Anthony, 23
paratheatrical and prototheatrical traditions, 37–44, 50–53, *52*
Parker, Alexander A., 180
pastoral literature, 224n46. See also Arcadia
Pedro, Valentín de, 106
Pérez de Montalbán, Juan, 31
Pérez-Magallón, Jesús, 14
perseguida triunfante, La (Zayas), 231n32
Persistence of Presence (Nelson), 23–24
Philip II of Spain, 269n76
Phocas (Focas), Byzantine emperor, 181–93
piedra filosofal, La (The Philosopher's Stone) (Candamo)
  Alfonso X's *Estoria* and, 117–20, 121
  cave in, 92, 120, 126
  empiricism and, 117–19, 124
  as national mythological drama, 10–11, 89–93
  natural magic and, 120–26
  wild figure in, 91–93, 120–26, 244n68
Piranesi, Giovanni Battista, 17
Pizarro, Francisco, 107
Pizarro, Gonzalo, 90, 92, 104–9, 115–16
Planet of the Apes (film franchise), 209–10n1
Polifemo y Circe (Amescua and Calderón de la Barca), 267n60
Polyphemus, 171
Poussin, Nicolas, 17, *19*
Pratt, Dale, 131
premio de la hermosura, El (Beauty's Prize) (Vega), 30
Prince, The (Machiavelli), 135–44
príncipe de los montes, El (The Forest Prince) (Pérez de Montalbán), 31

prudence
　in *En la vida todo es verdad y todo mentira* (Calderón de la Barca), 190–91, 193
　in *La lindona de Galicia* (Claramonte), 135–44, 257n77
　in *La sirena de Tinacria* (Figueroa y Córdoba), 150–51, 156
　in *La vida es sueño* (Calderón de la Barca), 175–76, 179
psychology, 2
puente de Mantible, La (The Bridge of Mantible) (Calderón de la Barca), 30
pureza de sangre (blood purity), 95

Quijano, Aníbal, 18–19

radical performances, 128–29
Radical Theatricality (Burningham), 57
reason of state, 135–44, 150–51. See also prudence
Regimiento de navegación (García de Céspedes), *118*, 124
Reichenberger, Arnold G., 131
Renaissance and Baroque (Wölfflin), 12–15, 16
Renaissance Clothing and the Materials of Memory (Jones and Stallybrass), 152
Rey Bueno, Mar, 269n76
Ribadeneira, Pedro de, 136, 138
Río Parra, Elena del, 60, 179
Rivers, Elias, 262n19
Rodrigo, 91–92, 102
Rodríguez, Juan Carlos, 44
Rodríguez de la Flor, Fernando, 96, 99
Rofé, Joshua. See *Sasquatch* (2021 film)
Romero de Cepeda, Joaquín, 30
Rowling, J. K., 209–10n1
Rozas, José Manuel, 98–99, 100, 101
Rubio Moraga, Angel Luis, 8
Rudolph II, Holy Roman Emperor, 269n76
rueda de la fortuna, La (Amescua), 167, 182–85, 254n52, 271n90

Ruiz, Teofilo, 121
Ryjik, Veronika, 92–93

Saavedra Fajardo, Diego de, 136, 139–40, 143
Salic Law, 183
salvaje en la Comedia del Siglo de Oro, El (Antonucci), 36, 37–38
San Pedro, Diego de, 126
Sancho III of Castile, 133–34
Sasquatch (Bigfoot), 33–34, 202–8, 235–36n71
Sasquatch (2021 film), 203, 204–7
science fiction, 243n64
sentimental romance, 2, 36–37
Shakespeare, William, 219n7, 231n32, 249n15
Simerka, Barbara, 231n32
sirena de Tinacria, La (Figueroa y Córdoba), 31, 147, 151–60, 254n52, 259n4
sirens, 151–52
Slater, John, 189
Spadaccini, Nicholas, 15, 59
Stallybrass, Peter, 152
Stelluti, Francesco, 188
Stern, Charlotte, 46–48
Surtz, Ronald, 47

talismans, 254n52
Taylor, Diana, 51, 53–54
Teodosio, 91–92, 102–3
Tesoro de la lengua castellana (Covarrubias), 49, 230n23
Tolkien, J. R. R., 209–10n1
totalitarian state. See tyranny
tower, 165–67, 169–72, 177–78, 180
tragedy, 106–8
tres mayores prodigios, Los (The Three Greatest Marvels) (Calderón de la Barca), 30
tyranny
　in *El animal de Hungría* (Vega), 79–80

tyranny (cont'd.)
    in *En la vida todo es verdad y todo mentira* (Calderón de la Barca), 184–85
    in *La lindona de Galicia* (Claramonte), 138–39
Tyrrell, Ian, 90–91

Uebel, Michael, 60
Unruly Women (Boyle), 161

Vaccari, Debora, 50
Valbuena Prat, Angel, 182–83
vampires, 58–59
Vega, Lope de
    gardens and, 215n55
    national identity and, 96–97. See also *Batuecas del Duque de Alba, Las* (Vega)
    wild figure as monster and, 1, 8–10, 60–61, 87–88. See also *hijo de los leones, El* (Vega); *nacimiento de Ursón y Valentín, El* (The Birth of Orson and Valentine) (Vega)
    wild man tradition and, 1, 6, 8–10, 48–49, 53–57, 69–71, 168
    See also specific works
Vélez de Guevara, Luis, 31, 32–33
vergonzoso en palacio, El (Bashful at Court) (Molina), 104
vida es sueño, La (Calderón de la Barca)
    animal pelts in, 165–68, 169–70, 177
    composition of, 166
    En la vida todo es verdad y todo mentira (Calderón de la Barca) and, 167, 181–82, 185–86
    exceptional wild figure in, 167–69, 180
    gendered performance of wildness and, 163
    El hijo de los leones (Vega) and, 84–85
    hybrid contradictions in, 166–67, 169–81

inequitable treatment of women in, 250n23
La lindona de Galicia (Claramonte) and, 144
La piedra filosofal (Candamo) and, 122, 124, 246n83
El príncipe de los montes (Pérez de Montalbán) and, 31
La rueda de la fortuna (Amescua) and, 167
tower in, 165–67, 169–72, 177–78, 180
wild figure as monster in, 172–81
wild man tradition and, 166–68
Virtudes vencen señales (Virtue Conquers Appearances) (Vélez de Guevara), 32–33
Visigoths, 91–92, 93–95, 99–104
Vitse, Marc, 169

Wallerstein, Immanuel, 21
Weiss, Julian, 14, 87–88
Where the Crawdads Sing (Owen), 209–10n11
White, Hayden, 35, 59
wild man
    in chivalric and sentimental romance, 2, 36–40
    comedia de corrales and, 50–57
    concept and evolution of, 1–12, 2–5, 7, 11, 25–26, 35–36
    in paratheatrical and prototheatrical traditions, 37–44, 40–42, 50–53, 52
    present-day conceptualizations of, 201–8
    See also Carnival
wild man in Baroque *comedia*
    concept and evolution of, 1–12, 195–200
    corpus and scope of study on, 30–34
    gendered performance of. *See* gender as marginal monster par excellence, 58–63. *See also* Vega, Lope de

national identity and, 81–82, 91–93. See also *Amazonas en las Indias, Las* (Molina); *Batuecas del Duque de Alba, Las* (Vega); *piedra filosofal, La* (Candamo)
scholarship on, 36, 37–38
Wild Man, The (1566 woodcut), *5*
Wild Men Storming the Castle of Love (glass roundel), *42*
Wilder Mann (Fréger), *7*, 272n9
Williams, Raymond, 15

Winter's Tale, The (Shakespeare), 231n32
Wölfflin, Heinrich, 12, 16

Yeti, 202

Zayas, María de, 231n32
Žižek, Slavoj, 62, 79
zombies, 58–59
Zugasti, Miguel, 104, 105, 109
Zurburán, Francisco de, *11*

www.ingramcontent.com/pod-product-compliance
Lightning Source LLC
Chambersburg PA
CBHW030524230426
43665CB00010B/755